Code x30

Ford Cortina Mk IV 1.6 & 2.0 Owners Workshop Manual

by J H Haynes Member of the Guild of Motoring Writers

Models covered
Ford Cortina Mk IV (including Cortina 80 often known as Mk V) 1.6 and 2.0 Saloon and Estate; 1593 cc & 1993 cc

Covers Carousel and Crusader limited edition models
Does not cover 1.3 or 2.3 models

ISBN 1 85010 170 1

© Haynes Publishing Group, 1977, 1980, 1981, 1982, 1985, 1987

Printed in England *(343 - 7N6)*

ABCD'

THE BOOK

Haynes Publishing Group
Sparkford Nr Yeovil
Somerset BA22 7JJ England

Haynes Publications, Inc
861 Lawrence Drive
Newbury Park
California 91320 USA

British Library Cataloguing in Publication Data
Haynes, J. H.
Ford Cortina Mk IV (& Mk V) 1.6 & 2.0 owners
workshop manual.–3rd ed.–
(Owners Workshop Manuals)
1. Cortina automobile
I. Title   II. Series
629.28'722   TL215.C568
ISBN 1–85010–170–1

Acknowledgements

Special thanks are due to the Ford Motor Company for the supply of technical information and certain illustrations. Castrol Limited provided lubrication data, and the Champion Sparking Company supplied the illustrations showing the various spark plug conditions.

The section of Chapter 10 dealing with the suppression of radio interference, was originated by Mr I.P. Davey, and was first published in *Motor* magazine.

Lastly, thanks are due to all of those people at Sparkford who helped in the production of this manual.

About this manual

Its aim

The aim of this manual is to help you get the best value from your vehicle. It can do so in several ways. It can help you decide what work must be done (even should you choose to get it done by a garage), provide information on routine maintenance and servicing, and give a logical course of action and diagnosis when random faults occur. However, it is hoped that you will use the manual by tackling the work yourself. On simpler jobs it may even be quicker than booking the car into a garage and going there twice, to leave and collect it. Perhaps most important, a lot of money can be saved by avoiding the costs a garage must charge to cover its labour and overheads.

The manual has drawings and descriptions to show the function of the various components so that their layout can be understood. Then the tasks are described and photographed in a step-by-step sequence so that even a novice can do the work.

Its arrangement

The manual is divided into thirteen Chapters, each covering a logical sub-division of the vehicle. The Chapters are each divided into Sections, numbered with single figures, eg 5; and the Sections into paragraphs (or sub-sections), with decimal numbers following on from the Section they are in, eg 5.1, 5.2, 5.3 etc.

It is freely illustrated, especially in those parts where there is a detailed sequence of operations to be carried out. There are two forms of illustration: figures and photographs. The figures are numbered in sequence with decimal numbers, according to their position in the Chapter – eg Fig. 6.4 is the fourth drawing/illustration in Chapter 6. Photographs carry the same number (either individually or in related groups) as the Section or sub-section to which they relate.

There is an alphabetical index at the back of the manual as well as a contents list at the front. Each Chapter is also preceded by its own individual contents list.

References to the 'left' or 'right' of the vehicle are in the sense of a person in the driver's seat facing forwards.

Unless otherwise stated, nuts and bolts are removed by turning anti-clockwise, and tightened by turning clockwise.

Vehicle manufacturers continually make changes to specifications and recommendations, and these, when notified, are incorporated into our manuals at the earliest opportunity.

Whilst every care is taken to ensure that the information in this manual is correct, no liability can be accepted by the authors or publishers for loss, damage or injury caused by any errors in, or omissions from, the information given.

Introduction to the Ford Cortina Mk IV

The Mk IV Cortina was first introduced in 1976 and was initially available with any one of three basic engine types, the 1.3 ohv engine or the 1.6 or 2.0 ohc engines. A further version became available in 1977 when the 2.3 litre V6 engine was added to the range. In this manual we deal with the 1.6 and 2.0 litre models, the 1.3 and 2.3 litre versions being covered in separate manuals.

The 1.6 engined model is available in the Base, L, GL or Ghia form, whilst the 2.0 litre model is available in the GL or Ghia form. The original 2 litre S version was discontinued in 1979 and in its place an 'S pack' became available on all except the Base model.

The 'S pack' is designed to provide a firmer suspension front and rear, large gas-filled shock absorbers being employed all round in place of the normal hydraulic types, alloy roadwheels are also fitted together with other refinements such as a 'hockey stick' gear lever, a tachometer, four-spoke steering wheel and bumper overriders. As an alternative on some Estate models, a 'Heavy Duty' pack is available. This offers a strengthened axle casing, larger rear brakes and reinforced radial ply tyres. The suspension is also uprated and the payload is increased from 935 lb to 1216 lb.

Contents

1980 model Cortina L Estate

Mk IV Cortina 2 litre 'S'

Jacking and Towing

Jacking points

To change a wheel in an emergency, use the jack supplied with the vehicle. Ensure that the roadwheel nuts are released before jacking-up the car and make sure that the arm of the jack is fully engaged with the body bracket and that the base of the jack is standing on a firm level surface.

The jack supplied with the vehicle is not suitable for use when raising the vehicle for maintenance or repair operations. For this work, use a trolley, hydraulic or screw type jack located under the front crossmember, bodyframe sidemembers or rear axle casing, as illustrated. Always supplement the jack with axle stands or blocks before crawling beneath the car.

Towing points

If your vehicle is being towed, make sure that the tow rope is attached to a towing eye or the front crossmember. If the vehicle is equipped with automatic transmission, the distance towed must not exceed 15 miles (24 km), nor the speed 30 mph (48 km/h), otherwise serious damage to the transmission may result. If these limits are likely to be exceeded, disconnect and remove the propeller shaft.

If you are towing another vehicle, attach the tow rope to the lower suspension arm bracket at the axle tube.

Using the vehicle jack

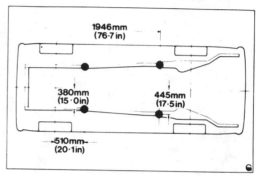

Vehicle jacking points (for maintenance and repair operations)

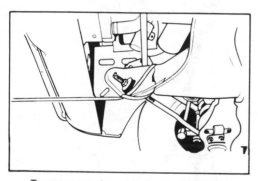

Tow rope attachment to front of vehicle

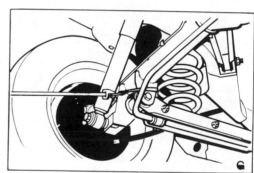

Tow rope attachment to rear of vehicle

Quick reference capacities

Engine oil capacity:

Excluding filter (oil change only)	5.5 pints (3.15 litres)
With new filter	6.2 pints (3.55 litres)

Cooling system:

1600 cc	10.1 pints (5.75 litres)
2000 cc	10.8 pints (6.13 litres)

Fuel tank capacity ... ... 12 gallons (54 litres)

Gearbox capacity:

1600 cc	1.6 pints (0.9 litre)
2000 cc	2.6 pints (1.5 litres)

Automatic transmission fluid capacity ... ... 11.1 pints (6.3 litres)

Rear axle capacity:

1600 cc	1.8 pints (1.0 litre)
2000 cc	1.9 pints (1.1 litres)

Buying spare parts
and vehicle identification numbers

Buying spare parts

Spare parts are available from many sources, for example: Ford garages, other garages and accessory shops, and motor factors. Our advice regarding spare part sources is as follows:

Officially appointed Ford garages - This is the best source of parts which are peculiar to your car and are otherwise not generally available (eg complete cylinder heads, internal gearbox components, badges, interior trim etc). It is also the only place at which you should buy parts if your car is still under warranty - non-Ford components may invalidate the warranty. To be sure of obtaining the correct parts it will always be necessary to give the storeman your car's vehicle identification number, and if possible, to take the 'old' part along for positive identification. Remember that many parts are available on a factory exchange scheme - any parts returned should always be clean! It obviously makes good sense to go straight to the specialists on your car for this type of part for they are best equipped to supply you.

Other garages and accessory shops - These are often very good places to buy materials and components needed for the maintenance of your car (eg oil filters, spark plugs, bulbs, fan belts, oils and greases, touch-up paint, filler paste, etc). They also sell general accessories, usually have convenient opening hours, charge lower prices and can often be found not far from home.

Motor factors - Good factors will stock all of the more important components which wear out relatively quickly (eg clutch components, pistons, valves, exhaust systems, brake cylinders/pipes/hoses/seals/shoes and pads etc). Motor factors will often provide new or reconditioned components on a part exchange basis - this can save a considerable amount of money.

Vehicle identification numbers

Although many individual parts, and in some cases sub-assemblies, fit a number of different models it is dangerous to assume that just because they look the same, they are the same. Differences are not always easy to detect except by serial numbers. Make sure therefore, that the appropriate identity number for the model or sub-assembly is known and quoted when a spare part is ordered.

The vehicle identification plate is mounted on the right-hand side of the front body panel and may be seen once the bonnet is open. Record the numbers from your car on the blank spaces of the accompanying illustration. You can then take the manual with you when buying parts; also the exploded drawings throughout the manual can be used to point out and identify the components required.

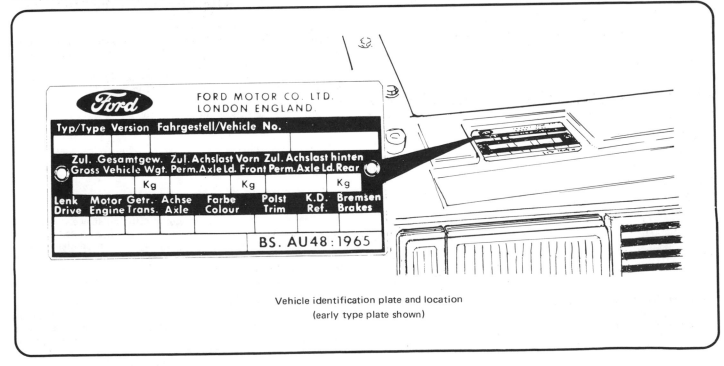

Vehicle identification plate and location
(early type plate shown)

Safety first!

Professional motor mechanics are trained in safe working procedures. However enthusiastic you may be about getting on with the job in hand, do take the time to ensure that your safety is not put at risk. A moment's lack of attention can result in an accident, as can failure to observe certain elementary precautions.

There will always be new ways of having accidents, and the following points do not pretend to be a comprehensive list of all dangers; they are intended rather to make you aware of the risks and to encourage a safety-conscious approach to all work you carry out on your vehicle.

Essential DOs and DON'Ts

DON'T rely on a single jack when working underneath the vehicle. Always use reliable additional means of support, such as axle stands, securely placed under a part of the vehicle that you know will not give way.

DON'T attempt to loosen or tighten high-torque nuts (e.g. wheel hub nuts) while the vehicle is on a jack; it may be pulled off.

DON'T start the engine without first ascertaining that the transmission is in neutral (or 'Park' where applicable) and the parking brake applied.

DON'T suddenly remove the filler cap from a hot cooling system – cover it with a cloth and release the pressure gradually first, or you may get scalded by escaping coolant.

DON'T attempt to drain oil until you are sure it has cooled sufficiently to avoid scalding you.

DON'T grasp any part of the engine, exhaust or catalytic converter without first ascertaining that it is sufficiently cool to avoid burning you.

DON'T allow brake fluid or antifreeze to contact vehicle paintwork.

DON'T syphon toxic liquids such as fuel, brake fluid or antifreeze by mouth, or allow them to remain on your skin.

DON'T inhale dust – it may be injurious to health (see *Asbestos* below).

DON'T allow any spilt oil or grease to remain on the floor – wipe it up straight away, before someone slips on it.

DON'T use ill-fitting spanners or other tools which may slip and cause injury.

DON'T attempt to lift a heavy component which may be beyond your capability – get assistance.

DON'T rush to finish a job, or take unverified short cuts.

DON'T allow children or animals in or around an unattended vehicle.

DO wear eye protection when using power tools such as drill, sander, bench grinder etc, and when working under the vehicle.

DO use a barrier cream on your hands prior to undertaking dirty jobs – it will protect your skin from infection as well as making the dirt easier to remove afterwards; but make sure your hands aren't left slippery.

DO keep loose clothing (cuffs, tie etc) and long hair well out of the way of moving mechanical parts.

DO remove rings, wristwatch etc, before working on the vehicle – especially the electrical system.

DO ensure that any lifting tackle used has a safe working load rating adequate for the job.

DO keep your work area tidy – it is only too easy to fall over articles left lying around.

DO get someone to check periodically that all is well, when working alone on the vehicle.

DO carry out work in a logical sequence and check that everything is correctly assembled and tightened afterwards.

DO remember that your vehicle's safety affects that of yourself and others. If in doubt on any point, get specialist advice.

IF, in spite of following these precautions, you are unfortunate enough to injure yourself, seek medical attention as soon as possible.

Asbestos

Certain friction, insulating, sealing, and other products – such as brake linings, brake bands, clutch linings, torque converters, gaskets, etc – contain asbestos. *Extreme care must be taken to avoid inhalation of dust from such products since it is hazardous to health.* If in doubt, assume that they *do* contain asbestos.

Fire

Remember at all times that petrol (gasoline) is highly flammable. Never smoke, or have any kind of naked flame around, when working on the vehicle. But the risk does not end there – a spark caused by an electrical short-circuit, by two metal surfaces contacting each other, by careless use of tools, or even by static electricity built up in your body under certain conditions, can ignite petrol vapour, which in a confined space is highly explosive.

Always disconnect the battery earth (ground) terminal before working on any part of the fuel or electrical system, and never risk spilling fuel on to a hot engine or exhaust.

It is recommended that a fire extinguisher of a type suitable for fuel and electrical fires is kept handy in the garage or workplace at all times. Never try to extinguish a fuel or electrical fire with water.

Fumes

Certain fumes are highly toxic and can quickly cause unconsciousness and even death if inhaled to any extent. Petrol (gasoline) vapour comes into this category, as do the vapours from certain solvents such as trichloroethylene. Any draining or pouring of such volatile fluids should be done in a well ventilated area.

When using cleaning fluids and solvents, read the instructions carefully. Never use materials from unmarked containers – they may give off poisonous vapours.

Never run the engine of a motor vehicle in an enclosed space such as a garage. Exhaust fumes contain carbon monoxide which is extremely poisonous; if you need to run the engine, always do so in the open air or at least have the rear of the vehicle outside the workplace.

If you are fortunate enough to have the use of an inspection pit, never drain or pour petrol, and never run the engine, while the vehicle is standing over it; the fumes, being heavier than air, will concentrate in the pit with possibly lethal results.

The battery

Never cause a spark, or allow a naked light, near the vehicle's battery. It will normally be giving off a certain amount of hydrogen gas, which is highly explosive.

Always disconnect the battery earth (ground) terminal before working on the fuel or electrical systems.

If possible, loosen the filler plugs or cover when charging the battery from an external source. Do not charge at an excessive rate or the battery may burst.

Take care when topping up and when carrying the battery. The acid electrolyte, even when diluted, is very corrosive and should not be allowed to contact the eyes or skin.

If you ever need to prepare electrolyte yourself, always add the acid slowly to the water, and never the other way round. Protect against splashes by wearing rubber gloves and goggles.

When jump starting a car using a booster battery, for negative earth (ground) vehicles, connect the jump leads in the following sequence: First connect one jump lead between the positive (+) terminals of the two batteries. Then connect the other jump lead first to the negative (–) terminal of the booster battery, and then to a good earthing (ground) point on the vehicle to be started, at least 18 in (45 cm) from the battery if possible. Ensure that hands and jump leads are clear of any moving parts, and that the two vehicles do not touch. Disconnect the leads in the reverse order.

Mains electricity

When using an electric power tool, inspection light etc, which works from the mains, always ensure that the appliance is correctly connected to its plug and that, where necessary, it is properly earthed (grounded). Do not use such appliances in damp conditions and, again, beware of creating a spark or applying excessive heat in the vicinity of fuel or fuel vapour.

Ignition HT voltage

A severe electric shock can result from touching certain parts of the ignition system, such as the HT leads, when the engine is running or being cranked, particularly if components are damp or the insulation is defective. Where an electronic ignition system is fitted, the HT voltage is much higher and could prove fatal.

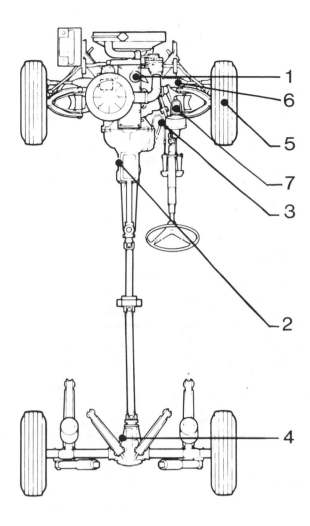

Recommended lubricants and fluids

Component or system	Lubricant type or specification
1 Engine	20W/50 multigrade engine oil
2 Gearbox (manual)	EP80 hypoid gear oil
3 Gearbox (automatic)	Ford auto trans fluid SQ-M2C-9007-AA
4 Rear axle (differential)	EP90 hypoid gear oil
5 Front wheel bearings	Lithium-based grease
6 Steering (manual)	EP90 hypoid gear oil
6 Steering (power-assisted)	Automatic transmission fluid
7 Brakes	Hydraulic fluid to SAE J1703

Note: The above are general recommendations. Lubrication requirements vary from territory to territory and depend on the usage to which the vehicle is put - consult the operators handbook supplied with your car.

Routine maintenance

Maintenance is essential for ensuring safety and desirable for the purpose of getting the best in terms of performance and economy from your car. Over the years the need for periodic lubrication - oiling, greasing, and so on - has been drastically reduced if not totally eliminated. This has unfortunately tended to lead some owners to think that because no such action is required, components either no longer exist, or will last for ever. This is a serious delusion. It follows therefore that the largest initial element of maintenance is visual examination. This may lead to repairs or renewals.

In the summary given here the 'essential for safety' items are shown in **bold type**. They must be attended to at the regular frequencies shown in order to avoid the possibility of accidents and loss of life. Other neglect results in unreliability, increased running costs, more rapid wear and more rapid depreciation of the vehicle in general.

Every 250 miles (400 km) or weekly - whichever comes first

Steering
Check the tyre pressures.
Examine tyres for wear or damage.
Is steering smooth and accurate?

Brakes
Check reservoir fluid level.
Is there any fall off in braking efficiency?
Try an emergency stop.

Lights, wipers and horns
Do all bulbs work at the front and rear?
Are the headlamp beams aligned properly?
Do the wipers and horns work?
Check washer fluid level(s).

Engine
Check the engine oil level and top-up if required.
Check the radiator coolant level and top-up if required.
Check the battery electrolyte level and top-up to the level of the separators with distilled water.

Seat belts
Check all belts for damage, wear and buckle operation.

Every 6,000 miles (9,600 km)

Check tension of alternator drivebelt (Chapter 2, Section 11).
Clean fuel pump filter (Chapter 3).
Check wear in disc pads (Chapter 9).
Check rear brake shoe lining wear (Chapter 9).
Renew engine oil and filter. Drain oil when engine is hot into a suitable container. Remove and renew the filter as given in

Chapter 1. Refit drain plug and top-up the engine oil level using the recommended grade of oil (page 12).
Check fluid level in brake master cylinder and top-up as necessary (Chapter 9).
Check manual transmission oil level and top-up if necessary. A combined level/filler plug is fitted and the level of oil must be up to the bottom of the plug hole.
Check power steering fluid level (if fitted).
Check automatic transmission oil level - see Chapter 6.
Check rear axle oil level and top-up if necessary. A combined level/filler plug is fitted - the level of oil to be up to the bottom of the plug hole.
Check and adjust the clutch cable free movement (early models - Chapter 5).
Inspect steering and suspension components for wear (Chapter 13).
Check and adjust valve clearances (Chapter 1).
Clean and re-gap spark plugs (Chapter 4).
Inspect brake lines and flexible hoses for damage or deterioration (Chapter 9).
Check exhaust system for leaks or broken mountings.
Check carburettor adjustment (Chapters 3 or 13).
Change position of roadwheels to even out tyre wear, if wished.
Lubricate door hinges, locks etc.
Clean crankcase ventilation PCV valve.
Clean and inspect the coil and distributor, including checking the condition and adjustment of the distributor points (Chapter 4).
Check generally, including underneath the car for evidence of fluid, exhaust, oil or water leaks.

Every 12,000 miles (19,000 km)

Check ignition timing (Chapter 4).
Check front wheel alignment (Chapter 11).
Check operation of handbrake - adjust if necessary (Chapter 9).
Remove and renew the spark plugs (Chapter 4).
Remove and renew the distributor contact points (Chapter 4).
Lubricate the handbrake linkages with medium grease.

Every 24,000 miles (38,000 km) or at two yearly intervals

Drain cooling system and refill with 'long-life' type antifreeze mixture.
Clean, repack with grease and adjust front wheel bearings.
Renew the air cleaner element (Chapter 3).

Every 36,000 miles (58,000 km)

Bleed hydraulic system, renew all system seals and refill with clean, fresh fluid.
Remove plugs and grease front suspension upper swivel balljoints.

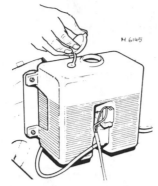

Checking windscreen washer fluid level

Engine oil dipstick

Removing radiator cap

Checking battery electrolyte level

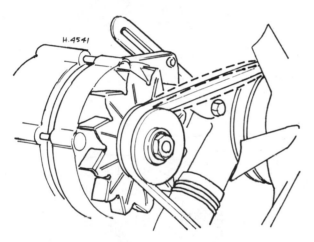

Checking alternator drivebelt tension

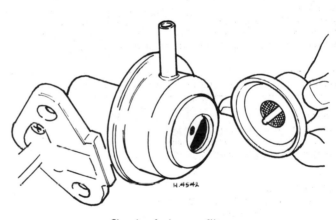

Cleaning fuel pump filter

Installing new oil filter

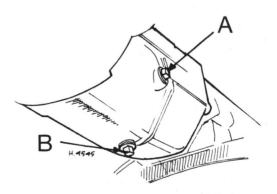

Manual gearbox filler (A) and drain plug (B)

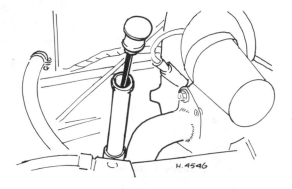

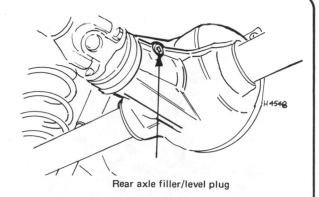

Rear axle filler/level plug

Automatic transmission dipstick and filler tube

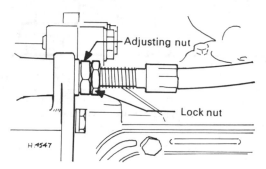

Adjusting nut

Lock nut

Clutch cable adjustment point (pre-1980 models)

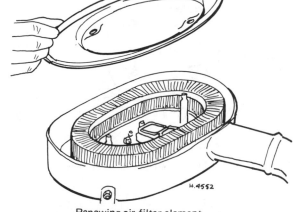

Adjusting valve clearances

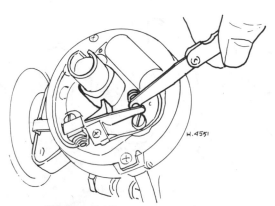

Checking distributor contact points gap

Renewing air filter element

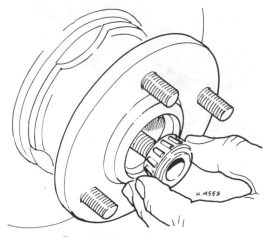

Removing front wheel outer bearing

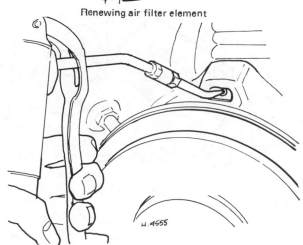

Greasing front suspension upper swivel balljoint using special adaptor

Chapter 1 Engine

For modifications, and information applicable to later models, see Supplement at end of manual

Contents

Specifications

Engine (general)

	1.6 HC Economy LSC	1.6 HC LCJ	2.0 HC NEG
Engine type		Four in-line, single overhead camshaft	
Engine marking	**1.6 HC Economy LSC**	**1.6 HC LCJ**	**2.0 HC NEG**
Firing order	1–3–4–2 (No 1 at timing belt end)		
Bore in (mm)	3.452 (87.67)	3.452 (87.67)	3.576 (90.82)
Stroke in (mm)	2.6 (66)	2.6 (66)	3.03 (76.95)
Cubic capacity (cc) (nominal)	1593	1593	1993
Compression ratio	9.2 : 1 (low compression 8.2 : 1)		
Compression pressure at starter speed lbf/in^2 (kgf/cm^2)		157 to 184 (11 to 13)	
Maximum engine speed rev/min ...	5800	5800	6300
Engine power (DIN) HP at rev/min ...	58 at 4500	71 at 5000	96 at 5200
Torque (DIN) lbf ft (kgf m)	82 (11.3)	87 (12.0)	111 (15.4)
at rev/min	2600	2700	3500

Cylinder block

	1600 (all models)		2000 (all models)	
Cast identification marks	16		20	
Number of main bearings	5		5	
Cylinder bore dia. grades:	inches	mm	inches	mm
Standard grade:				
1	3.4508–3.4512	(87.650–87.660)	3.5748–3.5752	(90.800–90.810)
2	3.4512–3.4516	(87.660–87.670)	3.5752–3.5756	(90.810–90.820)
3	3.4516–3.4520	(87.670–87.680)	3.5756–3.5760	(90.820–90.830)
4	3.4520–3.4524	(87.680–87.690)	3.5760–3.5764	(90.830–90.840)
Oversize A	3.4709–3.4713	(88.160–88.170)	3.5949–3.5953	(91.310–91.320)
Oversize B	3.4713–3.4717	(88.170–88.180)	3.5953–3.5957	(91.320–91.330)
Oversize C	3.4717–3.4720	(88.180–88.190)	3.5957–3.5961	(91.330–91.340)
Standard supp. in service	3.4520–3.4524	(87.680–87.690)	3.5760–3.5764	(90.830–90.840)
Oversize 0.5	3.4717–3.4720	(88.180–88.190)	3.5957–3.5961	(91.330–91.340)
Oversize 1.0	3.4913–3.4917	(88.680–88.690)	3.6154–3.6157	(91.830–91.840)

Centre main bearing width in (mm)	1.072–1.070 (27.22–27.17)
Main bearing liners fitted:	
Inner diameter (standard):	
RED in (mm)	2.2446–2.2456 (57.014–57.038)
BLUE in (mm)	2.2442–2.2452 (57.004–57.028)
Crankshaft:	
Undersize:	
0.25 RED in (mm)	2.2348–2.2357 (56.764–56.788)
BLUE in (mm)	2.2344–2.2354 (56.754–56.778)
0.50 in (mm)	2.2250–2.2263 (56.514–56.548)
0.75 in (mm)	2.2151–2.2164 (56.264–56.298)
1.00 in (mm)	2.2053–2.2066 (56.014–56.048)
Main bearing parent bore dia:	
RED in (mm)	2.3866–2.3870 (60.620–60.630)
BLUE in (mm)	2.3870–2.3874 (60.630–60.640)

Crankshaft

Endfloat in (mm)	0.0032–0.0110 (0.08–0.28)
Main bearing journal diameters:	
Standard:	
RED in (mm)	2.2441–2.2437 (57.000–56.990)
BLUE in (mm)	2.2437–2.2433 (56.990–56.980)
Undersize:	
0.25 in (mm)	2.2338–2.2335 (56.740–56.730)
0.50 in (mm)	2.2244–2.2240 (56.500–56.490)
0.75 in (mm)	2.2146–2.2142 (56.250–56.240)
1.00 in (mm)	2.2047–2.2043 (56.000–56.990)
Thrust washer thickness:	
Standard in (mm)	0.091–0.0925 (2.3–2.35)
Undersize in (mm)	0.098–0.100 (2.5–2.55)
Main bearing clearance in (mm)	0.0005–0.0019 (0.014–0.048)
Crankpin journal diameter:	
Standard:	
RED in (mm)	2.0472–2.0468 (52.000–51.990)
BLUE in (mm)	2.0468–2.0465 (51.990–51.980)
Undersize:	
0.25 RED in (mm)	2.0374–2.0370 (51.750–51.740)
0.25 BLUE in (mm)	2.0370–2.0366 (51.740–51.730)
0.50 in (mm)	2.0276–2.0272 (51.500–51.490)
0.75 in (mm)	2.0177–2.0173 (51.250–51.240)

Camshaft

Drive	Toothed belt
Thrust plate thickness:	
Type 1 in (mm)	0.158 (4.01)
Type 2 in (mm)	0.157 (3.98)
Width of camshaft groove in (mm)	$0.1600 {\,}^{+0.0028}_{-0.0000}$ ($4.064{\,}^{+0.070}_{-0.000}$)
	1600
Cam lift in (mm)	0.2348 (5.964)
Cam heel to toe dimensions in (mm)	1.387–1.417 (35.23–35.98)
	2000
Cam lift in (mm)	0.2493 (6.332)
Cam heel to toe dimensions in (mm)	1.428–1.441 (36.26–36.60)
Journal diameter (all models):	
Front in (mm)	1.6539–1.6531 (42.01–41.99)
Centre in (mm)	1.7571–1.7563 (44.63–44.61)

Rear in (mm)	...	...	...	...	...	...	...	1.7720–1.7713 (45.01–44.99)
Bearing - inside diameter (all models):								
Front in (mm)	...	...	...	...	...	...	...	1.6557–1.6549 (42.055–42.035)
Centre in (mm)	...	...	...	...	...	...	...	1.7588–1.7580 (44.675–44.655)
Rear in (mm)	...	...	...	...	...	...	...	1.7381–1.7730 (45.055–45.035)
Camshaft endfloat in (mm)	...	...	...	...	...	...	...	0.0016–0.0047 (0.04–0.12)
Identification colour	...	...	...	...	...	...	...	White (1600), Yellow (2000)

Pistons

						1600 (all models)	2000 (all models)
Piston diameter:							
Standard:							
Grade 1 in (mm)	...	...	...	...	...	3.4490–3.4494 (87.605–87.615)	3.5730–3.5734 (90.755–90.765)
2 in (mm)	...	...	...	...	...	3.4494–3.4498 (87.615–87.625)	3.5734–3.5738 (90.765–90.775)
3 in (mm)	...	...	...	...	...	3.4498–3.4502 (87.625–87.635)	3.5738–3.5742 (90.775–90.785)
4 in (mm)	...	...	...	...	...	3.4502–3.4506 (87.635–87.645)	3.5742–3.5746 (90.785–90.795)
Standard supplied in service in (mm)	...	...				3.4500–3.4510 (87.630–87.655)	3.5740–3.5750 (90.780–90.805)
Oversize supplied in service:							
0.5 in (mm)	...	...	...	...	...	3.4697–3.4707 (88.130–88.155)	3.5937–3.5947 (91.280–91.305)
1.0 in (mm)	...	...	...	...	...	3.4894–3.4904 (88.630–88.655)	3.6134–3.6144 (91.780–91.805)

						1600 and 2000 (all models)
Piston clearance in cylinder bore in (mm)	...	...	...	...		0.001–0.0024 (0.025–0.060)
Ring gap (in situ):						
Top in (mm) ...	...	...	...	...	...	0.015–0.023 (0.38–0.58)
Centre in (mm)	...	...	...	...	...	0.015–0.023 (0.38–0.58)
Bottom in (mm)	...	...	...	...	...	0.0157–0.055 (0.4–1.4)

Gudgeon pins

Length in (mm) ...	...	...	...	...	...	...	...	2.83–2.87 (72–72.8)
Diameter:								
RED in (mm)	...	...	...	...	...	...	...	0.94465–0.94476 (23.994–23.997)
BLUE in (mm)	...	...	...	...	...	...	...	0.94476–0.94488 (23.997–24.000)
YELLOW in (mm) ...	...	...	...	...	...	...		0.94488–0.94500 (24.000–24.003)
Interference fit in piston in (mm)	...	...	...	...	...			0.0002–0.00043 (0.005–0.011)
Clearance in small end bush in (mm)	...	...	...	...				0.0007–0.00153 (0.018–0.039)

Connecting rods

Big-end bore:								
RED in (mm)	...	...	...	...	...	...	...	2.1653–2.1657 (55.00–55.01)
BLUE in (mm)	...	...	...	...	...	...	...	2.1657–2.1661 (55.01–55.02)
Small end bush diameter in (mm)	...	...	...	...	...			0.9434–0.9439 (23.964–23.976)
Inside diameter:								
Standard:								
RED in (mm)	...	...	...	...	...	...	...	2.0478–2.0487 (52.014–52.038)
BLUE in (mm)	...	...	...	...	...	...	...	2.0474–2.0483 (52.004–52.028)
Undersize:								
0.25 RED in (mm)	...	...	...	...	...			2.0379–2.0388 (51.764–51.788)
0.25 BLUE in (mm)	...	...	...	...	...			2.0376–2.0385 (51.754–51.778)
0.50 in (mm)	...	...	...	...	...	...		2.0281–2.0294 (51.514–51.548)
0.75 in (mm)	...	...	...	...	...	...		2.0183–2.0196 (51.264–51.298)
1.00 in (mm)	...	...	...	...	...	...		2.0084–2.0100 (51.014–51.048)
Crankpin to bearing liner clearance:								
Standard in (mm)	...	...	...	...	...	...		0.00055–0.0018 (0.014–0.048)
Undersize in (mm)	...	...	...	...	...	...		0.00055–0.0023 (0.014–0.058)

Cylinder head

								1600 models	2000 models
Cast identification number	...	...	...	...	...	...	...	6	0

								1600 and 2000 (all models)
Valve seat angle ...	...	...	...	...	...	...	...	44º 30'–45º
Valve guide inside diameter, inlet and exhaust:								
Standard in (mm)	...	...	...	...	...	...		0.3174–0.3184 (8.063–8.088)
Oversize:								
0.2 in (mm)	...	...	...	...	...	...	...	0.3253–0.3263 (8.263–8.288)
0.4 in (mm)	...	...	...	...	...	...	...	0.3332–0.3342 (8.463–8.488)
Parent bore for camshaft bearing liners:								
Front in (mm)	...	...	...	...	...	...	...	1.7745–1.7757 (45.072–45.102)
Centre in (mm)	...	...	...	...	...	...	...	1.8776–1.8001 (47.692–45.722)
Rear in (mm)	...	...	...	...	...	...	...	1.8926–1.8938 (48.072–48.102)

Valves

								1600 and 2000 (all models)
Valve clearances (cold):								
Inlet in (mm)	...	...	...	...	...	...	...	0.008 (0.20)
Exhaust in (mm)	...	...	...	...	...	...	...	0.010 (0.25)

	1600 models	2000 models
Inlet opens	22° BTDC	24° BTDC
Inlet closes	54° ABDC	64° ABDC
Exhaust opens	64° BBDC	70° BBDC
Exhaust closes	12° ATDC	18° ATDC

Inlet valve

	1600 models	2000 models
Length in (mm)	4.449 ± 0.016 (113 ± 0.4)	4.3760 (111.15)
Valve head diameter in (mm)	1.654 ± 0.008 (42 ± 0.2)	1.654 ± 0.008 (42 ± 0.2)
Valve stem diameter:		
Standard in (mm)	0.3167–0.3159 (8.043–8.025)	
Oversize:		
0.2 in (mm)	0.3245–0.3238 (8.243–8.225)	
0.4 in (mm)	0.3324–0.3317 (8.443–8.425)	
Valve stem to guide clearance in (mm)	0.0008–0.0025 (0.020–0.063)	
Valve lift in (mm)	0.3741 (9.503)	0.3985 (10.121)

	1600 and 2000 (all models)
Valve spring free-length in (mm)	1.73 (44)

	1600 models	2000 models
Spring load, valve open lb (kg)	169.4 ± 6.6 (77 ± 3)	176 ± 6 (80 ± 3)

	1600 and 2000 (all models)
Spring load, valve closed lb (kg)	68 ± 4 (31 ± 2)
Spring length, compressed in (mm)	0.945 (24)

Exhaust valves

	1600 models	2000 models
Length in (mm)	4.431 ± 0.019 (112.55 ± 0.5)	4.35 ± 0.017 (110.6 ± 0.45)

	1600 models	2000 models
Valve head diameter in (mm)	1.34–1.35 (34.00–34.40)	1.41–1.42 (35.80–36.20)

	1600 and 2000 (all models)
Valve stem diameter:	
Standard in (mm)	0.3156–0.3149 (8.017–7.999)
Oversize:	
0.2 in (mm)	0.3235–0.3228 (8.217–8.199)
0.4 in (mm)	0.3314–0.3307 (8.417–8.399)
Valve stem to guide clearance in (mm)	0.0018–0.0035 (0.046–0.089)

	1600 models	2000 models
Valve lift in (mm)	0.3728 (9.47)	0.3992 (10.14)

	1600 and 2000 (all models)
Valve spring free length in (mm)	1.732 (44)

	1600 models	2000 models
Spring load, valve open lb (kg)	170 ± 6 (77 ± 3)	176 ± 6 (80 ± 3)

	1600 and 2000 (all models)
Spring load, valve closed lb (kg)	68.3 ± 4.4 (31 ± 2)
Spring length, compressed in (mm)	0.95 (24)

Engine lubrication data (all models)

Oil change without renewal of filter. Imp. pints (litres)	5.7 (3.25)
Oil change with renewal of filter. Imp. pints (litres)	6.6 (3.75)
Minimum oil pressure:	
At 700 rpm lb f/in^2 (kg f/cm^2) ...	30 (2.1)
At 1500 rpm lb f/in^2 (kg f/cm^2) ...	36 (2.5)
Relief valve opens at lb f/in^2 (kg f/cm^2) ...	57–67 (4.0–4.7)
Oil pump outer rotor and housing clearance in (mm)	0.006–0.012 (0.15–0.30)
Inner and outer rotor clearance in (mm)	0.002–0.008 (0.05–0.20)
Inner and outer rotor endfloat in (mm)	0.0012–0.004 (0.03–0.10)

Torque wrench settings

	lb f ft	kg fm
Main bearing caps	64.5–74.5	9.0–10.4
Flywheel	46.5–50.9	6.5–7.1
Big-end bolts	29.7–34.7	4.1 — 4.8

	lbf ft	kgf m
Oil pump	12—15	1.7—2.1
Oil pump cover	6.4—9.3	0.9—1.3
Oil sump:		
First stage	0.7—1.4	0.1—0.2
Second stage	4.3—5.7	0.6—0.8
Third stage	6—7.5	0.8—0.9
Oil drain plug	15—20	2.1—2.8
Cylinder head:		
First stage	15—30	2.0—4.1
Second stage	36—51	4.9—7.0
Third stage (after delay of twenty minutes)	54—61	7.4—8.4
Fourth stage (after warming up)	70—85	9.6—11.7
Rocker cover:		
1st to 6th bolt - Sequence (1)	3.5—5.0	0.5—0.7
7th and 8th bolt (2)	1.4—1.7	0.2—0.25
9th and 10th bolt (3)	3.5—5.0	0.5—0.7
7th and 8th bolt (4)	3.5—5.0	0.5—0.7
Spark plugs	14.3—20	2.0—2.8

1 General description

Engines fitted to models covered by this manual are of the four cylinder overhead camshaft design and available in two capacities, 1600 cc and 2000 cc. An exploded view identifying the main components is shown in Fig. 1.1.

The cylinder head is of the crossflow design with the inlet manifold one side and the exhaust manifold on the other. As flat top pistons are used the combustion chambers are contained in the cylinder head.

The combined crankcase and cylinder block is made of cast iron and houses the pistons and crankshaft. Attached to the underside of the crankcase is a pressed steel sump which acts as a reservoir for the engine oil. Full information on the lubricating system will be found in Section 24.

The cast iron cylinder head is mounted on top of the cylinder block and acts as a support for the overhead camshaft. The slightly angled valves operate directly in the cylinder head and are controlled by the camshaft via cam followers. The camshaft is operated by a toothed reinforced composite rubber belt from the crankshaft. To eliminate backlash and prevent slackness of the belt a spring loaded tensioner in the form of a jockey wheel is in contact with the back of the belt. It serves two further functions, to keep the belt away from the water pump and also to increase the contact area of the camshaft and crankshaft sprocket.

The drive belt also operates the auxiliary shaft sprocket and it is from this shaft that the oil pump, distributor and fuel pump operate.

The inlet manifold is mounted on the left-hand side of the cylinder head and to this the carburettor is fitted. A water jacket is incorporated in the inlet manifold so that the petrol/air charge may be pre-heated before entering the combustion chambers.

The exhaust manifold is mounted on the right-hand side of the cylinder head and connects to a single downpipe and silencer system.

Aluminium alloy pistons are connected to the crankshaft by 'H' section forged steel connecting rods and gudgeon pins. The gudgeon pin is a press fit in the small end of the connecting rod but a floating fit in the piston boss. Two compression rings and one scraper ring, all located above the gudgeon pin, are fitted.

The forged crankshaft runs in five main bearings and endfloat is accommodated by fitting thrust washers either side of the centre main bearing.

Before commencing any overhaul work on the engine refer to Section 8, where information is given about special tools that are required to remove the cylinder head, drive belt tensioner and oil pump.

2 Major operations possible with the engine in place

The following major operations can be carried out to the engine with it in place:
1 *Removal and replacement of camshaft (cylinder head removal)*
2 *Removal and replacement of cylinder head*
3 *Removal and replacement of camshaft drivebelt*
4 *Removal and replacement of oil pump*
5 *Removal and replacement of engine front mountings*
6* *Removal and replacement of the sump*
7* *Removal and replacement of the big end bearings*
8* *Removal and replacement of the pistons and connecting rods*

* In order to carry out these operations, the following additional work will be necessary:

Pre 1979 models
Disconnect the battery and drain the engine oil. Remove the front roadwheels. Disconnect the lower end of the steering shaft. Disconnect the brake lines and hoses from the panel brackets. Cap the pipe ends. Disconnect the fuel pipe from under the right-hand wing and from the fuel pump. Remove the starter motor. Unscrew the engine/transmission mounting bracket bolts and remove the flexible mounting pads from the front crossmember. Raise the engine/transmission on a hoist and unbolt and lower the front (engine) crossmember. The sump pan may now be unbolted and removed. Bleed the brakes after refitting and reassembly.

Post 1979 models
Disconnect the battery and drain the engine oil. Remove the starter motor and the engine/transmission support bracket bolts. Disconnect the ignition coil HT lead and the hose from the fuel pump. Unscrew the nuts from the flexible mountings on the front crossmember. Support the weight of the engine on a hoist and unbolt the right-hand mounting bracket from the engine. The sump pan may now to be unbolted and removed after swivelling it so that it can pass between the crossmember and the clutch housing.

3 Major operations requiring engine removal

The following major operations can be carried out with the engine out of the body frame on the bench or floor:

1 *Removal and replacement of the main bearings*
2 *Removal and replacement of the crankshaft*
3 *Removal and replacement of the flywheel*
4 *Removal and replacement of the crankshaft rear oil seal*

4 Methods of engine removal

The engine may be lifted out either on its own or in unit with the gearbox. On models fitted with automatic transmission it is recommended that the engine be lifted out on its own, unless a substantial crane or overhead hoist is available, because of the weight factor. If the engine and gearbox are removed as a unit they have to be lifted out at a very steep angle, so make sure that there is sufficient lifting height available.

5 Engine removal with gearbox

1 The do-it-yourselfer owner should be able to remove the power unit fairly easily in about four hours. It is essential to have a good hoist and two axle stands if an inspection pit is not available.
2 The sequence of operations listed in this Section is not critical as the position of the person undertaking the work, or the tool in his hand, will determine to a certain extent the order in which the work is tackled. Obviously the power unit cannot be removed until every-

thing is disconnected from it and the following sequence will ensure that nothing is forgotten.

3   Open the bonnet and using a soft pencil mark the outline position of both the hinges at the bonnet to act as a datum for refitting.

4   With the help of a second person to take the weight of the bonnet undo and remove the hinge to bonnet securing bolts with plain and spring washers. There are two bolts to each hinge.

5   Lift away the bonnet and put in a safe place where it will not be scratched. Remove the battery as described in Chapter 10, Section 2.

6   Place a container having a capacity of at least 8 Imp pints (4.5 litres) under the engine sump and remove the oil drain plug. Allow the oil to drain out and then refit the plug.

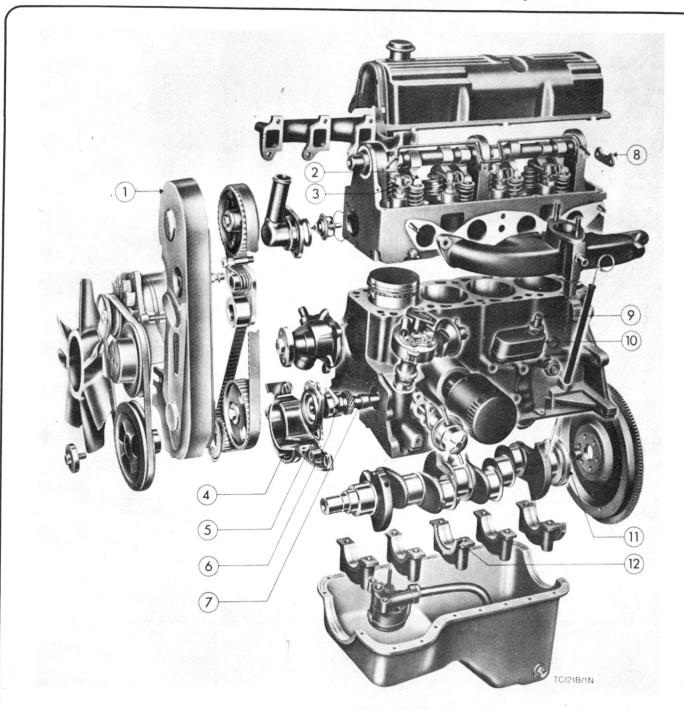

Fig. 1.1. Exploded view of the main engine components

1	Toothed belt guard	7	Auxiliary shaft
2	Cam follower	8	Camshaft thrust plate
3	Cam follower spring	9	P.C.V. valve
4	Crankshaft timing cover	10	Oil separator
5	Auxiliary shaft front cover	11	Crankshaft oil seal
6	Auxiliary shaft thrust plate	12	Thrust washer

7 Refer to Chapter 3, Section 2, and remove the air cleaner assembly from the top of the carburettor.

8 Mark the HT leads so that they may be refitted in their original positions and detach from the spark plugs.

9 Release the HT lead rubber moulding from the clip on the top of the cover.

10 Spring back the clips securing the distributor cap to the distributor body. Lift off the distributor cap.

11 Detach the HT lead from the centre of the ignition coil. Remove the distributor cap from the engine compartment.

12 Refer to Chapter 2, Section 2, and drain the cooling system.

13 Slacken the clip that secures the heater hose to the water pump. Pull off the hose.

14 Slacken the clip that secures the heater hose to the heater unit. Pull off the hose.

15 Slacken the clips that secure the hoses to the automatic choke and pull off the two hoses.

16 Slacken the clip securing the heater hose to the adaptor elbow on the side of the inlet manifold and pull off the hose.

17 Slacken the clip that secures the fuel feed pipe to the carburettor float chamber and pull off the hose. Plug the end to stop dirt ingress or fuel loss due to syphoning.

18 Detach the throttle control inner cable from the operating rod (photo).

19 Unscrew the throttle control outer cable securing nut and detach the cable from the mounting bracket (photo).

20 Detach the vacuum pipe from the vacuum unit on the side of the distributor (photo).

21 Undo and remove the four nuts and washers that secure the carburettor to the inlet manifold. Carefully lift the carburettor up and away from the studs on the manifold.

22 The combined insulation spacer and gasket may now be lifted from the studs. Note that it is marked 'TOP FRONT' and it must be refitted the correct way round.

23 Slacken the clip securing the hose to the manifold branch pipe adaptor and pull off the hose.

24 Slacken the clip securing the hose to the adaptor at the centre of the manifold and pull off the hose.

25 Undo and remove the self lock nuts and bolts securing the inlet manifold to the side of the cylinder head.

26 Note that one of the manifold securing bolts also retains the air cleaner support bracket (photo).

27 Lift away the inlet manifold (photo).

28 Carefully lift away the inlet manifold gasket.

29 Undo and remove the two nuts that secure the exhaust downpipe clamp plate to the exhaust manifold.

30 Slide the clamp plate down the exhaust pipe.

31 Refer to Chapter 2, Section 5, and remove the radiator.

32 Detach the temperature transmitter electric cable from the inlet manifold side of the cylinder head.

33 Pull the crankcase ventilation valve and hose from the oil separator located on the left-hand side of the cylinder block (photo).

34 Detach the oil pressure warning light cable from the switch located below the oil separator.

35 Detach the Lucar terminal connector from the starter motor solenoid (photo). Also detach the terminal connector from the rear of the alternator. If tight a screwdriver will be of assistance.

36 Make a note of the electrical cable connections on the rear of the starter motor solenoid and detach the cables (photos).

Note: Where a separate solenoid is mounted, on left-hand wing, just disconnect one cable from starter motor.

37 Undo and remove the distributor clamp bolt and clamp (photo). Lift away the distributor.

38 Undo and remove the bolt that secures the cable terminal to the engine just in front of the fuel pump (photo).

39 Undo and remove the two bolts and spring washers that secure the fuel pump to the cylinder block (photo).

40 Place the fuel pump on the battery tray (photo). Withdraw the pump operating rod from the cylinder block and put in a safe place.

41 Slacken the alternator securing bolts and push the alternator towards the engine. Lift away the fan belt.

42 Undo and remove the four bolts that secure the fan pulley to the

5.18 Detaching throttle cable from operating rod

5.19 Detaching throttle cable assembly from mounting bracket

5.20 Detaching vacuum pipe from distributor

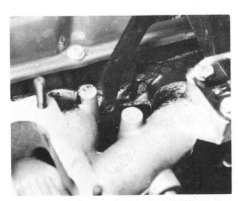

5.26 Air cleaner support bracket retained by one manifold bolt

5.27 Lifting away inlet manifold

5.33 Positive crankcase ventilation (PCV) valve removal

5.35 Removal of starter solenoid cable terminal

5.36A Detachment of cables at rear of solenoid

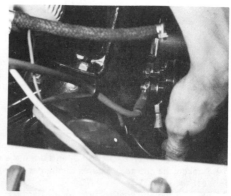

5.36B Detachment of third cable from rear of starter motor

5.37 Removal of distributor clamp bolt

5.38 Detachment of earth cable from engine

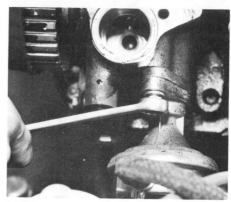

5.39 Removal of fuel pump securing bolts

5.40 Fuel pump removed from engine

5.42 Removal of fan and pulley

5.44 Detachment of exhaust pipe mounting rubber

5.55 Unhooking the clutch release cable

5.57A Supporting the weight of the gearbox

5.57B Lifting rope sling positioned around the engine mountings

5.63A Engine removal - Stage 1

5.63B Engine removal - Stage 2

water pump pulley hub. Lift away the fan and pulley (photo).
43 Working under the car slacken the exhaust downpipe to silencer clamp.
44 Detach the exhaust pipe rubber mounting from the body mounted bracket and pull the exhaust system to one side to give better access. Tie in position with string or wire (photo).
45 To remove centre console, refer to Chapter 12, Section 38.
46 Where parcel tray only is fitted, carefully ease the gearchange lever gaiter from the body panel and slide it up the gearlever.
47 *All models:* Using a screwdriver bend back the locking tabs on the lock ring and carefully unscrew the lock ring and gearchange lever retainer.
48 The gearchange lever can now be lifted upwards and away from the gearbox.
49 Mark the mating flanges of the propeller shaft and final drive so that they may be reconnected in their original positions and undo and remove the four securing bolts.
50 Where a split type propeller shaft is fitted, undo and remove the centre bearing retainer securing bolts, spring and plain washers.
51 Wrap some polythene around the end of the gearbox and secure with string or wire to stop oil running out.
52 Pull off the plug attached to the reverse light switch located on the side of the remote control housing.
53 Using a pair of circlip pliers remove the circlip retaining the speedometer drive cable end to the gearbox extension housing.
54 Pull the speedometer drive cable away from the side of the extension housing.
55 Using a pair of pliers detach the clutch operating cable from the actuating arm that protrudes from the side of the clutch housing. On some models it will be necessary to pull back the rubber gaiter first (photo).
56 Pull the clutch cable assembly through the locating hole in the flange on the clutch housing.
57 Suitably support the weight of the gearbox by using either a jack or an axle stand (photo). Using a rope sling passed under the engine mountings support the weight of the engine (photo).
58 Undo and remove the one bolt that secures the rubber mountings to the gearbox extension housing.
59 Undo and remove the four bolts, spring and plain washers that secure the gearbox support crossmember to the body. Lift away the crossmember.
60 Undo and remove the two engine mountings, lower securing nut and large washer.
61 Check that no electric cables or controls have been left connected and are tucked well out of the way.
62 The complete unit may now be removed from the car. Commence by removing the support from the rear of the gearbox and carefully lower the end to the ground. It will be beneficial if a piece of wood planking is placed between the end of the gearbox and the floor so that it can act as a skid.
63 Carefully raise the engine and pull slightly forward. It will now be necessary to tilt the engine at a very steep angle so that the sump clears the front grille panels. Continue to raise the engine until the sump is just above the front panel (photo).
64 A second person should now lift the rear of the gearbox over the front panel, and when all is clear lower the unit to the floor.
65 Thoroughly wash the exterior with paraffin or water soluble cleaner. Wash off with a strong water jet and dry thoroughly.

66 The gearbox may now be separated from the engine. Undo and remove the bolts that secure the starter motor to the bellhousing flange. Lift away the starter motor.
67 Remove the rear engine cover plate and bracket assembly from the clutch housing.
68 Undo and remove the remaining bolts that secure the clutch bell housing to the rear of the engine. The gearbox may now be parted from the engine. **DO NOT** allow the weight of the gearbox to hang on the input shaft (first motion shaft).

6 Engine removal without gearbox

1 Follow the instructions given in Section 5, paragraphs 1 to 44, inclusive.
2 Suitably support the weight of the gearbox by using either a jack or an axle stand. Using a rope sling passed under the engine mountings support the weight of the engine.
3 Undo and remove the two engine mounting lower securing nuts and large plain washers.
4 Undo and remove the bolts that secure the starter motor to the gearbox flange. Lift away the starter motor.
5 Remove the rear engine cover plate and bracket assembly from the clutch housing. Detach the bracket assembly from the cylinder block and swing it back out of the way.
6 Undo and remove the remaining bolts that secure the clutch bell housing to the rear of the engine.
7 Follow the instructions given in Section 5, paragraphs 61, 63 and 65.

7 Engine removal without automatic transmission

Because of weight considerations it is advisable to detach and remove the automatic transmission first, as described in Chapter 6, Section 10, and then remove the engine as described in Section 6, of this Chapter.

8 Engine - dismantling (general)

1 It is best to mount the engine on a dismantling stand, but if this is not available, stand the engine on a strong bench at a comfortable working height. Failing this, it will have to be stripped down on the floor.
2 During the dismantling process, the greatest care should be taken to keep the exposed parts free from dirt. As an aid to achieving this, thoroughly clean down the outside of the engine, first removing all traces of oil and congealed dirt.
3 A good grease solvent will make the job much easier, for after the solvent has been applied and allowed to stand for a time, a vigorous jet of water will wash off the solvent and grease with it. If the dirt is thick and deeply embedded, work the solvent into it with a strong stiff brush.
4 Finally wipe down the exterior of the engine with a rag and only then, when it is quite clean, should the dismantling process begin. As the engine is stripped, clean each part in a bath of paraffin or petrol.
5 Never immerse parts with oilways in paraffin eg; crankshaft. To clean these parts, wipe down carefully with a petrol dampened rag.

Oilways can be cleaned out with wire. If an airline is available, all parts can be blown dry and the oilways blown through as an added precaution.

6   Re-use of old gaskets is false economy. To avoid the possibility of trouble after the engine has been reassembled **always** use new gaskets throughout.

7   Do not throw away the old gaskets, for sometimes it happens that an immediate replacement cannot be found and the old gasket is then very useful as a template. Hang up the gaskets as they are removed.

8   To strip the engine, it is best to work from the top down. The crankcase provides a firm base on which the engine can be supported in an upright position. When the stage is reached where the crankshaft must be removed, the engine can be turned on its side and all other work carried out with it in this position.

9   Wherever possible, replace nuts, bolts and washers finger tight from wherever they were removed. This helps to avoid loss and muddle. If they cannot be replaced then arrange them in a fashion that it is clear from whence they came.

10 Before dismantling begins it is important that three special tools are obtained otherwise certain work cannot be carried out. The special tools are shown in the photo, and will enable the cylinder head bolts, the oil pump bolts, the timing belt tensioner plate and the valve springs to be removed.

9   Engine - removing ancillary components

Before basic engine dismantling begins, it is necessary to strip it of ancillary components

a) *Fuel system components*
   Carburettor and manifold assembly
   Exhaust manifold
   Fuel pump
   Fuel line
b) *Ignition system components*
   Spark plugs
   Distributor
c) *Electrical system components*
   Alternator
   Starter motor
d) *Cooling system components*
   Fan and hub
   Water pump
   Thermostat housing and thermostat
   Water temperature indicator sender unit
e) *Engine*
   Oil filter
   Oil pressure sender unit
   Oil level dipstick
   Oil filler cap and top cover
   Engine mountings
   Crankcase ventilation valve and oil separator
f) *Clutch*
   Clutch pressure plate assembly
   Clutch friction plate assembly

Some of these items have to be removed for individual servicing or renewal periodically and details can be found in the appropriate Chapter.

10 Cylinder head - removal (engine in car)

1   Open the bonnet and using a soft pencil mark the outline of both the hinges at the bonnet to act as a datum for refitting.
2   With the help of a second person to take the weight of the bonnet, undo and remove the hinge to bonnet securing bolts with plain and spring washers. There are two bolts to each hinge.
3   Lift away the bonnet and put in a safe place where it will not be scratched.
4   Refer to Chapter 10, Section 2, and remove the battery.
5   Place a container having a capacity of at least 8 Imp pints (4.5 litres) under the engine and sump and remove the oil drain plug. Allow the oil to drain out and then refit the plug.
6   Refer to Chapter 3, Section 2, and remove the air cleaner assembly from the top of the carburettor.

7   Mark the HT leads so that they may be refitted in their original postions and detach from the spark plugs.
8   Release the HT lead rubber moulding from the clip on the top of the cover.
9   Spring back the clips securing the distributor cap to the distributor body. Lift off the distributor cap.
10 Detach the HT lead from the centre of the ignition coil. Remove the distributor cap from the engine compartment.
11 Refer to Chapter 2, Section 2, and drain the cooling system.
12 Refer to Chapter 3, Section 18, and remove the carburettor.
13 The combined insulation spacer and gasket may now be lifted from the studs. Note that it is marked 'TOP FRONT' and it must be refitted the correct way round.
14 Slacken the clip securing the hose to the inlet manifold branch pipe adaptor and pull off the hose.
15 Slacken the clip securing the hose to the adaptor at the centre of the manifold and pull off the hose.
16 Undo and remove the self lock nuts and bolts securing the inlet manifold to the side of the cylinder head. Note that one of the manifold securing bolts also retains the air cleaner support bracket.
17 Lift away the inlet manifold and recover the manifold gasket.
18 Undo and remove the two nuts that secure the exhaust downpipe and clamp plate to the exhaust manifold.
19 Slide the clamp plate down the exhaust pipe.
20 Detach the temperature transmitter electric cable from the inlet manifold side of the cylinder head (photo).
21 Slacken the radiator top hose clips and completely remove the hose (photo).
22 Undo and remove the bolts, spring and plain washers that secure the top cover to the cylinder head (photos).
23 Lift away the top cover (photo).
24 Undo and remove the two self-locking nuts that secure the heat deflector plate to the top of the exhaust manifold. Lift away the deflector plate (photo).
25 Undo and remove the bolts, spring and plain washers that secure the toothed drivebelt guard (photo).
26 Lift away the guard (photo).
27 Release the tension from the drivebelt by slackening the spring loaded roller mounting plate securing bolt (photo).
28 Ease the toothed drivebelt from the camshaft sprocket (photo).
29 Using the special splined tool (21 - 002) together with a socket wrench (photo), slacken the cylinder head securing bolts in a diagonal and progressive manner until all are free from tension. Remove the ten bolts noting that because of the special shape of the bolt head no washers are used. Unfortunately there is no other tool suitable to slot into the bolt head so do not attempt to improvise which will only cause damage to the bolt (Fig. 1.2).
30 The cylinder head may now be removed by lifting upwards (photo). If the head is stuck, try to rock it to break the seal. Under no circumstances try to prise it apart from the cylinder block with a screwdriver or cold chisel, as damage may be done to the faces of the cylinder head and block. On no account turn the crankshaft in an attempt to use compression to break the cylinder head joint as the pistons may contact the valve heads resulting in severe damage. If this fails to work, strike the head sharply with a plastic headed or wooden hammer, or with a metal hammer with an interposed piece of wood to cushion the blow. Under no circumstances hit the head directly with a metal hammer as this may cause the casting to fracture. Several sharp taps with the hammer, at the same time pulling upwards, should free the head. Lift the head off and place to one side (photo).

11 Cylinder head - removal (engine on bench)

The procedure for removing the cylinder head with the engine on the bench is similar to that for removal when the engine is in the car, with the exception of disconnecting the controls and services. Refer to Section 10, and follow the sequence given in paragraphs 22 to 30, inclusive.

12 Auxiliary shaft - removal

1   Using a metal bar lock the shaft sprocket and with an open ended spanner undo and remove the bolt and washer that secures the sprocket to the shaft (photo).

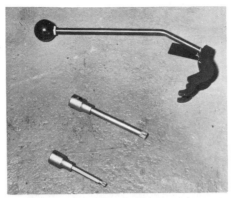

8.10 Three special tools necessary for dismantling

10.20 Temperature transmitter electric cable detachment

10.21 Slackening radiator top hose clip

10.22A Removing top cover front securing bolts

10.22B Top cover flange securing bolts

10.23 Top cover removal

10.24 Removing heat deflector plate

10.25 Removing belt guard securing bolts

10.26 Belt guard removal

10.27 Releasing belt tensioner mounting plate securing bolt

10.28 Removing belt from camshaft sprocket

10.29 Slackening cylinder head securing bolts

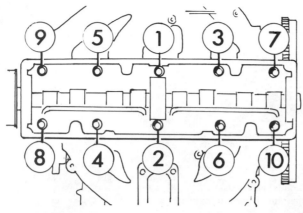

10.30A Cylinder head removal

Fig. 1.2. Correct order for slackening or tightening cylinder head bolts (Secs. 10 and 57)

10.30B Engine with cylinder head removed

12.1 Auxiliary shaft sprocket securing bolt removal

12.2 Removing auxiliary shaft timing cover securing bolts

12.3 Removing auxiliary shaft timing cover

12.4 Removal of auxiliary shaft thrust plate securing screws

12.5 Lifting away thrust plate

12.6 Withdrawal of auxiliary shaft

13.1 Removal of flywheel securing bolts

13.2 Lifting away flywheel

2 Undo and remove the three bolts and spring washers that secure the shaft timing cover to the cylinder block (photo).
3 Lift away the timing cover (photo).
4 Undo and remove the two crosshead screws that secure the shaft thrust plate to the cylinder block (photo).
5 Lift away the thrust plate (photo).
6 The shaft may now be drawn forwards and then lifted away (photo).

13 Flywheel and sump - removal

1 With the clutch removed, as described in Chapter 5, lock the flywheel using a screwdriver in mesh with the starter ring gear and undo the six bolts that secure the flywheel to the crankshaft in a diagonal and progressive manner (photo). Lift away the bolts.
2 Mark the relative position of the flywheel and crankshaft and then lift away the flywheel (photo).
3 Undo the remaining engine backplate securing bolts and ease the backplate from the two dowels. Lift away the backplate (photo).
4 Undo and remove the bolts that secure the sump to the underside of the crankcase (photo).
5 Lift away the sump and its gasket (photo).

14 Oil pump and strainer - removal

1 Undo and remove the screw and spring washer that secures the oil pump pick-up pipe support bracket to the crankcase.
2 Using special splined tool (21 - 012) undo the two special bolts that secure the oil pump to the underside of the crankcase. Unfortunately there is no other tool suitable to slot into the screw head so do not attempt to improvise which will only cause damage to the screw (photo).
3 Lift away the oil pump and strainer assembly (photo).
4 Carefully lift away the oil pump drive making a special note of which way round it is fitted (photo). (Sharply pointed end into crankcase).

15 Crankshaft pulley, sprocket and timing cover - removal

1 Lock the crankshaft using a block of soft wood placed between a crankshaft web and the crankcase then using a socket and suitable extension, undo the bolt that secures the crankshaft pulley. Recover the large diameter plain washer.
2 Using a large screwdriver ease the pulley from the crankshaft. Recover the large diameter thrust washer.
3 Again, using the screwdriver, ease the sprocket from the crankshaft (photo).
4 Undo and remove the bolts and spring washers that secure the timing cover to the front of the crankcase.
5 Lift away the timing cover and the gasket (photo).

16 Pistons, connecting rods and big-end bearings - removal

1 Note that the pistons have an arrow marked on the crown showing the forward facing side (photo). Inspect the big-end bearing caps and connecting rods to make sure identification marks are visible. This is to ensure that the correct end caps are fitted to the correct connecting rods and the connecting rods placed in their respective bores (Fig. 1.3).
2 Undo the big-end nuts and place to one side in the order in which they were removed.
3 Remove the big-end caps, taking care to keep them in the right order and the correct way round. Also ensure that the shell bearings are kept with their correct connecting rods unless the rods are to be renewed (photo).
4 If the big-end caps are difficult to remove, they may be gently tapped with a soft hammer.
5 To remove the shell bearings, press the bearing opposite the groove in both the connecting rod and its cap, and the bearing will slide out easily.
6 Withdraw the pistons and connecting rods upwards and ensure they are kept in the correct order for replacement in the same bore as they were originally fitted.

13.3 Backplate removal

13.4 Removal of sump securing bolts

13.5 Lifting away sump

14.2 Removal of oil pump securing bolts

14.3 Lifting away oil pump and pick-up pipe

14.4 Oil pump drive shaft removal

17 Crankshaft and main bearings - removal

With the engine removed from the car and separated from the gearbox, and the drivebelt, crankshaft pulley and sprocket, flywheel and backplate, oil pump, big-end bearings and pistons all dismantled, proceed to remove the crankshaft and main bearings.

1   Make sure that identification marks are visible on the main bearing end caps, so that they may be refitted in their original positions and also the correct way round (photo).
2   Undo by one turn at a time the bolts which hold the five bearing caps.
3   Lift away each main bearing cap and the bottom half of each bearing shell, taking care to keep the bearing shell in the right caps (photo).
4   When removing the rear main bearing end cap note that this also retains the crankshaft rear oil seal (photo).
5   When removing the centre main bearing, note the bottom semi-circular halves of the thrust washers, one half lying on either side of the main bearing. Lay them with the centre main bearing along the correct side.
6   As the centre and rear bearing end caps are accurately located by dowels it may be necessary to gently tap the end caps to release them.
7   Slightly rotate the crankshaft to free the upper halves of the bearing shells and thrust washers which can be extracted and placed over the correct bearing cap.
8   Carefully lift away the crankshaft rear oil seal (photo).
9   Remove the crankshaft by lifting it away from the crankcase (photo).

18 Camshaft drivebelt - removal (engine in car)

It is possible to remove the camshaft drivebelt with the engine in-situ but experience is such that this type of belt is very reliable and unlikely to break or stretch considerably. However, during a major engine overhaul it is recommended that a new belt is fitted. To renew the belt, engine in the car, first rotate the crankshaft to bring No.1 piston to TDC on its compression stroke then proceed in the following way.

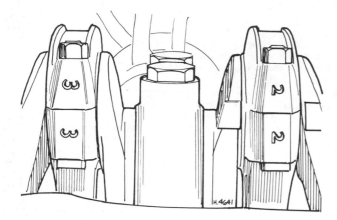

Fig. 1.3. Big-end bearing cap and connecting rod identification marks (Sec. 16)

15.3 Removal of sprocket from crankshaft

15.5 Removal of timing cover and gasket

16.1 Piston identification mark stamped on crown

16.3 Lifting away big-end cap

17.1 Main bearing cap - identification marks

17.3 Lifting away No. 2 main bearing cap

17.4 Rear main bearing cap removal

17.8 Lifting away crankshaft rear oil seal

17.9 Cylinder block and crankcase with crankshaft removed

18.6 Lifting away crankshaft pulley

18.8 Drive belt removal

19.2 Cam follower spring removal

19.4 Compressing valve spring

20.1 Removing camshaft lubrication pipe

20.2 Camshaft lubrication pipe oil holes

20.3 Using a metal bar to lock camshaft sprocket

20.4 Removal of camshaft sprocket

20.5 Removing camshaft thrust plate securing bolts

1 Refer to Chapter 2, Section 2, and drain the cooling system. Slacken the top hose securing clips and remove the top hose.
2 Slacken the alternator mounting bolts and push the unit towards the engine. Lift away the fan belt.
3 Undo and remove the bolts that secure the drivebelt guard to the front of the engine. Lift away the guard.
4 Slacken the belt tensioner mounting plate securing bolt and release the tension on the belt.
5 Place the car in gear (manual gearbox only), and apply the brakes firmly. Undo and remove the bolt and plain washer that secure the crankshaft pulley to the nose of the crankshaft. On vehicles fitted with automatic transmission, the starter must be removed and the ring gear jammed to prevent the crankshaft rotating.
6 Using a screwdriver carefully ease off the pulley (photo).
7 Recover the plain large diameter thrust washer.
8 The drivebelt may now be eased away (photo).
9 Do not rotate the crankshaft or camshaft whilst the drivebelt is off otherwise the valves may contact the pistons, resulting in damage.

19 Valves - removal

1 To enable the valve to be removed, a special valve spring compressor is required. This has a part number of '21 - 005'. However, it was found that it was just possible to use a universal valve spring compressor provided extreme caution was taken.
2 Make a special note of how the cam follower springs are fitted and using a screwdriver remove these from the cam followers (photo).
3 Back off fully the cam follower adjustment and remove the cam followers. Keep these in their respective order so that they can be refitted in their original positions.
4 Using the valve spring compressor, contract the valve springs and lift out the collets (photo).
5 Remove the spring cap and spring and using a screwdriver prise the oil retainer caps out of their seats. Remove each valve and keep in its respective order unless they are so badly worn that they are to be renewed. If they are going to be used again, place them in a sheet of card having eight numbered holes corresponding with the relative positions of the valves when fitted. Also keep the valve springs cups etc., in the correct order.
6 If necessary unscrew the ball head bolts.

20 Camshaft - removal

It is not necessary to remove the engine from the car in order to remove the camshaft. However, it will be necessary to remove the cylinder head first (Section 10) as the camshaft has to be withdrawn from the rear.
1 Undo and remove the bolts, and spring washers and bracket that secures the camshaft lubrication pipe. Lift away the pipe (photo).
2 Carefully inspect the fine oil drillings in the pipe to make sure that none are blocked (photo).
3 Using a metal bar lock the camshaft drive sprocket then undo and remove the sprocket securing bolt and washer (photo).
4 Using a soft faced hammer or screwdriver ease the sprocket from the camshaft (photo).

5 Undo and remove the two bolts and spring washers that secure the camshaft thrust plate to the rear bearing support (photo).
6 Lift away the thrust plate noting which way round it is fitted (photo).
7 Remove the cam follower springs and then the cam followers as detailed in Section 19, paragraphs 2 and 3.
8 The camshaft may now be removed by using a soft faced hammer and tapping rearwards. Take care not to cut the fingers when the camshaft is being handled as the sides of the lobes can be sharp (photo).
9 Lift the camshaft through the bearing inserts as the lobes can damage the soft metal bearing surfaces (photo).
10 If the oil seal has hardened or become damaged, it may be removed by prising it out with a screwdriver (photo).

21 Thermostat housing and belt tensioner - removal

1 Removal of these parts will usually only be necessary if the cylinder head is to be completely dismantled.
2 Undo and remove the two bolts and spring washers that secure the thermostat housing to the front face of the cylinder head.
3 Lift away the thermostat housing and recover its gasket (photo).
4 Undo and remove the bolt and spring washer that secures the belt tensioner to the cylinder head. It will be necessary to override the tension using a screwdriver as a lever (photos).
5 Using tool number '21 - 012' (the tool for removal of the oil pump securing bolts) unscrew the tensioner mounting plate and spring shaped bolt and lift away the tensioner assembly (photo).

22 Gudgeon pin - removal

Interference fit type gudgeon pins are used and it is important that no damage is caused during removal and refitting. Because of this, should it be necessary to fit new pistons, take the parts along to the local Ford garage who will have the special equipment to do this job.

23 Piston rings - removal

1 To remove the piston rings, slide them carefully over the top of the piston, taking care not to scratch the aluminium alloy; never slide them off the bottom of the piston skirt. It is very easy to break the cast iron piston rings if they are pulled off roughly, so this operation should be done with extreme care. It is helpful to make use of an old 0.020 inch (0.5 mm) feeler gauge.
2 Lift one end of the piston ring to be removed out of its groove and insert under it the end of the feeler gauge.
3 Turn the feeler gauge slowly round the piston and, as the ring comes out of its groove, apply slight upward pressure so that it rests on the land above. It can then be eased off the piston with the feeler gauge stopping it from slipping into an empty groove if it is any but the top piston ring that is being removed.

20.6 Camshaft thrust plate removal

20.8 Tapping camshaft through bearings

20.9 Camshaft removal

20.10 Camshaft oil seal removal

21.3 Thermostat housing removal

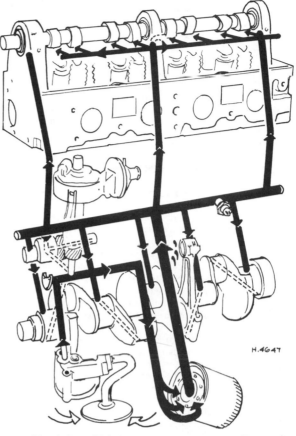

Fig. 1.4. Circulation of lubricant through the engine (Sec. 24)

H.4647

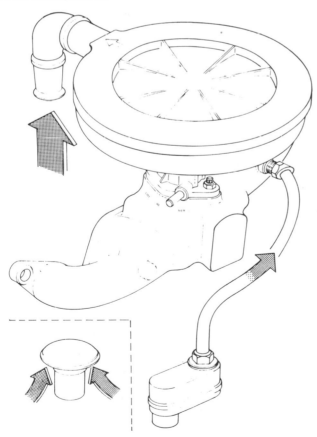

Fig. 1.5. The semi-enclosed engine ventilation system (Sec. 24)

21.4A Removal of belt tensioner mounting plate securing bolt

21.4B Easing off the belt spring tension with a screwdriver

24 Lubrication and crankcase ventilation system - description

1   The pressed steel oil sump is attached to the underside of the crankcase and acts as a reservoir for the engine oil (Fig. 1.4). The oil pump draws oil through a strainer located under the oil surface, passes it along a short passage and into the full flow oil filter. The freshly filtered oil flows from the centre of the filter element and enters the main gallery. Five small drillings connect the main gallery to the five main bearings. The big-end bearings are supplied with oil by the front and rear main bearings via skew oil bores.
     When the crankshaft is rotating, oil is thrown from the hole in each big-end bearing and splashes the thrust side of the piston and bore.
2   The auxiliary shaft is lubricated directly from the main oil gallery. The distributor shaft is supplied with oil passing along a drilling inside the auxiliary shaft.
3   A further three drillings connect the main oil gallery to the overhead camshaft. The centre camshaft bearing has a semi-circular groove from which oil is passed along a pipe running parallel with the camshaft. The pipe is drilled opposite to each cam and cam follower so providing lubrication to the cams and cam followers. Oil then passes back to the sump, via large drillings in the cylinder head and cylinder block.
     A semi enclosed engine ventilation system is used to control crankcase vapour. It is controlled by the amount of air drawn in by the engine when running and the throughput of the regulator valve (Fig. 1.5 and 1.6).
4   The system is known as the PCV system (Positive Crankcase Ventilation) and the advantage of the system is that should the 'blow-by' exceed the capacity of the PCV valve, excess fumes are fed into the engine through the air cleaner. This is caused by the rise in crankcase pressure which creates a reverse flow in the air intake pipe.
5   Periodically, pull the valve and hose from the rubber grommet of the oil separator and inspect the valve for free-movement. If it is stickly in action or is choked with sludge, dismantle it and clean the components.
6   Occasionally check the security and condition of the system connecting hoses.

25 Oil pump - dismantling, inspection and reassembly

1   If oil pump wear is suspected it is possible to obtain a repair kit. Check for wear first as described later in this Section and if confirmed, obtain an overhaul kit or a new pump. The two rotors are a matched pair and form a single replacement unit. Where the rotor assembly is to be re-used the outer rotor, prior to dismantling, must be marked on its front face in order to ensure correct reassembly.
2   Undo and remove the two bolts and spring washers that secure the intake cowl to the oil pump body. Lift away the cowl and its gasket (Fig. 1.7).
3   Note the relative position of the oil pump cover and body and then undo and remove the three bolts and spring washers. Lift away the cover.
4   Carefully remove the rotors from the housing.
5   Using a centre punch tap a hole in the centre of the pressure relief valve sealing plug, (make a note to obtain a new one).
6   Screw in a self tapping screw and, using an open ended spanner, withdraw the sealing plug as shown in Fig. 1.8.
7   Thoroughly clean all parts in petrol or paraffin and wipe dry using a non-fluffy rag. The necessary clearances may now be checked using a machined straight-edge (a good steel rule) and a set of feeler gauges. The critical clearances are between the lobes of the centre rotor and convex faces of the outer rotor; between the rotor and the pump body; and between both rotors and the end cover plate.
8   The rotor lobe clearance may be checked using feeler gauges and should be within the limits 0.002 - 0.008 in (0.05 - 0.20 mm).
9   The clearance between the outer rotor and pump body should be within the limits 0.006 - 0.012 in (0.15 - 0.30 mm) (Fig. 1.9).
10 The endfloat clearance may be measured by placing a steel straight-edge across the end of the pump and measuring the gap between the rotors and the straight-edge. The gap in either rotor should be within the limits 0.0012 - 0.004 in (0.03 - 0.10 mm), as shown in Fig. 1.10.
11 If the only excessive clearances are endfloat it is possible to reduce them by removing the rotors and lapping the face of the body on a flat bed until the necessary clearances are obtained. It must be

emphasised, however, that the face of the body must remain perfectly flat and square to the axis of the rotor spindle otherwise the clearances will not be equal and the end cover will not be a pressure tight fit to the body. It is worth trying, of course, if the pump is in need of renewal anyway but unless done properly, it could seriously jeopardise the rest of the overhaul. Any variations in the other two clearances should be overcome with a new unit.
12 With all parts scrupulously clean first refit the relief valve and spring and lightly lubricate with engine oil.
13 Using a suitable diameter drift drive in a new sealing plug, flat side outwards until it is flush with the intake cowl bearing face.
14 Well lubricate both rotors with engine oil and insert into the body. Fit the oil pump cover and secure with the three bolts in a diagonal and progressive manner to the final torque wrench setting stated in the Specifications.
15 Fit the intermediate shaft into the rotor driveshaft and make sure that the rotor turns freely.
16 Fit the cowl to the pump body, using a new gasket and secure with the two bolts.

26 Oil filter - removal and refitting

     The oil filter is a complete throw away cartridge screwed into the left-hand side of the cylinder block. Simply unscrew the old unit, clean the seating on the block and lubricate with engine oil. Screw the new one into position taking care not to cross the thread. Continue until the sealing ring just touches the block face then tighten one half turn using the hands only. Always run the engine and check for signs of leaks after installation.

27 Engine components - examination for wear

     When the engine has been stripped down and all parts properly cleaned, decisions have to be made as to what needs renewal and the following sections tell the examiner what to look for. In any border line case it is always best to decide in favour of a new part. Even if a part may still be serviceable its life will have been reduced by wear and the degree of trouble needed to replace it in the future must be taken into consideration. However, these things are relative and it depends on whether a quick 'survival' job is being done or whether the car as a whole is being regarded as having many thousands of miles of useful and economical life remaining.

21.5 Using special tool to remove mounting plate and spring securing bolt from belt tensioner

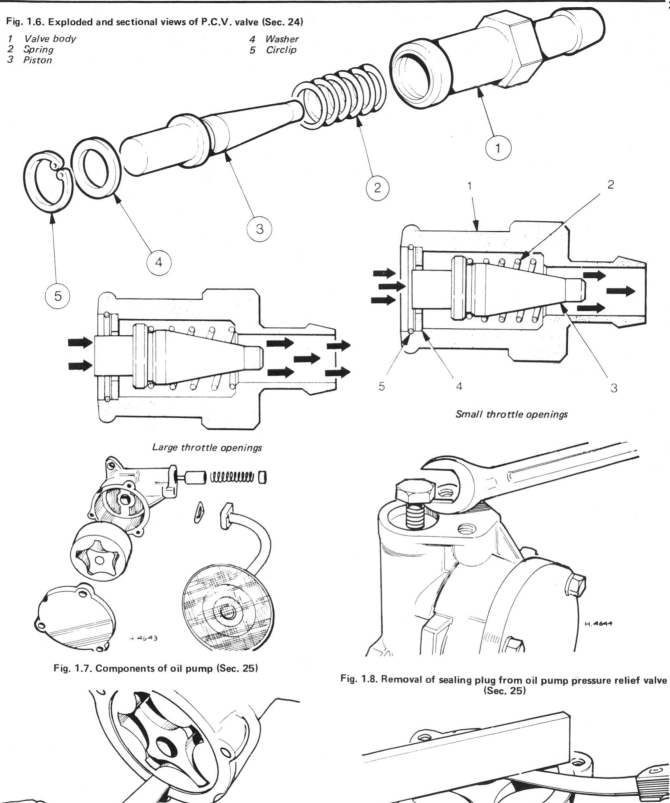

Fig. 1.6. Exploded and sectional views of P.C.V. valve (Sec. 24)

1   Valve body   4   Washer
2   Spring   5   Circlip
3   Piston

Large throttle openings

Small throttle openings

Fig. 1.7. Components of oil pump (Sec. 25)

Fig. 1.8. Removal of sealing plug from oil pump pressure relief valve (Sec. 25)

Fig. 1.9. Checking oil pump outer rotor and body clearance (Sec. 25)

Fig. 1.10. Checking oil pump endfloat clearance (Sec. 25)

28 Crankshaft - examination and renovation

1   Look at the main bearing journals and the crankpins and if there are any scratches or score marks then the shaft will need regrinding. Such conditions will nearly always be accompanied by similar deterioration in the matching bearing shells.
2   Each bearing journal should also be round and can be checked with a micrometer or caliper gauge around the periphery at several points. If there is more than 0.001 in of ovality regrinding is necessary.
3   A main Ford agent or motor engineering specialist will be able to decide to what extent regrinding is necessary and also supply the special undersize shell bearing to match whatever may need grinding off.
4   Before taking the crankshaft for regrinding check also the cylinder bore and pistons as it may be advantageous to have the whole engine done at the same time.

29 Crankshaft, main and big-end bearings - examination and renovation

1   With careful servicing and regular oil and filter changes bearings will last for a very long time but they can still fail for unforeseen reasons. With big-end bearings an indication is a regular rhythmic loud knocking from the crankcase. The frequency depends on engine speed and is particularly noticeable when the engine is under load. This symptom is accompanied by a fail in oil pressure although this is not normally noticeable unless an oil pressure gauge is fitted. Main bearing failure is usually indicated by serious vibration, particularly at higher engine revolutions, accompanied by a more significant drop in oil pressure and a 'rumbling' noise.
2   Big-end bearings can be removed with the engine still in the car. If the failure is sudden and the engine has a low mileage since new or overhaul this is possibly worth doing. Bearing shells in good condition have bearing surfaces with a smooth, even matt silver/grey colour all over. Worn bearings will show patches of a different colour when the bearing metal has worn away and exposed the underlay. Damaged bearings are pitted or scored. It is always well worthwhile fitting new shells as their cost is relatively low. If the crankshaft is in good condition, it is merely a question of obtaining another set of standard size shells. A reground crankshaft will need new bearing shells as a matter of course.

30 Cylinder bores - examination and renovation

1   A new cylinder is perfectly round and the walls parallel throughout its length. The action of the piston tends to wear the walls at right angles to the gudgeon pin due to side thrust. This wear takes place principally on that section of the cylinder swept by the piston rings.
2   It is possible to get an indication of bore wear by removing the cylinder head with the engine still in the car. With the piston down in the bore first signs of wear can be seen and felt just below the top of the bore where the top piston ring reaches and there will be a noticeable lip. If there is no lip it is fairly reasonable to expect that bore wear is not severe and any lack of compression or excessive oil consumption is due to worn or broken piston rings or pistons (see Section 31).
3   If it is possible to obtain a bore measuring micrometer, measure the bore in the thrust plane below the lip and again at the bottom of the cylinder in the same plane. If the difference is more than 0.003 inch (0.076 mm) then a rebore is necessary. Similarly, a difference of 0.003 inch (0.076 mm) or more between two measurements of the bore diameter taken at right angles to each other is a sign of ovality, calling for a rebore.
4   Any bore which is significantly scratched or scored will need reboring. This symptom usually indicates that the piston or rings are damaged also. In the event of only one cylinder being in need of reboring it will still be necessary for all four to be bored and fitted with new oversize pistons and rings. Your Ford agent or local motor engineering specialist will be able to rebore and obtain the necessary matched pistons. If the crankshaft is undergoing regrinding also, it is a good idea to let the same firm renovate and reassemble the crankshaft and pistons to the block. A reputable firm normally gives a guarantee for such work. In cases where engines have been rebored already to their maximum, new cylinder liners are available which may be fitted.

In such cases the same reboring processes have to be followed and the services of a specialist engineering firm are required.

31 Pistons and piston rings - inspection and testing

1   Worn pistons and rings can usually be diagnosed when the symptoms of excessive oil consumption and lower compression occur and are sometimes, though not always, associated with worn cylinder bores. Compression testers that fit into the spark plug hole are available and these can indicate where low compression is occurring. Wear usually accelerates the more it is left so when the symptoms occur, early action can possibly save the expense of a rebore.
2   Another symptom of piston wear is piston slap - a knocking noise from the crankcase not to be confused with big-end bearing failure. It can be heard clearly at low engine speed when there is no load (idling for example) and is much less audible when the engine speed increases. Piston wear usually occurs in the skirt or lower end of the piston and is indicated by vertical streaks in the worn area which is always on the thrust side. It can also be seen where the skirt thickness is different.
3   Piston ring wear can be checked by first removing the rings from the pistons as described in Section 23. Then place the rings in the cylinder bores from the top, pushing them down about 1½ inches (38.1 mm) with the head of a piston (from which the rings have been removed) so that they rest square in the cylinder. Then measure the gap at the ends of the ring with a feeler gauge. If it exceeds 0.023 inch (0.58 mm) for the two top compression rings, or 0.055 inch (1.4 mm) for the lower oil control ring then they need renewal.
4   The grooves in which the rings locate in the piston can also become enlarged in use. The clearance between ring and piston, in the groove, should not exceed 0.004 inch (0.102 mm) for the top two compression rings and 0.003 inch (0.076 mm) for the lower oil control ring.
5   However, it is rare that a piston is only worn in the ring grooves and the need to replace them for this fault alone is hardly ever encountered. Wherever pistons are renewed the weight of the four piston/connecting rod assemblies should be kept within the limit variations of 8 gms to maintain engine balance.

32 Connecting rods and gudgeon pins - examination and renovation

1   Gudgeon pins are a shrink fit into the connecting rods. Neither of these would normally need replacement unless the pistons were being changed, in which case the new pistons would automatically be supplied with new gudgeon pins.
2   Connecting rods are not subject to wear but in extreme circumstances such as engine seizure they could be distorted. Such conditions may be visually apparent but where doubt exists they should be changed. The bearing caps should also be examined for indications of filing down which may have been attempted in the mistaken idea that bearing slackness could be remedied in this way. If there are such signs then the connecting rods should be replaced.

33 Camshaft and camshaft bearings - examination and renovation

1   The camshaft bearing bushes should be examined for signs of scoring and pitting. If they need renewal they will have to be dealt with professionally as, although it may be relatively easy to remove the old bushes, the correct fitting of new ones requires special tools. If they are not fitted evenly and square from the very start they can be distorted thus causing localised wear in a very short time. See your Ford dealer or local engineering specialist for this work.
2   The camshaft itself may show signs of wear on the bearing journals, or cam lobes. The main decision to take is what degree of wear justifies replacement, which is costly. Any signs of scoring or damage to the bearing journals cannot be removed by regrinding. Renewal of the whole camshaft is the only solution. When overhauling the valve gear, check that oil is being ejected from the nozzles onto the cam followers. Turn the engine on the starter to observe this.
3   The cam lobes themselves may show signs of ridging or pitting on the high points. If ridging is light then it may be possible to smooth it out with fine emery. The cam lobes however, are surface hardened and once this is penetrated wear will be very rapid thereafter.

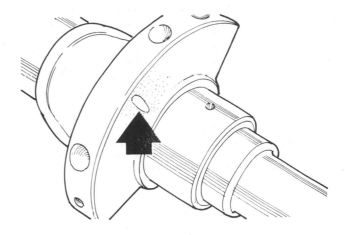

Fig.1.11 Crankshaft identification

A Crankcase main bearings
With either the crankshaft main or big-end bearings, a bearing consists of the crankcase journal bore, crankshaft journal and two bearing liner halves. The parent bore in the block will be standard or 0.015 in (0.38 mm) oversize. An oversize bore is apparent when the bearing caps are marked with white paint (arrowed). No paint markings indicate a standard bore

B Crankshaft — main bearing journal markings
The crankshaft journals were originally machined to standard size or 0.010 in (0.25 mm) undersize. Where the crankshaft web is marked with a green stripe (arrowed) the journals are undersize. If no marking is apparent they are standard

C Crankshaft big-end journal markings
Where the crankshaft big-end journals were originally machined to standard, no mark was made. Where the journal was machined 0.010 in (0.25 mm) undersize a green spot mark will be found on the web next to the journal

D A crankshaft with both main and big-end journals undersize is marked as shown

Fig.1.12 Big-end bearing identification

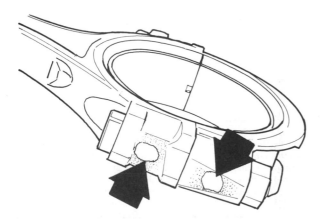

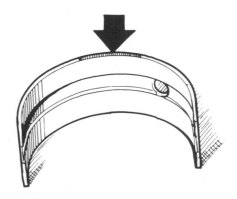

A Connecting rods/bearing caps
The connecting rod and its mating cap are marked on one side only with red paint (arrows). These colour markings must always be fitted onto the same side to avoid incorrect assembly

B Standard size bearing shells are not marked.
Bearing shells fitted to undersize crankshaft or oversize bores are marked on the back; colour markings on the edge (arrowed) denote first two undersizes, see Specifications

34 Cam followers - examination

The faces of the cam followers which bear on the camshaft should show no signs of pitting, scoring or other forms of wear. They should not be a loose sloppy fit on the ballheaded bolt.

Inspect the face which bears onto the valve stem and if pitted the cam follower must be renewed.

35 Valves and valve seats - examination and renovation

1   With the valves removed from the cylinder head examine the heads for signs of cracking, burning away and pitting of the edge where it seats in the port. The valve seats in the cylinder head should also be examined for the same signs. Usually it is the valve that deteriorates first but if a bad valve is not rectified the seat will suffer and this is more difficult to repair.

2   Provided there are no obvious signs of serious pitting the valve should be ground into its seat. This may be done by placing a smear of carborundum paste on the edge of the valve and, using a suction type valve holder, grinding the valve in situ. This is done with a semi-rotary action, rotating the handle of the valve holder between the hands and lifting it occasionally to redistribute the traces of paste. Use a coarse paste to start with. As soon as a matt grey unbroken line appears on both the valve and seat the valve is 'ground in'. All traces of carbon should also be cleaned from the head and neck of the valve stem. A wire brush mounted in a power drill is a quick and effective way of doing this.

3   If the valve requires renewal it should be ground into the seat in the same way as the old valve.

4   Another form of valve wear can occur on the stem where it runs in the guide in the cylinder head. This can be detected by trying to rock the valve from side to side. If there is any movement at all it is an indication that the valve stem or guide is worn. Check the stem first with a micrometer at points along and around its length and if they are not within the specified size new valves will probably solve the problem. If the guides are worn, however, they will need reboring for oversize valves or for fitting guide inserts. The valve seats will also need recutting to ensure they are concentric with the stems (Fig. 1.13). This work should be given to your Ford dealer or local engineering works.

5   When valve seats are badly burnt or pitted, requiring renewal, inserts may be fitted - or replaced if already fitted once before - and once again this is a specialist task to be carried out by a suitable engineering firm.

6   When all valve grinding is completed it is essential that every trace of grinding paste is removed from the valves and ports in the cylinder head. This should be done by thorough washing in petrol or paraffin and blowing out with a jet of air. If particles of carborundum should work their way into the engine they would cause havoc with bearings or cylinder walls.

36 Timing gears and belt - examination and renovation

1   Any wear which takes place in the timing mechanism will be on the teeth of the drive belt or due to stretch of the fabric. Whenever the engine is to be stripped for major overhaul a new belt should be fitted.

2   It is very unusual for the timing gears (sprockets) to wear at the teeth. If the securing bolt/nuts have been loose it is possible for the keyway or hub bore to wear. Check these two points and if damage or wear is evident a new gear must be obtained.

37 Flywheel ring gear - examination and renovation

1   If the ring gear is badly worn or has missing teeth it should be renewed. The old ring can be removed from the flywheel by cutting a notch between two teeth with a hacksaw and then splitting it with a cold chisel.

2   To fit a new ring gear requires heating the ring to 400°F (204°C). This can be done by polishing four equal spaced sections of the gear, laying it on a suitable heat resistant surface (such as fire bricks) and heating it evenly with a blow lamp or torch until the polished areas turn a light yellow tinge. Do not overheat or the hard wearing

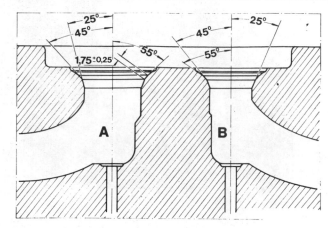

Fig. 1.13. Valve seat angles (Sec. 35)

A Inlet   B Exhaust

properties will be lost. The gear has a chamfered inner edge which should go against the shoulder when put on the flywheel. When hot enough place the gear in position quickly, tapping it home if necessary and let it cool naturally without quenching in any way.

38 Cylinder head and piston crowns - decarbonization

1   When the cylinder head is removed, either in the course of an overhaul or for inspection of bores or valve condition when the engine is in the car, it is normal to remove all carbon deposits from the piston crowns and heads.

2   This is best done with a cup shaped wire brush and an electric drill and is fairly straightforward when the engine is dismantled and the pistons removed. Sometimes hard spots of carbon are not easily removed except by a scraper. When cleaning the pistons with a scraper, take care not to damage the surface of the piston in any way.

3   When the engine is in the car certain precautions must be taken when decarbonising the piston crowns in order to prevent dislodged pieces of carbon falling into the interior of the engine which could cause damage to cylinder bores, piston and rings - or if allowed into the water passages - damage to the water pump. Turn the engine so that the piston being worked on is at the top of its stroke and then mask off the adjacent cylinder bores and all surrounding water jacket orifices with paper and adhesive tape. Press grease into the gap all round the piston to keep carbon particles out and then scrape all carbon away by hand carefully. Do not use a power drill and wire brush when the engine is in the car as it will virtually be impossible to keep all the carbon dust clear of the engine. When completed, carefully clear out the grease around the rim of the piston with a matchstick or something similar - bringing any carbon particles with it. Repeat the process on the other piston crown. It is not recommended that a ring of carbon is left round the edge of the piston on the theory that it will aid oil consumption. This was valid in the earlier days of long stroke low revving engines but modern engines, fuels and lubricants cause less carbon deposits anyway and any left behind tends merely to cause hot spots.

39 Valve guides - inspection

Examine the valve guides internally for wear. If the valves are a very loose fit in the guides and there is the slightest suspicion of lateral rocking using a new valve, then the guides will have to be reamed and oversize valves fitted. This is a job best left to the local Ford garage.

40 Sump - inspection

Wash out the sump in petrol and wipe dry. Inspect the exterior for signs of damage or excessive rust: If evident, a new sump must be obtained. To ensure an oil tight joint scrape away all traces of the old gasket from the cylinder block mating face.

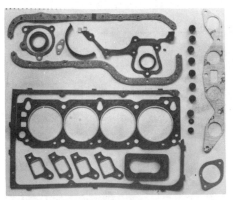

41.1 Items found in gasket set

42.3 Inserting bearing shells into crankcase

42.4 Main bearing cap identification marks

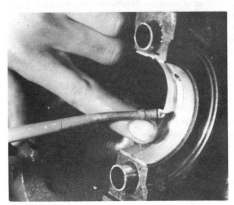

42.6 Fitting bearing shells to main bearing cap

42.7 Applying grease to either side of centre main bearing

42.8 Fitting thrust washers to centre main bearing

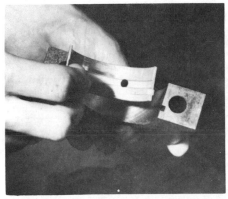

42.9 Lubricating bearing shells

42.10 Fitting crankshaft to crankcase

42.11 Refitting No. 1 main bearing cap. Note identification mark

42.12 Applying gasket cement to rear main bearing cap location

42.13 Refitting rear main bearing cap

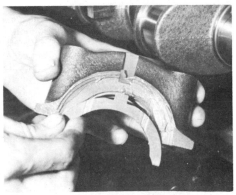

42.14 Fitting thrust washers to centre main bearing cap

42.15 All main bearing caps in position

42.16 Tighten main bearing cap securing bolts.

42.17 Using feeler gauge to check end-float

41 Engine reassembly - general

All components of the engine must be cleaned of oil, sludge and old gaskets and the working area should also be cleared and clean. In addition to the normal range of good quality socket spanners and general tools which are essential, the following must be available before reassembling begins:

1   Complete set of new gaskets (photo).
2   Supply of clean rags.
3   Clean oil can full of clean engine oil.
4   Torque spanner.
5   All new spare parts as necessary.

42 Crankshaft - installation

Ensure that the crankcase is thoroughly clean and that all oilways are clear. A thin twist drill or a piece of wire is useful for cleaning them out. If possible blow them out with compressed air.
Treat the crankshaft in the same fashion, and then inject engine oil into the crankshaft oilways.
Commence work of rebuilding the engine by replacing the crankshaft and main bearings:

1   Wipe the bearing shell locations in the crankcase with a soft, non-fluffy rag.
2   Wipe the crankshaft journals with a soft, non-fluffy rag.
3   If the old main bearing shells are to be renewed (not to do so is a false economy, unless they are virtually new) fit the five upper halves of the main bearing shells to their location in the crankcase (photo).
4   Identify each main bearing cap and place in order. The number is cast onto the cap and with intermediate caps an arrow is also marked which should point to front of engine (photo).
5   Wipe the end cap bearing shell location with a soft non-fluffy rag.
6   Fit the bearing half shell onto each main bearing cap (photo).
7   Apply a little grease to each side of the centre main bearing so as to retain the thrust washers (photo).
8   Fit the upper halves of the thrust washers into their grooves either side of the main bearing. The slots must face outwards (photo).
9   Lubricate the crankshaft journals and the upper and lower main bearing shells with engine oil (photo).
10 Carefully lower the crankshaft into the crankcase (photo).
11 Lubricate the crankshaft main bearing journals again and then fit No. 1 bearing cap (photo). Fit the two securing bolts but do not tighten yet.
12 Apply a little gasket cement to the crankshaft rear main bearing end cap location (photo).
13 Next fit No. 5 end cap (photo). Fit the two securing bolts but as before do not tighten yet.
14 Apply a little grease to either side of the centre main bearing end cap so as to retain the thrust washers. Fit the thrust washers with the tag located in the groove and the slots facing outwards (photo).
15 Fit the centre main bearing end cap and the two securing bolts. Then refit the intermediate main bearing end caps. Make sure that the arrows point towards the front of the engine (photo).
16 Lightly tighten all main cap securing bolts and then fully tighten in a progressive manner to the specified torque wrench setting.
17 Using a screwdriver ease the crankshaft fully forwards and with feeler gauges check the clearance between the crankshaft journal side

and the thrust washers. The clearance must not exceed 0.0032 - 0.0110 in (0.08 - 0.28 mm). Undersize thrust washers are available (photo).
18 Test the crankshaft for freedom of rotation. Should it be stiff to turn or possess high spots, a most careful inspection must be made with a micrometer, preferably by a qualified mechanic, to get to the root of the trouble. It is very seldom that any trouble of this nature will be experienced when fitting the crankshaft.

43 Pistons and connecting rods - reassembly

As a press type gudgeon pin is used (see Section 22) this operation must be carried out by the local Ford garage.

44 Piston rings - replacement

1   Check that the piston ring grooves and oilways are thoroughly clean and unblocked. Piston rings must always be fitted over the head of the piston and never from the bottom.
2   The easiest method to use when fitting rings is to wrap a .020 in (0.5080 mm) feeler gauge round the top of the piston and place the rings one at a time, starting with the bottom oil control ring, over the feeler gauge.
3   The feeler gauge, complete with ring can then be slid down the piston over the other piston ring grooves until the correct groove is reached. The piston ring is then slid gently off the feeler gauge into the groove.
4   An alternative method is to fit the rings by holding them slightly open with the thumbs and both of the index fingers. This method requires a steady hand and great care as it is easy to open the ring too much and break it.

45 Pistons - replacement

The piston, complete with connecting rods, can be fitted to the cylinder bores in the following sequence:
1   With a wad of clean rag wipe the cylinder bores clean.
2   The pistons, complete with connecting rods, are fitted to their bores from the top of the block.
3   Locate the piston ring gaps in the following manner (photo):
    Top: 150° from one side of the helical expander gap.
    Centre: 150° from the opposite side of the helical expander gap.
    Bottom: Helical expander: opposite the marked piston front side.
    Oil control ring rails: 1 inch (25 mm) each side of the helical expander gap.
4   Well lubricate the piston and rings with engine oil (photo).
5   Fit a universal piston ring compressor and prepare to insert the first piston into the bore. Make sure it is the correct piston-connecting rod assembly for that particular bore, that the connecting rod is the correct way round and that the front of the piston is towards the front of the bore, ie; towards the front of the engine (photo).
6   Again lubricate the piston skirt and insert into the bore up to the bottom of the piston ring compressor (photos).
7   Gently but firmly tap the piston through the piston ring compressor and into the cylinder bore with the wooden handle of a hammer (photo).

45.3 Positioning ring gaps

45.4 Lubrication pistons prior to refitting

45.5 Piston identification marks

45.6A Inserting connecting rod into cylinder bore

45.6B Piston ring compressor correctly positioned

45.7 Pushing piston down bore

46.6 Refitting big-end cap securing nuts

46.7 Tightening big-end cap securing nuts

Fig. 1.14 Alternative piston crown marking (notch to front) in relation to connecting rod oil hole (Sec. 45)

47.2 Inserting oil pump drive shaft

47.3 Tightening oil pump securing bolts

48.1 Fitting rectangular shaped seals to rear of crankshaft

48.2 Fitting seal into rear main bearing cap

48.3 Fitting crankshaft rear oil seal

48.4 Tapping crankshaft rear oil seal into position

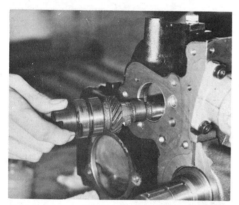

49.1 Refitting auxiliary shaft

49.2 Locating auxiliary shaft thrust plate

49.3 Tightening auxiliary shaft thrust plate securing screws

49.4 Positioning new gasket on cylinder block front face

49.6A Refitting crankshaft timing cover

49.6B Tightening crankshaft timing cover securing bolts

49.8 Tightening auxiliary shaft timing cover securing bolts

50.4 New gaskets fitted to greased underside of crankcase, ready for sump

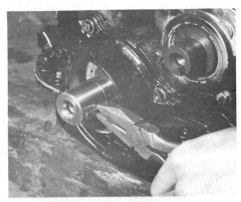
51.1 Refitting Woodruff key to crankshaft

51.2 Sliding on crankshaft sprocket

51.3 Fitting drive belt to crankshaft sprocket

51.4 Refitting large diameter plain washer

51.6 Fitting sprocket to auxiliary shaft

51.7 Refitting crankshaft pulley

51.8 Crankshaft pulley securing bolt and large washer

51.9 Tightening crankshaft pulley securing bolt

52.3 Water pump is offered up to mating face fitted with new gasket

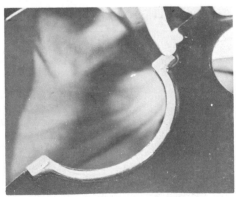
53.1 Fitting new gasket to backplate

46 Connecting rods to crankshaft - reassembly

1   Wipe clean the connecting rod half of the big-end bearing cap and the underside of the shell bearing and fit the shell bearing in position with its locating tongue engaged with the corresponding cut out in the rod.
2   If the old bearings are nearly new and are being refitted then ensure they are replaced in their correct locations on the correct rods.
3   Generously lubricate the crankpin journals with engine oil and turn the crankshaft so that the crankpin is in the most advantageous position for the connecting rods to be drawn onto it.
4   Wipe clean the connecting rod bearing cap and back of the shell bearing, and fit the shell bearing in position ensuring that the locating tongue at the back of the bearing engages with the locating groove in the connecting rod cap.
5   Generously lubricate the shell bearing and offer up the connecting rod bearing cap to the connecting rod.
6   Refit the connecting rod nuts (photo).
7   Tighten the bolts with a torque wrench to the specified setting (photo).
8   When all the connecting rods have been fitted, rotate the crankshaft to check that everything is free, and that there are no high spots causing binding. The bottom half of the engine is now nearly built up.

47 Oil pump - refitting

1   Wipe the mating faces of the oil pump and underside of the cylinder block.
2   Insert the hexagonal drive shaft into the end of the oil pump (photo).
3   Offer up the oil pump and refit the two special bolts. Using the special tool (21-012) and a torque wrench, tighten the two bolts to the specified setting. (photo).
4   Refit the one bolt and spring washer that secures the oil pump pick-up pipe support bracket to the crankcase)

48 Crankshaft rear oil seal - installation

1   Apply some gasket cement to the slot on either side of the rear main bearing end cap and insert a rectangular shaped seal (photo).
2   Apply some gasket cement to the slot in the rear main bearing end cap and carefully insert the shaped seal (photo).
3   Lightly smear some grease on the crankshaft rear oil seal and carefully ease it over the end of the crankshaft. The spring must be inwards (photo).
4   Using a soft metal drift carefully tap the seal into position (photo).

49 Auxiliary shaft and timing cover - refitting

1   Carefully insert the auxiliary shaft into the front face of the cylinder block (photo).
2   Position the thrust plate into its groove in the auxiliary shaft - countersunk faces of the holes facing outwards - and refit the two crosshead screws (photo).
3   Tighten the two crosshead screws using a crosshead screwdriver and an open-ended spanner (photo).
4   Smear some grease on the cylinder block side of a new gasket and carefully fit into position (photo).
5   Apply some gasket cement to the slot in the underside of the crankshaft timing cover. Insert the shaped seal.
6   Offer up the timing cover and secure with the bolts and spring washers (photos).
7   Smear some grease onto the seal located in the shaft timing cover and carefully ease the cover over the end of the auxiliary shaft.
8   Secure the auxiliary shaft timing cover with the four bolts and spring washers (photo).

Fig. 1.15. Correct fitment of sump gasket at front and rear main bearing caps (Sec. 50)

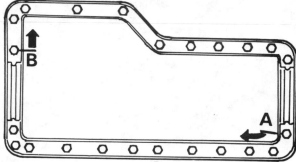

Fig. 1.16. Correct order for tightening sump bolts (Sec. 50)

50 Sump - installation

1   Wipe the mating faces of the underside of the crankcase and the sump.
2   Smear some Castrol LM Grease on the underside of the crankcase.
3   Fit the sump gasket making sure that the bolt holes line up (Fig. 1.15).
4   Offer the sump up to the gasket taking care not to dislodge the gasket and secure in position with the bolts (photo).
5   Tighten the sump bolts in a progressive manner to the specified torque wrench setting (Fig. 1.16).

51 Crankshaft sprocket and pulley and auxiliary shaft sprocket - refitting

1   Check that the keyways in the end of the crankshaft are clean and the keys are free from burrs. Fit the keys into the keyways (photo).
2   Slide the sprocket into position on the crankshaft. This sprocket is the small diameter one (photo).
3   Ease the drive belt into mesh with the crankshaft sprocket (photo).
4   Slide the large diameter plain washer onto the crankshaft (photo).
5   Check that the keyway in the end of the auxiliary shaft is clean and the key is free of burrs. Fit the key to the keyway.
6   Slide the sprocket onto the end of the auxiliary shaft (photo).
7   Slide the pulley onto the end of the crankshaft (photo).
8   Refit the bolt and thick plain washer to the end of the crankshaft (photo).
9   Lock the crankshaft pulley with a metal bar and using a socket wrench fully tighten the bolt (photo).

52 Water pump - refitting

1   Make sure that all traces of the old gasket are removed and then smear some grease on the gasket face of the cylinder block.
2   Fit a new gasket to the cylinder block.
3   Offer up the water pump and secure in position with the four bolts and spring washers (photo).

53.2 Backplate located on dowels in rear of cylinder block

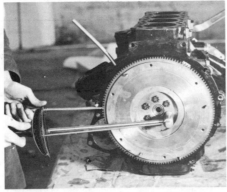
53.5 Tightening flywheel securing bolts

53.6 Refitting clutch

53.8 Fully tightening clutch securing bolts once disc has been centralised

54.1 Inserting valve into valve guide

54.2 Sliding seal down valve stem

54.3 Replacing valve spring cap

54.4 Refitting valve collets

55.1 Camshaft oil seal correctly fitted

55.3 Threading camshaft through bearings

55.4 Lubricating camshaft bearings

55.6 Locating camshaft thrust plate

53 Flywheel and clutch - refitting

1   Remove all traces of the shaped seal from the backplate and apply a little adhesive to the backplate. Fit a new seal to the backplate (photo).
2   Wipe the mating faces of the backplate and cylinder block and carefully fit the backplate to the two dowels (photo).
3   Wipe the mating faces of the flywheel and crankshaft and offer up the flywheel to the crankshaft aligning the previously made marks unless new parts have been fitted.
4   Fit the six crankshaft securing bolts and lightly tighten.
5   Lock the flywheel using a screwdriver engaged in the starter ring gear and tighten the securing bolts in a diagonal and progressive manner to the specified torque wrench setting (photo).
6   Refit the clutch disc and pressure plate assembly to the flywheel making sure the disc is the right way round (photo).
7   Secure the pressure plate assembly with the six retaining bolts and spring washers.
8   Centralise the clutch disc using an old input shaft or piece of wooden dowel and fully tighten the retaining bolts (photo).

54 Valves - refitting

1   With the valves suitably ground in (see Section 35) and kept in their correct order, start with No. 1 cylinder and insert the valve into its guide (photo).
2   Lubricate the valve stem with engine oil and slide on a new oil seal. The spring must be uppermost as shown in the photo.
3   Fit the valve spring and cap (photo).
4   Use either the special valve spring compressor, part number '21-005', or carefully use a universal valve spring compressor. Compress the valve spring until the split collets can be slid into position (photo). Note these collets have serrations which engage in slots in the valve stem. Release the valve spring compressor.
5   Repeat this procedure until all eight valves and valve springs are fitted.

55 Camshaft - installation

1   If the oil seal was removed (Section 20) a new one should be fitted taking care that it is fitted the correct way round. Gently tap it into position so that it does not tilt (photo).
2   Apply some grease to the lip of the oil seal. Wipe the three bearing surfaces with a clean, non-fluffy rag.
3   Lift the camshaft through the bearing taking care not to damage the bearing surfaces with the sharp edges of the cam lobes. Also take care not to cut the fingers (photo).
4   When the journals are ready to be inserted into the bearings, lubricate the bearings with engine oil (photo).
5   Push the camshaft through the bearings until the locating groove in the rear of the camshaft is just rearwards of the bearing carrier.
6   Slide the thrust plate into engagement with the camshaft taking care to fit it the correct way round as previously noted (photo).
7   Secure the thrust plate with the two bolts and spring washers (photo).
8   Check that the keyway in the end of the camshaft is clean and the key is free of burrs. Fit the key into the keyway (photo).
9   Locate the tag on the camshaft sprocket backplate in the second groove in the camshaft sprocket (photo).
10 Fit the camshaft sprocket backplate, tag facing outwards (photo).
11 Fit the camshaft sprocket to the end of the camshaft and with a soft faced hammer make sure it is fully home (photo).
12 Refit the sprocket securing bolt and thick plain washer (photo).

56 Cam followers - refitting

1   Undo the ball headed bolt locknut and screw down the bolt fully. This will facilitate refitting the cam followers (photo).
2   Rotate the camshaft until the cam lobe is away from the top of the cylinder head. Pass the cam follower under the back of the cam until the cup is over the ball headed bolt (photo).
3   Engage the cup with the ball headed bolt (photo).

55.7 Tightening camshaft thrust plate retaining bolts

55.8 Fitting Woodruff key to camshaft

55.9 Camshaft sprocket backplate tag

55.10 Camshaft sprocket backplate refitted

55.11 Refitting camshaft sprocket

55.12 Camshaft sprocket securing bolt and plain washer

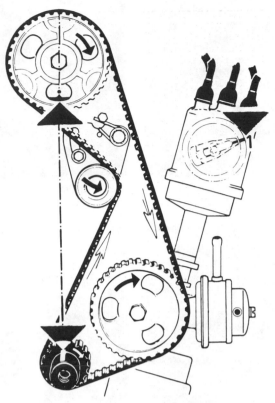

Fig. 1.17. Camshaft, ignition and crankshaft timing (Sec. 59)

56.1 Slackening ball headed bolt locknut

56.2 Passing cam follower under camshaft

56.3 Cup located over ball headed bolt

56.4 Cam follower spring engaged with the anchor

56.5A Cam follower spring being lifted over cam follower

56.5B Cam follower springs correctly fitted

56.7 Replacing lubrication pipe

57.2 Positioning cylinder head gasket on top of cylinder block

57.3 Lowering cylinder head onto gasket

57.4 Refitting cylinder head bolts

57.5 Special tool engaged in cylinder head bolt

57.6 Tightening cylinder head bolts

58.1 Refitting drive belt tensioner

58.3 Using screwdriver to relieve tension of spring

59.1 Lining up camshaft timing marks

59.5 Drive belt fitted

59.6A Replacing drive belt guard

59.6B Locating guard between washer and pedestal

60.2 Checking cam follower clearance

60.3 Slackening ball headed bolt locknut

60.4 Adjusting ball headed bolt

61.3 Gearbox located ready for attachment to engine

61.5A Refitting starter motor

61.5B Securing starter motor to engine

61.6 Refit the engine support bar

62.3 Engine positioned over front panels

62.4 Gearbox placed ready for pushing down below bulkhead

62.5 Trolley jack under rear of gearbox extension housing

62.7 Engine mounting being aligned on crossmember

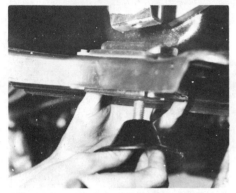

62.9 Gearbox crossmember attachment to gearbox extension housing

62.10 Crossmember to body mounted bracket attachment

62.12 Connector being attached to reverse light switch

4   Refit the cam follower spring by engaging the ends of the spring with the anchor on the ball headed bolt (photo).
5   Using the fingers pull the spring up and then over the top of the cam follower (photos).
6   Repeat the above sequence for the remaining seven cam followers.
7   Check that the jet holes in the camshaft lubrication pipe are free and offer up to the camshaft bearing pedestals (photo).
8   Refit the pipe securing bolts and spring washers.

57 Cylinder head – refitting

1   Wipe clean the mating faces of the cylinder head and cylinder block.
2   Carefully place a new gasket on the cylinder block making sure that it is the correct way up and the right way round (photo). Rotate the crankshaft so that No.1 piston is at TDC and then rotate the camshaft until the pointer on the sprocket is aligned with the dot on the front bearing pedestal. Do not rotate the crankshaft or camshaft once the cylinder head is fitted or the valves may contact the pistons.
3   Gently lower the cylinder head into place being as accurate as possible first time, so that the gasket is not dislodged (photo).
4   Refit the cylinder head bolts ensuring that the threads are cleaned and lightly oiled before doing so. Using the special tool (21-012) lightly tighten all the bolts.
5   Progressively tighten the cylinder head bolts in the sequence shown in Fig. 1.2. Tighten the bolts in four stages to the torque settings given in the Specifications.
6   Run the engine at a fast idle for 15 minutes then re-tighten the cylinder head bolts in the following way. Slacken the first bolt in sequence (Fig. 1.2) through half a turn and then re-tighten it to the fourth stage torque given in Specifications. Re-tighten the remaining bolts in sequence, loosening and re-tightening one at a time.

58 Camshaft drivebelt tensioner and thermostat housing - refitting

1   Thread the shaped bolt through the spring and tensioner plate and screw the bolt into the cylinder head (photo).
2   Tighten the bolt securely using special tool 21 - 012.
3   Using a screwdriver to overcome the tension of the springs, position the plate so that its securing bolt can be screwed into the cylinder head (photo).
4   Clean the mating faces of the cylinder head and thermostat housing and fit a new gasket.
5   Offer up the thermostat housing and secure in position with the two bolts and spring washers.
6   Tighten the bolts to the specified torque wrench setting.

59 Camshaft drivebelt - refitting and timing

1   Check that the crankshaft is positioned with No 1 piston at TDC, as indicated by the sprocket keyway being uppermost. The camshaft sprocket pointer should be aligned with the dot mark on the front bearing pedestal (photo). If the distributor is fitted, its rotor arm should be pointing to No 1 spark plug segment in the distributor cap — see Fig. 1.20.
2   If it is necessary to turn the crankshaft or camshaft to achieve the correct alignment, do so with great caution, as piston-valve contact may occur. The safest procedure is to rotate the crankshaft 90° anti-clockwise from TDC, thus positioning the pistons half way down the bores, then aligning the camshaft sprocket mark, and finally returning the crankshaft to the TDC position.
3   Engage the drivebelt with the crankshaft sprocket and auxiliary shaft sprocket. Pass the back of the belt over the tensioner jockey wheel and then slide it into mesh with the camshaft sprocket.

62.14 Speedometer cable secured by circlip

62.16 Clutch cable threaded through rubber gaiter

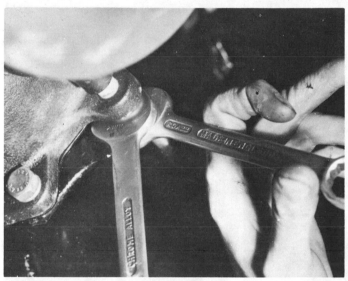
62.17 Clutch cable adjustment

62.18 Rubber gaiter refitted to clutch housing

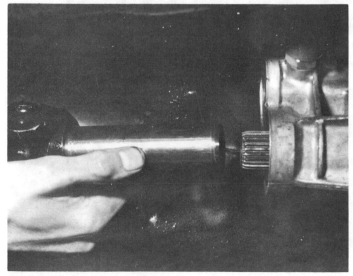
62.20 Sliding propeller shaft into engagement with mainshaft

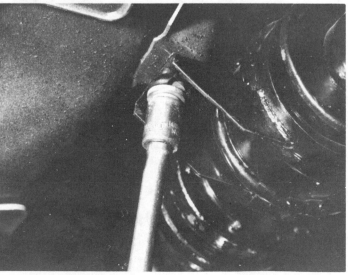
62.21 Propeller shaft centre bearing housing attachment to body

62.22 Propeller shaft and final drive flange reconnection

62.24 Exhaust pipe rubber mounting reconnected to body mounting bracket

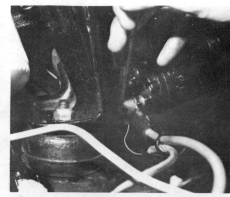

62.27 Reconnecting starter motor cables

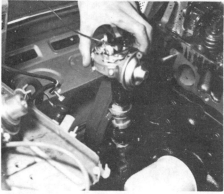

62.30A Replacing distributor

62.30B Securing distributor with clamp and bolt

62.32 Inserting fuel pump operating rod

62.33 Securing fuel pump to cylinder block

62.34 Reconnecting earth cables to cylinder block

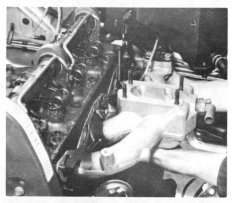

62.38 Refitting inlet manifold to cylinder head, fitted with new gasket

62.40 The carburettor insulator washer and gasket. The gasket face is marked TOP FRONT to ensure correct fitment

62.43 Connecting water hose to automatic choke and inlet manifold

62.44 Connecting crankcase breather hose to inlet manifold

4 Slacken the tensioner plate securing bolt and allow the tensioner to settle by rotating the crankshaft twice. Retighten the tensioner plate securing bolt.

5 Line up the timing marks and check that these are correct indicating the belt has been correctly refitted (photo).

6 Refit the drivebelt guard, easing the guard into engagement with the bolt and large plain washer located under the water pump (photos).

7 Refit the guard securing bolts and tighten fully.

60 Valve clearances - checking and adjustment

1 With the engine top cover removed, turn the crankshaft until the two cams of one cylinder point upwards to form a 'V'. This will ensure that the cam follower will be at the back of the cam.

2 Using feeler gauges as shown in this photo check the clearance which will be found in the Specifications.

3 If adjustment is necessary, using open ended spanners slacken the ball headed bolt securing locknut (photo).

4 Screw the ball headed bolt up or down as necessary until the required clearance is obtained (photo). Retighten the locknut.

5 An alternative method of adjustment is to work to the following table:

Valves open	Valves to adjust
1 ex and 4 in	6 in and 7 ex
6 in and 7 ex	1 ex and 4 in
2 in and 5 ex	3 ex and 8 in
3 ex and 8 in	2 in and 5 ex

61 Engine/gearbox - reconnecting

If the engine was removed in unit with the gearbox it may be reattached in the following manner:

1 With the engine on the floor and a wood block under the front of the sump, lift up the gearbox and insert the gearbox input shaft into the centre of the clutch and push, so that the input shaft splines pass through the internal splines of the clutch disc.

2 If difficulty is experienced in engaging the splines, try turning the gearbox slightly but on no account allow the weight of the gearbox to rest on the input shaft as it is easily bent.

3 With the gearbox correctly positioned on the engine backplate support its weight using a wooden block (photo).

4 Secure the gearbox to the engine and backplate with the bolts and spring washers.

5 Refit the starter motor to its aperture in the backplate and secure with the bolts and spring washers (photos).

6 Refit the support bar located between the engine and clutch bellhousing (photo).

62 Engine - installation (with gearbox)

1 Pass a rope sling around the engine mountings and raise the complete power unit from the floor.

2 Check that all cables and controls in the engine compartment are tucked well out of the way and that the exhaust downpipe is tied to the steering column.

3 Place an old blanket over the front of the car to avoid scratching of the grille or front panel. Lift up the power unit sufficiently so that the sump passes over the front panel.

4 An assistant should now lift up the gearbox extension housing whilst the engine is pushed rearwards. Ease the gearbox through the engine compartment and then gradually lower the engine (photo).

5 If a trolley jack is available have it ready under the car to accept the weight of the rear of the gearbox. Alternatively, use a piece of wood (photo).

6 Continue to lower the engine and ease the gearbox rearwards until the engine is central within the engine compartment.

7 Locate the engine front mounting studs within the bracket in the front crossmember using a metal bar (photo).

8 Jack up the rear of the gearbox and secure the engine mountings with the nuts and plain washers.

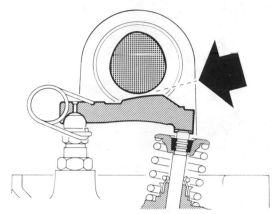

Fig. 1.18. Cam follower and camshaft clearance

9 Attach the gearbox crossmember to the gearbox extension housing and secure with the shaped metal plate and bolt (photo).

10 Secure the gearbox crossmember to the body attached brackets using the four special dowel bolts and spring washers (photo).

11 Remove the engine suspension rope and the trolley jack (if used) from the gearbox.

12 Working under the car first reconnect the reverse light switch terminal connector (photo).

13 Reconnect the speedometer inner cable to the drive gear and push the outer cable fully up to the extension housing machined recess.

14 Secure the speedometer cable to the gearbox using the circlip. Make sure that it is correctly seated (photo).

15 Check that the clutch release cable nylon bush is correctly located in the gearbox clutch housing flange and fixed through the clutch release cable.

16 Thread the clutch cable through the rubber gaiter (if fitted) and re-connect the clutch inner cable to the release arm (photo).

17 Adjust the cable until there is 1 to 1.2 in (25 to 30 mm) clutch pedal free travel (photo).(See also Chapter 5, Section 2).

18 Refit the rubber gaiter (if fitted) (photo).

19 Wipe clean the gearbox mainshaft splines and lubricate with a little Castrol Hypoy Light (EP 80).

20 Offer up the propeller shaft and engage the propeller shaft splines with those of the mainshaft (photo).

21 Where a split type propeller shaft is fitted secure the centre bearing housing to the brackets mounted on the body with the two bolts, spring and plain washers (photo).

22 Align the marks that were previously made on the propeller shaft and final drive flanges and secure with the four bolts and spring washers (photo).

23 Release the exhaust downpipe and offer up the exhaust manifold. Push up the clamp plate and secure with the two nuts. These nuts should be tightened a turn at a time to ensure that the downpipe seats correctly.

24 Reconnect the exhaust pipe intermediate support rubber to the body mounted bracket (photo).

25 Remove the gearbox filler plug and check the oil level. Top-up as necessary with gearbox oil. The total capacity is 1.6 Imp pints (0.9 litres) for 1600 engine, 2.6 Imp pints (1.5 litres) for 2000 engine.

26 Refit the filler plug and lightly tighten. The plug has a ½ inch square socket so if a socket set is available the ratchet wrench will just fit nicely.

27 Now turning to the engine compartment reconnect the cables to the rear of the starter motor or solenoid as noted upon removal. Secure with the nut (photo).

28 The distributor may now be refitted. Look up the initial static advance for the particular model in the specifications given in Chapter 4.

29 Turn the engine until No. 1 piston is coming up to TDC on the compression stroke. This can be checked by removing No. 1 spark plug and feeling the pressure being developed in the cylinder. Alternatively remove the oil filler cap and note when the cam is in the upright position.

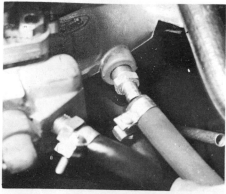

62.45 Connecting servo unit vacuum hose to inlet manifold

Fig. 1.19. Tightening order for engine top cover securing bolts (Sec. 62)

62.46 Connecting throttle control rod to carburettor

62.47 Reconnecting throttle control cable to operating rod

62.48 Reconnecting fuel pipe to float chamber

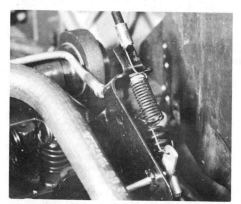

62.49 Throttle return spring refitted

62.50 Alternator lower mounting bolts

62.53 Spring clip securing alternator connector

62.55 Refitting radiator cowl

62.56 Reconnecting radiator top hose

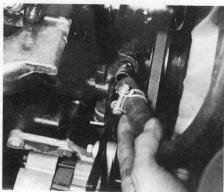

62.57 Heater hose being reconnected to water pump

30 Refer to Chapter 4, Section 12, and refit the distributor to the engine (photos).

31 Wipe the oil filter mating face of the cylinder block and smear a little grease on the oil filter seal. Screw the new unit into position taking care not to cross the thread. Continue until the sealing ring just touches the block face then tighten a half turn.

32 Insert the fuel pump operating rod in the side of the cylinder block just below the distributor body (photo).

33 Refit the fuel pump and insulation washer and secure with the two bolts and spring washers (photo).

34 Refit the earth cable to the side of the cylinder block just below the fuel pump and secure with the bolt and washer (photo).

35 Refit the main fuel line connection to the fuel pump.

36 Refit the water pump pulley and fan blades to the water pump hub and secure with the four bolts, plain and spring washers. Tighten these bolts to the specified torque wrench setting.

37 Remove all traces of old gasket from the inlet manifold side of the cylinder head and inlet manifold. Fit a new gasket.

38 Refit the inlet manifold to the side of the cylinder head (photo).

39 Secure the inlet manifold with the nuts, bolts and washers.

40 Fit the insulator washer to the inlet manifold taking care to ensure that it is the correct way round (photo).

41 Refit the carburettor to the inlet manifold

42 Secure the carburettor to the inlet manifold studs with the nuts and spring washers.

43 Reconnect the hose located between the automatic choke and inlet manifold. Tighten the two clips (photo).

44 Reconnect the crankcase breather pipe to the union adjacent to the water hose connection on the inlet manifold. Tighten the hose clip (photo).

45 Refit the servo unit vacuum hose to the union on the pipe of the inlet manifold. Tighten the hose clip (photo).

46 Reconnect the throttle control rod to the carburettor (photo).

47 Reconnect the throttle control cable to the carburettor throttle operating rod (photo).

48 Refit the fuel pipe from the fuel pump to the carburettor. Tighten the hose clip (photo).

49 Reconnect the throttle return spring (photo).

50 The alternator may now be refitted. Offer it up to its mounting bracket on the right-hand side of the cylinder block and insert the two lower mounting bolts with spring washers and spacer on the bolt and plain washer on the front (photo).

51 Refit the adjustment link to the side of the cylinder block and then attach the alternator to the adjustment link. Adjust the tension until there is 0.5 in (12.7 mm) of lateral movement at the mid point position of the belt run between the alternator pulley and the water pump. Tighten all securing bolts.

52 Refit the terminal connector to the rear of the alternator.

53 Secure the terminal connector with the spring clip (photo).

54 Carefully replace the radiator and secure with the four bolts and plain washers.

55 Locate the cowl on the rear of the radiator (if fitted) and secure with the four bolts and washers (photo).

56 Reconnect the radiator top and bottom hoses and tighten the hose clips (photo).

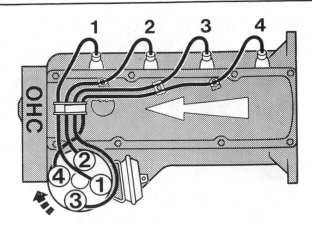

Fig. 1.20. Correct fitment of HT leads (Sec. 62)

57 Refit the heater hose to the union on the side of the water pump and secure with the clips (photo).

58 Place new gaskets on the engine top cover and position on the top of the cylinder head (photo).

59 Secure the top cover with the ten bolts and spring washers see photo, and Fig. 1.19.

60 Make sure the sump drain is tight and then refill the engine with 6.6 Imp pints (3.75 litres) of engine oil.

61 Reconnect the lower heater hose to the thermostatic choke union on the side of the carburettor. Secure with the hose clip.

62 Place the battery on its tray and secure with the clamp, bolt and washers.

63 Reconnect the battery positive and then negative terminals. Also reconnect the distributor HT leads to the spark plugs and to the centre of the ignition coil (Fig. 1.20).

64 Screw in the oil pressure switch and tighten with an open ended spanner. Reconnect the electric terminal (photo).

65 Refit the oil separator to the left-hand side of the engine the correct way round as shown in this photo and insert the PCV valve in the top.

66 Refit the air cleaner to the carburettor, as described in Chapter 3, Section 2.

67 Reconnect the LT cable to the side of the distributor.

68 Refill the cooling system as described in Chapter 2, Section 4.

69 Refer to Chapter 12, Section 38 to refit centre console.

70 Apply some grease to the end of the gearchange lever and lower it into engagement with the selector rod (photo).

71 Carefully screw on the lock ring and gearchange lever retainer. Using a screwdriver, bend down several of the lock ring locking tabs.

72 Refit the gaiter over the gearchange lever and re-attach it to the body panel.

62.58 Refitting top cover, complete with new gaskets

62.59 Securing top cover to cylinder head and drive belt guard

62.64 Refitting oil pressure switch

62.65 Refitting oil separator to crankcase

62.70 Selector rod in extension housing ready to accept gear change lever

73 Refer to Chapter 3, Section 2, and refit the air cleaner assembly.
74 With the help of an assistant refit the bonnet and secure the hinges with the bolts, spring and plain washers in their original positions.
75 Generally check that all wires, hoses, controls and attachments have been reconnected and the engine should be ready to start.
76 On vehicles having emission control systems, reconnect components and hoses.

63 Engine - installation (without gearbox)

The sequence of operations is basically identical to that for refitting the engine with the gearbox attached. The exception being work carried out on detaching the gearbox. These differences will have become evident during the removal stage. Follow the instructions found in Section 62, leaving out the paragraphs referring to the gearbox.

64 Engine - initial start-up after major overhaul or repair

1 Make sure that the battery is fully charged and that all lubricants, coolant and fuel are replenished.
2 If the fuel system has been dismantled it will require several revolutions of the engine on the starter motor to pump the petrol up to the carburettor. An initial 'prime' of about 1/3 of a cupful of petrol poured down the air intake of the carburettor will help the engine to fire quickly, thus relieving the load on the battery. Do not overdo this however, as flooding may result.
3 As soon as the engine fires and runs, keep it going at a fast tick-over only (no faster) and bring it up to normal working temperature.
4 As the engine warms up there will be odd smells and some smoke from parts getting hot and burning off oil deposits. The signs to look for are leaks of water or oil which will be obvious, if serious. Check also the exhaust pipe and manifold connections as these do not always find their exact gas tight position until the warmth and vibration have acted on them and it is almost certain that they will need tightening further. This should be done, of course, with the engine stopped.
5 When normal running temperature has been reached, adjust the engine idle speed as described in Chapter 3.
6 Stop the engine and wait a few minutes to see if any lubricant or coolant is dripping out when the engine is stationary.
7 After the engine has run for 15 minutes remove the engine top cover and retorque the cylinder head bolts. Also check the tightness of the sump bolts.
8 Road test the car to check that the timing is correct and that the engine is giving the necessary smoothness and power. Do not race the engine - if new bearings and/or pistons have been fitted it should be treated as a new engine and run in at a reduced speed for the first 1000 miles (2000 km).

65 Fault diagnosis - Engine

Symptom	Cause	Remedy
Engine turns over but will not start	Ignition damp or wet	Wipe dry the distributor cap and ignition leads.
	Ignition leads to spark plugs loose	Check and tighten at both spark plug and distributor cap ends.
	Shorted or disconnected low tension leads	Check the wiring on the low tension terminals of the coil and to the distributor.
	Dirty, incorrectly set or pitted contact breaker points	Clean, file smooth and adjust.
	Faulty condenser	Check contact breaker points for arcing, remove and fit new condenser.
	Defective ignition switch	Bypass switch with wire.
	Ignition LT leads connected wrong way round	Remove and replace leads to coil in correct order.
	Faulty coil	Remove and fit new coil.
	Contact breaker point spring earthed or broken	Check spring is not touching metal part of distributor. Check insulator washers are correctly placed. Renew points if the spring is broken.
	No petrol in petrol tank	Refill tank!
	Vapour lock in fuel line (in hot conditions or at high altitude)	Blow into petrol tank, allow engine to cool, or apply a cold wet rag to the fuel line in engine compartment.
	Blocked float chamber needle valve	Remove, clean and replace.
	Fuel pump filter blocked	Remove, clean and replace.
	Choked or blocked carburettor jets	Dismantle and clean.
	Faulty fuel pump	Remove, overhaul and replace.
	Too much choke allowing too rich a mixture to wet plugs	Remove and dry spark plugs or with wide open throttle, push-start the car (manual gearbox only).
	Float damaged or leaking or needle not seating	Remove, examine, clean and replace float and needle valve as necessary.
	Float lever incorrectly adjusted	Remove and adjust correctly.
Engine stalls and will not start	Ignition failure - sudden	Check over low and high tension circuits for breaks in wiring.
	Ignition failure - misfiring precludes total stoppage	Check contact breaker points, clean and adjust. Renew condenser if faulty.
	Ignition failure - in severe rain or after traversing water splash	Dry out ignition leads and distributor cap.
	No petrol in petrol tank	Refill tank.
	Petrol tank breather choked	Remove petrol cap and clean out breather hole or pipe.
	Sudden obstruction in carburettor	Check jets, filter, and needle valve in float chamber for blockage.
	Water in fuel system	Drain tank and blow out fuel lines.
Engine misfires or idles unevenly	Ignition leads loose	Check and tighten as necessary at spark plug and distributor cap ends.
	Battery leads loose on terminals	Check and tighten terminal leads.
	Battery earth strap loose on body attachment point	Check and tighten earth lead to body attachment point.
	Engine earth lead loose	Tighten lead.
	Low tension leads to terminals on coil loose	Check and tighten leads if found loose.
	Low tension lead from coil to distributor loose	Check and tighten if found loose.
	Dirty, or incorrectly gapped spark plugs	Remove, clean and regap.
	Dirty, incorrectly set or pitted contact breaker points	Clean, file smooth and adjust.
	Tracking across distributor cap	Remove and fit new cap.
	Ignition too retarded	Check and adjust ignition timing.
	Faulty coil	Remove and fit new coil.
	Mixture too weak	Check jets, float chamber needle valve and filters for obstruction. Clean as necessary. Carburettor incorrectly adjusted.
	Air leak in carburettor	Remove and overhaul carburettor.
	Air leak at inlet manifold to cylinder head, or inlet manifold to carburettor	Test by pouring oil along joints. Bubbles indicate leak. Renew manifold gasket as appropriate.
	Incorrect valve clearances	Adjust cam follower clearances.
	Burnt out exhaust valves	Remove cylinder head and renew defective valves.
	Sticking or leaking valves	Remove cylinder head, clean, check and renew valves as necessary.
	Wear or broken valve springs	Check and renew as necessary.
	Worn valve guides or stems	Renew valves.
	Worn pistons and piston rings	Dismantle engine, renew pistons and rings.

Symptom	Cause	Remedy
Lack of power and poor compression	Burnt out exhaust valves	Remove cylinder head, renew defective valves.
	Sticking or leaking valves	Remove cylinder head, clean, check and renew valves as necessary.
	Worn valve guides and stems	Remove cylinder head and renew valves.
	Weak or broken valve springs	Remove cylinder head, renew defective springs.
	Blown cylinder head gasket (accompanied by increase in noise)	Remove cylinder head and fit new gasket.
	Worn pistons and piston rings	Dismantle engine, renew pistons and rings.
	Worn or scored cylinder bores	Dismantle engine, rebore, renew pistons and rings.
	Ignition timing wrongly set. Too advanced or retarded	Check and reset ignition timing.
	Contact breaker points incorrectly gapped	Check and reset contact breaker points.
	Incorrect valve clearances	Adjust cam follower clearances.
	Incorrectly set spark plugs	Remove, clean and regap.
	Carburettor too rich or too weak	Tune carburettor for optimum performance.
	Dirty contact breaker points	Remove, clean and replace.
	Fuel filters blocked causing top end fuel starvation	Dismantle, inspect, clean and replace all fuel filters.
	Distributor automatic balance weights or vacuum advance and retard mechanisms not functioning correctly	Overhaul distributor.
	Faulty fuel pump giving top end fuel starvation	Remove, overhaul, or fit exchange reconditioned fuel pump.
Excessive oil consumption	Badly worn, perished or missing valve stem oil seals	Remove, fit new oil seals to valve stems.
	Excessively worn valve stems and valve guides	Remove cylinder head and fit new valves.
	Worn piston rings	Fit oil control rings to existing pistons or purchase new pistons.
	Worn pistons and cylinder bores	Fit new pistons and rings, rebore cylinders.
	Excessive piston ring gap allowing blow-by	Fit new piston rings and set gap correctly.
	Piston oil return holes choked	Decarbonise engine and pistons.
Oil being lost due to leaks	Leaking oil filter gasket	Inspect and fit new gasket as necessary.
	Leaking top cover gasket	Inspect and fit new gasket as necessary.
	Leaking timing case gasket	Inspect and fit new gasket as necessary.
	Leaking sump gasket	Inspect and fit new gasket as necessary.
	Loose sump plug	Tighten, fit new gasket as necessary.
Unusual noises from engine	Worn valve gear (noisy tapping from top cover	Inspect and renew cam followers and ball headed bolts.
	Worn big-end bearing (regular heavy knocking)	Drop sump, if bearings broken up clean out oil pump and oilways, fit new bearings. If bearings not broken but worn fit bearing shells.
	Worn main bearings (rumbling and vibration)	Drop sump, remove main bearing caps. If bearings worn or broken up, renew. If broken up strip oil pump and clean out.
	Worn crankshaft (knocking, rumbling and vibration)	Regrind crankshaft, fit new main and big-end bearings.
Engine fails to turn over when starter button operated	Discharged or defective battery	Charge or renew battery, push-start car (manual gearbox only).
	Dirty or loose battery leads	Clean and tighten both terminals and earth ends of earth lead.
	Defective starter solenoid or switch	Run a heavy duty wire direct from the battery to the starter motor or by-pass the solenoid.
	Engine earth strap disconnected	Check and retighten strap.
	Defective starter motor	Remove and recondition.

Chapter 2 Cooling system

For modifications, and information applicable to later models, refer to Supplement at end of manual

Contents

Specifications

System type ... Pressurised, assisted by pump and fan

Thermostat
Type ...	Wax
Location ...	Top water outlet tube
Starts to open ...	82 - 92°C (180 - 198°F)
Fully open ...	99 - 102°C (210 - 216°F)

Radiator
Type ...	Corrugated fin
Pressure cap opens ...	13 lb f/in^2 (0.91 kg f/cm^2)

Fan
1600 models ...	7 blades 12.5 in (317.5 mm)
2000 models:	
Standard ...	7 blades 12.5 in (317.5 mm)
Optional ...	6 blades 14.0 in (355.6 mm)

Cooling system capacity (including heater)
1600 models ...	10.0 Imp. pints (5.8 litres)
2000 models ...	10.75 Imp. pints (6.1 litres)

Torque wrench settings
	lb f ft	kg fm
Fan blade ...	5 - 7	0.69 - 0.97
Water pump ...	5 - 7	0.69 - 0.97
Thermostat housing ...	12 - 15	1.66 - 2.07

1 General description

The engine cooling water is circulated by a thermo-syphon, water pump assisted system, and the whole system is pressurised. This both to prevent the loss of water down the overflow pipe with the radiator cap in position and to prevent premature boiling in adverse conditions. The radiator cap is pressurised to 13 lb f in^2 (0.91 kg f m^2). This has the effect of increasing the boiling point of the coolant. If the water temperature goes above the increased boiling point the extra pressure in the system forces the internal part of the cap off its seat, thus exposing the overflow pipe down which the steam from the boiling water escapes thereby relieving the pressure. It is, therefore, important to check that the radiator cap is in good condition and that the spring behind the sealing washer has not weakened. The cooling system comprises the radiator, top and bottom water hoses, heater hoses, the impeller water pump (mounted on the front of the engine, it carries the fan blades, and is driven by the fan belt), the thermostat and the drain tap in the engine block. The inlet manifold is water heated, and some variants have an automatic choke operated by the coolant. On automatic transmission vehicles a transmission oil cooler is located in the radiator bottom tank.

The system functions in the following fashion: Cold water in the bottom of the radiator circulates up the lower radiator hose to the water pump where it is pushed round the water passages in the cylinder block, helping to keep the cylinder bores and pistons cool.

The water then travels down the radiator where it is rapidly cooled by the in-rush of cold air through the radiator core, which is created by both the fan and the motion of the car. The water, now much cooler, reaches the bottom of the radiator when the cycle is repeated.

When the engine is cold the thermostat (which is a valve that opens and closes according to the temperature of the water) maintains the circulation of the same water in the engine.

Only when the correct minimum operating temperature has been reached, as shown in the Specification, does the thermostat begin to open, allowing water to return to the radiator.

2 Cooling system - draining

1   If the engine is cold, remove the filler cap from the radiator by turning the cap anti-clockwise. If the engine is hot, then turn the filler cap to the first stop, and leave until the pressure in the system has had time to be released. Use a rag over the cap to protect your hand from escaping steam. If with the engine very hot the cap is released suddenly, the drop in pressure can result in the water boiling. With the pressure released the cap can be removed.
2   If antifreeze is used in the cooling system, drain it into a bowl having a capacity of at least 12 Imp pints (7 litres) for re-use.
3   Disconnect lower radiator hose and allow to drain. Also remove the engine drain plug which is located at the rear left-hand side of the cylinder block (photo).
4   When the water has finished draining, probe the drain plug orifice with a short piece of wire to dislodge any particles of rust or sediment which may be causing a blockage.
5   It is important to note that the heater cannot be drained completely during the cold weather so an antifreeze solution must be used. Always use an antifreeze with an ethylene glycol or glycerine base.

3 Cooling system - flushing

1   In time the cooling system will gradually lose its efficiency as the radiator becomes choked with rust, scale deposits from the water, and other sediment. To clean the system out, remove the radiator filler cap and engine drain plug and leave a hose running in the filler cap neck for ten to fifteen minutes.
2   In very bad cases the radiator should be reverse flushed. This can be done with the radiator in position. The cylinder block plug is removed and a hose with a suitable tapered adaptor placed in the drain plug hole. Water under pressure is then forced through the radiator and out of the header tank filler cap neck.
3   It is recommended that some polythene sheeting is placed over the

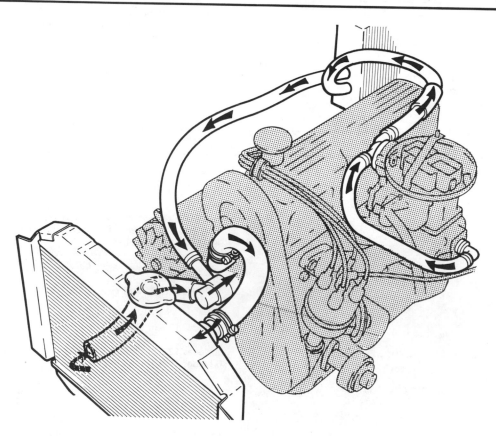

Fig. 2.1. Cooling system water circulation (Sec. 1)

engine to stop water finding its way into the electrical system.

4   The hose should now be removed and placed in the radiator cap filler neck, and the radiator washed out in the usual manner.

4   Cooling system - filling

1   Refit the cylinder block drain plug and reconnect the lower radiator hose.

2   Fill the system slowly to ensure that no air lock develops. If a heater is fitted, check that the valve in the heater is open (control at HOT), otherwise an air lock may form in the heater. The best type of water to use in the cooling system is rain water; use this whenever possible.

3   Do not fill the system higher than within a ½ inch (12.7 mm) of the filler neck. Overfilling will merely result in wastage, which is especially to be avoided when antifreeze is in use.

4   It is usually found that air locks develop in the heater radiator so the system should be vented during refilling by detaching the heater supply hose from the elbow connection on the water outlet housing.

5   Pour coolant in to the radiator filler neck whilst the end of the heater supply hose is held at the elbow connection height. When a constant stream of water flows from the supply hose quickly refit the hose. If venting is not carried out it is possible for the engine to overheat. Should the engine overheat for no apparent reason then the system should be vented before seeking other causes.

6   Only use antifreeze mixture with a glycerine or ethylene glycol base.

7   Replace the filler cap and turn it firmly clockwise to lock it in position.

5   Radiator - removal, inspection and cleaning

1   Drain the cooling system, as described in Section 2 of this Chapter.

2   Slacken the two clips which hold the top and bottom radiator hoses on the radiator and carefully pull off the two hoses.

3   Undo and remove the four bolts that secure the radiator shroud to the radiator side panels and move the shroud over the fan blades. This is only applicable when a shroud is fitted (photo).

4   *Vehicles with automatic transmission.* Position a drain tray beneath the radiator, disconnect both oil cooler pipes and pull clear of radiator Fig. 2.2.

5   Undo and remove the four bolts that secure the radiator to the front panel. The radiator may now be lifted upwards and away from the engine compartment. The fragile matrix must not be touched by the fan blades as it easily punctures (photo).

6   Lift the radiator shroud from over the fan blades and remove from the engine compartment.

7   With the radiator away from the car any leaks can be soldered or repaired with a suitable substance. Clean out the inside of the radiator by flushing as described earlier in this Chapter. When the radiator is out of the car it is advantageous to turn it upside down and reverse flush. Clean the exterior of the radiator by carefully using a compressed air jet or a strong jet of water to clear away any road dirt, flies etc.

8   Inspect the radiator hoses for cracks, internal or external perishing and damage by overtightening of the securing clips. Also inspect the overflow pipe. Renew the hoses if suspect. Examine the radiator hose clips and renew them if they are rusted or distorted.

9   The drain plug and washer should be renewed if leaking or with worn threads, but first ensure the leak is not caused by a faulty fibre washer.

6   Radiator - installation

1   Refitting the radiator and shroud (if fitted) is the reverse sequence to removal (see Section 5).

2.3 Cylinder block drain plug removal

5.3 Radiator shroud repositioned over fan blades

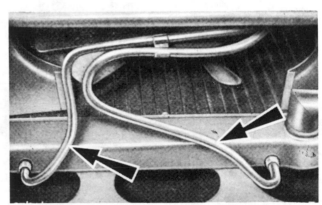

Fig. 2.2. Automatic transmission oil cooler pipes (Sec. 5)

5.5 Radiator removal

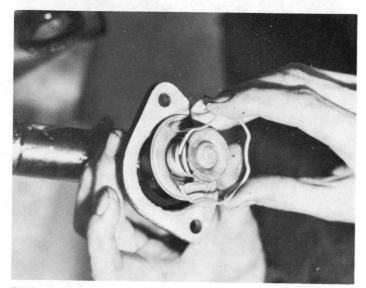

7.5 Removal of thermostat retaining clip

7.6 Removal of sealing ring

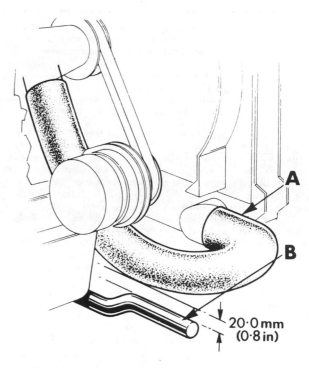

Fig. 2.3. Radiator bottom hose (A) to stabilizer bar (B) clearance diagram (Sec. 6)

20·0mm (0·8in)

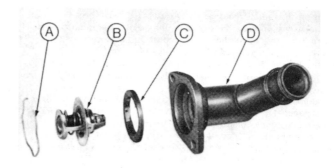

Fig. 2.4. (A) Retaining clip (B) Thermostat (C) Sealing ring (D) Thermostat housing (Sec. 7)

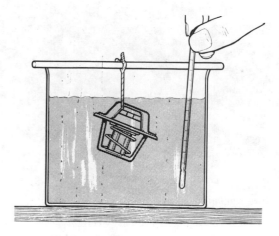

Fig. 2.5. Thermostat testing (Sec. 7)

2 If new hoses are to be fitted they can be a little difficult to fit
on to the radiator so lubricate them with a little soap.
3 Refill the cooling system, as described in Section 4.
4 *Vehicles with automatic transmission.* Refer to Chapter 6, Section
9 and check and top up the automatic transmission fluid.
5 A clearance of 0.8 in (20.0 mm) must be maintained between the
bottom hose and the stabilizer bar to prevent chafing. Make sure that
the upper end of the hose is pushed well up onto the water pump
(Fig. 2.3).

7 Thermostat - removal , testing and refitting

1 Partially drain the cooling system (usually 4 Imp pints (2.27 litres)
is enough), as described in Section 2.
2 Slacken the top radiator hose to the thermostat housing and
remove the hose.
3 Undo and remove the two bolts and spring washers that secure
the thermostat housing to the cylinder head.
4 Carefully lift the thermostat housing away from the cylinder head.
Recover the joint washer adhering to either the housing or cylinder
head.
5 Using a screwdriver ease the clip securing the thermostat to the
housing (Fig. 2.4). Note which way round the thermostat is
fitted in the housing and also that the bridge is 90° to the outlet (photo).
6 The thermostat may now be withdrawn from the housing. Recover
the seal from inside the housing (photo).
7 Test the thermostat for correct functioning by suspending it on
a string in a saucepan of cold water together with a thermometer
(Fig. 2.5). Heat the water and note the temperature at which the
thermostat begins to open. This should be 82 - 92°C (180 - 198°F).
It is advantageous in winter to fit a thermostat that does not open too
early. Continue heating the water until the thermostat is fully open.
Then let it cool down naturally.
8 If the thermostat does not fully open in boiling water, or does not
close down as the water cools, then it must be discarded and a new
one fitted. Should the thermostat be stuck open when cold this will
usually be apparent when removing it from the housing.
9 Refitting the thermostat is the reverse sequence to removal. Always
ensure that the thermostat housing and cylinder head mating faces are
clean and flat. If the thermostat housing is badly corroded fit a new
housing. Always use a new paper gasket. Tighten the two securing bolts
to the specified torque wrench setting.
10 If a new winter thermostat is fitted, provided the summer one is
still functioning correctly, it can be stored away and refitted in the
spring. Thermostats should last for two to three years before renewal
becomes desirable.

8 Water pump - removal and refitting

1 Drain the cooling system, as described in Section 2.
2 Refer to Section 5 and remove the radiator (and shroud if fitted).
3 Slacken the alternator mounting bolts and push the alternator
towards the cylinder block. Lift away the fan belt.
4 Undo and remove the four bolts and washers that secure the fan
assembly to the water pump spindle hub. Lift away the fan and pulley
(Fig. 2.6).
5 Slacken the clip that secures the heater hose to the water pump.
Pull the hose from its union on the water pump.
6 Slacken the clamp that secures the lower hose to the water pump.
Pull the hose from the pump.
7 Remove three bolts and take off timing belt cover (Fig. 2.7).
8 Undo and remove the four bolts and spring washers that secure
the water pump to the cylinder block. Lift away the water pump and
recover the gasket (Fig. 2.8).
9 Refitting the water pump is the reverse sequence to removal. The
following additional points should, however, be noted:

   a) *Make sure the mating faces of the cylinder block and water
      pump are clean. Always use a new gasket.*
   b) *Tighten the water pump securing bolts to the specified torque
      wrench setting.*
   c) *Tighten the water pump fan and pulley bolts to the specified
      torque wrench setting.*

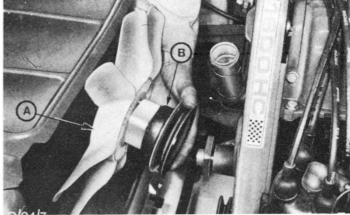

Fig. 2.6. Removing fan (A) and water pump pulley (B) (Sec. 8)

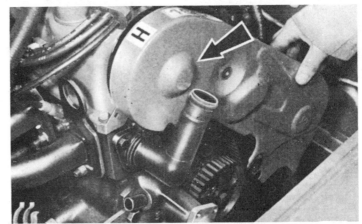

Fig. 2.7. Removing timing belt cover (Sec. 8)

Fig. 2.8. Lifting out water pump (Sec. 8)

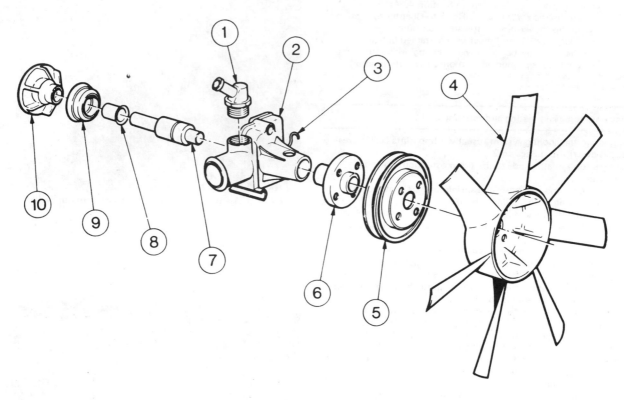

Fig. 2.9. Water pump components (Sec. 9)

1 *Heater connection*	3 *Bearing retainer*	5 *Fan pulley*	8 *Slinger*
2 *Pump body*	4 *Cooling fan*	6 *Pulley hub*	9 *Seal assembly*
		7 *Shaft and bearing assembly*	10 *Impeller*

9 Water pump - dismantling and overhaul

1 Before undertaking the dismantling of a water pump to effect a repair, check that all parts are available. It may be quicker and more economical to replace the complete unit.

2 Refer to Fig. 2.9 and using a universal three leg puller and suitable thrust block draw the hub from the shaft.

3 Carefully pull out the bearing retaining clip from the slot in the water pump housing. On some water pumps this clip is not fitted.

4 Using a soft faced hammer drive the shaft and bearing assembly out towards the rear of the pump body.

5 The impeller vane is removed from the spindle by using a universal three leg puller and suitable thrust block.

6 Remove the seal and the slinger by splitting the latter with the aid of a sharp cold chisel.

7 Carefully inspect the condition of the shaft and bearing assembly and if it shows signs of wear or corrosion, new parts should be obtained. If it was found that coolant was leaking from the pump, a new seal should be obtained. If it was evident that the pulley hub or impeller were a loose fit they must be renewed. The repair kit available comprises a new shaft and bearing assembly, a slinger seal, bush, clip and gasket.

8 To reassemble the water pump first fit the shaft and bearing assembly to the housing, larger end of the shaft to the front of the housing, and press the assembly into the housing until the front of the bearing is flush with the pump housing.

9 Refit the bearing locating wire.

10 Next press the pump pulley onto the front end of the shaft until the end of the shaft is flush with the end of the hub.

11 Press the new slinger (flanged end first) onto the shaft until the non-flanged end is approximately 0.5 in (13 mm) from the shaft end. To act as a rough guide the flanged end of the slinger will be just in line with the impeller side of the window in the water pump body.

12 Place the new seal over the shaft and into the counterbore shaft until a clearance of 0.03 in (0.76 mm) is obtained between the impeller and the housing face (Fig. 2.10). Whilst this is being carried out the slinger will be pushed into its final position by the impeller.

10 Fan belt - removal and refitting

If the fan belt is worn or has stretched unduly, it should be renewed. The most usual reason for replacement is that the belt has broken in service. It is recommended that a spare belt be always carried in the car.

1 Loosen the alternator mounting bolt and move the alternator towards the engine (Fig. 2.11).

2 Slip the old belt over the crankshaft, alternator and water pump pulley wheels and lift it off over the fan blades.

3 Put a new belt onto the three pulleys and adjust it as described in Section 11. **Note:** After fitting a new belt it will require adjustment after approximately 250 miles (400 km).

11 Fan belt - adjustment

1 It is important to keep the fan belt correctly adjusted and it is considered that this should be a regular maintenance task every 6,000 miles (10,000 km). If the belt is loose it will slip, wear rapidly and cause the alternator and water pump to malfunction. If the belt is too tight the alternator and water pump bearings will wear rapidly causing premature failure of these components.

2 The fan belt tension is correct when there is 0.5 in (12.7 mm) of lateral movement at the mid-point position of the belt run between the alternator pulley and the water pump (Fig. 2.12).

3 Adjust the fan belt, slacken the alternator securing bolts and move the alternator in or out until the correct tension is obtained. It is

easier if the alternator bolts are only slackened a little so it requires some effort to move the alternator. In this way the tension of the belt can be arrived at more quickly than by making frequent adjustment.

4 When the correct adjustment has been obtained fully tighten the alternator mounting bolts.

12 Temperature gauge - fault diagnosis

1 If the temperature gauge fails to work, either the gauge, the sender unit, the wiring or the connections are at fault.

2 It is not possible to repair the gauge or the sender unit and they must be replaced by new units if at fault.

3 First check the wiring connections are sound. Check the wiring for breaks using an ohmmeter. The sender unit and gauge should be tested by substitution.

13 Temperature gauge and sender unit - removal and refitting

1 Information on the removal of the gauge will be found in Chapter 10.

2 To remove the sender unit, disconnect the wires leading into the unit at its connector and unscrew the unit with a spanner. The unit is located in the cylinder head just below the manifold on the left-hand side. Refitting is the reverse sequence to removal.

14 Antifreeze precautions

1 In circumstances where it is likely that the temperature will drop below freezing it is essential that some of the water is drained and adequate amount of ethylene glycol antifreeze such as Castrol antifreeze, added to the cooling system.

2 If Castrol antifreeze is not available, any antifreeze which conforms with specifications BS3151 or BS3152 can be used. Never use an antifreeze with an alchohol base as evaporation is too high.

3 Castrol antifreeze with an anti-corrosion additive can be left in the cooling system for up to two years, but after six months it is advisable to have the specific gravity of the coolant checked at your local garage, and thereafter once every three months.

4 The table below gives the amount of antifreeze and degree of protection.

Anti-freeze %	Commences to freeze ^oC	^oF	Frozen solid ^oC	^oF	Amount of anti-freeze Imp pints	litres
25	-13	9	-26	-15	2½	1½
33	-19	-2	-36	-33	3	2
50	-36	-33	-48	-53	5	3

Note: Never use antifreeze in the windscreen washer reservoir as it will cause damage to the paintwork.

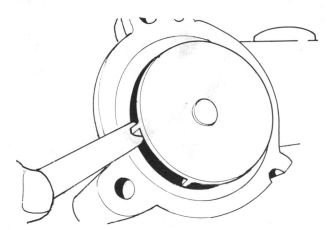

Fig. 2.10. Checking slinger clearance with feeler gauges (Sec. 9)

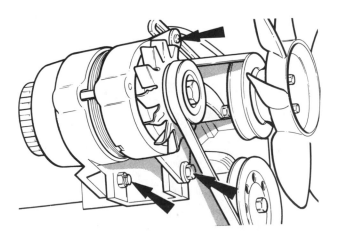

Fig. 2.11. Alternator mounting bolts (Sec. 10)

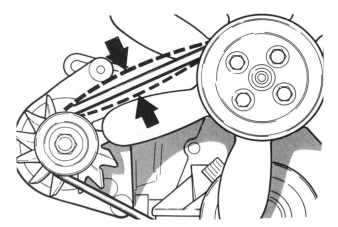

Fig. 2.12. Fan belt tension measurement point (Sec. 11)

15 Fault diagnosis - Cooling system

Symptom	Cause	Remedy
Overheating	Insufficient water in cooling system	Top up radiator.
	Fan belt slipping (accompanied by a shrieking noise on rapid engine acceleration)	Tighten fan belt to recommended tension or replace if worn.
	Radiator core blocked or radiator grille restricted	Reverse flush radiator, remove obstructions.
	Bottom water hose collapsed, impeding flow	Remove and fit new hose.
	Thermostat not opening properly	Remove and fit new thermostat.
	Ignition advance and retard incorrectly set (accompanied by loss of power, and perhaps misfiring)	Check and reset ignition timing.
	Carburettor incorrectly adjusted (mixture too weak)	Tune carburettor.
	Exhaust system partially blocked	Check exhaust pipe for constrictive dents and blockages.
	Oil level in sump too low	Top up sump to full mark on dipstick.
	Blown cylinder head gasket (water/steam being forced down the radiator overflow pipe under pressure)	Remove cylinder head, fit new gasket.
	Engine not yet run-in	Run-in slowly and carefully.
	Brakes binding	Check and adjust brakes if necessary.
Cool running	Thermostat jammed open	Remove and renew thermostat.
	Incorrect thermostat fitted allowing premature opening of valve	Remove and replace with new thermostat which opens at a higher temperature.
	Thermostat missing	Check and fit correct thermostat.
Loss of cooling water	Loose clips on water hose	Check and tighten clips if necessary.
	Top, bottom or by-pass water hoses perished and leaking	Check and replace any faulty hoses.
	Radiator core leaking	Remove radiator and repair.
	Thermostat gasket leaking	Inspect and renew gasket.
	Radiator pressure cap spring worn or seal ineffective	Renew radiator pressure cap.
	Blown cylinder head gasket (pressure in system forcing water/steam down overflow pipe)	Remove cylinder head and fit new gasket.
	Cylinder wall or head cracked	Dismantle engine, despatch to engineering works for repair.

Chapter 3 Carburation; fuel and exhaust systems

For modifications, and information applicable to later models, refer to Supplement at end of manual

Contents

Specifications

Fuel pump

Type	Mechanical driven by pushrod from auxiliary shaft
Delivery pressure	3.75 to 5.0 lb/in^2 (0.26 - 0.35 kg/cm^2)
Inlet vacuum	8.5 in (21.60 cm) Hg

Fuel tank

Capacity	12 Imp. gallons (54 litres)

Fuel filter ... ...   Nylon mesh, located in fuel line

Air cleaner ... ...   Replaceable paper element

Ford single venturi carburettors - 1600 cc engines (except Ghia)

Throttle barrel diameter	1.42 in (36.0 mm)
Venturi diameter	1.06 in (27.0 mm)
Main jet - manual choke	137
Main jet - automatic choke	135
Mixture - % carbon monoxide	0.8 to 1.2
Idle speed	775 to 825 rpm
Fast idle - manual choke	900 to 1100 rpm
- automatic choke - manual transmission	1900 to 2100 rpm
- automatic transmission	2100 to 2200 rpm
Float level	1.11 to 1.17 in (28.25 to 29.75 mm)
Choke plate pull down	0.12 to 0.14 in (3.05 to 3.55 mm)
Accelerator pump stroke	0.11 in (2.9 mm)
V mark setting:	
Manual transmission	0.20 in (5.0 mm)
Automatic transmission	0.18 in (4.5 mm)
De-choke setting	0.19 to 0.23 in (4.8 to 5.8 mm)
Vacuum pull down:	
Manual transmission	0.14 to 0.16 in (3.55 to 4.05 mm)
Automatic transmission	0.11 to 0.13 in (2.75 to 3.25 mm)

Weber twin venturi carburettors - all 2000 cc engines and Ghia 1600*

Venturi diameter:	
Primary	1.02 in (26 mm)
Secondary	1.06 in (27 mm)
Main jet - primary:	
Manual transmission	137
Automatic transmission	135
Main jet - secondary	127
Air correction jet:	
Primary	170
Secondary	125
Diffuser tube:	
Primary	F66
Secondary	F66
Idling jet:	
Primary	45
Secondary	60
Mixture - % carbon monoxide	1.3 to 1.7
Idling speed	800 to 850 rpm
Fast idle speed	1900 to 2100 rpm
Float level:	
Brass float	1.59 to 1.63 in (40.5 to 41.5 mm)
Plastic float	1.37 to 1.41 in (34.8 to 35.5 mm)
Vacuum pull down setting	0.27 to 0.29 in (6.75 to 7.25 mm)
Choke phasing setting	0.06 in (1.52 mm)

Torque wrench settings

	lb f ft	kg fm
Fuel pump to cylinder block	12 to 15	1.7 to 2.1
Air cleaner body to carburettor	6 to 9	0.9 to 1.2
Air cleaner cover	2.5 to 3	0.4
Carburettor attachment nuts	5 to 7	0.7 to 1.0
Fuel tank retaining straps	Tighten until 1.6 to 1.8 in (40 to 45 mm) of thread protrudes through nut	
Exhaust manifold clamp	15 to 20	2.1 to 2.8
Exhaust pipe 'U' bolts	15 to 20	2.1 to 2.8

*Typical calibration. For specific carburettor number, consult your dealer

1 General description

The fuel system comprises an 12 Imp. gallon (54.0 litre) fuel tank, a mechanically operated fuel pump, a filter and a Ford or Weber carburettor.

The fuel tank is positioned below the luggage compartment and is held in position by two retaining straps. The filler pipe neck is integral with the tank and passes through the right-hand quarter panel.

The combined fuel outlet and sender unit is located in the front face of the tank. Fuel tank ventilation is via the filler cap.

The mechanical fuel pump is connected to the fuel tank by a nylon pipe. It is located on the left-hand side of the engine and is driven by an auxiliary shaft. Located in the fuel pump is a nylon filter and access is gained via a sediment cap.

A Nitrile rubber flexible hose connects the carburettor to the fuel pump.

Incorporated in the hose between the carburettor and fuel pump is a line filter and the direction of petrol flow is indicated by an arrow on the housing.

The air cleaner fitted to all models is of the renewable paper element type, and has an adjustable spout which can be manually set for winter or summer operation.

2 Air cleaner - removal, refitting and servicing

The renewable paper element type air cleaner is fitted onto the top of the carburettor installation and is retained in position by securing nuts and washers, on a flange at the top of the carburettor. Additional support brackets are used. To remove the air cleaner assembly proceed as follows:
1 Note the direction in which the air intake is pointing.
2 Undo and remove the bolt and spring washer that secures the support bracket to the top cover.
3 Undo and remove the bolt and spring washer that secures the air cleaner long support bracket located next to the distributor.
4 Undo and remove the self-tapping screws on the top cover.
5 There is one additional screw that should be removed and this is located above the air intake on 2V models.
6 Carefully lift away the top cover (photo). At this stage the element may be lifted out.
7 If it is necessary to remove the lower body on 2V models, bend back the lock tabs and undo and remove the four securing nuts (photo).
8 Lift away the two tab washers and the reinforcement plate (photo).
9 The lower body together with the support brackets may now be removed from the top of the carburettor (photo).
10 Refitting the air cleaner is the reverse sequence to removal.

Servicing

The element may be cleaned by using a compressed air jet in the reverse direction to air flow by holding the jet nozzle at least 5 inches (127 mm) away from the element at its centre and blowing outwards. Then hold the element in the vertical position and gently tap until all dirt and dust is removed.

Inspect the element for signs of splitting, cracking, pin holes or permanent distortion and, if evident, a new element should be fitted. A new element must be fitted after 15,000 miles (25,000 km) or earlier if the car is being operated in very dusty conditions.

3 Fuel pump - routine servicing

1 At intervals of 3,000 miles (5,000 km), undo and pull the fuel pipe from the pump inlet tube.
2 Undo and remove the centre screw and 'O' ring and lift off the sediment cap, filter and seal (photo).
3 Thoroughly clean the sediment cap, filter and pumping chamber using a paintbrush and clean petrol to remove any sediment (photo).
4 Reassembly is the reverse sequence to dismantling. Do not over-tighten the centre screw as it could distort the sediment cap.

2.6 Lifting away air cleaner top

2.7 Undoing four air cleaner body to carburettor retaining nuts

2.8 Lifting away reinforcement plate

2.9 Removal of air cleaner body

3.2 Lifting away fuel pump sediment cap, filter and seal

3.3 Removal of filter from sediment cap of fuel pump

4 Fuel pump - description

The mechanical fuel pump is mounted on the left-hand side of the engine and is driven by an auxiliary shaft. It is not possible for this type of pump to be dismantled for repair other than cleaning the filter and sediment cap. Should a fault appear in the pump it may be tested and if confirmed, it must be discarded and a new one obtained. One of two designs may be fitted, this depending on the availability at the time of production of the car.

5 Fuel pump - removal and refitting

1   Remove the inlet and outlet pipes at the pump and plug the ends to stop petrol loss or dirt finding its way into the fuel system.
2   Undo and remove two bolts and spring washers that secure the pump to the cylinder block.
3   Lift away the fuel pump and gasket and recover the pushrod.
4   Refitting the fuel pump is the reverse sequence to removal but there are several additional points that should be noted:

   a) Do not forget to refit the pushrod.
   b) Tighten the pump securing bolts to the specified torque wrench setting.
   c) If a crimped type hose clamp was fitted, it will have been damaged on removal, and should be replaced by a suitable screw type clamp (Fig. 3.1).
   d) Before reconnecting the pipe from the fuel tank to the pump inlet, move the end to a position lower than the fuel tank so that fuel can syphon out. Quickly connect the pipe to the pump inlet.
   e) Disconnect the pipe at the carburettor and turn the engine over until petrol issues from the open end. Quickly connect the pipe to the carburettor union.

6 Fuel pump - testing

Presuming that the fuel lines and unions are in good condition and that there are no leaks anywhere, check the performance of the fuel pump in the following manner. Disconnect the fuel pipe at the carburettor inlet union, and the high tension lead to the coil and, with a suitable container or large rag in position to catch the ejected fuel, turn the engine over. A good spurt of petrol should emerge from the end of the pipe every second revolution.

7 Fuel tank - removal and refitting

1   The fuel tank is positioned at the rear of the car and is supported on two straps.
2   Remove the filler cap and, using a length of rubber hose or plastic pipe approximately 0.25 in (6.35 mm) bore, syphon as much petrol out as possible until the level is below the level of the sender unit.
3   Disconnect the battery earth terminal, release the fuel gauge sender unit wire and the fuel feed pipe from the sender unit. Certain vehicles have a fuel return pipe fitted. In this case, take a careful note of correct pipe connections (Fig. 3.1).
4   Plug the ends of the pipes to stop petrol loss or dirt ingress.
5   Using two screwdrivers in the slots in the sender unit retaining ring unscrew the sender unit from the fuel tank. Lift away the sealing ring and the sender unit noting that the float must hang downwards.
6   Undo and remove the tank strap retaining nuts and lower the tank.
7   Refitting is the reverse sequence to removal. Tighten the support strap securing nuts until 1.6 - 1.8 in (40 - 45 mm) of thread is protruding through the nut.
8   Refill the fuel tank and reconnect the battery earth terminal. Test the operation of the fuel gauge sender unit by switching on the ignition. Wait 30 seconds and observe the gauge reading.

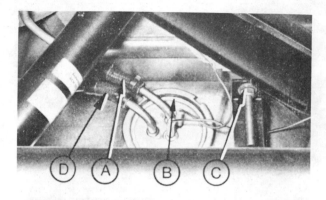

Fig. 3.1 Fuel return (A), Sender unit (B), Tank securing strap (C) and Fuel outlet (D). Fuel return on 2000 cc engines (Sec 7)

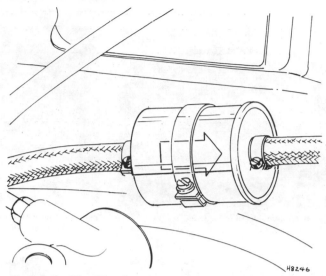

Fig. 3.2. Fuel line filter (arrow shows direction of flow) (Sec. 10)

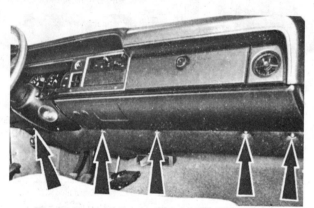

Fig. 3.3. Lower trim panel screws (Sec. 11 and 12)

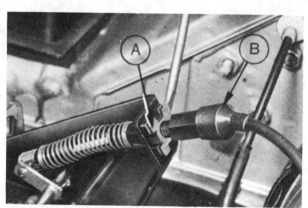

Fig. 3.4. Retaining clip (A) and accelerator cable (B) (Sec. 12)

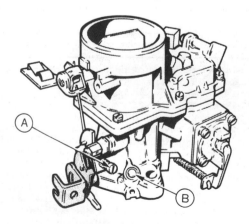

Fig. 3.5. Ford carburettor - Idle speed screw (A), Mixture adjusting screw plug (B) (Sec. 16)

Fig. 3.6. Accelerator cable adjusting nut (Sec. 13)

8 Fuel tank - cleaning

1   With time it is likely that sediment will collect in the bottom of the fuel tank. Condensation, resulting in rust and other impurities will usually be found in the fuel tank of any car more than three or four years old.
2   When the tank is removed it should be vigorously flushed out and turned upside down. If facilities are available at the local garage the tank may be steam cleaned and the exterior repainted with a lead based paint.
3   Never weld or bring a naked light close to an empty fuel tank until it has been steam cleaned out for at least two hours or, washed internally with boiling water and detergent and allowed to stand for at least three hours.
4   Any small holes may be repaired using a special preparation such as Holts Petro-Patch which gives satisfactory results provided that the instructions are rigidly adhered to.

9 Fuel gauge sender unit - removal and refitting

1   The fuel gauge sender unit can be removed with the fuel tank in position. (Refer to Section 7, paragraphs 2 to 5).
2   If the operation of the sender unit is suspect, check that the rheostat is not damaged and that the wiper contact is bearing against the coil.
3   Replacement is a straightforward reversal of the removal sequence. Always fit a new seal to the recess in the tank to ensure no leaks develop.
4   The float arm should hang downwards. Test the operation of the fuel gauge sender unit by switching on the ignition. Wait 30 seconds and observe the gauge reading.

10 Fuel line filter - removal and refitting

1   Slacken the two hose clips and ease off the inlet and outlet pipes. Plug the ends of the pipes to stop dirt ingress or loss of petrol. Lift away the filter (Fig. 3.2).
2   The filter should be renewed at intervals of 18,000 miles (30,000 km) or when fuel starvation symptoms are experienced.
3   Refitting the fuel line filter is the reverse sequence to removal. There is an arrow on the filter body which indicates the direction of fuel flow as it must not be fitted the wrong way round.

11 Accelerator pedal and shaft - removal and refitting

1   Remove the five screws and take out the lower trim panel (Fig. 3.3).
2   Prise up and remove the spring clip from the top of the accelerator pedal shaft, pull back and remove the throttle cable.
3   Withdraw the two shaft retaining clips and slide out the shaft. It will be found beneficial if one bush is rotated through 90° and with a screwdriver, ease the bush from the bracket.
4   If desired, the pedal may be detached from the pedal shaft spigot by prising the pedal flange out of engagement with a screwdriver. Lift away the pedal spring.
5   Inspect the pedal shaft bushes and if worn they should be renewed.
6   It will now be necessary to check the adjustment as described in Section 13.

12 Accelerator cable - removal and refitting

1   Remove the five screws and take out the lower trim panel (Fig. 3.4).
2   Prise up and remove the spring clip from the top of accelerator pedal shaft, pull back and remove the throttle cable.
3   From under the bonnet, undo and remove the screw, thereby releasing the throttle cable from the engine compartment rear bulkhead panel.
4   Slide the clip from the inner cable socket and the throttle shaft ball so as to disconnect the inner cable.
5   Prise out the cable retaining clip from the bracket on the inlet manifold (Fig. 3.4). Depress the lugs individually with a screwdriver and twist out the throttle cable retainer.
6   Refitting and reconnecting the accelerator cable is the reverse sequence to removal.

7   It will now be necessary to adjust the linkage, as described in Section 13.

13 Accelerator linkage - adjustment

1   Refer to Section 2, and remove the air cleaner.
2   Fully depress the accelerator pedal and wedge with a length of wood between the pedal and front seat.
3   Wind back the adjusting nut until the throttle plate is just fully open, with no slack in the cable and no strain in the linkage (Fig. 3.6).
4   *Automatic transmission vehicles.* Refer to Chapter 6, Section 13, and check downshift cable adjustment to ensure this does not prevent the throttle plate from fully opening.
5   Release the accelerator pedal and refit the air cleaner.

14 Carburettors - general description

1   *Ford Single venturi carburettor:* This carburettor incorporates basic and bypass idle, main, power valve and accelerator pump systems. The float chamber is externally vented. The carburettor comprises two castings, the upper and lower bodies. The upper body incorporates the float chamber cover and pivot brackets, fuel inlet components, choke plate and the main and power valve system, idling systems and accelerator pump discharge nozzle.

The lower body incorporates the float chamber, the throttle barrel and venturi, throttle valve components, adjustment screws, accelerator pump and distributor vacuum connection.

In addition, the idle mixture adjustment screw is 'tamper proofed'. (Refer to Section 15).
2   *Weber Dual venturi carburettor:* This carburettor operates on similar principles to the single venturi type and incorporates a fully automatic strangler type choke to ensure easy starting whilst the engine is cold. The float chamber is internally vented.

The carburettor body comprises two castings which form the upper and lower bodies. The upper incorporates the float chamber cover, float pivot brackets, fuel inlet and return unions, gauze filter, spring-loaded needle valve, twin air intakes, choke plates and the section of the power valve controlled by vacuum.

Incorporated in the lower body is the float chamber, accelerator pump, two throttle barrels and integral main ventures, throttle plates, spindles, levers, jets and the petrol power valve.

The throttle plate opening is in a preset sequence so that the primary starts to open first and is then followed by the secondary, in such a manner that both plates reach full throttle position at the same time. The primary barrel, throttle plate and venturi are smaller than the secondary, whereas the auxiliary venturi size is identical in both the primary and secondary barrels.

All the carburation systems are located in the lower body and the main progression systems operate in both barrels, whilst the idling and the power valve systems operate in the primary barrel only and the full load enrichment system in the secondary barrel.

The accelerator pump discharges fuel into the primary barrel.

A connection for the vacuum required to control the distributor advance/retard vacuum unit is located on the lower body.

In addition, the idle mixture adjustment and basic idle adjustment screws are 'tamper-proofed'. (Refer to Section 15).

15 Slow running adjustment - general

1   In view of the increasing awareness of the dangers of exhaust pollution and the very low levels of carbon monoxide (CO) emission for which these carburettors are designed, the slow running mixture setting, and the **basic** idle setting on Weber carburettors, should **not** be adjusted without the use of a proper CO meter (exhaust gas analyser).
2   Even if such equipment is available, the plastic 'tamper-proof' plugs can only be removed by destroying them.

16 Slow running adjustment

1   Warm up the engine to its normal operating temperature.
2   Connect a CO meter and a tachometer, if the latter is not already fitted to the car, according to manufacturer's instructions.

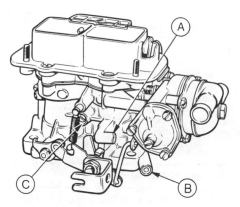

Fig. 3.7. Weber carburettor slow running adjustment points (Sec. 16)

A   Idle speed adjustment screw
B   Idle mixture adjustment screw
C   Bypass idle speed screw (where fitted)

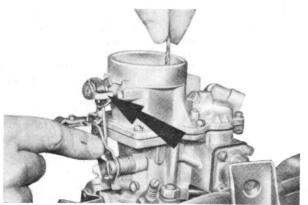

Fig. 3.8. Choke plate pull down adjusting tag (Sec. 17)

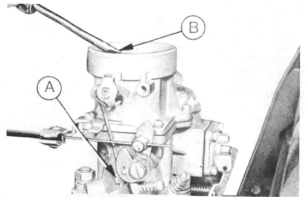

Fig. 3.9. Fast idle adjusting tag (A), Choke plate open (B) (Sec. 17)

3   Clear the engine exhaust gases by running the engine at 3000 rpm for approximately 30 seconds and allow the engine to idle.
4   Wait for the meter to stabilise and compare the CO and idle speed readings against those given in the Specifications at the beginning of this Chapter.
5   Adjust the idle speed screw (or bypass idle speed screw on Weber carburettors so equipped) to give the correct rpm. If the correct rpm cannot be achieved using the bypass idle screw (when fitted) on Weber carburettors, the tamper-proof plug will have to be removed from the idle mixture adjustment screw and adjustment made there.
6   During normal routine maintenance servicing, normally no adjustment of the mixture (CO level) will be required. If however the CO level is found to be incorrect the following procedure should be adopted.
7   Remove the air cleaner assembly as described in Section 2.
8   Using a small electrician's screwdriver, prise out the tamper-proof plug covering the mixture adjusting screw.
9   Loosely refit the air cleaner, it is not necessary to bolt it in position.
10 Clear the engine exhaust gases by runnning the engine at 3000 rpm for approximately 30 seconds and allow the engine to idle.
11 Adjust the mixture screw and the idle screw until the correct idle speed and CO reading are obtained. If the correct readings are not obtained within 10 to 30 seconds, clear the engine exhaust gases as described in paragraph 10 and repeat the adjustment procedure until correct readings are obtained.
12 Refit the air cleaner and a new tamper-proof plug.

17 Ford manual choke carburettor - fast idle adjustment

1   Refer to Section 16 and adjust idle speed.
2   Refer to Section 2 and remove the air cleaner.
3   Rotate the cable operating cam to its stop and hold the choke mechanism in this position.
4   Open the choke plate to its stop and measure the clearance between the choke plate and the throttle barrel with a suitably sized drill bit.
5   This measurement is the choke plate pull down. Adjust as required by bending the tag (Fig. 3.8).
6   With the engine at its normal running temperature, hold the choke plate fully open, and move the control mechanism as far as possible without moving the choke plate. Check the fast idle speed at this position.
7   Bend the adjusting tag (Fig. 3.9) to achieve the specified speed.

18 Carburettor - removal and refitting

1   Disconnect the battery earth lead.
2   Remove the air cleaner, as described in Section 2.
3   On Weber carburettors, peen back the lock tabs then remove the four nuts and take off the air cleaner mounting plate.
4   *Automatic choke:* Remove, then refit, the radiator cap to depressurize the cooling system. Disconnect the water hoses from the choke housing, then plug the hose ends to prevent loss of coolant.
5   *Manual choke:* Disconnect the choke inner and outer cables from the carburettor linkage and bracket.
6   Disconnect the throttle cable from the carburettor. Where applicable, disconnect the kick-down linkage.
7   Disconnect the fuel, vacuum, emission control and vent pipes from the carburettor. Where crimped hoses are used, the clips must be prised open.
8   Remove the retaining nuts and lift off the carburettor. Remove the gasket (and spacer, if fitted).
9   Installation is the reverse of the removal procedure, but the following points must be noted:
   a) Ensure that all mating surfaces are clean and that new gaskets are used.
   b) Where a spacer is used, position a gasket on each side of it.
   c) Screw-type hose clips should be used as replacements for crimped-type clips.
   d) Top up the cooling system before running the engine (automatic choke models).
   e) On manual choke models adjust the choke cable by pulling out the dash knob approximately ¼ in (6 mm), then connect the cable to the carburettor, eliminating all the cable slackness.
   f) Adjust the carburettor, as described in Sections 16 and 17.

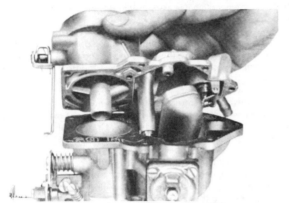

Fig. 3.10. Removing upper body (Sec. 20)

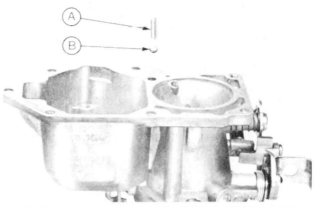

Fig. 3.11. Accelerator valve (B) and Weight (A) (Sec. 20)

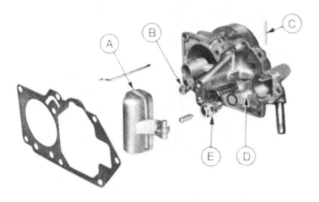

Fig. 3.12. Float (A), Main jet (B), Retaining pin (C), Inlet filter (D), Valve housing (E) (Sec. 20)

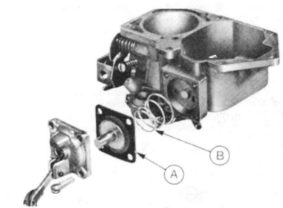

Fig. 3.13. Accelerator pump diaphragm (A) and Return spring (B) (Sec. 20)

Fig. 3.14. Main items to be cleaned (Sec. 20)

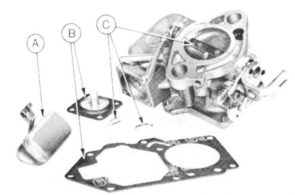

Fig. 3.15. Check (A) for leaks, (B) for splits or damage and (C) for wear or damage (Sec. 20)

19 Carburettors - dismantling and reassembly (general)

1 With time, the component parts of the carburettor will wear and petrol consumption increase. The diameter of drillings and jets may alter, and air and fuel leaks may develop around spindles and other moving parts. Because of the high degree of precision involved it is best to purchase an exchange carburettor. This is one of the few instances where it is better to take the latter course rather than to rebuild the component oneself.

2 It may be necessary to partially dismantle the carburettor to clear a blocked jet. The accelerator pump itself may need attention and gaskets may need renewal and providing care is taken, there is no reason why the carburettor may not be completely reconditioned at home, but ensure a full repair kit can be obtained before you strip the carburettor down. **Never** poke out jets with wire or similar to clean them, but blow them out with compressed air or air from a car tyre pump.

20 Ford single venturi carburettor - cleaning, inspection and adjustment

1 Initially remove the carburettor from the car as described in Section 10, then clean the exterior with a water soluble cleaner.

2 *Manual choke:* Remove the screws and lift off the carburettor body. Disconnect the choke link and move it clear of the carburettor body (Fig. 3.10).

3 *Automatic choke:* Remove the screws and lift off the carburettor body. Disconnect the choke mechanism by removing the single screw securing the fast idle cam to the main body of the carburettor.

4 Invert the carburettor and allow the accelerator weight and ball valve to fall out (Fig. 3.11).

5 Tap out the float retaining pin and lift out the float and needle valve.

6 Unscrew the valve housing and detach the filter (Fig. 3.12).

7 Unscrew the main jet.

8 Remove the screws from the accelerator pump assembly, take off the cover then remove the component parts. Do not lose the return spring (Fig. 3.13).

9 Before attempting to remove the mixture screw, refer to Section 15.

10 Unscrew the jets.

11 Clean the jets and passageways shown in Fig. 3.14 using clean, dry compressed air.

12 Check the float for signs of damage or leaking. Inspect the pump diaphragm and gasket for splits or deterioration. Examine the mixture screw, throttle spindle and needle valve seat for signs of wear. Replace parts as necessary (Fig. 3.15).

13 When reassembling first fit the mixture screw and spring in the same position as originally fitted.

14 Reassemble the accelerator pump. The sealing washer is fitted with the steel side outwards and the main return spring has the smaller diameter inwards (Fig. 3.13).

15 Refit the needle valve assembly and float. Ensure that the filter and sealing washer are fitted to the valve housing before fitting to the carburettor upper body (Fig. 3.12).

16 *Float level adjustment:* Hold the upper body vertically so that the needle valve is closed by the float, then measure the dimension from the face of the upper body to the base of the float. Bend the tag A (Fig. 3.16) to obtain the dimension given in the Specifications.

17 Refit the main jet.

18 Refit the accelerator ball valve and weight.

19 Using a new gasket, fit the upper body to the main body, and reconnect the choke operating linkage. On manual choke carburettors hold the choke mechanism fully closed so that the cam does not go over-centre when the upper body is fitted.

20 *Carburettors with manual choke:* Rotate cable operated cam to stop and hold. Open choke plate to stop and measure the choke plate pull down with a suitably sized twist drill. Adjust to the specified figure by bending the tag B (Fig. 3.17).

21 *Accelerator pump stroke:* Screw the idle adjusting screw clear of the linkage, so that the throttle is fully closed. Push the accelerator pump diaphragm fully in and measure the clearance between the pump lever and the diaphragm. Bend the control link at the U-section to obtain the dimension given in the Specifications.

22 Refit the automatic choke (Section 21).

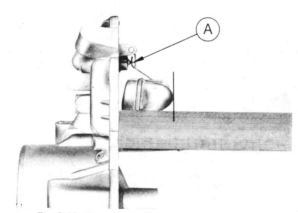

Fig. 3.16. Float level adjusting tag (Sec. 20)

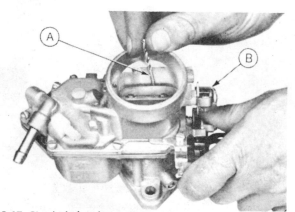

Fig. 3.17. Check choke plate pull down with drill (A) and adjust at tag (B) (Sec. 20)

Fig. 3.18. Removing automatic choke (Sec. 21)

21 Ford single venturi carburettor automatic choke - removal, overhaul and refitting

1   Disconnect the battery earth lead.

2   Remove the air cleaner, as described in Section 2.

3   Remove the three choke cover retaining screws, detach the cover and move it clear of the carburettor. Remove the gasket (Fig. 3.18).

4   Remove the two screws securing the choke body and the single screw securing the linkage to the operating spindle. Detach the choke assembly (Fig. 3.19 and 3.20).

5   Remove the single screw, detach the choke operating spindle, and pull out the linkage and piston.

6   Clean all the components, inspect them for damage and wipe them dry with a lint-free cloth. Do not use any lubricants during reassembly.

7   Reassemble the vacuum piston, operating spindle and operating linkage; do not forget the plastic sleeve on the spindle and ensure that the link rod of the piston assembly is in the outer hole of the lever (Fig. 3.22).

8   Position the sealing rubber between the main choke body and the carburettor. Reconnect the choke linkage to the spindle and fit the choke body.

9   Adjust the V-mark setting, de-choke setting and vacuum pull down as described in Section 22.

10 Using a new gasket on the choke cover, connect the bi-metal spring into the centre slot in the operating link, position the cover and loosely fit the three retaining screws.

11 Rotate the cover until the marks are aligned then tighten the three screws (Fig. 3.21).

12 Reconnect the battery, run the engine and adjust the fast idle speed as described in Section 22.

13 Refit the air cleaner (Section 2).

22 Ford single venturi carburettor automatic choke - adjustment

Note: The procedure is described for a carburettor which is fitted in the car but, with the exception of fast idle speed and vacuum pull-down adjustments, can be carried out on the bench if required where the carburettor has been removed.

1   Disconnect the battery earth lead.

2   Remove the air cleaner, as described in Section 2.

3   Remove the three choke cover retaining screws, detach the cover and move it clear of the carburettor. Remove the gasket.

4   *V-mark setting:* Fit an elastic band to the choke lever plate so that the plate is held closed. Open, then release, the throttle to ensure that the choke plate closes fully. Position a suitable twist drill shank between the edge of the choke plate and the air horn wall on the accelerator pump side of the carburettor. Partially open the throttle to allow the fast idle cam to drop into its operating position. With the choke control rod located at the end of the slot in the fast idle cam, bend the rod at the point arrowed in Fig. 3.23 so that the V-mark on the cam aligns with the end of the throttle lever (Fig. 3.24). Remove the twist drill.

5   *De-choke setting:* Hold the choke lever plate closed with the elastic band as described in the previous paragraph. Fully open the throttle and check that the de-choke operates just before full throttle is reached. The adjustment is checked by measuring between the edge of the choke plate and the air horn wall on the accelerator pump side of the carburettor using a specified drill shank; the de-choke is adjusted to specification by bending the lever on the fast idle cam (Fig. 3.25). Take care that the drill does not fall into the inlet manifold as the choke plate opens. Remove the drill.

6   *Vacuum pull-down:* The use of a special tool is necessary to check this item. The tool may be obtained under tool number MS69 'Auto-choke pre-load tool', or manufactured to the dimensions shown in Fig. 3.26. This tool should be made **accurately** from mild steel to ensure it has a weight of 1.76 to 2.29 oz (50 to 65 gms). Locate the throttle on the 'High Cam' (Fig. 3.27), start the engine and position the tool. Now measure the gap between the choke plate and the air horn wall on the accelerator pump side of the carburettor using a suitable drill shank. Adjust the pull-down by bending the lever shown (Fig. 3.27).

7   Position the gasket on the choke cover and connect the bi-metal spring into the centre slot in the operating link. Position the cover and loosely fit the retaining screws.

8   Rotate the cover until the marks are aligned, then tighten the three

Fig. 3.19. Choke housing screws (Sec. 21)

Fig. 3.20. Disconnecting choke linkage (Sec. 21)

Fig. 3.21. Alignment marks (Sec. 21)

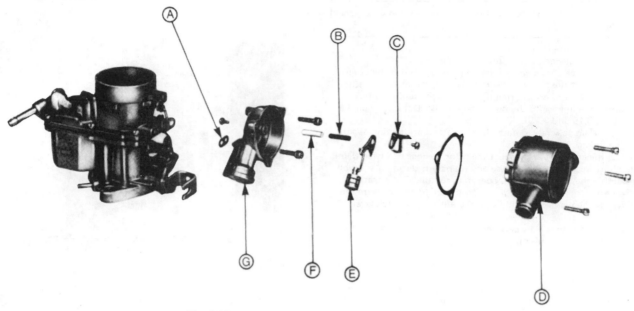

Fig. 3.22. Ford automatic choke components (Sec. 21)

A Gasket   C Operating link   E Vacuum piston assembly   G Main housing
B Operating spindle   D Outer housing   F Spindle sleeve

Fig. 3.23. 'V' mark adjustment point (Sec. 22)

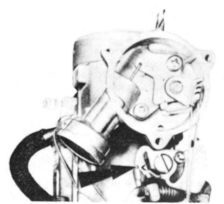

Fig. 3.24. 'V' mark alignment point (Sec. 22)

retaining screws.

9   Reconnect the battery, run the engine and adjust the fast idle speed, as described in the following paragraph.

10 *Fast idle adjustment:* **Note** - Ideally a tachometer will be required in order to set the fast idle rpm to the specified value. Run the engine up to normal operating temperature then switch off and connect the tachometer (where available). Open the throttle and locate the fast idle cam in the fast idle position (with the V-mark in line with the throttle lever). Release the throttle to hold the cam in this position and check that the choke plate is fully open (if it is not fully open, the assembly is faulty or the engine is not at operating temperature). Without touching the accelerator pedal, start the engine and bend the tag on the throttle lever as necessary to obtain the correct fast idle rpm.

11 Finally refit the air cleaner (Section 2).

23 Weber dual venturi carburettor - cleaning, inspection and adjustment

1   Initially remove the carburettor from the car as described in Section 18, then clean the exterior with a water soluble cleaner.

2   Carefully prise out the U-clip with a screwdriver and disconnect the choke plate operating link (Fig. 3.28).

3   Remove the six screws and detach the carburettor upper body (Fig. 3.29).

4   Unscrew the brass nut located at the fuel intake and detach the fuel

filter.

5   Tap out the float retaining pin, and detach the float and needle valve (Fig. 3.30).

6   Remove the three screws and detach the power valve diaphragm assembly.

7   Unscrew the needle valve housing.

8   Unscrew the jets and jet plugs from the carburettor body, noting the positions in which they are fitted (Fig. 3.31).

9   From the carburettor body, remove the two primary diffuser tubes (Fig. 3.32).

10 Remove four screws and detach the accelerator pump diaphragm, taking care that the spring is not lost (Fig. 3.33).

11 Before attempting to remove the mixture screw, refer to Section 15.

12 Remove four screws and detach the anti-stall diaphragm, taking care that the spring is not lost (Fig. 3.34). **Note:** This is only fitted on certain variants.

13 Clean the jets and passageways using clean, dry compressed air (Fig. 3.32). Check the float assembly for signs of damage or leaking. Inspect the power valve and pump diaphragms and gaskets for splits or deterioration. Examine the mixture screw, needle valve seat and throttle spindle for signs of wear. Replace parts as necessary (Fig. 3.35).

14 When reassembling, refit the accelerator pump diaphragm assembly (Fig. 3.36).

15 Fit the mixture screw and spring in the same position as originally fitted.

16 Slide the two diffuser tubes into position, then refit the jets and jet plugs.

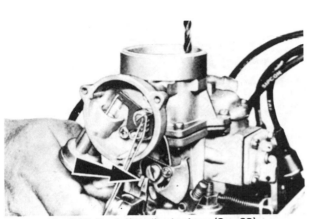

Fig. 3.25. De-choke adjusting lever (Sec. 22)

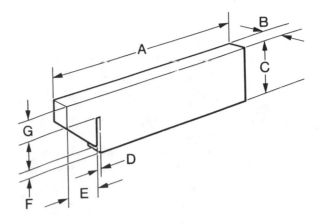

Fig. 3.26. Pre-load tool (A) = 2.63 in (67 mm), (B) = 0.25 in (6.4 mm),
(C) = 0.75 in (19 mm), (D) = 0.06 in (1.6 mm), (E) = 0.37 in (9.5 mm),
(F) = 0.12 in (3.0 mm, (G) = 0.25 in (6.4 mm) (Sec. 22)

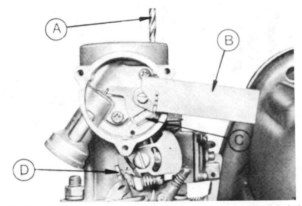

Fig. 3.27. Pull down adjustment - Twist drill (A), Pre-load tool (B),
Adjusting lever (C), Throttle in 'high cam' position (D) (Sec. 22)

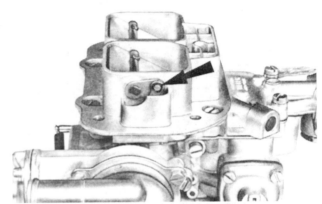

Fig. 3.28. Choke link U-circlip (Sec. 23)

Fig. 3.29. Removing carburettor upper body (Sec. 23)

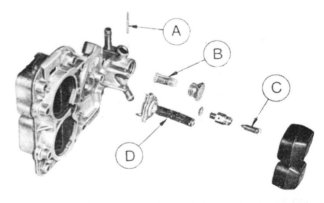

Fig. 3.30. Float retaining pin (A), Filter (B), Needle valve (C), Power
valve (D) (Sec. 23)

Fig. 3.31. Remove main correction jets (A) and main jets (B) for cleaning (Sec. 23)

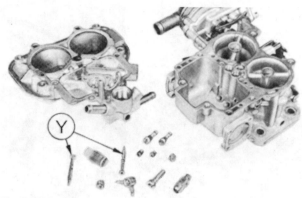

Fig. 3.32. Items to be cleaned (Y-primary diffuser tubes) (Sec. 23)

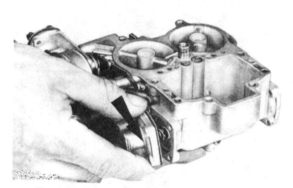

Fig. 3.33. Removing accelerator pump diaphragm (Sec. 23)

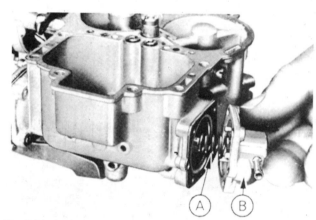

Fig. 3.34. Anti-stall diaphragm spring (A) and housing (B) (Sec. 23)

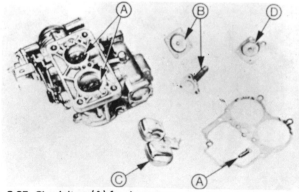

Fig. 3.35. Check item (A) for damage or wear, (B) for splitting, (C) for leaking and (D) (where fitted) for splitting (Sec. 23)

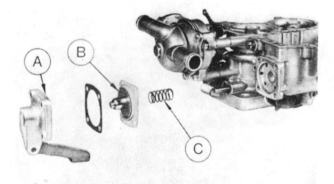

Fig. 3.36. Accelerator pump housing (A), diaphragm (B) and return spring (C) (Sec. 23)

17 Refit the anti-stall diaphragm assembly, if applicable (Fig. 3.37).
18 Loosely fit the three screws to retain the power valve diaphragm assembly, then compress the return spring so that the diaphragm is not twisted or distorted. Lock the retaining screws and release the return spring (Fig. 3.38).
19 Hold the diaphragm down, block the air bleed with a finger then release the diaphragm. If the diaphragm stays down it has correctly sealed to the housing.
20 Refit the needle valve housing, needle valve and float assembly to the upper body (Fig. 3.30).
21 *Float level adjustment:* Hold the upper body vertically so that the needle valve is closed by the float, then measure the dimension from the face of the upper body to the base of the float. Adjust to the specified figure by bending the tag (Fig. 3.39).
22 Refit the fuel inlet filter and brass nut.
23 Position a new gasket and refit the carburettor upper body to the main body. Ensure that the choke link locates correctly through the upper body. Apply thread locking fluid to the upper body screw threads.
24 Reconnect the choke link and refit the U-circlip.

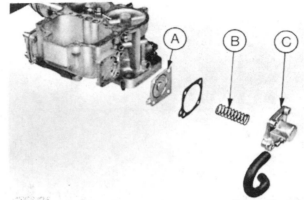

Fig. 3.37. Anti-stall diaphragm (A), return spring (B) and housing (C) (Sec. 23)

24 Weber dual venturi carburettor automatic choke - removal, overhaul and refitting

1 Disconnect the battery earth lead.
2 Remove the air cleaner, as described in Section 2.
3 Remove the three screws, detach the cover and move it clear of the carburettor. For access to the lower screw it will be necessary to make up a suitably cranked screwdriver.
4 Detach the internal heat shield.
5 Remove the single U-circlip and disconnect the choke plate operating link.
6 Remove the three screws, disconnect the choke link at the operating lever and detach the choke assembly. For access to the lower screw the cranked screwdriver will again be required (Fig. 3.40).
7 Remove the three screws and detach the vacuum diaphragm assembly.
8 Dismantle the remaining parts of the choke mechanism.
9 Clean all the components, inspect them for wear and damage and wipe them dry with a lint-free cloth. Do not use any lubricants during reassembly.
10 Reassemble the choke mechanism, after checking the diaphragm and sealing ring for splits (Fig. 3.41).
11 Refit the vacuum diaphragm and housing, ensuring that the diaphragm is flat before the housing is fitted (Fig. 3.42).
12 Ensure that the O-ring is correctly located in the choke housing then reconnect the lower choke link. Position the assembly and secure it with the three screws; ensure that the upper choke link locates correctly through the carburettor body.
13 Reconnect the upper choke link to the choke spindle.

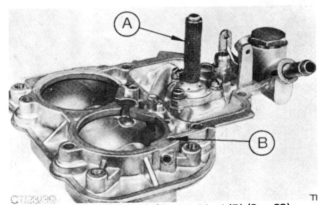

Fig. 3.38. Power valve (A) and air bleed (B) (Sec. 23)

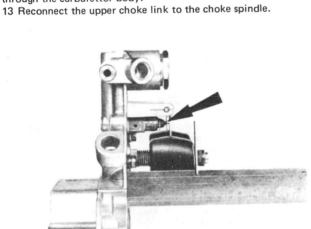

Fig. 3.39. Float level adjusting tag (Sec. 23)

Fig. 3.40. Automatic choke securing screws (Sec. 24)

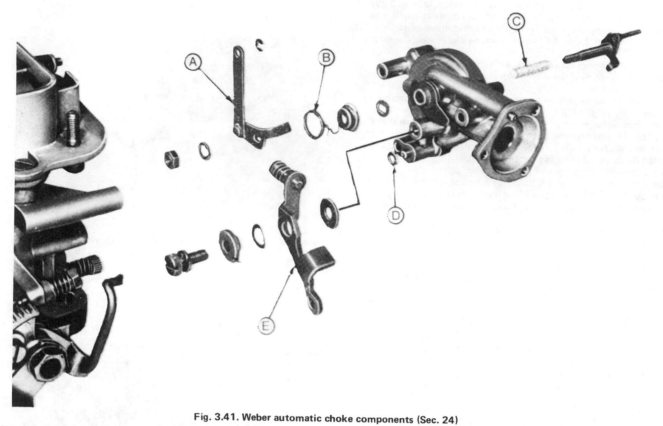

Fig. 3.41. Weber automatic choke components (Sec. 24)

A *Upper choke link*

B *Fast idle cam spring*

C *Spindle sleeve*

D *Sealing ring*
E *Choke link with adjusting screw*

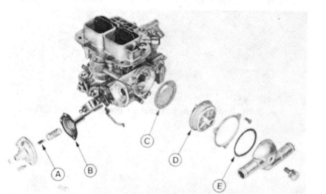

Fig. 3.42. Vacuum diaphragm (B) and adjusting screw (A). Internal heat shield (C), housing assembly (D) and gasket (E) (Sec. 24)

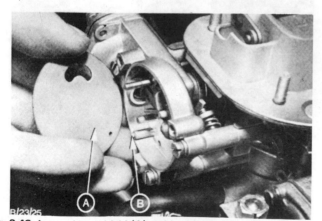

Fig. 3.43. Internal heat shield (A) and locating peg (B) (Sec. 24 and 25)

14 Check the vacuum pull-down and choke phasing, as described in Section 25.

15 Refit the internal heat shield ensuring that the hole in the cover locates correctly onto the peg cast in the housing (Fig. 3.43).

16 Connect the bi-metal spring to the choke lever, position the choke cover and loosely fit the three retaining screws.

17 Rotate the cover until the marks are aligned, then tighten the three screws (Fig. 3.44).

18 Reconnect the battery, run the engine and adjust the fast idle speed, as described in Section 25.

19 Refit the air cleaner (Section 2).

25 Weber dual venturi carburettor automatic choke - adjustment

Note: The procedure is described for a carburettor which is fitted in the car, but with the exception of fast idle speed adjustment, can be carried out on the bench if required where the carburettor has been removed.

1   Disconnect the battery earth lead.

2   Remove the air cleaner, as described in Section 2.

3   Remove the three screws, detach the choke cover and move it clear of the carburettor. For access to the lower screw it will be necessary to make up a suitable cranked screwdriver (Fig. 3.45).

4   Detach the internal heat shield.

5   *Vacuum pull-down:* Fit an elastic band to the choke plate lever and position it so that the choke plates are held closed. Open, then release, the throttle to ensure that the choke plates close fully. Unscrew the plug from the diaphragm unit then manually push open the diaphragm up to its stop from inside the choke housing. Do not push on the rod as it is spring loaded but push on the diaphragm plug body. The choke plate pull-down should now be measured, using an unmarked twist drill shank between the edge of the choke plate and the air horn wall, and compared with the specified figure (Fig. 3.46). Adjust, if necessary, by screwing the adjusting screw in or out, using a short bladed screwdriver (Fig. 3.47). Refit the end plug and detach the elastic band on completion.

Fig. 3.44. Correct choke housing alignment mark (B) (Sec. 24 and 25)

Fig. 3.45. Housing securing screws (Sec. 45)

Fig. 3.46. Elastic band (A), twist drill (B) and operating rod (C) (Sec. 25)

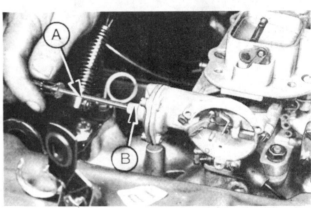

Fig. 3.47. Adjust vacuum pull down at (B) with screwdriver (A) (Sec. 25)

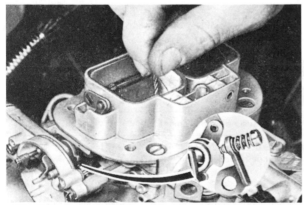

Fig. 3.48. Fast idle screw on upper section of cam (Sec. 25)

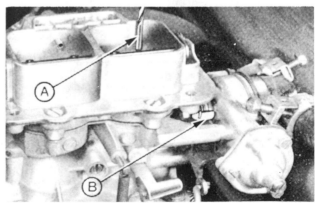

Fig. 3.49. Adjust choke phasing tag (B) with specified drill in position (A) (Sec. 25)

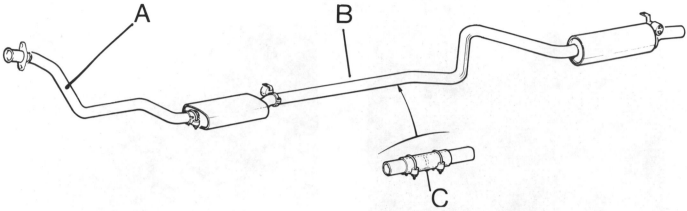

Fig. 3.50. Downpipe (A), resonator and muffler assembly (B) and service joint (C) (Sec. 26)

Fig. 3.51. Fast idle adjustment (B) with choke plates open (A) (Sec. 25)

26.2 Exhaust pipe attached to floor pan

6   *Choke phasing:* Hold the throttle partly open and position the fast idle cam so that the fast idle adjusting screw locates on the upper section of the cam. Release the throttle to hold the cam in this position, then push the choke plates down until the step on the cam jams against the adjusting screw (Fig. 3.48). Measure the clearance between the edge of the choke plate and the air horn wall using a specified sized drill. Adjust, if necessary, by bending the tag (3.49).

7   Refit the internal heat shield ensuring that the hole in the cover locates correctly onto the peg cast in the housing (Fig. 3.43).

8   Connect the bi-metal spring to the choke lever, position the choke cover and loosely fit the three retaining screws.

9   Rotate the cover until the marks are aligned then tighten the three screws (Fig. 3.44).

10 Reconnect the battery, run the engine and adjust the fast idle speed as described in the following paragraph.

11 *Fast idle speed adjustment:* **Note** - Ideally a tachometer will be required in order to set the fast idle rpm to the specified value. Run the engine up to normal operating temperature, then switch off and connect the tachometer (where available). Open the throttle partially, hold the choke plates fully closed then release the throttle so that the choke mechanism is held in the fast idle position. Release the choke plates, checking that they remain fully open (if they are not open, the assembly is faulty or the engine is not at operating temperature). Without touching the accelerator pedal, start the engine and adjust the fast idle screw as necessary to obtain the correct fast idle rpm (Fig. 3.51).

12 Finally refit the air cleaner (Section 2).

26 Exhaust system - general description

1   The exhaust system consists of a cast iron manifold, a down pipe and a single piece front resonator and rear muffler assembly (Fig. 3.50).

2   The system is flexibly attached to the floor pan by two circular rubber mountings (photo).

3   At regular intervals the system should be checked for corrosion, joint leakage, the condition and security of the flexible mountings and the tightness of the joints.

27 Exhaust system - replacement

Note: This Section describes the procedures for replacement of the complete one-piece exhaust system. If only the front resonator is to be replaced it is not necessary to remove the rear muffler. If only the rear muffler is to be replaced it is not necessary to remove the front resonator. However, if either of these parts is to be replaced individually, it is important to make the sawcut described in paragraph 5 in the position stated. Where a replacement muffler or resonator is being used on what was originally a one-piece exhaust system, a service sleeve and U-clamps will be required to connect the two parts of the system.

1   Disconnect the battery earth lead.

2   If possible, raise the car on a ramp or place it over an inspection pit.

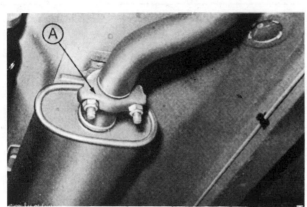

Fig. 3.52. 'U'-bolt clamp at downpipe to resonator joint (Sec. 27)

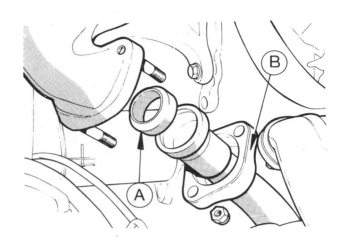

Fig. 3.53. Manifold clamp (B) and sealing ring (A) (Sec. 27)

Alternatively jack up the car and support it to obtain the maximum amount of working room underneath.

3   Cut through the exhaust with a hacksaw on the section to the rear of the resonator. If the complete exhaust is being replaced the position of the sawcut is not important. If the resonator only is being replaced the sawcut should be made 29.5 in (750 mm) from the rear face of the resonator. If the muffler only is being replaced, the sawcut should be made 29.0 in (735 mm) from the rear face of the resonator. Ensure that the sawcut is at 90° to the pipe. Where a 2-piece exhaust system is fitted, separate the two parts by removing the U-clamps at the service sleeve behind the resonator.

4   Unhook the rear muffler from the rubber insulator and guide over the axle and pull clear of the vehicle.

5   Remove the two securing nuts and separate the exhaust pipe at the manifold clamp. Remove the sealing ring.

6   Unhook the front resonator from the rubber insulator and guide clear of the car.

7   Remove the securing nuts and detach the two exhaust support brackets. Remove the 'U' bolt clamp that secures the downpipe to the front resonator (Fig. 3.52).

8   Separate the downpipe from the front resonator, cutting if necessary, and remove the manifold clamp ring.

9   Clean the contacting faces of the sealing ring, manifold and clamp with emery cloth. Examine the two rubber insulators for deterioration and replace if necessary.

10 Scribe a line 3 in (75 mm) from the end of the front resonator pipe and slide on the service joint. Slide the manifold clamp ring onto the downpipe.

11 Connect the front resonator and the downpipe and clamp loosely (Fig. 3.53).

12 Position the front part of the exhaust system under the car, and suspend from the front rubber insulator and the manifold clamp. Do not tighten the nuts.

13 Scribe a line 2 in (50 mm) from the end of the muffler pipe, position the muffler under the vehicle and slide into the service joint up to the scribed line. Suspend from the rear rubber insulator and loosely fit the 'U' bolt clamps to the service joint.

14 Align the exhaust system, ensuring there is a minimum clearance of 0.8 in (20 mm) between any part of the system and the body or body components.

15 Tighten the manifold clamp and the three 'U' bolt clamps to the correct torque.

16 Reconnect the battery, run the engine to check for exhaust leaks then lower the car to the ground.

Fault diagnosis overleaf

28 Fault diagnosis - fuel system and carburation

Symptom	Cause	Remedy
Fuel consumption excessive	Air cleaner choked and dirty giving rich mixture	Remove, clean and replace air cleaner element.
	Fuel leaking from carburettor, fuel pumps, or fuel lines	Check for and eliminate all fuel leaks. Tighten fuel line union nuts.
	Float chamber flooding	Check and adjust float level.
	Generally worn carburettor	Remove, overhaul and replace.
	Distributor condenser faulty	Remove and fit new unit.
	Balance weights or vacuum advance mechanism in distributor faulty	Remove and overhaul distributor.
	Carburettor incorrectly adjusted, mixture too rich	Tune and adjust carburettor.
	Idling speed too high	Adjust idling speed.
	Contact breaker gap incorrect	Check and reset gap.
	Valve clearances incorrect	Check cam follower to valve stem clearances and adjust as necessary.
	Incorrectly set spark plugs	Remove, clean and re-gap.
	Tyres under-inflated	Check tyre pressures and inflate if necessary.
	Wrong spark plugs fitted	Remove and replace with correct units.
	Brakes dragging	Check and adjust brakes.
Insufficient fuel delivery or weak mixture due to air leaks	Petrol tank air vent restricted	Remove petrol cap and clean out air vent.
	Partially clogged filters in pump and carburettor	Remove and clean filters. Remove and clean out float chamber and needle valve assembly.
	Incorrectly seating valves in fuel pump	Remove, and fit new fuel pump.
	Fuel pump diaphragm leaking or damaged	Remove and fit new fuel pump.
	Gasket in fuel pump damaged	Remove, and fit new fuel pump.
	Fuel pump valves sticking due to petrol gumming	Remove and thoroughly clean fuel pump.
	Too little fuel in fuel tank (prevalent when climbing steep hills)	Refill fuel tank.
	Union joints on pipe connections loose	Tighten joints and check for air leaks.
	Split in fuel pipe on suction side of fuel pump	Examine, locate and repair.
	Inlet manifold to block or inlet manifold to carburettor gasket leaking	Test by pouring oil along joints - bubbles indicate leak. Renew gasket as appropriate.

Chapter 4 Ignition system

For modifications, and information applicable to later models, refer to Supplement at end of manual

Contents

Specifications

Spark plugs

Type	1600 Autolite BF 22 2000 Autolite BF 32
Size	18 mm
Plug gap	0.025 in (0.60 mm)

Coil

Type	Oil filled low voltage used in conjunction with 1.5 ohm ballast resistor
Resistance at 20°C (68°F)	
Primary	0.95 - 1.60 ohms
Secondary	5000 - 9300 ohms

Distributor

Type	Ford (Motorcraft) or Bosch	
Application:		Colour code
1600	Bosch 76 HF - 12100 - HA	Red/Purple
2000	Bosch 76 HF - 12100 - CA	Yellow/Green
	or	
1600	Ford 76 HF - 12100 - GA	Yellow/Brown
2000	Ford 76 HF - 12100 - DA	Yellow
Contact points gap setting:		
Bosch	0.018 in (0.45 mm)	
Ford (Motorcraft)	0.025 in (0.64 mm)	
Rotation of rotor	Clockwise from top	
Automatic advance	Mechanical and vacuum	
Drive	Skew gear	
Initial advance: (static and dynamic)		
1600 (except 1600 Ghia)	6° BTDC at 800 rpm	
2000 and 1600 Ghia	8° BTDC at 800 rpm	
Firing order	1, 3, 4, 2	
Condenser capacity - Ford	0.21 - 0.25 m fd	
Condenser capacity - Bosch	0.18 - 0.26 m fd	
Dwell angle	48° - 52°	

1 General description

In order that the engine can run correctly it is necessary for an electrical spark to ignite the fuel/air mixture in the combustion chamber at exactly the right moment in relation to engine speed and load.

The ignition system is divided into two circuits, low tension and high tension.

The low tension (LT), or primary circuit, consists of the battery ignition switch, low tension or primary coil windings, and the contact breaker points and condenser, both located at the distributor.

The high tension (HT), or secondary circuit, consists of the high tension or secondary coil winding, the heavy ignition lead from the centre of the coil to the distributor cap, and the rotor arm and the spark plug leads.

The ignition system is based on feeding low tension voltage from the battery to the coil where it is converted to high tension voltage. The high tension voltage is powerful enough to jump the spark plug gap in the cylinders many times a second under high compression pressures, providing that the system is in good condition and that all adjustments are correct.

The wiring harness includes a high resistance wire in the ignition coil feed circuit and it is very important that only a 'ballast resistor' type ignition coil of the 7 volt type is used. This lead is identified by its white with pink colour tracer colour coding.

During starting this 'ballast resistor' wire is by-passed, allowing the full available battery voltage to be fed to the coil (Fig. 4.1). This ensures that during cold starting, when the starter motor current draw would be high, sufficient voltage is still available at the coil to produce a powerful spark. It is therefore essential that only the correct type of coil is used. Under normal running the 12 volt supply is directed through the ballast resistor before reaching the coil (Fig. 4.2).

The ignition advance is controlled both mechanically and by vacuum to ensure that the spark occurs at just the right instant for the particular engine load and speed. The mechanical governor comprises two lead weights, which move out from the distributor shaft as the engine speed rises, due to centrifugal force.

The vacuum control consists of a diaphragm, one side of which is connected via a small bore tube to the carburettor, and the other side to the contact breaker plate. Depression in the inlet manifold and carburettor, which varies with engine speed and throttle opening, causes the diaphragm to move, so moving the contact breaker plate, and advancing or retarding the spark.

Two makes of distributor are used on the Cortina, Ford (black cap) and Bosch (red cap). They are similar in design, with the exception of the condenser location, which is external on the Bosch unit (Fig. 4.3).

Components located beneath the base plate, and the drive gear, are only available for Ford distributors. It will be found that the base plate is sealed in the casing on Bosch distributors, and should not be removed.

2 Contact breaker points - adjustment

1 To adjust the contact breaker points to the correct gap, first release the two clips securing the distributor cap to the distributor body, and lift away the cap. Clean the cap inside and out with a dry cloth. It is unlikely that the four segments will be badly burned or scored, but, if they are, the cap will have to be renewed.

2 Inspect the carbon brush contact located in the top of the cap to ensure that it is not broken and stands proud of the plastic surface.

3 Lift away the rotor arm and check the contact spring on the top of the rotor arm. It must be clean and have adequate tension to ensure good contact.

4 Gently prise the contact breaker points open to examine the condition of their faces. If they are rough, pitted or dirty it will be necessary for replacement points to be fitted.

5 Presuming the points are satisfactory, or that they have been replaced, measure the gap between the points with feeler gauges, by turning the crankshaft until the heel of the breaker arm is on a high point of the cam. The gap should be:

Bosch   *0.018 in (0.45 mm)*
Ford   *0.025 in (0.60 mm)*

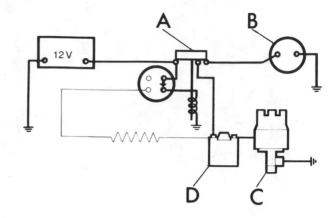

Fig. 4.1. Ignition switch in 'start' position. Starter solenoid (A), Starter motor (B), Distributor (C), Ignition coil (D) (Sec. 1)

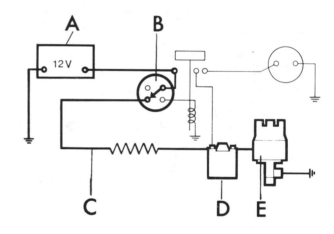

Fig. 4.2. Ignition switch in 'on' position. Battery (A), Ignition switch (B), Ballast resistor (C), Coil (D), Distributor (E) (Sec. 1)

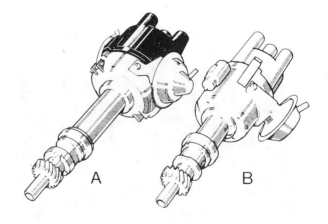

Fig. 4.3. Ford (A) and Bosch (B) distibutors (Sec. 1)

Measuring plug gap. A feeler gauge of the correct size (see ignition system specifications) should have a slight 'drag' when slid between the electrodes. Adjust gap if necessary

Adjusting plug gap. The plug gap is adjusted by bending the earth electrode inwards, or outwards, as necessary until the correct clearance is obtained. Note the use of the correct tool

Normal. Grey-brown deposits, lightly coated core nose. Gap increasing by around 0.001 in (0.025 mm) per 1000 miles (1600 km). Plugs ideally suited to engine, and engine in good condition

Carbon fouling. Dry, black, sooty deposits. Will cause weak spark and eventually misfire. Fault: over-rich fuel mixture. Check: carburettor mixture settings, float level and jet sizes; choke operation and cleanliness of air filter. Plugs can be re-used after cleaning

Oil fouling. Wet, oily deposits. Will cause weak spark and eventually misfire. Fault: worn bores/piston rings or valve guides; sometimes occurs (temporarily) during running-in period. Plugs can be re-used after thorough cleaning

Overheating. Electrodes have glazed appearance, core nose very white — few deposits. Fault: plug overheating. Check: plug value, ignition timing, fuel octane rating (too low) and fuel mixture (too weak). Discard plugs and cure fault immediately

Electrode damage. Electrodes burned away; core nose has burned, glazed appearance. Fault: pre-ignition. Check: as for 'Overheating' but may be more severe. Discard plugs and remedy fault before piston or valve damage occurs

Split core nose (may appear initially as a crack). Damage is self-evident, but cracks will only show after cleaning. Fault: pre-ignition or wrong gap-setting technique. Check: ignition timing, cooling system, fuel octane rating (too low) and fuel mixture (too weak). Discard plugs, rectify fault immediately

6 If the gap varies from the amount stated, slacken the contact plate
securing screw/s. Bosch distributor 1 screw. Ford distributor 2 screws
(Fig. 4.5 and photo).

7 Adjust the contact gap by moving the contact breaker plate. When
the gap is correct, tighten the securing screw/s and recheck the gap
(photo).

8 Replace the rotor arm and distributor cap. Retain in position with
the two clips.

9 On modern engines, setting the contact breaker gap in the
distributor using feeler gauges must be regarded as a basic adjustment
only. For optimum engine performance, the dwell angle must be
checked. The dwell angle is the number of degrees through which the
distributor cam turns during the period between the instance of
closure and opening of the contact breaker points. Checking the dwell
angle not only gives a more accurate setting of the contact breaker gap
but also evens out any variations in the gap which could be caused by
wear in the distributor shaft or its bushes, or difference in height of any
of the cam peaks.

10 The angle should be checked with a dwell meter connected in
accordance with the maker's instructions. Refer to the Specifications
for the correct dwell angle. If the dwell angle is too large, increase the
points gap, if too small, reduce the points gap.

11 The dwell angle should always be adjusted before checking and
adjusting the ignition timing.

2.6 Ford contact breaker adjusting screws

3 Contact breaker points - removal and refitting

1 Disconnect the battery positive terminal.

2 Unplug the spark plug leads, unclip the distributor cap and lift clear.

3 Remove the rotor arm by pulling it straight up from the top of the
cam spindle.

4 If the contact breaker points are burned, pitted or badly worn, they
must be renewed, since attempting to file or grind them will destroy
the special facing.

5 Detach the LT lead at the points:

   Bosch   pull off lead
   Ford   slacken the screw and slide out the forked ends
                  (photo)

6 Remove the securing screw/s and lift out the contact breaker points
(Fig. 4.6 and 4.7).

7 To refit the points is the reverse sequence to removal. Smear a trace
of grease onto the cam to lubricate the moving heel, then reset the
gap, as described in Section 2.

8 Push the rotor arm onto the cam spindle, ensuring that the locating
boss is aligned with the slot.

9 Place the distributor cap squarely on the distributor and retain in
position with the two clips.

10 Push the leads onto the plugs, in the correct order, and reconnect
the battery.

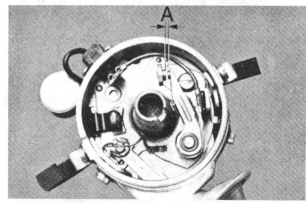

Fig. 4.5. Bosch contact breaker points gap (A) (Sec. 2)

4 Condenser - removal, testing and refitting

1 The purpose of the condenser (sometimes known as a capacitor)

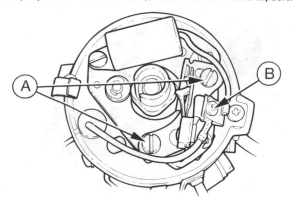

Fig. 4.6. Contact breaker screws (A) and low tension lead connection
(B) in Ford distributor (Sec. 3)

2.7 Check Ford contact breaker points gap

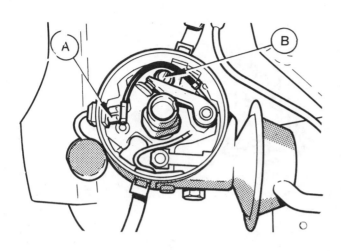

Fig. 4.7. Low tension lead connection (A) and contact breaker screw (B) in Bosch distributor (Sec. 3)

3.5 Detaching Ford LT lead

is to ensure that when the contact breaker points open there is no sparking across them which would waste voltage and cause wear.

2 The condenser is fitted in parallel with the contact breaker points. If it develops a short circuit, it will cause ignition failure as the contact breaker points will be prevented from correctly interrupting the low tension circuit.

3 If the engine becomes very difficult to start or begins to miss after several miles of running and the breaker points shown signs of excessive burning, then the condition of the condenser must be suspect. One further test can be made by separating the points by hand with the ignition switched on. It this is accompanied by a bright flash, it is indicative that the condenser has failed.

4 Without special test equipment the only safe way to diagnose condenser trouble is to replace a suspected unit with a new one and note if there is any improvement.

5 To remove the condenser from the distributor take off the distributor cap and rotor arm.

6 *Bosch:* Disconnect the low tension leads from the coil and to the contact breaker points. Release the condenser cable from the side of the distributor body and then undo and remove the screw that secures the condenser to the side of the distributor body. Lift away the condenser.

7 *Ford:* Slacken the self tapping screw holding the condenser lead and low tension lead to the contact breaker points (photo). Slide out the forked terminal on the end of the condenser low tension lead. Undo and remove the condenser retaining screw and remove the condenser from the breaker plate.

8 To refit the condenser, simply reverse the order of removal.

Fig. 4.8. Distributor securing bolt (Sec. 6)

5 Distributor - lubrication

1 It is important that the distributor cam is lubricated with vaseline (petroleum jelly) or grease at 6,000 miles (10,000 km) or 6 monthly intervals. Also the automatic timing control weights and cam spindle are lubricated with engine oil.

2 Great care should be taken not to use too much lubricant as any excess that finds its way onto the contact breaker points could cause burning and misfiring.

3 To gain access to the cam spindle, lift away the distributor cap and rotor arm. Apply no more than two drops of engine oil onto the felt pad. This will run down the spindle when the engine is hot and lubricate the bearings.

4 To lubricate the automatic timing coltrol, allow a few drops of oil to pass through the holes in the contact breaker base plate through which the four sided cam emerges. Apply not more than one drop of oil to the pivot post of the moving contact breaker point. Wipe away excess oil and refit the rotor arm and distributor cap.

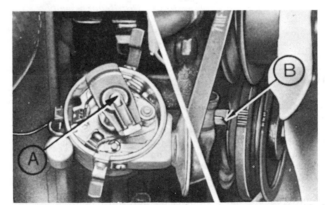

Fig. 4.9. Rotor facing No. 1 contact (A) with crankshaft pulley timing mark (B) aligned (Sec. 6)

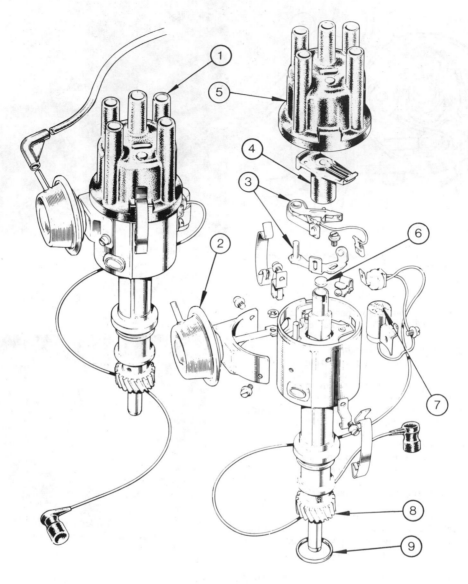

Fig. 4.10. Bosch distributor assembly (Sec. 7)

1	Distributor assembly	4	Rotor arm
2	Vacuum unit	5	Cap
3	Contact breaker	6	Felt wick

7	Condenser
8	Drive gear
9	Seal

6 Distributor - removal

1   To remove the distributor from the engine, mark the four spark plug leads so that they may be refitted to the correct plugs and pull off the four spark plug lead connectors.

2   Disconnect the high tension lead from the centre of the distributor cap by gripping the end cap and pulling. Also disconnect the low tension lead from the ignition coil.

3   Pull off the rubber union holding the vacuum pipe to the distributor vacuum advance housing. Refer to the note in paragraph 5.

4   Remove the distributor body clamp bolt which holds the distributor clamp plate to the engine and lift out the distributor (Fig. 4.8).

5   **Note:** If it is not wished to disturb the timing turn the crankshaft until the timing marks are in line and the rotor arm is pointing to number 1 spark plug segment in the distributor cap (Fig. 4.9). This will facilitate refitting the distributor providing the crankshaft is not moved whilst the distributor is away from the engine. Mark the position

of the rotor in relation to the distributor body, *after* it has been lifted clear.

7 Distributor (Bosch) - dismantling

1   With the distributor on the bench, release the two spring clips retaining the cap and lift away the cap (Fig. 4.10).

2   Pull the rotor arm off the distributor cam spindle.

3   Remove the contact breaker points, as described in Section 3.

4   Unscrew and remove the condenser securing screw and lift away the condenser and connector.

5   Next carefully remove the 'U' shaped clip from the pull rod of the vacuum unit.

6   Undo and remove the two screws that secure the vacuum unit to the side of the distributor body. Lift away the vacuum unit.

7   The distributor cap spring clip retainers may be removed by undoing and removing the screws and lifting away the clips and retainers.

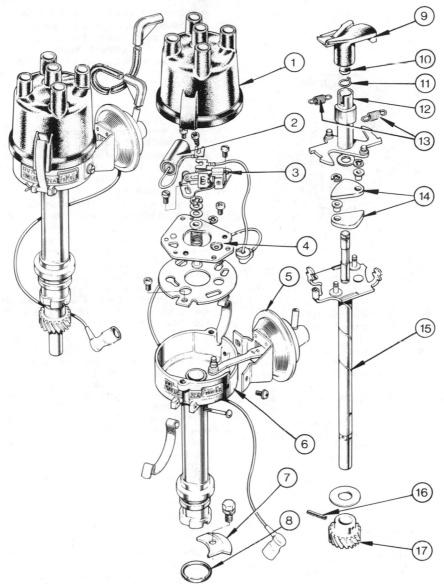

Fig. 4.11. Ford distributor assembly (Sec. 8)

1	Cap	7	Distributor clamp	13	Advance springs
2	Condenser	8	Seal	14	Advance weights
3	Contact breakers	9	Rotor arm	15	Shaft
4	Base plate	10	Felt wick	16	Pin
5	Vacuum unit	11	Spring clip	17	Drive gear
6	Body	12	Cam		

Note: This is the limit of the dismantling which should be attempted, since none of the parts beneath the breaker plate, including the drive gear can be renewed.

8 Distributor (Ford) - dismantling

1 Refer to Section 7, and follow the instructions given in paragraphs 1 to 3. The component parts are shown in Fig. 4.11.
2 Next prise off the small circlip from the vacuum unit pivot post.
3 Take out the two screws that hold the breaker plate to the distributor body and lift away.
4 Undo and remove the condenser retaining screw and lift away the condenser.
5 Take off the circlip, flat washer and two wave washers from the pivot post. Separate the two plates. Be careful not to lose the spring now left on the pivot post.
6 Pull the low tension wire and grommet from the lower plate.
7 Undo the two screws holding the vacuum unit to the body. Take

off the unit.
8 Make a sketch of the position of the cam plate assembly in relation to the bumpstop, noting the identification letters. Also note which spring - thick or thin - is fitted to which post (Fig. 4.12).
9 Dismantle the spindle by taking out the felt pad in the top. Remove the spring clip using small electrical pliers.
10 Prise off the bumpstop and lift out the cam plate assembly. Remove the thrust washer.
11 It is only necessary to remove the spindle and lower plate if it is excessively worn. If this is the case, with a suitable diameter parallel pin punch tap out the gear lock pin.
12 The gear may now be drawn off the shaft with a universal puller. If there are no means of holding the legs these must be bound together with wire to stop them springing apart during removal.
13 Finally withdraw the shaft from the distributor body.

9 Distributor - inspection and repair

1 Check the contact breaker points for wear, burning or pitting.

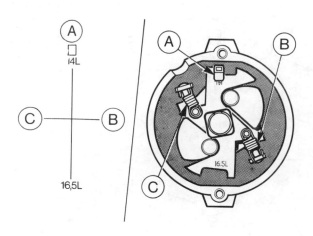

Fig. 4.12. Typical sketch only, showing location of bump stop (A), Thin spring (B) and Thick spring (C) (Sec. 8)

Check the distributor cap for signs of tracking indicated by a thin black line between the segments. Renew the cap if any signs of tracking are found.

2   If the metal portion of the rotor arm is badly burned or loose, renew the arm. If only slightly burned clean the end with a fine file. Check that the contact spring has adequate pressure and the bearing surface is clean and in good condition.

3   Check that the carbon brush in the distributor cap is unbroken and stands proud of its holder.

4   Examine the centrifugal weights and pivots for wear and the advance springs for slackness. They can be checked by comparing with new parts. If they are slack they must be renewed.

5   Check the points assembly for fit on the breaker plate, and the cam follower for wear.

6   Examine the fit of the spindle in the distributor body. If there is excessive side movement it will be necessary to obtain a new body as small items are not available.

10 Distributor (Bosch) - reassembly

1   Place the distributor cap retaining spring clip and retainers on the outside of the distributor body and secure the retainers with the two screws.

2   Position the contact breaker point assembly in the breaker plate in such a manner that the entire lower surface of the assembly contacts the plate. Refit the contact breaker point assembly securing screw but do not fully tighten yet.

3   Hook the diaphragm assembly pull rod into contact with the pivot pin.

4   Secure the diaphragm to the distributor body with the two screws. Also refit the condenser to the terminal side of the diaphragm bracket securing screw. The condenser must firmly contact its lower stop on the housing.

5   Apply a little grease or petroleum jelly to the cam and also to the heel of the breaker lever.

6   Reset the contact breaker points, as described in Section 2, and then replace the rotor arm and distributor cap.

11 Distributor (Ford) - reassembly

1   Reassembly is a straightforward reversal of the dismantling process but there are several points which must be noted.

2   Check that the drive gear is not 180° out of position, as the pin bores may be slightly misaligned. Secure it with a new pin.

3   Coat the upper shaft with a lithium base grease, ensuring that the undercut is filled.

4   When fitting the cam spindle assembly, first replace the thrust washer, then refer to the sketch made in Section 8, item 8. Check that

the assembly moves freely without binding.

5   Position the spring clip legs opposite the rotor arm slot.

6   Before assembling the breaker plates make sure that the nylon bearing studs are correctly located in their holes in the upper breaker plate, and the small earth spring is fitted on the pivot post.

7   When all is assembled reset the contact breaker points, as described in Section 2.

12 Distributor - installation

1   If a new shaft or gear has not been fitted (ie; the orignial parts are still being used), it will not be necessary to re-time the ignition.

2   Align the rotor arm with the mark on the distributor body (Section 6, item 5). Insert the distributor into its location with the vacuum advance assembly to the rear.

3   Notice that the rotor arm rotates as the gears mesh. The rotor arm must settle in exactly the same direction that it was in before the distributor was removed. To do this lift out the assembly far enough to rotate the shaft one tooth at a time, lowering it home to check the direction with the assembly fully home fit the distributor clamp plate, bolt the plain washer.

4   With the distributor assembly fitted reconnect the low tension lead from the side of the distributor to the CB or negative (−) terminal on the coil. Reconnect the HT lead to the centre of the distributor cap and refit the rubber union of the vacuum pipe which runs from the induction manifold to the side of the vacuum advance unit.

5   If the engine has been disturbed, refer to Section 14.

13 Spark plugs and HT leads

1   The correct functioning of the spark plugs is vital for the correct running and efficiency of the engine.

2   At intervals of 6,000 miles (10,000 km), the plugs should be removed, examined, cleaned, and if worn excessively, renewed. The condition of the spark plugs will also tell much about the overall condition of the engine (see page 83).

3   If the insulator nose of the spark plug is clean and white, with no deposits, this is indicative of a weak mixture, or too hot a plug (a hot plug transfers heat away from the electrode slowly - a cold plug transfers it away quickly).

4   The plugs fitted as standard are as listed in Specifications at the head of this Chapter. If the tip and insulator nose are covered with hard black looking deposits, then this is indicative that the mixture is too rich. Should the plug be black and oily, then it is likely that the engine is fairly worn, as well as the mixture being too rich.

5   If the insulator nose is covered with light tan to greyish brown deposits, then the mixture is correct and it is likely that the engine is in good condition.

6   If there are any traces of long brown tapering stains on the outside of the white portion of the plug, then the plug will have to be renewed, as this shows that there is a faulty joint between the plug body and the insulator, and compression is being allowed to leak away.

7   Plugs should be cleaned by a sand blasting machine which will free them from carbon more thoroughly than cleaning by hand. The machine will also test the condition of the plugs under compression. Any plugs that fails to spark at the recommended pressure should be renewed.

8   The spark plug gap is of considerable importance, as, if it is too large or too small, the size of the spark and its efficiency will be seriously impaired. The spark plug gap should be set to the figure given in Specifications at the beginning of this Chapter.

9   To set it, measure the gap with a feeler gauge, and then bend open, or close, the outer plug electrode until the correct gap is achieved. The centre electrode should never be bent as this may crack the insulation and cause plug failure if nothing worse.

10   When replacing the plugs, remember to use new plug washers, and replace the leads from the distributor in the correct firing order, which is 1, 3, 4, 2 (No. 1 cylinder being the one nearest the radiator).

11   The plug leads require no routine attention other than being kept clean and wiped over regularly.

12   At intervals of 6,000 miles (10,000 km) or 6 months, however, pull the leads off the plugs and distributor one at a time and make sure no water has found its way onto the connections. Remove any corrosion from the brass ends, wipe the collars on top of the distributor, and refit the leads.

14 Ignition timing

1 When a new gear or shaft has been fitted or the engine has been rotated, or if a new assembly is being fitted, it will be necessary to retime the ignition. Carry it out this way:

2 Look up the initial advance (static) for the particular model in the Specifications at the beginning of this Chapter.

3 Turn the engine until No. 1 piston is coming up to TDC on the compression stroke. This can be checked by removing No. 1 spark plug and feeling the pressure being developed in the cylinder or by removing the oil filler cap and noting when the cam is in the upright position. If this check is not made it is all too easy to set the timing 180° out. The engine can most easily be turned by placing a suitable sized socket and a ratchet on the crankshaft pulley bolt. Alternatively, it may be turned by engaging top gear and edging the car along (except automatic).

4 Continue turning the engine until the appropriate timing mark on the crankshaft pulley is in line with the pointer. This setting must be correct for the initial advance for the engine which has already been established from the Specifications.

5 This photo shows the crankshaft pulley at TDC (top dead centre) position - zero degrees advance. **Note:** Marks occasionally vary, but the heavy mark is always at TDC, each mark to the right (clockwise) being 2° before, and marks to the left each being 2° after.

6 Now with the vacuum advance unit pointing to the rear of the engine and the rotor arm in the same position as was noted before removal insert the distributor into its location. Notice that the rotor arm rotates as the gears mesh. Lift out the distributor far enough to rotate the shaft one tooth at a time, lowering it home to check the direction of the rotor arm. When it points in the desired direction with the assembly fully home fit the distributor clamp plate, bolt and plain washer. Do not fully tighten yet.

7 Gently turn the distributor body until the contact breaker points are just opening when the rotor is pointing at the contact in the distributor cap which is connected to No. 1 spark plug. A convenient way is to put a mark on the outside of the distributor body in line with the segment in the cover, so that it shows when the cover is removed.

8 If this position cannot be reached check that the drive gear has meshed on the correct tooth by lifting out the distributor once more. If necessary, rotate the drive shaft gear one tooth and try again.

9 Tighten the distributor body clamp enough to hold the distributor, but do not overtighten.

10 Have the engine at normal operating temperature, idling at specified speed and the distributor advance vacuum pipe disconnected from the distributor and plugged.

11 Connect a stroboscope in accordance with the manufacturer's instructions and direct the light onto the timing scale adjacent to the crankshaft pulley.

12 The notch in the pulley should be in alignment with the specified (BTDC) mark on the timing scale. The mark and notch can be painted white to improve clarity (photo).

13 If the marks are not in alignment, release the distributor clamp plate bolt and rotate the distributor until they are.

14 Tighten the clamp plate bolt, switch off the engine, reconnect the vacuum pipe and remove the stroboscope.

15 The setting of a distributor including the amount of vacuum and mechanical advance can only be accurately carried out on an electric tester. Alterations to the vacuum advance shims or tension on the mechanical advance unit springs will change the characteristics of the unit.

15 Ignition system - fault finding

By far the majority of breakdown and running troubles are caused by faults in the ignition system either in the low tension or high tension circuits.

There are two main symptoms indicating ignition faults. Either the engine will not start or fire, or the engine is difficult to start and misfires. If it is a regular misfire, ie; the engine is running on only two or three cylinders, the fault is almost sure to be in the secondary or high tension circuit. If the misfiring is intermittent, the fault could be in either the high or low tension circuits. If the car stops suddenly, or will not start at all, it is likely that the fault is in the low tension circuit. Loss of power and overheating, apart from faulty carburation settings, are normally due to faults in the distributor or to incorrect ignition timing.

16 Fault diagnosis - engine fails to start

1 If the engine fails to start and the car was running normally when it was last used, first check there is fuel in the petrol tank. If the engine turns over normally on the starter motor and the battery is evidently well charged, then the fault may be in either the high or low tension circuits. First check the HT circuit. **Note:** If the battery is known to be fully charged, the ignition light comes on, and the starter motor fails to turn the engine **check the tightness of the leads on the battery terminals** and also the secureness of the earth lead to its connection to the body. It is quite common for the leads to have worked loose, even if they look and feel secure. If one of the battery terminal posts gest very hot when trying to work the starter motor this is a sure indication of a faulty connection to that terminal.

2 One of the commonest reasons for bad starting is wet or damp spark plug leads and distributor. Remove the distributor cap. If condensation is visible internally dry the cap with a rag and also wipe over the leads. Replace the cap.

3 If the engine still fails to start, check that current is reaching the plugs, by disconnecting each plug lead in turn at the spark plug end, and holding the end of the cable about 3/16 inch (5mm) away from the cylinder block. Spin the engine on the starter motor.

4 Sparking between the end of the cable and the block should be fairly strong with a strong regular blue spark. (Hold the lead with rubber to avoid electric shocks). If current is reaching the plugs, then remove them and clean and regap them to 0.025 inch (0.60 mm). The engine should now start.

5 If there is no spark at the plug leads take off the HT lead from the centre of the distributor cap and hold it to the block as before. Spin the engine on the starter once more. A rapid succession of blue sparks between the end of the lead and the block indicate that the coil is in order and that the distributor cap is cracked, the rotor arm faulty, or the carbon brush in the top of the distributor cap is not making good contact with the spring on the rotor arm. Possibly, the points are in bad condition. Renew them as described in this Chapter, Section 2 or 3.

6 If there are no sparks from the end of the lead from the coil check the connections at the coil end of the lead. If it is in order start checking the low tension circuit.

7 Use a 12v voltmeter or a 12v bulb and two lengths of wire. With the ignition switched on and the points open, test between the low tension wire to the coil (it is marked SW or +) and earth. No reading indicates a break in the supply from the ignition switch. Check the connections at the switch to see if any are loose. Refit them and the engine should run. A reading shows a faulty coil or condenser, or broken lead between the coil and the distributor.

14.5 Crankshaft pulley timing marks and timing pointer

8 Take the condenser wire off the points assembly and with the points open test between the moving point and earth. If there now is a reading then the fault is in the condenser. Fit a new one as described in this Chapter, Section 4, and the fault is cleared.

9 With no reading from the moving point to earth, take a reading between earth and the CB or negative (–) terminal of the coil. A reading here shows a broken wire which will need to be replaced between the coil and distributor. No reading confirms that the coil has failed and must be replaced, after which the engine will run once more. Remember to refit the condenser wire to the points assembly. For these tests it is sufficient to separate the points with a piece of dry paper while testing with the points open.

17 Fault diagnosis - engine misfires

1 If the engine misfires regularly run it at a fast idling speed. Pull off each of the plug caps in turn and listen to the note of the engine. Hold the plug cap in a dry cloth or with a rubber glove as additional protection against a shock from the HT supply.

2 No difference in engine running will be noticed when the lead from the defective circuit is removed. Removing the lead from one of the good cylinders will accentuate the misfire.

3 Remove the plug lead from the end of the defective plug and hold it about 3/16 inch (5 mm) away from the block. Re-start the engine. If the sparking is fairly strong and regular the fault must lie in the spark plug.

4 The plug may be loose, the insulation may be cracked, or the points may have burnt away giving too wide a gap for the spark to jump. Worse still, one of the points may have broken off.

5 If there is no spark at the end of the plug lead, or if it is weak and intermittent, check the ignition lead from the distributor to the plug. If the insulation is cracked or perished, renew the lead. Check the connections at the distributor cap.

6 If there is still no spark, examine the distributor cap carefully for tracking. This can be recognised by a very thin black line running between two or more electrodes, or between an electrode and some other part of the distributor. These lines are paths which now conduct electricity across the cap thus letting it run to earth. The only answer is a new distributor cap.

7 Apart from the ignition timing being incorrect, other causes of misfiring have already been dealt with under the section dealing with the failure of the engine to start. To recap - these are that:

a) *The coil may be faulty giving an intermittent misfire;*
b) *There may be a damaged wire or loose connection in the low tension circuit;*
c) *The condenser may be short circuiting; or*
d) *There may be a mechanical fault in the distributor (broken driving spindle or contact breaker spring).*

8 If the ignition timing is too far retarded, it should be noted that the engine will tend to overheat, and there will be a quite noticeable drop in power. If the engine is overheating and the power is down, and the ignition timing is correct, then the carburettor should be checked, as it is likely that this is where the fault lies.

Chapter 5 Clutch

For modifications, and information applicable to later models, refer to Supplement at end of manual

Contents

Specifications

Type	Single dry plate, diaphragm spring, cable operated	
	1600 cc	**2000 cc**
Lining diameter		
Inner	5 in (127 mm)	4.49 in (114 mm)
Outer	7.44 in (189 mm)	8.46 in (215 mm)
Lining thickness	0.12 in (3.2 mm)	0.15 in (3.8 mm)
Number of torsion springs	4	6
Pedal free-play	1.06 - 1.22 in (27 - 31 mm)	
Total pedal stroke	6.69 in (170 mm)	

Torque wrench settings	lb f ft	kg fm
Pressure plate to flywheel bolts	14	2
Bellhousing to gearbox:		
2000 cc	46	6.3
1600 cc	42	5.8

1 General description

All models covered by this manual are fitted with a single diaphragm spring clutch. The unit comprises a steel cover which is dowelled and bolted to the rear face of the flywheel and contains the pressure plate, diaphragm spring and fulcrum rings.

The clutch disc is free to slide along the splined first motion shaft and is held in position between the flywheel and the pressure plate by the pressure of the pressure plate spring. Friction lining material is rivetted to the clutch disc and it has a spring cushioned hub to absorb transmission shocks and to help ensure a smooth take off.

The circular diaphragm spring is mounted on shoulder pins and held in place in the cover by two fulcrum rings. The spring is also held to the pressure plate by three spring steel clips which are rivetted in position.

The clutch is actuated by a cable controlled by the clutch pedal. The clutch release mechanism consists of a release fork and bearing which are in permanent contact with the release fingers on the pressure plate assembly. There should therefore never be any free play at the release fork. Wear of the friction material in the clutch is adjusted out by means of a cable adjuster at the lower end of the cable where it passes through the bellhousing.

Depressing the clutch pedal actuates the clutch release arm by means of the cable. The release arm pushes the release bearing forwards to bear against the release fingers so moving the centre of the diaphragm spring inwards. The spring is sandwiched between two annular rings which act as fulcrum points. As the centre of the spring is pushed in, the outside of the spring is pushed out, so moving the pressure plate backwards and disengaging the pressure plate from the clutch disc.

When the clutch pedal is released the diaphragm spring forces the pressure plate into contact with the high friction linings on the clutch disc and at the same time pushes the clutch disc a fraction of an inch forwards on its splines so engaging the clutch disc with the flywheel. The clutch disc is now firmly sandwiched between the pressure plate and the flywheel so the drive is taken up.

2 Routine maintenance and clutch adjustment

1   Every 6,000 miles (10,000 km) adjust the clutch cable to compensate for wear in the linings.
2   The clutch should be adjusted until there is a free-play of 1.06 - 1.22 in (27 - 31 mm) at the pedal, as shown in Fig. 5.2.
3   To obtain the correct adjustment, slacken off the locknut and turn the adjusting nut until the correct free-play is obtained.
4   Hold the adjusting nut steady to prevent it moving and retighten the locknut. Check the clearance again.
5   When a new clutch friction plate has been fitted it will be found that the cable will require fairly extensive adjustment, particularly if the old friction plate was well worn before renewal.

3 Clutch - removal

This job may be carried out with the engine either in or out of the car. The gearbox must be detached from the rear of the engine as described in Chapter 6. Then proceed as follows:
1   With a file or scriber mark the relative position of the clutch cover and flywheel which will ensure identical positioning on replacement. This is not necessary if a new clutch is to be fitted.
2   Undo and remove, in a diagonal and progressive manner, the six bolts and spring washers that secure the clutch cover to the flywheel. This will prevent distortion of the cover and also the cover suddenly flying off due to binding on the dowels.
3   With all the bolts removed lift the clutch assembly from the locating dowels. Note which way round the friction plate is fitted and lift it from the clutch cover.

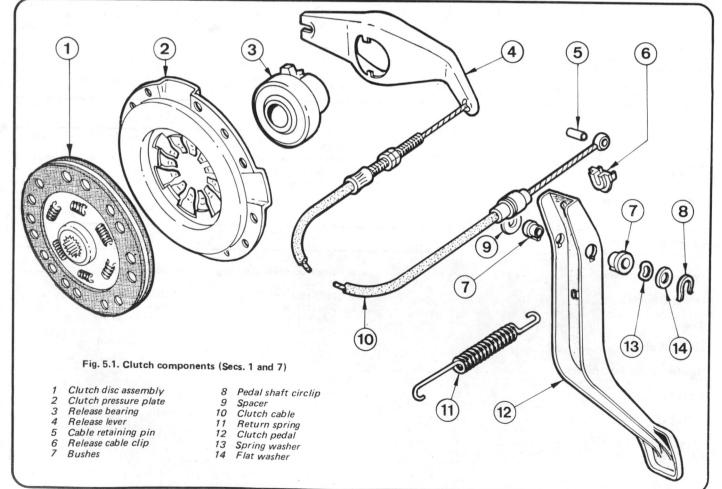

Fig. 5.1. Clutch components (Secs. 1 and 7)

1	Clutch disc assembly	8	Pedal shaft circlip
2	Clutch pressure plate	9	Spacer
3	Release bearing	10	Clutch cable
4	Release lever	11	Return spring
5	Cable retaining pin	12	Clutch pedal
6	Release cable clip	13	Spring washer
7	Bushes	14	Flat washer

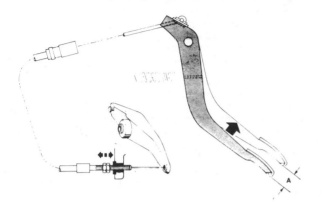

Fig. 5.2. Clutch pedal free play (A) (Sec. 2)

Fig. 5.3. Centralising the clutch disc (Sec. 5)

4 Clutch - dismantling and inspection

1 It is not practical to dismantle the pressure plate assembly and the term 'dismantling' is usually used for simply fitting a new clutch friction plate.

2 If a new clutch disc is being fitted it is a false economy not to renew the release bearing at the same time. This will preclude having to replace it at a later date when wear on the clutch linings is still very small.

3 If the pressure plate assembly requires renewal an exchange unit must be purchased. This will have been accurately set up and balanced to very fine limits.

4 Examine the clutch disc friction linings for wear and loose rivets and the disc for rim distortion, cracks, broken hub springs, and worn splines. The surface of the friction linings may be highly glazed, but as long as the clutch material pattern can be clearly seen this is satisfactory. Compare the amount of lining wear with a new clutch disc at the stores in your local garage. If worn the friction plate must be renewed.

5 It is always best to renew the clutch driven plate as an assembly to preclude further trouble, but, if it is wished to merely renew the linings, the rivets should be drilled out and not knocked out with a punch. The manufacturers do not advise that only the linings be renewed and personal experience dictates that it is far more satisfactory to renew the driven plate complete rather than to try and economise by only fitting new friction linings.

6 Check the machined faces of the flywheel and the pressure plate. If either is grooved it should be machined until smooth, or renewed.

7 If the pressure plate is cracked or split it is essential that an exchange unit is fitted, also if the pressure of the diaphragm spring is suspect.

8 Check the release bearing for smoothness of operation. There should be no harshness or slackness in it. It should spin reasonably freely bearing in mind it has been pre-packed with grease. **Note**: When the clutch disc is removed, a certain amount of asbestos dust is likely to be present. This **should not** be inhaled: the best method of cleaning is to use a vacuum cleaner.

5 Clutch - refitting

1 It is important that no oil or grease gets on the clutch plate friction linings, or the pressure plate and flywheel faces. It is advisable to replace the clutch with clean hands and to wipe down the pressure plate and flywheel faces with a clean rag before assembly begins.

2 Place the clutch plate against the flywheel, ensuring that it is the correct way round. The projecting torsion spring plate should be furthest from the flywheel.

3 Replace the clutch cover assembly loosely on the dowels. Replace the six bolts and spring washers and tighten them finger tight so that the clutch plate is gripped but can still be moved.

4 The clutch disc must now be centralised so that when the engine and gearbox are mated, the gearbox first motion shaft splines will pass through the splines in the centre of the driven plate.

5 Centralisation can be carried out quite easily by inserting a round bar or long screwdriver through the hole in the centre of the clutch, so that the end of the bar rests in the small hole in the end of the crankshaft containing the spigot bush. Ideally an old Ford first motion shaft should be used (Fig. 5.3).

6 Using the first motion shaft spigot bush as a fulcrum, moving the bar sideways or up and down will move the clutch disc in whichever direction is necessary to achieve centralisation.

7 Centralisation is easily judged by removing the bar and viewing the driven plate hub in relation to the hole in the centre of the clutch cover plate diaphragm spring. When the hub appears exactly in the centre of the hole all is correct. Alternatively the first motion shaft will fit the bush and centre of the clutch hub exactly, obviating the need for visual alignment.

8 Tighten the clutch bolts firmly in a diagonal sequence to ensure that the cover plate is pulled down evenly and without distortion of the flange. Finally tighten the bolts to a torque wrench setting of 12 - 15 lb f ft (1.6 - 2.07 kg fm).

6 Clutch cable - removal and refitting

1 Open the bonnet, and for safety reasons disconnect the battery.

2 Chock the rear wheels, jack up the front of the car and support on firmly based stands. Ease off the rubber grommet from the side of the clutch housing located as shown in Fig. 5.4.

3 Push the clutch pedal hard against the stop and with an open ended spanner slacken the locknut and clutch adjustment nut. These are located on the clutch bellhousing.

4 It will now be possible to lift the cable ball end from the slotted end of the release lever. Whilst this is being done take great care not to accidentally disengage the release lever from the bearing hub.

5 Lever the cable eye end and pin from the cable retention bush in the pedal with a small screwdriver (see Fig. 5.5).

6 Withdraw the pin from the eye and withdraw the cable assembly from the abutment tube in the dash panel.

7 Replacement is a straightforward reversal of the removal sequence. Well lubricate the pivot pin. Refer to Section 2, and adjust the cable.

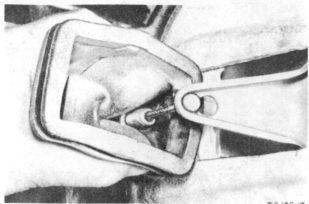

Fig. 5.4. Removing clutch cable grommet from the bellhousing (Sec. 6)

Fig. 5.5. Clutch cable retaining pin (Sec. 6)

Fig. 5.6. Clutch release arm and bearing (Sec. 7)

7 Clutch release bearing - removal and refitting

1   With the gearbox and engine separated to provide access to the clutch, attention can be given to the release bearing located in the bellhousing, over the input shaft (Fig. 5.6).
2   The release bearing is a relatively inexpensive but important component and unless it is nearly new it is a mistake not to replace it during an overhaul of the clutch.
3   The release bearing and arm can be withdrawn from the clutch housing.
4   To free the bearing from the release arm, simply rotate the bearing through 90° and remove. Note which way round the bearing is fitted (Fig. 5.1).
5   Refitting is a straightforward reversal of removal.

8 Clutch pedal - removal and refitting

1   Release the clutch cable from the pedal, refer to Section 6.
2   Disconnect the clutch pedal return spring (Fig. 5.7).
3   Remove the pedal shaft circlip (Fig. 5.8), flat washer and spring washer. Pull the pedal sideways off the shaft. Press out the clutch pedal spacers by hand.
4   Refitting is a straightforward reversal of removal.

9 Fault diagnosis - clutch

There are four main faults to which the clutch and release mechanism are prone. They may occur by themselves or in conjunction with any of the other faults. They are clutch squeal, slip, spin and judder.

Clutch squeal
1   If on taking up the drive or when changing gear, the clutch squeals, this is a good indication of a badly worn clutch release bearing.
2   As well as regular wear due to normal use, wear of the clutch release bearing is much accentuated if the clutch is ridden, or held down for long periods in gear, with the engine running. To minimise wear of this component the car should always be taken out of gear at traffic lights and for similar holdups.

Clutch slip
3   Clutch slip is a self-evident condition which occurs when the clutch pedal free-travel is insufficient, the clutch friction plate is badly worn, when oil or grease have got onto the flywheel or pressure plate faces, or when the pressure plate itself is faulty.
4   The reason for clutch slip is that, due to one of the faults listed above, there is either insufficient pressure from the pressure plate, or

Fig. 5.7. Clutch pedal return spring (Sec. 8)

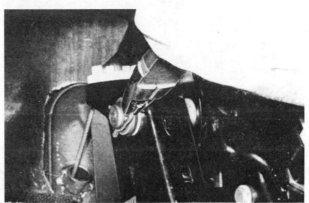

Fig. 5.8. Removing pedal shaft circlip (Sec. 8)

insufficient friction from the friction plate to ensure solid drive.

5 If small amounts of oil get onto the clutch, they will be burnt off under the heat of clutch engagement, and in the process, gradually darken the linings. Excessive oil on the clutch will burn off leaving a carbon deposit which can cause quite bad slip, or fierceness, spin and judder.

6 If clutch slip is suspected, and confirmation of this condition is required, there are several tests which can be made.

7 With the engine in second or third gear and pulling lightly up a moderate incline sudden depression of the accelerator pedal may cause the engine to increase its speed without any increase in road speed. Easing off on the accelerator will then give a definite drop in engine speed without the car slowing.

8 In extreme cases of clutch slip the engine will race under normal acceleration conditions.

9 If slip is due to oil or grease on the linings a temporary cure can sometimes be effected by squirting carbon tetrachloride into the clutch. The permanent cure is, of course, to renew the clutch driven plate and trace and rectify the oil leak.

Clutch spin

10 Clutch spin is a condition which occurs when the release arm travel is excessive, there is an obstruction in the clutch either on the primary gear splines or in the operating lever itself, or the oil may have partially burnt off the clutch linings and have left a resinous deposit which is causing the clutch disc to stick to the pressure plate or flywheel.

11 The reason for clutch spin is that due to any, or a combination of, the faults just listed, the clutch pressure plate is not completely freeing from the centre plate even with the clutch pedal fully depressed.

12 If clutch spin is suspected, the condition can be confirmed by extreme difficulty in engaging first gear from rest, difficulty in changing gear, and very sudden take up of the clutch drive at the fully depressed end of the clutch pedal travel as the clutch is released.

13 Check that the clutch cable is correctly adjusted and, if in order, the fault lies internally in the clutch. It will then be necessary to remove the clutch for examination, and to check the gearbox input shaft.

Clutch judder

14 Clutch judder is a self evident condition which occurs when the gearbox or engine mountings are loose or too flexible, when there is oil on the faces of the clutch friction plate, or when the clutch pressure plate has been incorrectly adjusted during assembly.

15 The reason for clutch judder is that due to one of the faults just listed, the clutch pressure plate is not freeing smoothly from the friction disc, and is snatching.

16 Clutch judder normally occurs when the clutch pedal is released in first gear or reverse gear, and the whole car shudders as it moves backwards or forwards.

Chapter 6
Manual gearbox and automatic transmission

For modifications, and information applicable to later models, refer to Supplement at end of manual

Contents

Specifications

Manual gearbox

Number of gears	4 forward, 1 reverse	
Type of gears	Helical, constant mesh	
Synchromesh	All forward gears	
Gearbox type designation	Type B or C	
Gearbox application:		
1600 cc engine	Type C	
2000 cc engine	Type B	
Gear ratios:	**Type B**	**Type C**
First	3.65 : 1	3.58 : 1
Second	1.97 : 1	2.01 : 1
Third	1.37 : 1	1.40 : 1
Fourth	1.00 : 1	1.00 : 1
Reverse	3.66 : 1	3.324 : 1
Lubricant type	SAE 80 EP gear oil	
Lubricant capacity:		
Type C	1.6 pints (0.9 litres)	
Type B	2.6 pints (1.5 litres)	
Countershaft cluster gear endfloat	0.006 to 0.018 in (0.15 to 0.45 mm)	
Thrust washer thickness	0.061 to 0.063 in (1.55 to 1.60 mm)	
Diameter of countershaft	0.68 in (17.3 mm)	
	0.66 in (16.7 mm)	

Automatic transmission

Manufacture	Ford
Type	Bordeaux (C3)
Selector lever positions	P, R, N, D, 2, 1
Gear ratios:	
First	2.47 : 1
Second	1.47 : 1
Third	1 : 1
Reverse	2.11 : 1
Converter ratio:	
1600 cc	2.02 : 1
2000 cc	2.35 : 1
Transmission fluid specification	SQM-2C-9007-AA/ESW-M2C33-G*
Fluid capacity (approx)	11.4 pints (6.5 litres)

* Castrol TQF meets this specification.

Torque wrench settings (manual gearbox)

	lb f ft	kg fm
Type B		
Transmission cover bolts	6.6 to 8.0	0.9 to 1.1
Extension housing retaining bolts	33 to 36	4.5 to 4.9
Drive gear bearing retainer bolts	6.6 to 8.0	0.9 to 1.1
Clutch bellhousing to transmission	43 to 51	5.8 to 6.9
Clutch bellhousing to engine	33 to 40	4.5 to 5.5
Gearbox mounting to floorpan bolts	13 to 16	1.8 to 2.2
Type C		
Transmission cover bolts	15 to 18	2.1 to 2.5
Extension housing retaining bolts	33 to 36	4.5 to 4.9
Clutch housing to transmission	40 to 45	5.5 to 6.2
Clutch housing to engine	33 to 40	4.5 to 5.5
Gearbox mounting to floor pan bolts	13 to 16	1.8 to 2.2

Torque wrench settings (automatic transmission)

	lb f ft	kg fm
Torque converter housing to transmission	27 to 39	3.6 to 5.3
Disc to converter	27 to 30	3.6 to 4.1
Oil sump bolts	12 to 17	1.6 to 2.4
Downshift cable bracket	12 to 17	1.6 to 2.4
Downshift lever nut:		
Outer	7 to 11	1.0 to 1.5
Inner	30 to 40	4.1 to 5.4
Inhibitor switch	12 to 15	1.6 to 2.0
Brake band adjusting screw locknut	35 to 45	4.7 to 6.1
Fluid line to connector	7 to 10	0.9 to 1.4
Connector to transmission housing	10 to 15	1.4 to 2.0
Torque converter housing to engine	22 to 27	3.0 to 3.7
Torque converter drain plug	20 to 29	2.7 to 4.0
Oil cooler line to connector	12 to 15	1.6 to 2.0

1 Manual gearbox - general description

The manual gearboxes used on the models covered by this manual are equipped with four forward and one reverse gear. All forward gears are engaged through blocker ring syncromesh units to obtain smooth silent gearchanges.

The bellhousing and gearbox case are of cast iron, and are bolted together on all type C, and certain type B gearboxes, while other type B gearboxes have a one-piece bellhousing and gearbox.

The cast aluminium extension housing incorporates the remote control gearchange mechanism, which consists of a single selector rod.

The selector forks are free to slide on the selector rod which also serves as the gearchange shaft. At the gearbox end of this rod lies the selector arm, which, depending on the position of the gearlever, places the appropriate selector fork in the position necessary for the synchroniser sleeve to engage with the dog teeth on the gear selected.

It is impossible to select two gears at once because of an interlock guard plate which pivots on the right-hand side of the gearbox casing. The selector forks, when not in use, are positively held by the guard plate in their disengaged positions.

All forward gears on the mainshaft and input shaft are in constant mesh with their corresponding gears on the countershaft gear cluster and are helically cut to achieve quiet running.

The countershaft reverse gear has straight-cut spur teeth that drives the toothed 1st/2nd gear selector sleeve on the mainshaft through an interposed sliding idler gear.

The gearbox is of simple design using a minimum number of components. Where close tolerances and limits are required, manufacturing tolerances are compensated for and excessive endfloat or backlash eliminated by the fitting of selective circlips. When overhauling the gearbox always use new circlips, never replace ones that have already been used.

2 Gearbox - removal and refitting

The gearbox can be removed in unit with the engine through the engine compartment as described in Chapter 1, Section 5. Alternatively, the gearbox can be separated from the rear of the engine at the bellhousing and the gearbox lowered from under the car. The latter method is easier and quicker than the former.

1 If a hoist or an inspection pit is not available then run the back of the car up a pair of ramps or jack it up and fit axle stands. Next jack up the front of the car and support on axle stands.

2 For safety reasons, disconnect the battery earth terminal.

3 Working inside the car, push the front seats rearwards as far as possible.

4 Refer to Chapter 12, Section 38 to remove the centre console, if fitted.

5 Carefully ease the gearchange lever gaiter from the body panel and slide it up the gear lever (photo).

6 Using a screwdriver bend back the locking tabs on the lock ring and very carefully unscrew the lock ring and gearchange lever retainer (photo).

7 The gearchange lever can now be lifted upwards and away from the gearbox (photo).

8 Mark the mating flanges of the propeller shaft and final drive so that they may be reconnected in their original positions and undo and remove the four securing bolts.

9 Where a split type propeller shaft is fitted, undo and remove the centre bearing retainer securing bolts, spring and plain washers (photo).

10 Draw the propeller shaft rearwards so detaching the front end from the rear of the gearbox and lift away from under the car.

11 Wrap some polythene around the end of the gearbox and secure with string or wire to stop any oil running out.

12 Make a note of the cable connections to the starter motor and detach the cables.

13 Undo and remove the three bolts that secure the starter motor to the gearbox flange. Lift away the starter motor.

14 Remove the rear engine cover plate and bracket assembly from the clutch housing. Detach the bracket assembly from the cylinder block and swing it back out of the way. This bracket is shown in Fig. 6.1.

15 Pull off the plug attached to the reverse light switch located on the side of the remote control housing.

16 Pull the speedometer drive cable away from the side of the extension housing.

17 Using a pair of pliers detach the clutch operating cable from the actuating arm that protrudes from the side of the clutch housing (photo). On some models it will be necessary to pull back the rubber gaiter first.

18 Pull the clutch cable assembly through the locating hole in the flange on the clutch housing.

19 Suitably support the weight of the gearbox by either using a jack or an axle stand. Insert a wooden chock between the sump and engine support so that the engine does not drop when the gearbox is removed.

20 Undo and remove the remaining bolts that secure the clutch bellhousing to the rear of the engine.

21 Undo and remove the exhaust pipe securing nuts at the exhaust manifold and the exhaust mounting bracket. Push the assembly away from the gearbox and tie back with string.

22 Undo and remove the one bolt that secures the rubber mounting to the gearbox extension housing.

23 Undo and remove the four bolts, spring and plain washers that secure the gearbox support crossmember to the body. (photo).

24 Lift away the crossmember (photo).

25 Using a pair of circlip pliers remove the circlip retaining the speedometer drive cable end to the gearbox extension housing (photo).

26 The assistance of a second person is now required who should be ready to help in taking the weight of the gearbox.

27 **Do not** allow the weight of the gearbox to hand on the input shaft (first motion shaft) as it is easily bent. Carefully separate the gearbox from the engine by sliding it rearwards out of the clutch housing. It will be necessary to lower the jack or stand to give clearance of the gearbox from the underside of the body.

28 If major work is to be undertaken on the gearbox it is recommended that the exterior be washed with paraffin or 'Gunk' and dried with a non-fluffy rag.

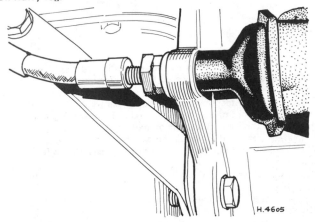

Fig. 6.1. Location of bracket between engine and clutch housing (Sec. 2)

29 Refitting the gearbox is the reverse sequence to removal but the following additional points should be noted:

  a) *Make sure that the engine cover plate bracket is correctly positioned.*
  b) *Adjust the clutch cable, refer to Chapter 5 Section 2.*
  c) *Before refitting the gearchange lever well grease the fork ends*
  d) *Refill the gearbox with the correct gear oil*
  e) *Refer to Chapter 7 Section 2 to refit the propeller shaft*

3 Gearbox - dismantling

1 Place the complete unit on a firm bench or table and ensure that you have the following tools available, in addition to the normal range of spanners etc.

  a) *Good quality circlip pliers, 2 pairs - 1 expanding and 1 contracting*
  b) *Soft-faced mallet, at least 2 lb (1 kg)*
  c) *Drifts, steel and brass 0.375 inch (9.525 mm) diameter*
  d) *Small containers fro needle rollers*
  e) *Engineer's vice mounted on firm bench*
  f) *Selection of metal tubing*

Any attempt to dismantle the gearbox without the foregoing is not impossible, but will certainly be very difficult and inconvenient.

2 Read the whole of this Section before starting work.

3 The internal parts of the gearboxes are shown in Fig. 6.2 and 6.3.

4 Detach the release bearing from the release lever by turning the carrier through 90° and pulling forwards (photo).

5 This photo shows the cut-outs in the release bearing carrier that have to be lined up with the two protrusions in the release lever to enable removal of the bearing carrier.

6 Undo and remove the four bolts and spring washers that secure the clutch housing to the gearbox main case (photo).

7 Draw the clutch housing forwards away from the main case.

8 Using a suitable drift, working through the gear lever aperture, tap out the extension housing rear cover (photo). Unscrew the reversing lamp switch.

Gearbox B (2000 cc) - selector mechanism

9 Remove the eight top cover bolts, and remove the cover and gasket.

10 Turn the gearbox through 180° and allow the oil to drain.

11 Remove the side plug (Fig. 6.4) and remove the spring, detent ball and plunger (photo).

12 Remove the blanking plug from the rear of the gearbox casing and drive out the lock plate spring pin using a suitable pin punch.

13 Remove the spring pin from the reverse selector boss (photo). Remove the selector rail rearwards (photo).

14 Lift out both selector forks, the lock plate and the selector boss (photo).

2.5 Sliding gaiter up gear lever

2.6 Bending back lock ring tabs with screwdriver

2.7 Lifting away gearchange lever

2.9 Removal of centre bearing retainer securing bolt

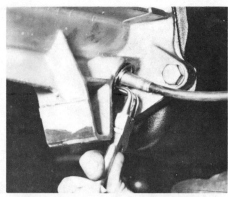

2.16 Speedometer cable retaining circlip

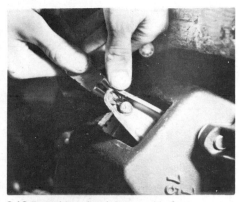

2.18 Detaching clutch inner cable from actuating arm

2.24 Removal of gearbox support cross-member to body securing bolt

2.25 Crossmember removal

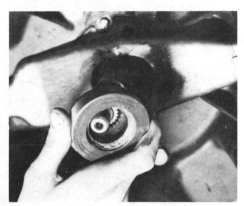

3.4 Release bearing removal

3.5 Release bearing located in release lever

3.6 Removal of clutch housing to gearbox securing bolts

3.8 Extension housing rear cover removal. Note reversing light switch (arrowed)

3.11 Detent ball, spring and plunger removal - Gearbox B

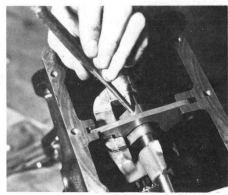

3.13A Reverse selector boss spring pin removal - Gearbox B

3.13B Selector rail removal - Gearbox B

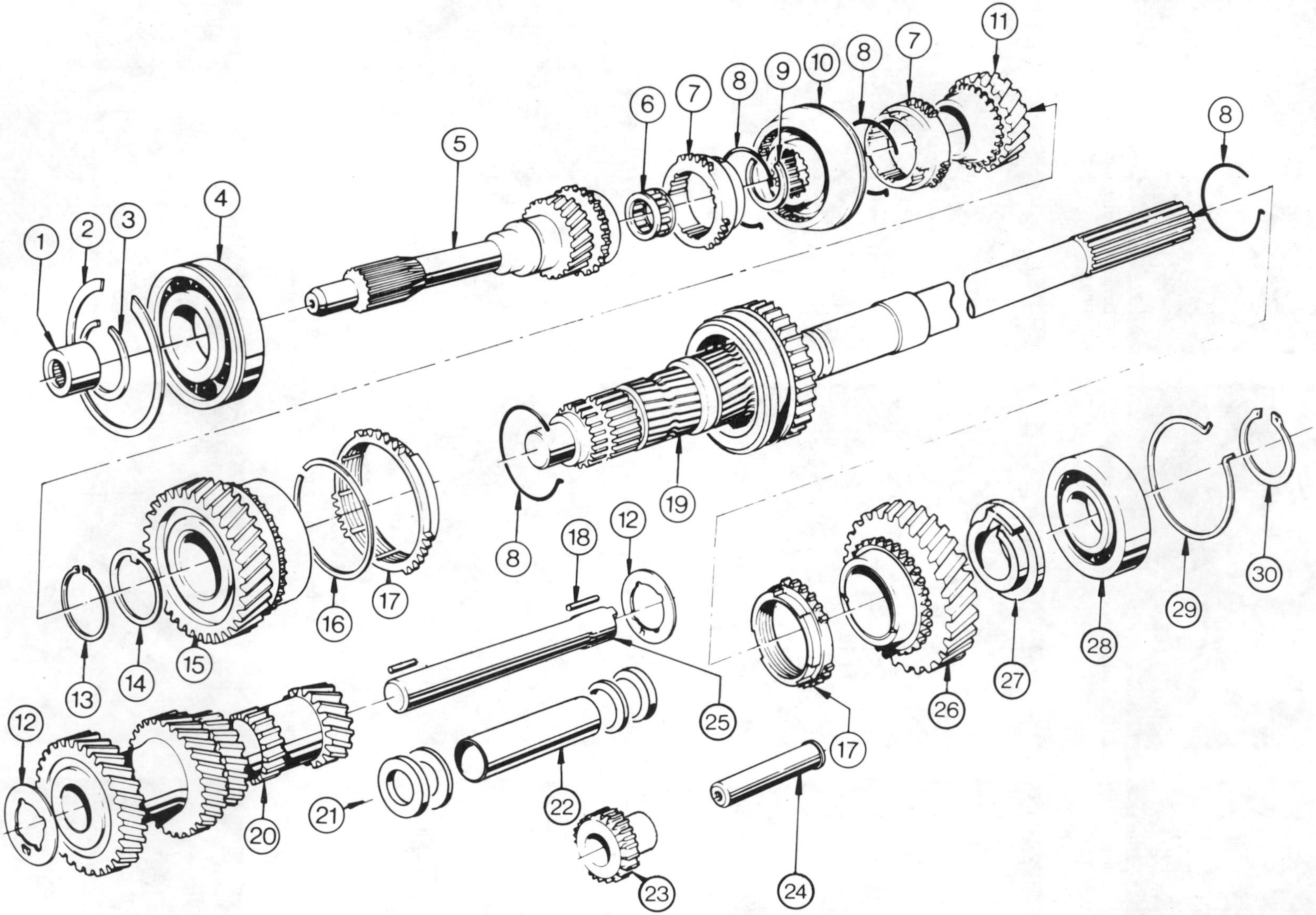

Fig. 6.2. Gearbox B internal components (Sec. 3)

1 Input shaft guide bearing
2 Input shaft retaining circlip
3 Input shaft bearing circlip
4 Input shaft bearing
5 Input shaft
6 Needle roller bearing
7 3rd/4th synchroniser baulk ring
8 Synchroniser spring clip
9 3rd/4th synchroniser retaining circlip
10 3rd/4th gear selector sleeve

11 3rd gear
12 Countershaft gear thrust washer
13 Thrust washer retaining circlip
14 Thrust washer
15 2nd gear
16 Circlip
17 1st/2nd synchroniser baulk ring
18 Countershaft needle rollers (19 each end)
19 Mainshaft with 1st/2nd gear selector sleeve
20 Countershaft gear train

21 Countershaft spacer shims
22 Countershaft spacer tube
23 Reverse idler gear
24 Reverse idler shaft
25 Countershaft
26 1st gear
27 Oil scoop ring
28 Mainshaft bearing
29 Mainshaft to extension housing circlip
30 Mainshaft bearing retaining circlip

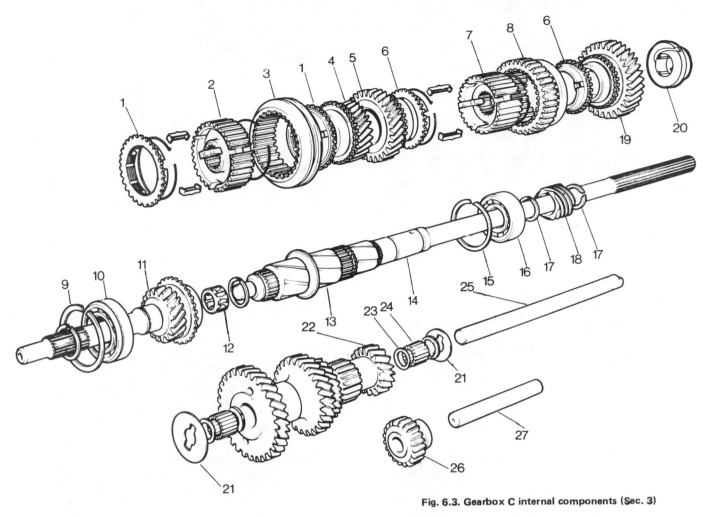

Fig. 6.3. Gearbox C internal components (Sec. 3)

Gearbox C(1600 cc) - selector mechanism

15 Remove the four top cover bolts, and remove the cover and gasket. Note selector rail detent spring and ball location (Fig. 6.5).

16 Remove the detent spring and ball. This can either be removed using a magnet or a screwdriver with a blob of grease on the end.

17 Invert the gearbox and drain out the oil.

18 Using a suitable pin punch tap out the selector boss spring pin (Fig. 6.6). To do this, press the selector rod forward to avoid damaging first gear.

19 Remove the selector to the rear and remove the selector boss and lock plate.

20 Select second gear, press the reverse relay lever backwards and lift out both selector forks (Fig. 6.7).

All models

21 Unscrew and remove the bolts and spring washers that secure the extension housing to the main casing.

22 Rotate the extension housing until the cutaway is in such a position that the countershaft can be drawn from the maincasing.

23 Using a suitable diameter soft metal drift tap the countershaft rearwards until it is possible to pull it from the rear face of the main case (photo).

24 Remove the countershaft from the main case (photo).

25 Allow the countershaft gear train to drop to the bottom of the main case.

26 Remove the gearbox extension housing and mainshaft assembly from the gearbox (photo).

27 Remove the input shaft needle roller bearing.

28 Undo and remove the bolts and spring washers that secure the spigot bearing to the front face of the main case.

29 Lift away the spigot bearing from over the input shaft. Recover the 'O' ring (photo).

1	3rd/4th synchroniser baulk ring	16	Mainshaft bearing
2	3rd/4th synchroniser hub	17	Retaining circlip
3	3rd/4th gear selector sleeve	18	Speedometer drive gear
4	3rd gear	19	1st gear
5	2nd gear	20	Oil scoop ring
6	1st/2nd synchroniser baulk ring	21	Countershaft gear thrust washer
7	1st/2nd synchroniser hub	22	Countershaft gear train
8	1st/2nd gear selector sleeve	23	Countershaft spacer shims
9	Input shaft retaining circlip	24	Countershaft needle rollers (20 each end)
10	Input shaft bearing	25	Countershaft
11	Input shaft	26	Reverse idler gear
12	Needle roller bearing	27	Reverse idler shaft
13	Mainshaft with thrust washer		
14	Speedometer gear locking ball		
15	Mainshaft to extension housing circlip		

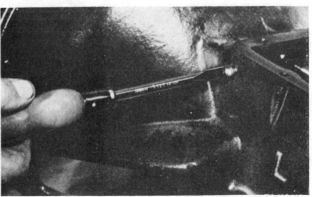

Fig. 6.4. Removing the locking bar plug - Gearbox B (Sec. 3)

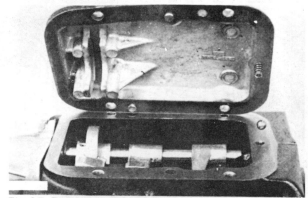

Fig. 6.5. Removing top cover - Gearbox C. Note spring and ball locations (Sec. 3 and 7)

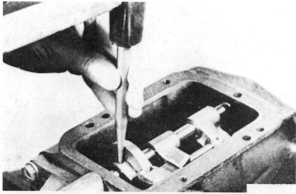

Fig. 6.6. Removing selector spring pin - Gearbox C (Sec. 3)

Fig. 6.7. Removing selector forks - Gearbox C (Sec. 3)

Fig. 6.8. Removing the input shaft - Gearbox C (Sec. 3)

Fig. 6.9. Removing reverse gear idler shaft (Sec. 3)

Fig. 6.10. Removing mainshaft retaining circlip (Sec. 3)

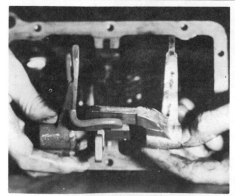

3.14 Selector fork removal - Gearbox B

3.23 Countershaft removal using a drift

3.24 Lifting away countershaft

3.26 Removal of extension housing and mainshaft assembly

3.29 Spigot bearing and 'O' ring removal

3.30 Prising bearing outer track from main casing with screwdriver

Fig. 6.11. Removing 3rd gear and synchroniser - Gearbox C (Sec. 6)

3.31 Countershaft gear train removal

30 Remove the input shaft assembly. On type B gearboxes, this is removed forward (photo). On type C gearboxes, remove the large circlip and tap on the bearing outer race to release it (Fig. 6.8). Remove to the rear.

31 Lift the countershaft geartrain from inside the main case. Note which way round it is fitted (photo). Recover the two countershaft thrust washers.

32 Insert a suitable bolt into the reverse gear idler shaft with a nut, washer and suitable socket. Tighten the nut and withdraw the idler shaft (Fig. 6.9).

33. Withdraw the circlip from the pin, and remove the reverse gear relay lever.

34 Prise out the speedometer drive gear cover from the extension housing, and withdraw the drive gear.

35 Remove the mainshaft bearing circlip from the extension housing (Fig. 6.10). Drive the mainshaft assembly from the extension housing using a soft-faced mallet (photo).

---

4 Gearbox - inspection

1 Thoroughly clean the interior of the gearbox, and check for dropped needle rollers and spring pins.

2 Carefully clean and then examine all the component parts for general wear, distortion, slackness of fit, and damage to machined faces and threads.

3 Examine the gearwheels for excessive wear and chipping of the teeth. Renew them as necessary.

4 Examine the countershaft for signs of wear, where the needle rollers bear. If a small ridge can be felt at either end of the shaft it will be necessary to renew it. Renew the thrust washers at each end.

5 The four synchroniser baulk rings are bound to be badly worn and it is false economy not to renew them. New rings will improve the smoothness, and speed of the gearchange considerably.

6 The needle roller bearing and cage, located between the nose of the mainshaft and the annulus in the rear of the input shaft, is also liable to wear, and should be renewed as a matter of course.

7 Examine the condition of the two ball bearing assemblies, one on the input shaft and one on the mainshaft. Check them for noisy operation, looseness between the inner and outer races, and for general wear. Normally they should be renewed on a gearbox that is being rebuilt.

8 If either of the synchroniser units are worn it will be necessary to buy a complete assembly as the parts are not sold individually. Also check the sliding keys for wear.

9 Examine the ends of the selector forks where they rub against the channels in the periphery of the synchroniser units. If possible compare the selector forks with new units to help determine the wear that has occurred. Renew them if worn.

10 If the bearing bush in the extension is badly worn it is best to take the extension to your local Ford garage to have the bearing pulled out and a new one fitted.

Note: This is normally done with the mainshaft assembly still located in the extension housing.

11 The oil seals in the extension housing and main drive gear bearing retainer should be renewed as a matter of course. Drive out the old seal with the aid of a drift or broad screwdriver. It will be found that the seal comes out quite easily.

With a piece of wood or suitable sized tube to spread the load evenly, carefully tap a new seal into place ensuring that it enters the bore squarely.

---

5 Input shaft - dismantling and reassembly

1 The input shaft assembly may be dismantled by first removing the circlip using a pair of circlip pliers (photo).

2 Place the drive gear on the top of the vice with the outer track of the race resting on soft faces.

3 Using a soft faced hammer drive the input shaft through the race inner track. The strain placed on the bearing does not matter, as the bearing would not be removed unless it was being renewed. Alternatively use a three legged universal puller.

4 Lift away the race from the drive gear noting that the circlip groove on the outer track is offset towards the front.

5 To assemble the input shaft, place the race against soft metal (old shell bearing suitably straightened) on the top of the jaws of the vice and, using a drift located in the mainshaft spigot bearing hole in the rear of the input shaft, drift the shaft into the bearing. Make quite sure the bearing is the correct way round. Alternatively use a piece of long tube of suitable diameter (photo).
6 Refit the circlip that secures the bearing.
On type B gearboxes, also fit the circlip in the outer bearing race.

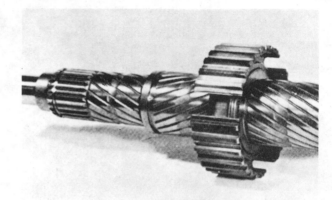

Fig. 6.12. Gearbox B mainshaft and 1st/2nd synchroniser hub (Sec. 6)

---

6 Mainshaft - dismantling and reassembly

---

1 With the mainshaft on the bench, remove the synchroniser sleeve from the front.
2 Using a pair of circlip pliers, expand the circlip that retains the third and top synchromesh hub on the mainshaft (photo).
3 Remove the third and top synchromesh assembly from the end of the mainshaft. Remove the synchroniser baulk ring away from the third gear. Remove the third gear.
Note: On type C gearboxes the synchroniser assembly and third gear are removed with a standard two-legged puller (Fig. 6.11).
4 Expand and remove the circlip retaining the speedometer drive gear and remove the gear locking ball (C type gearbox only).
5 Using a pair of circlip pliers expand the circlip located at the rear of the mainshaft bearing, lift it from its groove and slide it down the mainshaft (photo).
6 Place the mainshaft on soft faces placed on the jaws of a vice so that the rear end is uppermost and the face of the first gear is on the vice.
7 Using a soft faced mallet, drive the mainshaft through the gear and bearing assembly.
8 Lift away the speedometer gear, bearing, large circlip, oil scoop ring, 1st gear and synchroniser baulk ring.
9 Remove the circlip and remove the 1st and 2nd synchroniser assembly (C type gearbox), thrust washer (B type gearbox), 2nd gear and the synchroniser baulk ring.
10 Note that on the B type gearbox, the synchroniser hub (Fig. 6.12).

Fig. 6.13. Synchroniser hub - exploded (Sec. 6)

3.35 Mainshaft being tapped through extension housing

5.1 Input shaft bearing retaining circlip

5.5 Input shaft bearing refitting

6.2 Circlip removal from end of mainshaft

6.5 Mainshaft rear bearing retaining circlip removal

6.17 Synchromesh sleeve being slid into hub

cannot be removed from the mainshaft, while on the C type gearbox, the thrust washer is an integral part (Fig. 6.3).

11 Mark the synchromesh sleeve, hub and sliding keys for each synchromesh unit so that they may be refitted in their original positions.

12 Slide the synchromesh sleeve from the hub and lift away the sliding keys and springs (Fig. 6.13).

13 When new synchroniser assemblies are being fitted, they should be dismantled and thoroughly cleaned of all traces of preservative.

14 Lightly lubricate all parts with gearbox oil before reassembly.

15 The main reassembly procedure can now be commenced but first note that selective circlips will be needed at some stages during reassembly. It is therefore necessary to read through the procedure before reassembly commences so that the necessary circlips can be obtained.

16 Assemble the synchronisers by sliding the sleeve onto the hub with the mating marks aligned. Fit the sliding keys and springs, with the springs staggered, and the tagged ends of the springs in the same key (Fig. 6.14).

17 On B type gearboxes, the 1st and 2nd synchroniser hub is a unit

Fig. 6.16. Fitting oil scoop ring (Sec. 6)

with the mainshaft. Fit the selector sleeve with the groove to the front (photo).

18 *B type gearbox* Slide the 2nd gear baulk ring and second gear onto the mainshaft with the cone facing the rear (photo). Fit the thrust washer and secure with a circlip.

19 *C type gearbox* Slide the 2nd gear, with the cone facing the rear (Fig. 6.15). Slide the 2nd gear baulk ring onto the mainshaft, and fit the synchroniser assembly with the selector groove to the rear. Secure with the circlip.

20 *All versions* Fit the 1st and 2nd baulk ring, and the first gear with the cone facing the front. Slide on the oil scoop ring noting the different way round that it is fitted according to transmission type B or C (Figs. 6.2 or 6.3).

21 It will now be necessary to select a new large circlip to eliminate endfloat of the mainshaft. To do this, first fit the original circlip in its groove in the gearbox extension and draw it outwards (ie; away from the rear of the extension). Now accurately measure the dimension from the base of the bearing housing to the outer edge of the circlip and record the figure. Also accurately measure the thickness of the bearing outer track (Fig. 6.17) and subtract this figure from the depth already recorded. This will give the required circlip thickness.

22 Loosely fit the selected circlip, lubricate the bearing contact surfaces then press it onto the shaft. To press the bearing home, close the jaws of the vice until they are not quite touching the mainshaft, and with the bearing resting squarely against the side of the vice jaws draw the bearing on by tapping the end of the shaft with a soft faced mallet.

23 Refit the small circlip retaining the main bearing in place. This is also a selective circlip and must be fitted so that all endfloat between the bearing inner track and the circlip edge is eliminated (photo).

24 Refit the speedometer drive gear retaining ball (C type gearbox), speedometer drive gear and circlip (C type gearbox).

Note: On B type gearboxes the drive gear should be drifted on using a suitable diameter tube until the dimension A (Fig. 6.18) is 1.44 in (49.25 mm).

25 Slide on the 3rd gear with the cone facing the front, the baulk ring and the synchroniser assembly (photo).

26 Using a suitable piece of tube, drift on the synchroniser assembly, with the longer hub to the front. Secure with the circlip (Fig. 6.19).

Fig. 6.14. Synchroniser spring clip alignment (Sec. 6)

Fig. 6.15. Fitting second gear (Gearbox C) (Sec. 6)

6.18 2nd gear synchroniser baulk ring and 2nd gear being fitted to mainshaft

6.23 Rear bearing retaining circlip refitting

6.26 3rd gear, synchroniser baulk ring and synchro

Fig. 6.17. Extension housing circlip thickness (Sec. 6)

Fig. 6.18. B type gearbox speedometer gear location (Sec. 6)

Fig. 6.19. Fitting 3rd/4th synchroniser retaining circlip (Sec. 6)

Fig. 6.20. Gearbox B countershaft gear train (Sec. 7)

7 Gearbox - reassembly

1 Lay the extension housing on its side and carefully insert the mainshaft (photo).

2 Place the extension housing on the edge of the bench so that the mainshaft end can protrude when fully home. Using a soft-faced mallet drive the mainshaft bearing into the extension housing bore (photo).

3 Using a pair of pointed pliers and small screwdriver refit the bearing retaining circlip. This is a fiddle and can take time (photo).

4 Apply grease to the mating face of the extension housing and fit a new gasket (photo).

5 Refit the reverse relay arm and spring onto the pivot pin, and secure with a circlip.

6 Place the reverse idler gear into its location in the main casing and engage it with the reverse relay arm. Slide in the idler shaft, and tap home with a mallet (photo).

7 The countershaft gear train needle roller bearings are next reassembled.

8 *B type gearbox* This countershaft has a spacer tube and 19 needle rollers at each end. The longer rollers must be fitted at the rear end, and thick spacers at the outside ends (Fig. 6.20).

9 *C type gearbox* This countershaft has 20 needle rollers at each end. All rollers are the same size and the four spacers are the same size (Fig. 6.21).

10 *B type gearbox* Slide the spacer tube into the countershaft geartrain bore.

11 Smear some grease in both ends of the bore.

12 Insert one of the spacer shims (photo).

13 Fit the needle rollers into the forward end of the bore. Do not handle the needle rollers more than absolutely necessary as they will warm up and therefore not adhere to the grease (photo).

14 With the first set of needle rollers in position carefully fit the second spacer shim (photo).

15 Obtain a piece of bar or tube having approximately the same diameter as the countershaft and the same length as the countershaft gear train. Slide this halfway into the bore of the countershaft gear

train so acting as a retainer for the needle rollers.

16 Insert a spacer shim into the rear end of the countershaft gear train bore and fit the second set of needle rollers in the same manner as for the first set (photo).

17 Fit the last spacer shim and push the previously obtained bar or tube through the second set of needle roller bearings.

18 Smear grease on each thrust washer face of the countershaft gear train.

19 Fit the thrust washers to the countershaft gear train (photo).

20 Carefully lower the countershaft gear train into the main casing making sure that the thrust washers are not dislodged (photo).

21 Support the main casing on the bench so that it is upright and insert the input shaft.

Note: On B type gearboxes this is inserted from the front. On C type gearboxes this is inserted from inside the housing until the bearing is clear, and retained with a circlip (Fig. 6.22).

22 Smear some grease on the groove in the front face of the main casing and fit a new 'O' ring seal.

23 Slide the spigot bearing over the input shaft. Make sure the slight internal recess is towards the bottom, or line up the marks made during dismantling (photo).

24 Secure the spigot bearing with bolts and spring washers (photo). Tighten in a diagonal manner to ensure that the 'O' ring seals correctly.

25 Apply some grease to the caged bearing that fits into the bore in the rear of the input shaft. Fit the bearing into the bore.

26 Fit the baulk ring to the taper on the rear of the input shaft.

27 Carefully insert the mainshaft through the rear face of the main casing (photo).

28 Turn the extension housing until the cutaway is positioned such that the countershaft can be inserted through the main casing rear face.

29 Turn the input shaft and mainshaft so that the countershaft gear train can drop into engagement. Visually line up the countershaft bore hole in the main case with the centre of the countershaft gear train and slide the countershaft into position. The milled end of the countershaft is towards the rear of the main case (photo).

30 Turn the countershaft until it is positioned as shown in Fig. 6.23 or 6.24. Tap in until the main part of the shaft is flush with rear face.

Fig. 6.21. Gearbox C countershaft gear train (Sec. 7)

7.1 Fitting mainshaft into extension housing - stage 1

7.2 Drifting mainshaft bearing into extension housing - stage 2

7.3 Fitting bearing retaining circlip

7.4 Fitting new gasket to greased face of extension housing

7.6 Fitting reverse idler gear and shaft into main casing

7.12 Inserting spacer shim into countershaft bore

7.13 Fitting needle rollers into countershaft bore

7.14 Inserting second spacer shim into countershaft bore

Fig. 6.22. Gearbox C input shaft retaining circlip (Sec. 7)

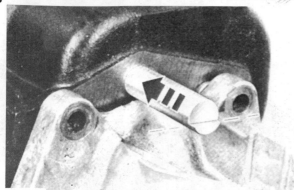

Fig. 6.23. Fitting gearbox B countershaft (Sec. 7)

Fig. 6.24. Fitting gearbox C countershaft (Sec. 7)

7.16 Fitting second set of needle rollers into countershaft bore

7.19 Fitting thrust washers to greased face of countershaft gear train

7.20 Fitting countershaft gear train into main casing

7.23 Sliding spigot bearing over input shaft

7.24 Securing spigot bearing to main casing

7.27 Inserting mainshaft into main casing

7.29 Inserting countershaft into main casing

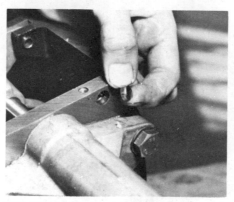

7.34 Fitting blanking plug to main case rear face - Gearbox B

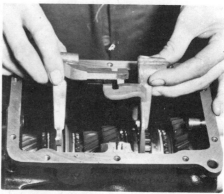

7.35A Fitting selector forks to main casing - Gearbox B

7.35B Sliding reverse selector boss into the lock plate - Gearbox B

7.36 Fitting spring pin to reverse selector boss and rail - Gearbox B

7.46 Securing clutch housing with bolts and spring washers

Fig. 6.25. Gearbox C selector forks (Sec. 7)

Fig. 6.26. Fitting gearbox C selector forks (Sec. 7)

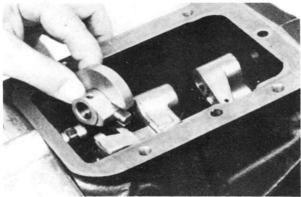

Fig. 6.27. Fitting gearbox C selector boss and lock plate (Sec. 7)

31 Check that the idler shaft and countershaft protrusions will line up with the slots in the extension housing and push the extension housing up to the rear face of the main casing.
32 Secure the extension housing with the bolts and spring washers.
33 Refit the speedometer driven gear and tap home the cover.

Gearbox B (2000 cc) - selector mechanism
34 Fit the selector lock plate and secure with the spring pin. Fit a new blanking plug at the rear of the housing (photo).
35 Insert both selector forks (photo) and the reverse selector boss (photo).
36 Slide the selector rail, from the rear through the bosses, and lock with the spring pin (photo).
37 Refit the detent ball, plunger and spring and screw plug into the side of the housing.
38 Replace the top cover and secure with eight bolts.

Gearbox C (1600 cc) - selector mechanism
39 Assemble the two selector forks and fit the spring pin (Fig. 6.25).
40 To insert the selector forks, engage 2nd gear and press the reverse relay lever to the rear (Fig. 6.26).
41 Slide the lock plate over the selector boss, and hold them in line with the selector rail bore (Fig. 6.27).
42 Slide the selector rail in from the rear and secure with a spring pin, Fit the pin with the slot to the rear and drive in about 0.04 in (1 mm).
43 Insert the detent ball into the casing, and the spring into the top cover and hold in place with some grease (Fig. 6.5). Fit the top cover and tighten the bolts.

All models
44 Fit the extension housing rear cover, coated with sealing compound. Secure with three blows from a pin punch, spread around the edge. Screw in the reversing lamp switch.
45 Wipe the mating faces of the clutch housing and main casing and offer up the clutch housing.
46 Secure the clutch housing with the bolts and spring washers (photo).
47 Fit the clutch release arm to the clutch housing and then the release bearing to the release arm. Turn through 90° to lock.
48 The gearbox is now ready for refitting. Do not forget to refill with the correct grade of oil.

8 Automatic transmission - general description

The automatic transmission takes the place of the clutch and gearbox, which are, of course, mounted behind the engine.
The unit has a large aluminium content which helps to reduce its overall weight and it is of compact dimensions. A transmission oil cooler is fitted as standard and ensures cooler operation of the transmission under trailer towing conditions. A vacuum connection to the inlet manifold provides smoother and more consistent downshifts under load than is the case with units not incorporating this facility.
The system comprises two main components:
a) A three element hydrokinetic torque converter coupling, capable of torque multiplication at an infinitely variable ratio.

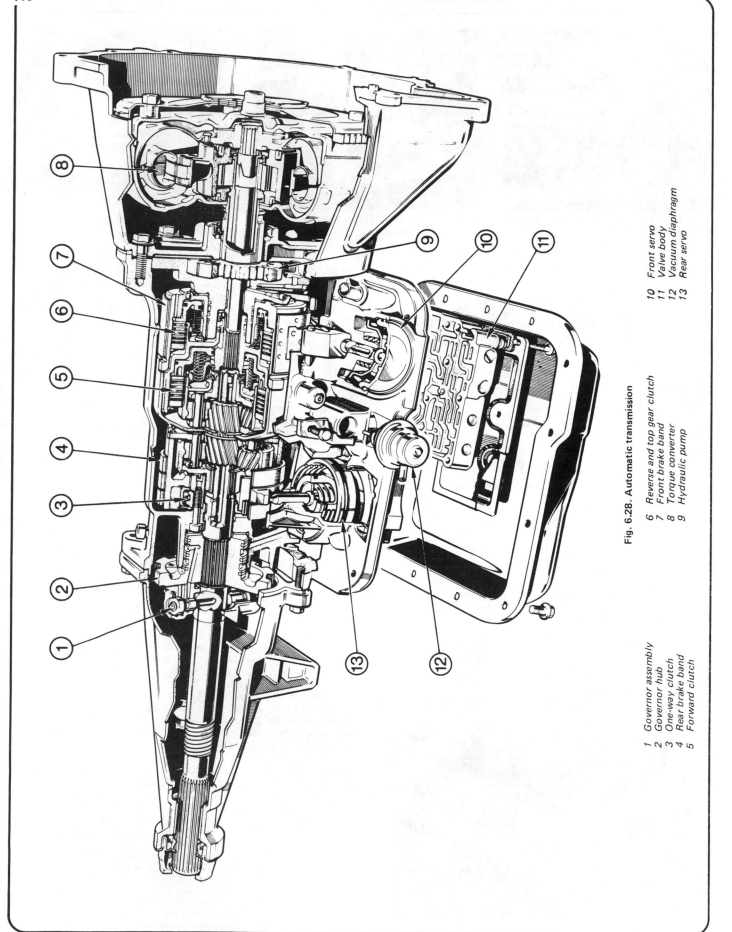

Fig. 6.28. Automatic transmission

1   Governor assembly
2   Governor hub
3   One-way clutch
4   Rear brake band
5   Forward clutch

6   Reverse and top gear clutch
7   Front brake band
8   Torque converter
9   Hydraulic pump

10   Front servo
11   Valve body
12   Vacuum diaphragm
13   Rear servo

b) A torque/speed responsive and hydraulically operated epicyclic gearbox comprising planetary gearsets providing three forward ratios and one reverse ratio. Due to the complexity of the automatic transmission unit, if performance is not up to standard, or overhaul is necessary, it is imperative that this be left to the local main agents who will have the special equipment for fault diagnosis and rectification.

The content of the following sections is therefore confined to supplying general information and any service information and instruction that can be used by the owner.

9 Automatic transmission - fluid level checking

1 Every 6,000 miles (10,000 km) bring the engine transmission to its normal operating temperature. Running the vehicle on the road for a minimum distance of 5 miles (8 km) will achieve this.
2 Select 'P' and allow the engine to idle for two or three minutes.
3 With the engine still idling, withdraw the transmission dipstick. Wipe it clean, re-insert it, withdraw it for the second time and read off the level.
4 If necessary top up with the specified oil, through the dipstick tube, to the 'MAX' mark.
5 Always keep the exterior of the transmission unit clean and free from mud and oil and the air intake grilles must not be obstructed.

10 Automatic transmission - removal and refitting

Any suspected faults must be referred to the main agent before unit removal, as with this type of transmission the fault must be confirmed, using specialist equipment, before it has been removed from the car.
1 Open the engine compartment lid and place old blankets over the wings to prevent accidental scratching of the paintwork.
2 Undo and remove the battery earth connection nut and bolt from the battery terminal.
3 Remove the starter motor.
4 Position the vehicle on a ramp or over an inspection pit or, if these are not available, jack it up and support securely under the bodyframe. Make sure that there is sufficient clearance under the vehicle to permit withdrawal of the transmission.
5 Unscrew and remove the upper bolts which secure the torque converter housing to the engine. One of these bolts secures the dipstick tube support bracket.
6 Disconnect the 'kick-down' cable from the transmission downshift lever and bracket (Fig. 6.29).
7 Disconnect the plug from the reverse inhibitor switch.
8 Unscrew the lock plate bolt and remove the speedometer cable (Fig. 6.30).
9 Refer to Chapter 7, and remove the propeller shaft. To stop accidental dirt ingress, wrap some polythene around the end of the automatic transmission unit and secure with string or wire.
10 Undo and remove the two nuts that secure the exhaust down pipe to the manifold studs. Ease the coupling from the studs, lower the down pipe and recover the sealing cone.
11 Disconnect the oil cooler pipes from the transmission (Fig. 6.31). Plug the pipe ends to prevent dirt ingress.
12 Remove the two selector rod spring clips and take out the selector rod (Fig. 6.32).
13 Disconnect the vacuum pipe from the vacuum diaphragm (Fig. 6.33).
14 The torque converter should next be disconnected from the crankshaft driving plate. Rotate the crankshaft until each bolt may be seen through the starter motor aperture. Undo each bolt and turn one at a time until all the bolts are free (Fig. 6.34).
15 Place an additional jack under the automatic transmission unit and remove the two bolts and spring washers that secure the unit to the crossmember. Also remove the four bolts that locate the crossmember to the underside of the floor panel (Fig. 6.36).
16 Slowly lower the transmission unit and engine jacks until there is sufficient clearance for the dipstick tube to be removed.
17 Withdraw the dipstick and pull the oil filler tube (dipstick tube) sharply from the side of the transmission unit. Recover the 'O' ring.

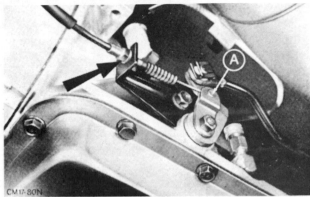
Fig. 6.29. Disconnecting downshift cable (Sec. 10)

Fig. 6.30. Speedometer cable (A) and lock plate (Sec. 10)

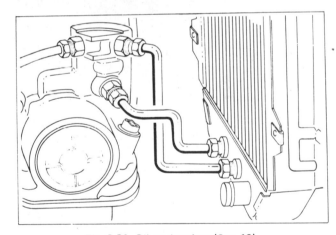
Fig. 6.31. Oil cooler pipes (Sec. 10)

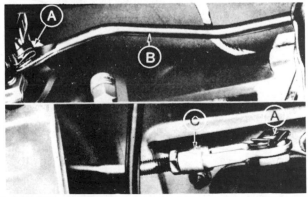
Fig. 6.32. Selector rod (B), spring clips (A) and adjuster (C) (Sec. 10)

Fig. 6.33. Disconnect the vacuum pipe

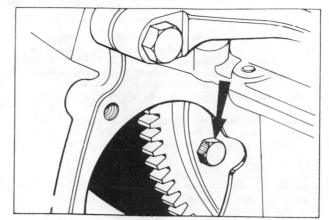

Fig. 6.34. Torque converter to crankshaft bolt (Sec. 10)

Fig. 6.35. Selector mechanism with both
levels in position 'D' (Secs. 11 and 12)

A   Selector inhibitor pawl
B   Selector inhibitor cable
C   Inhibitor push button
D   Selector lever handle
E   Adjusting link
F   Selector rod

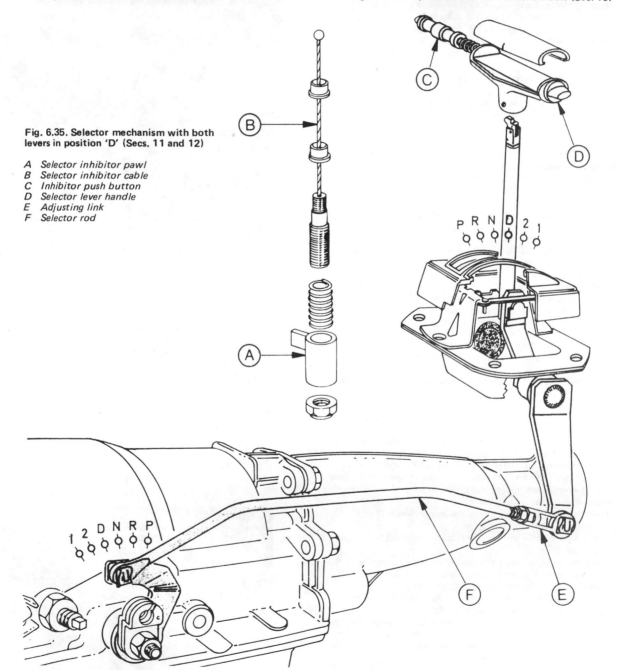

Fig. 6.36. Removing the rear crossmember bolts (Sec. 10)

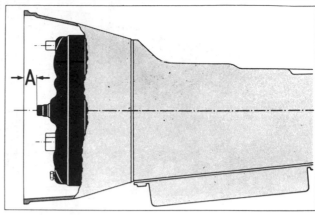

Fig. 6.37. Checking torque converter engagement (Sec. 10)

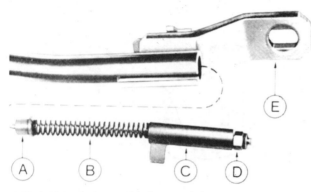

Fig. 6.38. Inhibitor cable bush (A), spring (B), pawl (C) and locknut (D) and selector lever (E) (Sec. 11)

18 Undo and remove the remaining bolts and spring washers that secure the converter housing to the engine.
19 Continue to lower the jacks until there is sufficient clearance between the top of the converter housing and underside of the floor for the transmission unit to be satisfactorily withdrawn.
20 Check that no cables or securing bolts have been left in position and tuck the speedometer cable out of the way.
21 The assistance of at least one other person is now required because of the weight of the complete unit.
22 Carefully pull the unit rearwards and, when possible, hold the converter in place in the housing as it will still be full of hydraulic fluid.
23 Finally withdraw the unit from under the car and place on wooden blocks so that the selector lever is not damaged or bent.
24 To separate the converter housing from the transmission case first lift off the converter from the transmission unit, taking suitable precautions to catch the fluid upon separation. Undo and remove the six bolts and spring washers that secure the converter housing to the transmission case. Lift away the converter housing.
25 Installation is a reversal of removal but ensure that the torque converter drain plug is in line with the hole in the driveplate. To check that the torque converter is positively engaged, measure the distance 'A' between the converter housing to engine mating face and the end of stub shaft. This should be at least 10 mm (Fig. 6.37).
26 Adjust the selector cable and inhibitor switch as described later in this Chapter.
27 Refill the transmission unit with the specified fluid before starting the engine and check the oil level as described in Section 9.

11 Automatic transmission selector mechanism - removal, overhaul and refitting - Fig. 6.35

1   Prise off the selector lever escutcheon, and withdraw the illumination mounting from the selector lever.
2   Remove the spring clip and detach the selector rod from the selector lever.

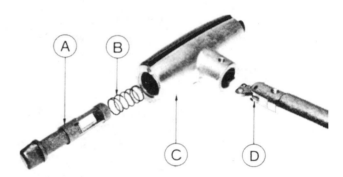

Fig. 6.39. Inhibitor push button (A), spring (B), selector handle (C) and lever (D) (Sec. 11)

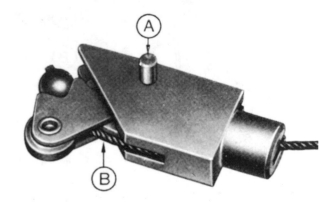

Fig. 6.40. Remove straight pin (A) and inhibitor cable (B) (Sec. 11)

3   If required, remove the spring clip and detach the selector rod from the transmission selector lever.
4   Remove the four bolts retaining the selector lever housing to the transmission tunnel and remove the housing.
5   Remove the rubber plug from the side of the selector lever housing, unscrew the nut and press the lower lever out of the housing.
6   Unscrew the locknut on the inhibitor cable and withdraw the pawl, spring and guide bush (Fig. 6.38).
7   Remove the Allen screw from the T handle and remove the handle. Remove the push button and spring (Fig. 6.39).
8   Using a pin punch, drive out the retaining pin and remove the inhibitor mechanism and inhibitor cable (Fig. 6.40).
9   Refitting is a reversal of the above procedure noting that the T handle Allen screw is inserted from the front, so that the push button is nearest the driver (Fig. 6.35).
10 Adjust the mechanism, refer to Section 12.

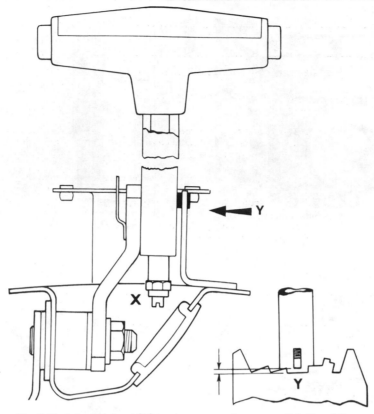

Fig. 6.41. Adjust locknut (X) to give correct clearance at (Y) (Sec. 12)

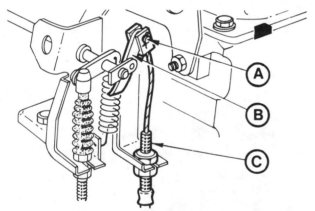

Fig. 6.42. Downshift cable retaining pin (A), connecting lever (B) and threaded sleeve (C) (Sec. 13)

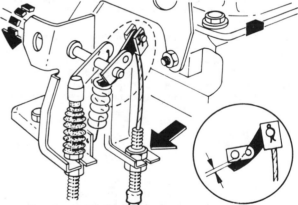

Fig. 6.43. Adjusting the downshift cable (Sec. 13)

12 Automatic transmission selector mechanism - adjustment

Two adjustments can be made to the selector mechanism.
1   Prise off the selector lever escutcheon, and from underneath the car, remove the plug in the side of the selector housing.
2   Adjust the inhibitor cable locknut (X) to give a dimension at (Y) of 0.004 to 0.008 in (0.1 to 0.2 mm), using feeler blades (Fig. 6.41).
3   Replace the plug and escutcheon.
4   With the transmission shift lever and the manual selector lever in 'D', adjust the selector rod link until it can be reconnected without strain (Fig. 6.35).

13 Downshift cable - removal, refitting and adjustment

1   Remove the split pin and disconnect the cable from the carburettor linkage (Fig. 6.42).
2   Slacken the adjusting nut from the mounting bracket, pull back the outer sheath and unhook the cable from the slot.

3   Unhook the cable from the transmission lever and bracket (Fig. 6.29).
4   Refitting is a reversal of the above, but the inner nut at the upper end should be screwed on completely, and the outer nut only a few turns.
5   Depress the accelerator pedal fully, and check that the throttle plate is fully open.
6   Using a screwdriver, lever the downshift cable lever upwards, pulling the inner cable fully upwards.
7   Turn the adjusting nut to lengthen or shorten the cable to give a clearance of 0.02 to 0.05 in (0.5 to 2.3 mm) between the down-shift lever and the accelerator shaft (Fig. 6.43). Tighten the locknut.

14 Starter inhibitor/reverse lamp switch - removal and refitting

1   This switch is non-adjustable and any malfunction must be due to a wiring fault, a faulty switch or wear in the internal actuating cam.
2   When removing and installing the switch, always use a new 'O' ring seal and tighten to specified torque.

15 Fault diagnosis - manual gearbox

Symptom	Reason/s	Remedy
Weak or ineffective synchromesh	Synchronising cones worn, split or damaged	Dismantle and overhaul gearbox. Fit new gear wheels and synchronising cones.
	Baulk ring synchromesh dogs worn, or damaged	Dismantle and overhaul gearbox. Fit new synchromesh baulk ring.
Jumps out of gear	Broken gearchange fork rod spring	Dismantle and replace spring.
	Gearbox coupling dogs badly worn	Dismantle gearbox. Fit new coupling dogs.
	Selector fork rod groove badly worn	Fit new selector fork rod.
Excessive noise	Incorrect grade of oil in gearbox or oil level too low	Drain, refill or top up gearbox with correct grade of oil.
	Bush or needle roller bearings worn or damaged	Dismantle and overhaul gearbox. Renew bearings.
	Gear teeth excessively worn or damaged	Dismantle, overhaul gearbox. Renew gear wheels.
	Countershaft thrust washers worn allowing excessive end play	Dismantle and overhaul gearbox. Renew thrust washers.
Excessive difficulty in engaging gear	Clutch cable adjustment incorrect	Adjust clutch cable correctly.

16 Fault diagnosis - automatic transmission

Faults in these units are nearly always the result of low fluid level or incorrect adjustment of the selector linkage or downshift cable. Internal faults should be diagnosed by your main Ford dealer who has the necessary equipment to carry out the work.

Chapter 7 Propeller shaft

Contents

Specifications

		1600 cc		2000 cc	
		Manual gearbox	**Automatic transmission**	**Manual gearbox**	**Automatic transmission**
Type (all two piece) ...	...	With rubber coupling	With constant velocity (CV) joint	With rubber coupling	With CV joint
Length*		49.9 in (1267.5 mm)	51.12 in (1298.5 mm)	49.9 in (1267.5 mm)	51.12 in (1298.5 mm)
Number of splines		20 (except 1600 Ghia)	25	25 (and 1600 Ghia)	25
Yoke outside diameter ...		1.186 in (30.15 mm) (except 1600 Ghia)	1.375 in (34.93 mm)	1.375 in (34.93 mm) (and 1600 Ghia)	1.375 in (34.93 mm)

Note: Length of driveshafts with constant velocity joint is measured from the rear axle flange to the centre of the front universal joint. Length of driveshafts with rubber coupling is measured from the centre of the rearmost universal joint to the centre of the rubber coupling.

Constant velocity joint grease ... . S - M1C - 45 15 - A

Torque wrench settings				lbf ft	kgf m
Propeller shaft to drive pinion flange ...	...	...	... ...	43 - 47	6 - 6.5
Driveshaft centre bearing support bolts	...	...	... ...	13 - 17	1.8 - 2.3
Constant velocity joint bolts	...	...	... ...	30	4.1

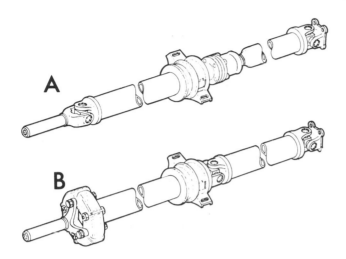

Fig. 7.1. Propeller shaft with constant velocity (CV) joint (A) and with rubber coupling (B) (Sec. 1)

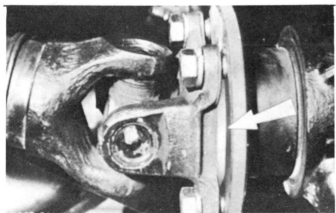

Fig. 7.2. Removing centre bearing - note shims (Sec. 2)

Fig. 7.3. Fit spacer between shaft and axle flanges (Sec. 2)

1 General description

Drive is transmitted from the gearbox to the rear axle by means of a finely balanced tubular propeller shaft. Fitted to each shaft are two universal joints which allow for vertical movement of the rear axle. Each universal joint comprises a four legged centre spider, four needle roller bearings and two yokes.

Fore-and-aft movement of the rear axle is absorbed by a sliding spline in the front of the propeller shaft which slides over a mating spline on the rear of the gearbox mainshaft.

Cortina 1600 and 2000 models have a two piece propeller shaft fitted. Most variants employ a constant velocity joint to the rear of the centre bearing. Vehicles with 2000 cc engine, and a manual gearbox have two universal joints in the rear part of the shaft, and a rubber coupling to the rear of the gearbox splines (Fig. 7.1).

All models are fitted with sealed universal joints.

The propeller shaft assembly is a relatively simple component and therefore reliable in service. Unfortunately it is not possible to obtain spare parts for the staked type universal joints, therefore when these are worn a new assembly must be fitted.

2 Propeller shaft - removal and refitting

1 Jack-up the rear of the car, or position the rear of the car over a pit or on a ramp.
2 If the rear of the car is jacked-up, supplement the jack with axle stands so that danger is minimised should the jack collapse.
3 If the rear wheels are off the ground place the car in gear and apply the handbrake to ensure that the propeller shaft does not turn when an attempt is made to loosen the four nuts securing the propeller shaft to the rear axle.
4 The propeller shaft is carefully balanced to fine limits and it is important that it is replaced in exactly the same position it was in prior to removal. Scratch marks on the propeller shaft and rear axle flanges to ensure accurate mating when the time comes for reassembly.
5 Unscrew and remove the four bolts and spring washers which hold the flange on the propeller shaft to the flange on the rear axle.
6 Slightly push the shaft forward to separate the two flanges, then lower the end of the shaft.
7 To detach the centre bearing support, undo and remove the two bolts, spring and plain washers securing it to the underside of the body. Retain any mounting shims, noting their location (Fig. 7.2).
8 Lower the shaft and pull it rearwards to disengage the gearbox mainshaft splines.
9 Place a large can or a tray under the rear of the gearbox extension to catch any oil which is likely to leak past the oil seal when the propeller shaft is removed.
10 Slide the front of the propeller shaft into the transmission, taking care not to damage the oil seal.
11 *Propeller shaft with rubber coupling*. Loosely fit the centre bearing, refitting the shims which were removed.
12 With the weight of the car on the wheels, fit a 0.16 in (4 mm) spacer between the propeller shaft and axle flange (Fig. 7.3). Tighten the bolts.
13 Position the centre bearing parallel to the shaft, and tighten the mounting bolts.
14 Remove the spacer and fully tighten the bolts with the mating marks aligned.
15 *Propeller shaft with CV joint*. Loosely fit the centre bearing, refitting the shims which were removed.
16 Align the pinion flange mating marks and tighten the bolts.
17 With the rear of the car jacked-up, so that the rear axle hangs down, pull the front of the shaft, and the centre bearing forward.
18 When the CV joint is felt to bear against the rear of the centre bearing, tighten the centre bearing bolts, **ensuring that the bearing is square to the shaft.**
19 *All versions.* Lower the car to the ground, and top-up the transmission with specified oil.

3 Propeller shaft centre bearing - removal and refitting

1 Refer to Section 2 and remove the complete propeller shaft assembly.

2 Using a blunt chisel carefully prise open the centre bearing support retaining bolt locking tab.

3 Slacken the bolt located in the end of the yoke and with a screwdriver ease out the 'U' shaped retainer through the side of the yoke. These parts are shown in Fig. 7.4.

4 Mark the propeller shaft and yoke for correct refitting. Disconnect the propeller shaft from the yoke and lift off the insulator rubber together with collar from the ball race.

5 Part the insulator rubber from the collar.

6 Refer to Fig. 7.5 and using a universal two legged puller draw the bearing together with cup from the end of the propeller shaft.

7 To fit a new bearing and cup onto the end of the propeller shaft use a piece of suitable diameter tube and drive into position. Fill the space between bearing and caps with specified grease.

8 With a pair of pliers bend the six metal tongues of the collar slightly outwards and carefully insert the insulator rubber. It is important that the flange of the insulator rubber, when fitted into the support, is uppermost see 'A' (Fig. 7.4).

9 Using a pair of 'parrot jaw' pliers or chisel bend the metal tongues rearwards over the rubber lip as shown in Fig. 7.6.

10 Next slide the support with the insulator rubber over the ball race.

11 Screw in the bolt together with locking tab into the propeller shaft forward end bearing leaving just sufficient space for the 'U' shaped retainer to be inserted.

12 Assemble the two propeller shaft halves in their original positions as denoted by the two previously made marks or by the double tooth (Fig. 7.7).

13 Refit the 'U' shaped retainer with the boss towards the splines (Fig. 7.8).

14 Finally tighten the retainer securing bolt and bend over the lockwasher.

4 Constant velocity joint - renewal

1 Remove the propeller shaft, as previously described.

2 Place alignment marks on the constant velocity joint flange and the rear section of the propeller shaft so that the original balance can be maintained.

3 Remove the six bolts and circlip from the front face of the constant velocity joint.

4 Remove the joint from the splined shaft and then extract the cup spring through the opening of the rubber sleeve.

5 No further dismantling should be carried out, but the old joint should be discarded and a new one purchased.

6 Commence reassembly by inserting the cup spring through the rubber sleeve so that the spring rests against the outer circumference of the constant velocity joint.

7 Attach the joint to the flange with two bolts only, inserted fingertight.

8 Offer up the propeller shaft (marks made before dismantling in alignment) and engage the splines. Now remove the two bolts, push the joint against the cup spring and fit the circlip.

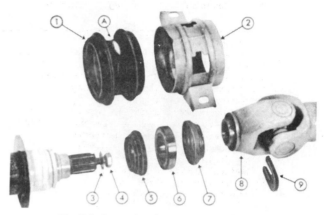

Fig. 7.4. Centre bearing components (Sec. 3)

1   Rubber bush   6   Ball race
2   Bearing housing and retainer   7   Dust cover
3   Washer   8   Yoke
4   Bolt   9   U shaped retainer
5   Dust cover

'A' shows flange which must be located at top of housing

Fig. 7.5. Pulling off the bearing and caps (Sec. 3)

Fig. 7.6 Bending the six metal tabs over the rubber lip (Sec. 3)

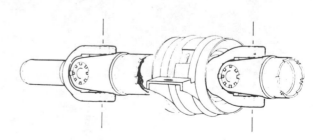

Fig. 7.7. Installed position of driveshaft halves (Sec. 3)

9 Fill the constant velocity joint with 30 grams of specified grease, once again align the marks and connect the propeller shaft section. Insert the bolts and tighten to a torque of 30 lbf ft (41. kgf m).

5 Universal joints - tests for wear

1 Wear in the needle roller bearings is characterised by vibration in the transmission, 'clonks' on taking up the drive, and in extreme cases of lack of lubrication, metallic squeaking and ultimately grating and shrieking sound as the bearings break up.

2 It is easy to check if the needle roller bearings are worn with the propeller shaft in position, by trying to turn the shaft with one hand, the other hand holding the rear axle flange when the rear universal joint is being checked, and the front half coupling when the front universal joint is being checked. Any movement between the propeller shaft and the front and the rear half couplings is indicative of considerable wear. If worn, a new assembly will have to be obtained. Check also by trying to lift the shaft and noticing any movement of the joints.

3 The centre bearing is a little more difficult to test for wear when mounted on the car. Undo and remove the two support securing bolts, spring and plain washers and allow the propeller shaft centre to hang down. Test the centre bearing for wear by grabbing the support and rocking it. If movement is evident the bearing is probably worn and should be renewed, as described in Section 3.

Fig. 7.8. Inserting 'U' retainer. Note position of boss (Sec. 3)

6 Fault diagnosis - propeller shaft

Symptom	Reason/s	Remedy
Vibration when car running on road	Out of balance shaft	Renew
	Wear in splined sleeve	Renew
	Loose flange bolts	Tighten
	Worn shaft joints	Renew joints or exchange complete assembly as appropriate

Chapter 8 Rear axle

Contents

Specifications

Axle type
1600 cc	Salisbury, Type A
2000 cc	Salisbury, Type B

Axle ratio
1600 saloon, standard	3.89 : 1
1600 saloon option and estate car	4.11 : 1
2000 all variants	3.75 : 1

Number of gearteeth
Crownwheel:
3.75 : 1	45
3.89 : 1	35
4.11 : 1	37

Drive pinion:
3.75 : 1	12
3.89 : 1	9
4.11 : 1	9

Backlash and preloads
Crownwheel and pinion backlash	0.004 - 0.008 in (0.10 - 0.20 mm)
Pinion bearing preload	0.001 - 0.003 in (0.03 - 0.07 mm)
Collapsible spacer length	0.453 - 0.461 in (11.5 - 11.7 mm)

Oil capacity and type
Type A axle	1.75 Imp. pints (1 litre)
Type B axle	1.90 Imp. pints (1.1 litre)
Specification	5QM-2C9002AA (SAE 90)

Torque wrench settings
	lb f ft	kg f m
Drive pinion self-locking nut	Refer to text (Section 4)	
Rear axle housing cover	22 - 29	3 - 4
Axle-shaft to side flange retainer plate	19 - 23	2.7 - 3.2
Propeller shaft to drive pinion flange	43 - 47	6 - 6.5
Propeller shaft centre bearing bolts	13 - 17	1.8 - 2.3
Filler/level plug	25 - 30	3.5 - 4.2

1 General description

The rear axle is of the semi-floating type and held in place by two lower swinging arms which are able to pivot on brackets welded to the chassis. Coil springs are located between the underside of the body and the swinging arms. Longitudinal and diagonal location of the rear axle is also controlled by two upper swinging arms which locate between the underside of the body and the outer ends of the final drive housing.

The differential unit is of the two pinion design and driven by a hypoid crownwheel and pinion. It is mounted in a cast iron differential housing into which the halfshaft and hub outer tubes are pressed.

The drive pinion is mounted in two taper roller bearings which are specially preloaded using a collapsible type spacer (Fig. 8.1).

The differential cage is also mounted on two taper roller bearings which are preloaded by spreading the differential carrier. The drive is taken through two differential side-gears to both axle-shafts. The axle-shafts are splined to the differential side-gears and run in ball races at their outer ends. These ball races have integral oil seals.

Two types of axle are used, the light (A type) and the heavier (B type) axle. Construction is identical, the only external differences being the axle housing and the pinion flange (Fig. 8.2).

2 Oil level - checking

1 At the routine service intervals, the axle oil level should be checked and topped-up as required.
2 With the car standing on a *level* surface, remove the combined filler/level plug (fig. 8.3).
3 The oil level should be up to the bottom edge of the hole. Add specified oil as necessary and refit the plug.

3 Rear axle - removal and refitting

1 Remove the rear wheel trims and slacken the roadwheel nuts. Chock the front wheels, jack-up the rear of the car and place on axle stands located beneath the lower radius arms. Remove the two rear wheels.
2 Support the weight of the rear axle by placing the saddle of a jack (preferably trolley type) under the centre of the rear axle.
3 With a scriber or file mark a line across the propeller shaft and pinion driving flanges so that they may be refitted together in their original positions.
4 Refer to Chapter 7, Section 2, and remove the propeller shaft.
5 Release the handbrake. Undo and remove the two cheese head screws that secure the brake drums to the axle-shaft. Using a soft-faced hammer carefully tap outwards on the circumference of each brake drum and lift away the brake drums.
6 Using a screwdriver placed between the brake shoe and relay lever, ease the handbrake cable relay lever inwards. Grip the handbrake cable end with a pair of pliers and release it from the relay lever. Pull the handbrake cable through each brake backplate (Fig. 8.4).
7 Wipe the top of the brake master cylinder reservoir and unscrew the cap. Place a piece of polythene sheeting over the reservoir neck and refit the cap. This is to stop hydraulic fluid syphoning out during subsequent operations.
8 Wipe the area around the brake flexible pipe to metal pipe union just in front of the rear axle and referring to Chapter 9, Section 3, detach the brake flexible hose from the metal pipe (Fig. 8.5).
9 With a trolley jack, slightly raise the axle and undo and remove the bolt, nut and plain washer that secures each shock absorber to the rear axle. Contract the shock absorbers (Fig. 8.6).
10 Undo and remove the bolt, nut and plain washer that secures each upper and each lower radius arm to the axle housing (Fig. 8.7).
11 Lower the rear axle and remove both coil springs, retaining the upper mounting rubber rings.

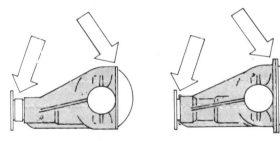

Fig. 8.2. Differences between axle type A (left) and axle type B (right) (Sec. 1)

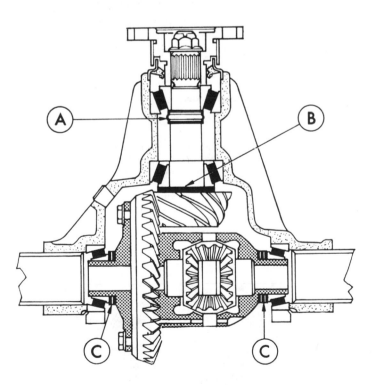

Fig. 8.1. Collapsible spacer (A), drive pinion shim (B), differential bearing shims (C) (Sec. 1)

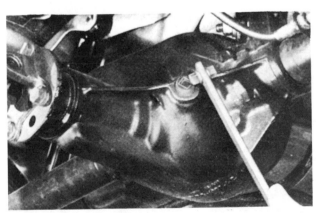

Fig. 8.3. Removing filler/level plug (Sec. 2)

Fig. 8.4. Removing the handbrake cable (Sec. 3)

Fig. 8.5. Remove the brake flexible hose from the brake pipe (Sec. 3)

Fig. 8.6. Remove the shock absorber from axle casing (Sec. 3)

Fig. 8.7. Removing the lower (A) and upper (B) radius arms (Sec. 3)

12 The complete rear axle assembly may now be withdrawn.

13 Refit the rear axle in the reverse sequence to removal. Realign the marks on the propeller shaft and pinion flange.

14 Refer to Chapter 7, Section 3 to refit the centre bearing.

15 The radius arm mounting bolts must only be tightened to a torque wrench setting of 42 - 50 lb f ft (5.8 - 6.9 kg f m) when the roadwheels have been refitted and the car is standing on the ground.

16 It will be necessary to bleed the brake hydraulic system as described in Chapter 9, Section 2.

17 Check the amount of oil in the rear axle and top-up if necessary.

---

4   Drive pinion oil seal - renewal

Note: *Renewal of the drive pinion oil seal requires a great deal of care and the use of some special equipment. Without these, the collapsible spacer can be damaged which will require its renewal, and this operation is outside the scope of the do-it-yourself motorist because a special tool is required for removal of the pinion bearing. Whenever the pinion oil seal is renewed, it is essential that the self-locking pinion nut is also renewed.*

1   Jack up the rear of the vehicle and support it securely under the bodyframe.

2   Remove the rear roadwheels and brake drums.

3   Disconnect the propeller shaft from the rear axle drive pinion after marking them for correct alignment.

4   Using a spring balance and length of cord wound round the drive pinion flange, determine the torque required to turn the drive pinion and record it. Alternatively, a socket wrench fitted to the pinion nut and a suitable torque wrench may be used.

5   Mark the coupling in relation to the pinion splines to ensure that they are refitted in the same position.

6   Hold the pinion coupling flange by placing two 2 inch long bolts through two opposite holes, bolting them up tight; undo the self-locking nut whilst holding a large screwdriver or tyre lever between the two bolts for leverage. Using a standard two or three-leg puller, remove the coupling flange from the pinion shaft.

7   Using a hammer and a small chisel or screwdriver, remove the oil seal from the pinion housing. During this operation great care must be taken to ensure that the pinion shaft is not scored in any way. Note that there will be some spillage of the axle oil as the seal is removed.

8   Carefully clean the contact area inside the pinion housing, then apply a film of general purpose grease to this surface and between the lips of the new oil seal. Do not remove the existing grease from the replacement seal.

9   Using a tube of suitable diameter, press in the new seal to its full depth in the pinion housing.

10   Refit the coupling in its correct relative position to the pinion shaft.

11   Using a new self-locking nut, prevent the flange from turning, then carefully and slowly tighten the nut until the same turning torque is achieved as recorded at paragraph 4. Continue tightening until an additional 2 to 3 lbf in (2 to 4 kfg cm) is achieved, to

Fig. 8.8. Removing the bearing retainer plate (Sec. 5)

allow for the friction of the new oil seal. After this torque has been obtained, do not tighten the self-locking nut or the collapsible spacer will be damaged (see note at beginning of Section).

12 Remove the two bolts from the coupling flange then refit the propeller shaft taking note of the alignment marks made when removing.

13 Top up the rear axle with the correct grade of oil, then refit the brake drums and roadwheels.

14 Lower the car to the ground.

5 Axle-shaft (halfshaft) - removal and refitting

1 Chock the front wheels, remove the rear wheel trim and slacken the wheel nuts. Jack-up the rear of the car and support on firmly based axle stands. Remove the roadwheel and release the handbrake.

2 Undo and remove the cheese head screw that secures the brake drum to the axle-shaft. Using a soft faced hammer, carefully tap outwards on the circumference of the brake drum and lift away the brake drum.

3 Using a socket wrench placed through the holes in the axle shaft flange, undo and remove the four bolts that secure the bearing retainer plate to the axle casing (Fig. 8.8).

4 Place a container under the end of the rear axle to catch any oil that may drain out once the axle-shaft has been removed.

5 The axle-shaft may now be withdrawn from the rear axle.

6 It is possible for the ball races to bind onto the axle-shaft in which case screw in two long bolts through the end of the axle tube and thereby ease the axle-shaft assembly out (Fig. 8.9).

7 Before refitting the axle-shaft assembly, smear a little grease along the length of the axle-shaft and also on the ball race to prevent corrosion due to moisture.

8 Insert the axle-shaft into the rear axle tube, keep the shaft horizontal until its splines are felt to engage with those of the differential gears.

9 Secure the bearing retainer with the four bolts which should be tightened to a torque wrench setting of 19 - 23 lb f ft (2.7 - 3.2 kg f m).

10 Refit the brake drum and secure with the cheesehead screw.

11 Refit the roadwheel and lower the car to the ground.

6 Axle-shaft (Halfshaft) - bearing/oil seal - renewal

1 Remove the axle-shaft, as described in the preceding Section.

2 Secure the axle-shaft in a vice fitted with jaw protectors and then carefully drill a hole in the bearing retaining collar. Do not drill right through the collar or the axle-shaft will be damaged. Use a sharp cold chisel and cut the collar from the shaft (Fig. 8.10).

3 A press or suitable bearing extractor will be required to remove the bearing from the shaft. Do not damage the retainer plate during this operation.

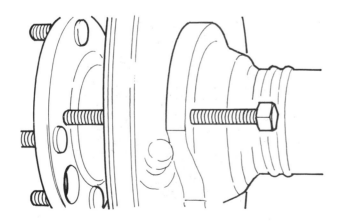

Fig. 8.9. Using long bolts to assist withdrawal of axle shaft (Sec. 5)

Fig. 8.10. Removing the bearing retaining ring (Sec. 6)

Fig. 8.11. Replacing a wheel stud (Sec. 7)

4 Commence installation by fitting the retainer plate to the axle-shaft, followed by the bearing (oil seal away from axle-shaft flange) and a new bearing retaining collar.

5 Using a press or two-legged puller, apply pressure to the collar to draw all three components into their correct positions, tight against the axle-shaft end-flange.

6 Apply a little grease to the bearing recess in the end of the axle tube and install the axle-shaft, as described in Section 5.

7 Roadwheel retaining studs - renewal

1 A wheel retaining stud which has broken or whose threads have stripped may be removed and the new one installed using a number of washers, built up to the thickness of the flange, and a wheel nut with its conical face outwards (Fig. 8.11).

2 When installing the new stud, make sure that its securing splines are correctly aligned with those in the axle-shaft flange before applying pressure.

8 Rear axle - repair and overhaul

1 It is not recommended that servicing of the rear axle should go beyond the operations described in this Chapter.

2 Special tools and gauges are required to set up the differential, and dismantling and reassembly should be left to your Ford main dealer.

3 The latest trend is in fact for rear axle components not to be supplied individually but the complete factory-built unit only to be supplied as a spare.

4 Reference to the Fault Diagnosis chart will however assist the home mechanic in eliminating some sources of noise and wear before deciding that it is the rear axle which is undoubtedly due for major overhaul or reconditioning.

9 Fault diagnosis - rear axle

Symptom	Reason/s	Remedy
Oil leakage	Faulty pinion oil seal Faulty axle-shaft oil seals Defective cover gasket	Renew. Renew. Renew.
Noise	Lack of oil Worn bearings General wear	Top-up. Renew. Have assembly reconditioned or purchase a new unit.
'Clonk' on taking up drive and excessive backlash	Incorrectly tightened pinion nut Worn components Worn axle-shaft splines Elongated roadwheel bolt holes	Check (see Section 3). Renew or recondition unit. Renew unit. Renew wheels.

Chapter 9 Braking system

For modifications, and information applicable to later models, refer to Supplement at end of manual

Contents

Specifications

System type	Hydraulic, servo assisted on all four wheels
Front	Dual line disc, self adjusting
Rear	Dual line drum, self adjusting
Handbrake	Mechanical, on rear wheels only

Front brakes

Disc diameter	9.74 in (247.5 mm)
Max disc runout (total)	0.0035 in (0.09 mm)
Cylinder diameter	2.13 in (54.0 mm)
Minimum pad thickness	0.06 in (1.5 mm)

Rear brakes

	1600	2000 and 1600 2V HC
Drum diameter	8.0 in (203 mm)	9.0 in (229 mm)
Shoe width	1.5 in (38 mm)	1.75 in (44.5 mm)
Wheel cylinder diameter	0.75 in (19 mm)	0.70 in (17.8 mm)
Minimum lining thickness	0.40 in (1.0 mm)	0.40 in (1.0 mm)

Vacuum servo unit

Type	38
Boost ratio	2.2 : 1

Torque wrench settings	lb f ft	kg f m
Brake caliper to front suspension	45 - 50	6.22 - 6.91
Brake disc to hub	30 - 34	4.15 - 4.70
Rear brake backplate to axle housing	15 - 18	2.07 - 2.49
Hydraulic pipe union	5 - 7	0.70 - 1
Bleed screw	5 - 7	0.70 - 1
Master cylinder - tipping valve securing nut	35 - 45	4.8 - 6.22
Master cylinder to servo	17	2.3

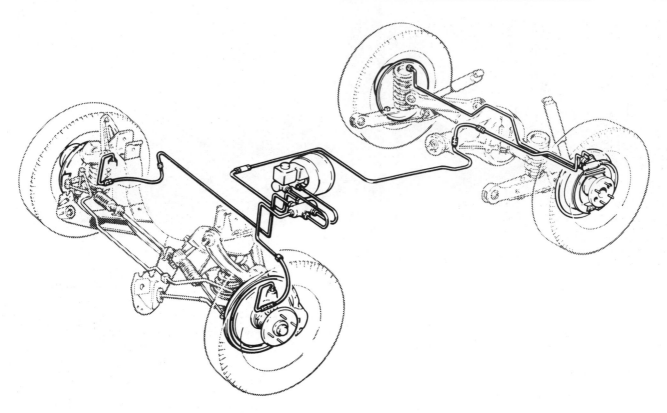

Fig. 9.1. Hydraulic braking system layout (Sec. 1)

1 General description

Disc brakes are fitted to the front wheels and drum brakes to the rear. All are operated under servo assistance from the brake pedal, this being connected to the master cylinder and servo assembly, mounted on the bulkhead.

The hydraulic system is of the dual line principle whereby the front disc brake calipers have a separate hydraulic system to that of the rear drum brake wheel cylinders, so that, if failure of the hydraulic pipes to the front or rear brakes occurs, half the braking system is still operative (Fig. 9.1). Servo assistance in this condition is still available.

The front brake disc is secured to the hub flange and the caliper mounted on the steering knuckle and wheel stub, so that the disc is able to rotate in between the two halves of the calipers. Inside each half of the caliper is a hydraulic cylinder, this being interconnected by a drilling which allows hydraulic fluid pressure to be transmitted to both halves. A piston operates in each cylinder, and is in contact with the outer face of the brake pad. By depressing the brake pedal, hydraulic fluid pressure is increased by the servo unit and transmitted to the caliper by a system of metal and flexible hoses, whereupon the pistons are moved outwards so pushing the pads onto the face of the disc and slowing down the rotational speed of the disc.

The rear drum brakes have one cylinder operating two shoes. When the brake pedal is depressed, hydraulic fluid pressure, increased by the servo unit, is transmitted to the rear brake wheel cylinders by a system of metal and flexible pipes. The pressure moves the pistons outwards so pushing the shoe linings into contact with the inside circumference of the brake drum and slowing down the rotational speed of the drum.

The handbrake provides an independent means of rear brake application.

Also, attached to each of the brake units is an automatic adjuster which operates in conjunction with the footbrake.

Whenever it is necessary to obtain spare parts for the braking system great care must be taken to ensure that the correct parts are obtained because of the varying types of braking components fitted to the Cortina Mk IV range of cars.

2 Bleeding the hydraulic system

1 Removal of all the air from the hydraulic system is essential to the correct working of the braking system, and before undertaking this, examine the fluid reservoir cap to ensure that the vent hole is clear. Check the level of fluid in the reservoir, and top-up if required, ensuring that both halves are fitted.
2 Check all brake line unions and connections for possible seepage, and at the same time check the condition of the rubber hoses which may be perished.
3 If the condition of the caliper or wheel cylinders is in doubt, check for possible signs of fluid leakage.
4 If there is any possibility that incorrect fluid has been used in the system, drain all the fluid out and flush through with methylated spirits. Renew all piston seals and cups since they will be affected and could possibly fail under pressure.
5 Gather together a clean jam jar, a 12 inch (300 mm) length of tubing which fits tightly over the bleed screws and a tin of the correct brake fluid.
6 To bleed the system, clean the area around the bleed valves and start on the front right-hand bleed screw by first removing the rubber cup over the end of the bleed screw (Fig. 9.2).
7 Place the end of the tube in a clean jar which should contain sufficient fluid to keep the end of the tube underneath during the operation.
8 Open the bleed screw ½ turn with a spanner and depress the brake pedal. After slowly releasing the pedal, pause for a moment to allow the fluid to recoup in the master cylinder and then depress it again. This will force air from the system. Continue until no more air bubbles can be seen coming from the tube. At intervals make certain that the reservoir is kept topped-up, otherwise air will enter at this point again.
9 Finally press the pedal down fully and hold it there whilst the bleed screw is tightened. To ensure correct seating it should be tightened to a torque wrench setting of 5 - 7 lb f ft (0.70 - 1.0 kg f m).
10 Repeat this operation on the second front brake, and then the rear brakes, starting with the right-hand brake unit.
11 When completed check the level of the fluid in the reservoir and then

4.4 Spring clips (A), retaining pins (B), and anti-rattle clips (C)

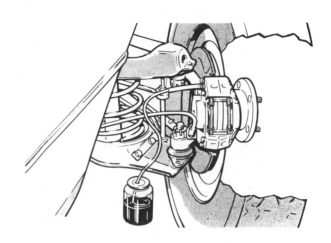

Fig. 9.2. Bleeding the front right-hand brake (Sec. 2)

check the feel of the brake pedal, which should be firm and free from any 'spongy' action, which is normally associated with air in the system.
12 It will be noticed that during the bleeding operation the effort required to depress the pedal the full stroke will increase because of the loss of vacuum assistance as it is destroyed by repeated operation of the servo unit. Although the servo unit will be inoperative as far as assistance is concerned it does not affect the brake bleed operation.

3 Flexible hose - inspection, removal and refitting

1   Inspect the condition of the flexible hydraulic hoses leading to each of the front disc brake calipers and also the one at the front of the rear axle. If they are swollen, damaged or chafed, they must be renewed.
2   Wipe the top of the brake master cylinder reservoir and unscrew the cap. Place a piece of polythene sheet over the top of the reservoir and refit the cap. This is to stop hydraulic fluid syphoning out during subsequent operations.
3   To remove a front flexible hose, wipe the union and brackets free of dust and undo the union nuts from the metal pipe ends.
4   Undo and remove the locknuts and plain washers securing each flexible hose end to the bracket and lift away the flexible hose.
5   To remove the rear flexible hose follow the instructions for the front flexible hose.
6   Refitting in both cases is the reverse sequence to removal. It will be necessary to bleed the brake hydraulic system as described in Section 2. If one hose has been removed it is only necessary to bleed either the front or rear brake hydraulic system.

4 Front brake pads - inspection, removal and refitting

1   Apply the handbrake, remove the front wheel trim, slacken the wheel nuts, jack-up the front of the car and place on firmly based axle stands. Remove the front wheel.
2   Inspect the amount of friction material left on the pads. The pads must be renewed when the thickness has been reduced to a minimum of 0.12 inch (3.0 mm).
3   If the fluid level in the master cylinder reservoir is high, when the pistons are moved into their respective bores to accomodate new pads the level could rise sufficiently for the fluid to overflow. Place absorbent cloth around the reservoir or syphon a little fluid out so preventing paintwork damage caused by being in contact with the hydraulic fluid.
4   Using a pair of long nosed pliers extract the two small spring clips that hold the main retaining pins in place (photo).
5   Remove the main retaining pins and wire anti-rattle clips.
6   The friction pads can now be removed from the caliper. If they prove difficult to remove by hand, a pair of long nosed pliers can be used. Lift away the shims.

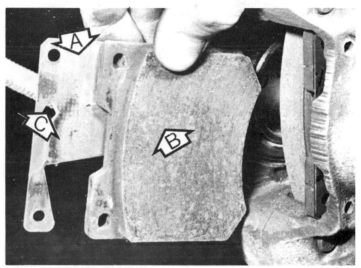

4.9 Shim (A), brake pad (B) and arrow (C) which must point upwards

7   Carefully clean the recesses in the caliper in which the friction pads and shims lie, and the exposed faces of each piston from all traces of dust or rust.
8   Using a piece of wood carefully retract the pistons.
9   Fit new friction pads and shims, with the arrow on the shim pointing upwards (photo). Insert the pad retaining pins and anti-rattle clips (photo 4.4) and secure with the spring clips.
10 Refit the roadwheel and lower the car. Tighten the wheel nuts securely and replace the wheel trim.
11 To correctly seat the pistons pump the brake pedal several times and finally top-up the hydraulic fluid level in the master cylinder reservoir as necessary.

5 Front brake caliper - removal and refitting

1   Apply the handbrake, remove the front wheel trim, slacken the wheel nuts, jack-up the front of the car and place on firmly based axle stands. Remove the front wheel.
2   Wipe the top of the brake master cylinder reservoir and unscrew the cap. Place a piece of polythene sheet over the top of the reservoir and refit the cap. This is to stop hydraulic fluid syphoning out during subsequent operations.
3   Remove the friction pads, as described in Section 4.
4   If it is intended to fit new caliper pistons and/or the seals, depress the brake pedal to bring the pistons into contact with the disc and so assist subsequent removal of the pistons.

5   Wipe the area clean around the flexible hose bracket and detach the pipe as described in Section 3. Tape up the end of the pipe to stop the possibility of dirt ingress.

6   Using a screwdriver or chisel, bend back the tabs on the locking plate and undo the two caliper body mounting bolts. Lift away the caliper from its mounting flange on the steering knuckle and wheel stub.

7   To refit the caliper, position it over the disc and move it until the mounting bolt holes are in line with the two front holes in the steering knuckle and wheel stub mounting flange.

8   Fit the caliper retaining bolts through the two holes in a new locking plate and insert the bolts through the caliper body. Tighten the bolts to a torque wrench setting of 45 - 50 lb f ft (6.22 - 6.91 kg f m).

9   Using a screwdriver, pliers or chisel, bend up the locking plate tabs so as to lock the bolts.

10 Remove the tape from the end of the flexible hydraulic pipe and reconnect it to the union on the hose bracket. Be careful not to cross thread the union nut during the initial turns. The union nut should be tightened securely, if possible using a torque wrench, and special slotted end ring spanner attachment set to 5 - 7 lb f ft (0.70 - 1.00 kg f m).

11 Push the pistons into their respective bores so as to accommodate the pads. Watch the level of hydraulic fluid in the master cylinder reservoir as it can overflow if too high whilst the pistons are being retracted. Place absorbent cloth around the reservoir or syphon a little fluid out so preventing paintwork damage caused by being in contact with the hydraulic fluid.

12 If the old pads are being re-used, refit them into their respective original positions. If new pads are being used it does not matter which side they are fitted. Replace the shims, and clips.

13 Insert the two pad and shim retaining pins and secure in position with the spring clips.

14 Bleed the hydraulic system as described in Section 2. Replace the roadwheel and lower the car.

6   Front brake caliper - dismantling and reassembly

1   The pistons should be removed first. To do this, half withdraw one piston from its bore in the caliper body. (See Fig. 9.3).

2   Carefully remove the securing circlip and extract the sealing bellows from their location in the lower part of the piston skirt. Completely remove the piston.

3   If difficulty is experienced in withdrawing the piston use a jet of compressed air or a foot pump to move it out of its bore.

4   Remove the sealing bellows from their location in the annular ring which is machined in the cylinder bore.

5   Remove the piston sealing ring from the cylinder bore using a small screwdriver but do take care not to scratch the fine finish of the bore.

6   To remove the second piston repeat the operations in paragraphs 1 - 5 inclusive.

7   It is important that the two halves of the caliper are not separated under any circumstances. If hydraulic fluid leaks are evident, from the joint, the caliper must be renewed.

8   Thoroughly wash all parts in methylated spirits or clean hydraulic fluid. During reassembly new rubber seals must be fitted and these should be well lubricated with clean hydraulic fluid.

9   Inspect the pistons and bores for signs of wear, score marks or damage, and if evident, new parts should be obtained ready for fitting or a new caliper obtained.

10 To reassemble, fit one of the piston seals into the annular groove in the cylinder bore.

11 Fit the rubber bellows to the cylinder bore groove so that the lip is turned outwards.

12 Lubricate the seal and rubber bellows with clean hydraulic fluid. Push the piston, crown first, through the rubber sealing bellows and then into the cylinder bore. Take care as it is easy for the piston to damage the rubber bellows.

13 With the piston half inserted into the cylinder bore fit the inner edge of the bellows into the annular groove that is in the piston skirt.

14 Push the piston down the bore as far as it will go. Secure the rubber bellows to the caliper with the circlip.

15 Repeat the operations in paragraphs 10 to 14 inclusive for the second piston.

16 The caliper is now ready for refitting. It is recommended that the hydraulic pipe end is temporarily plugged to stop any dirt ingress whilst being refitted, before the pipe connection is made.

7   Front brake disc and hub - removal and refitting

1   After jacking-up the car and removing the front wheel, remove the caliper as described in Section 5.

2   By judicious tapping and levering remove the dust cap from the centre of the hub.

3   Remove the split pin from the nut retainer and lift away the adjusting nut retainer.

4   Unscrew the adjusting nut and lift away the thrust washer and outer tapered bearing.

5   Pull off the complete hub and disc assembly from the stub axle.

6   From the back of the hub assembly carefully prise out the grease seal and lift away the inner tapered bearing (Fig. 9.4).

7   Carefully clean out the hub and wash the bearings with petrol making sure that no grease or oil is allowed to get onto the brake disc.

8   Should it be necessary to separate the disc from the hub for renewal or regrinding, first bend back the locking tabs and undo the four securing bolts. With a scriber mark the relative positions of the hub and disc to ensure refitting in their original positions and separate the disc from the hub.

9   Thoroughly clean the disc and inspect for signs of deep scoring or excessive corrosion. If these are evident, the disc may be reground but no more than a maximum total of 0.060 inch (1.524 mm) may be removed. It is, however, desirable to fit a new disc which must be of the same part number as the original. If not, renew both discs as a matching pair.

10 To reassemble make quite sure that the mating faces of the disc and hub are very clean and place the disc on the hub, lining up any previously made marks.

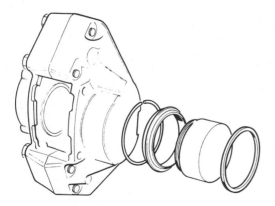

Fig. 9.3. Brake caliper body and one piston assembly (Sec. 6)

Fig. 9.4. Front hub assembly with disc removed (Sec. 7)

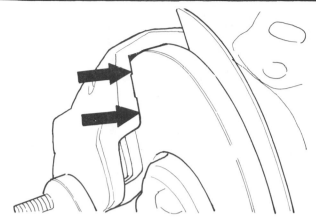

Fig. 9.5. Disc runout check points when using feeler gauges (Sec. 7)

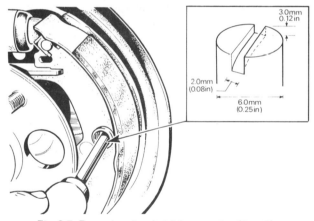

Fig. 9.6. Disconnecting shoe return spring (Sec. 8)

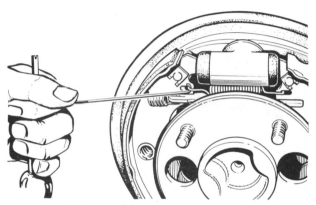

Fig. 9.7. Removing shoe hold down spring (Sec. 8)

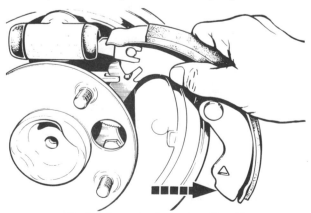

Fig. 9.8. Removing front shoe (Sec. 8)

11 Fit the four securing bolts and two new tab washers and tighten the bolts in progressive and diagonal manner to a final torque wrench setting of 30 - 34 lb f ft (4.15 kg f m). Bend up the locking tabs.

12 Work some grease well into the bearing, fully pack the bearing cages and rollers. **Note:** leave the hub and grease seal empty to allow for subsequent expansion of the grease.

13 To reassemble the hub, first fit the inner bearing and then gently tap the grease seal back into the hub. A new seal must always be fitted as during removal it was probably damaged. The lip must face inwards to the hub.

14 Replace the hub and disc assembly on the stub axle and slide on the outer bearing and thrust washer.

15 Refit the adjusting nut and tighten it to a torque wrench setting of 27 lb f ft (3.7 kg f m) whilst rotating the hub and disc to ensure free movement and centralisation of the bearings. Slacken the nut back by 90° which will give the required endfloat of 0.001 - 0.005 inch (0.03 - 0.13 mm). Fit the nut retainer and a new split pin but at this stage do not lock the split pin.

16 If a dial indicator gauge is available, it is advisable to check the disc for run out. The measurement should be taken as near to the edge of the worn yet smooth part of the disc as possible. and must not exceed 0.0035 inch (0.09 mm). If the figure obtained is found to be excessive, check the mating surfaces of the disc and hub for dirt or damage and also check the bearings and cups for excessive wear or damage.

17 If a dial indicator gauge is not available the runout can be checked by means of a feeler gauge placed between the casting of the caliper and the disc (Fig. 9.5). Establish a reasonably tight fit with the feeler gauge between the top of the casting and the disc and rotate the disc and hub. Any high or low spot will immediately become obvious by extra tightness or looseness of the fit of the feeler gauge. The amount of runout can be checked by adding or subtracting feeler gauges as necessary. It is only fair to point out that this method is not as accurate as when using a dial indicator gauge owing to the rough nature of the caliper casting.

18 Once the disc runout has been checked and found to be correct bend the ends of the split pin back and replace the dust cap.

19 Reconnect the brake hydraulic pipe and bleed the brakes as described in Section 2 of this Chapter.

8 Drum brake shoes (8 inch (203 mm) - 1600) - Inspection, removal and refitting

After high mileages, it will be necessary to fit replacement shoes with new linings. Refitting new linings to shoes is not considered economic, or possible without the use of special equipment as the linings are bonded to the shoes.

Ensure that the correct specification linings are fitted.

1 Chock the front wheels, jack-up the rear of the car and place on firmly based axle stands. Remove the roadwheel.

2 Release the handbrake, and remove the brake drum retaining screw (if fitted). Using a soft-faced mallet on the outer circumference, remove the brake drum.

3 The brake linings must be renewed when the lining material has worn down to 0.06 in (1.52 mm) at its thinnest part.

4 Using a hooked piece of wire, disconnect both brake shoe return springs (Fig. 9.6).

5 Release and remove the shoe hold-down springs. A rod or old screwdriver, slotted at the end is useful to first depress and then unhook the spring from its retaining bracket (Fig. 9.7).

6 Pull the bottom of the front brake shoe towards the front of the vehicle. This will actuate the self-adjusting mechanism to the point where the two ratchets slip out of engagement. Now twist the brake shoe to release it from the spacer strut and remove it (Fig. 9.8).

7 Move the rear shoe away from and below the backplate and at the same time disconnect the handbrake operating cable from the shoe lever (Fig. 9.9).

8 The rear brake shoe can be dismantled by removing the clip from the pivot pin and extracting the pin. Lever the strut from the shoe and detach the lever return spring (Fig. 9.10 and 9.11).

9 The front brake shoe can be dismantled by removing the clip and separating the longer ratchet lever from the shoe. Remove and discard the spring washer and then separate the shorter ratchet lever and spring from the shoe (Fig. 9.12).

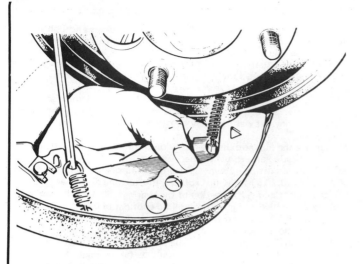

Fig. 9.9. Disconnecting handbrake cable (Sec. 8)

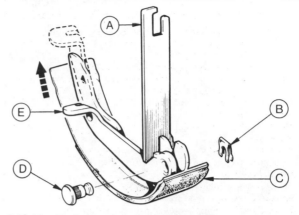

Fig. 9.10. Handbrake operating lever (A), clip (B), brake shoe (C), pivot pin (D), and strut (E) (Sec. 8)

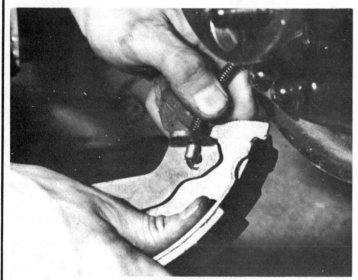

8.9 Disconnection of handbrake cable from relay lever

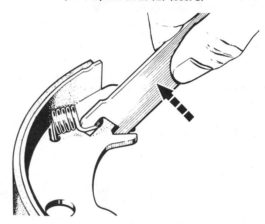

Fig. 9.11. Dismantling rear shoe (Sec. 8)

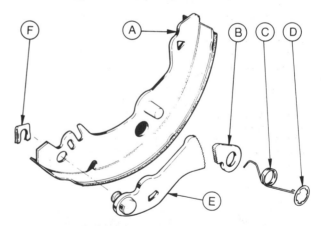

Fig. 9.12. Front shoe (A), short ratchet (B), ratchet spring (C), spring washer (D), long ratchet (E) and clip (F) (Sec. 8)

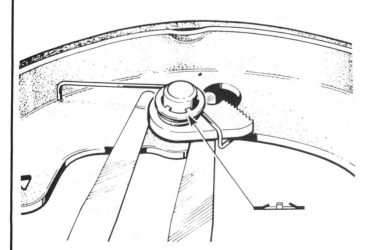

Fig. 9.13. Reassembling short ratchet, spring and washer (Sec. 8)

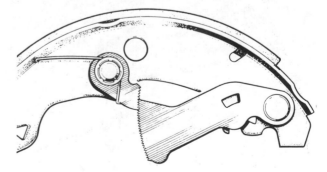

Fig. 9.14. Ratchet overlap on front shoe (Sec. 8)

10 Reassembly of the new shoes is a reversal of removal and dismantling, but note the following points:

i) No lubricant must be applied to the components.

ii) When assembling the smaller ratchet, spring and pivot pin to the front brake shoe, slide two 0.008 in (0.2 mm) feeler blades between the shoe and the ratchet before installing a new spring washer. This will provide the necessary rotational clearance. Make sure that the retaining tabs are correctly positioned as shown in Fig. 9.13.

iii) Having fitted the longer ratchet and securing clip, arrange the engagement of both ratchets to provide an overlap of 4 or 5 teeth (Fig. 9.14).

iv) The spring loaded ratchet lever must be pulled down with a hooked piece of wire so that the second ratchet can be pushed forward to the minimum adjustment position (Fig. 9.15).

v) The double coil shoe return spring is located at the top of the brake assembly.

11 Once the brake drum has been installed, apply the foot brake pedal several times to adjust the shoes to their minimum drum clearance position.

9 Drum brake shoes (9 inch (228 mm) - 2000) - inspection, removal and refitting

After high mileages, it will be necessary to fit replacement shoes with new linings. Refitting new brake linings to shoes is not considered economic, or possible without the use of special equipment as the linings are bonded to the shoes. Ensure that the correct specification linings are fitted to the shoes.

1 Chock the front wheels, jack-up the rear of the car and place on firmly based axle stands. Remove the roadwheel.

2 Release the handbrake, remove the brake drum retaining screw, (if fitted) and using a soft-faced mallet on the outer circumference of the brake drum remove the brake drum.

3 Should the situation exist whereby the shoes foul the drum making removal impossible, the shoes must be collapsed by detaching the handbrake cable from the body mounted brackets and then the plunger assembly removed from the backplate. Whenever the plunger is removed it must be discarded and a new one obtained.

4 The brake linings should be renewed when the lining material has worn down to 0.06 inch (1.52 mm) at its thinnest part.

5 Depress each shoe holding down spring and rotate the spring retaining washer through 90° to disengage it from the pin secured to the backplate. Lift away the washer and spring (Fig. 9.16).

6 Ease each shoe from its location slot in the fixed pivot and then detach the other end of each shoe from the wheel cylinder.

7 Note which way round and into which holes in the shoes the two retracting springs fit and detach the retracting springs.

Fig. 9.15. Adjusting ratchets to minimum position (Sec. 8)

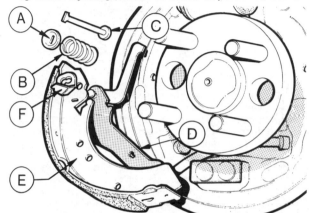

Fig. 9.16. Rear shoes assembly (Sec. 9), retaining washer (A), hold down spring (B), pin (C), relay lever (D), rear shoe (E), retaining bracket (F)

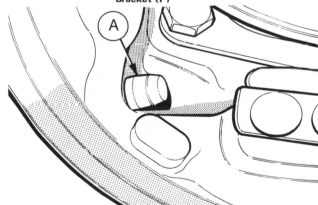

Fig. 9.17. Handbrake lever stop (A) (Sec. 9)

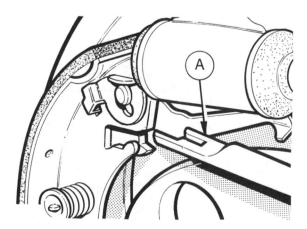

Fig. 9.18. Correct location of adjusting strut (A) (Sec. 9)

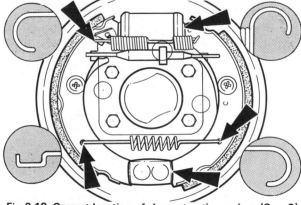

Fig. 9.19. Correct location of shoe retracting springs (Sec. 9)

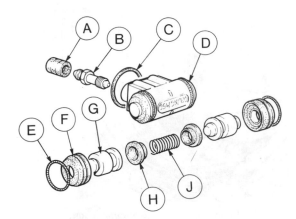

Fig. 9.20. Rear wheel cylinder (Sec. 10)

A Dust cap (where fitted)   F Dust cover
B Bleed nipple (where fitted) G Piston
C Seal (where fitted)   H Piston seal
D Wheel cylinder   J Return spring
E Retaining ring

8 Lift away the front shoe followed by the self adjusting pushrod and ratchet assembly.
9 Completely remove the handbrake cable from the body mounted brackets and disconnect the cable from the relay lever (photo).
10 Lift away the rear shoe together with the self adjusting mechanism (Fig. 9.16).
11 If the shoes are to be left off for a while, place a warning on the steering wheel as accidental depression of the brake pedal will eject the pistons from the wheel cylinder.
12 To remove the relay lever assembly, release the shoe retaining bracket and lift away the relay lever assembly (Fig. 9.16).
13 Thoroughly clean all traces of dust from the shoes, backplates and brake drums using a stiff brush. It is recommended that compressed air is **not** used as it blows up dust which should **not** be inhaled. Brake dust can cause judder or squeal and, therefore, it is important to clean out as described.
14 Check that the pistons are free in the cylinder, that the rubber dust covers are undamaged and in position, and that there are no hydraulic fluid leaks.
15 Prior to reassembly smear a trace of brake grease on the shoe support pads, brake shoe pivots and on the ratchet wheel face and threads.
16 Reassembly of the new shoes is a reversal of the removal and dismantling procedure, but note the following points:

 i) Renew the handbrake lever stop, by withdrawing it from the carrier plate, if it is damaged or stiff to move (Fig. 9.17).
 ii) Check that the handbrake lever is positioned over its stop
 iii) The longer fork of the adjusting strut must be positioned against the rear brake shoe (Fig. 9.18).
 iv) Fit the upper retracting spring to the front shoe, then to the rear shoe retaining bracket (Fig. 9.19). Ensure that the tag on this bracket is located in the cut-out in the shoe
 v) Expand the adjusting strut to remove all slack, and check that the pawl is correctly engaged in the ratchet wheel

17 Once the brake drum has been installed, apply the foot brake several times to adjust the shoes to their minimum drum clearance position.

10 Drum brake cylinder - removal, inspection and overhaul, and refitting

If hydraulic fluid is leaking from the brake wheel cylinder, it will be necessary to dismantle it and replace the seals. Should brake fluid be found running down the side of the wheel, or if it is noticed that a pool of liquid forms alongside one wheel or the level in the master cylinder drops it is also indicative of failed seals.

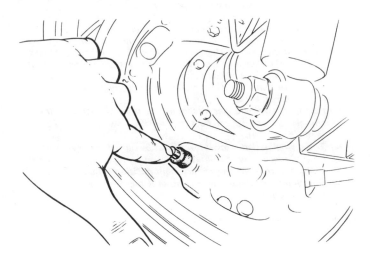

Fig. 9.21. Rear wheel adjustment plunger (Sec. 12)

1 Refer to Section 8 or 9 and remove the brake drum and shoes. Clean down the rear of the backplate using a stiff brush. Place a quantity of rag under the backplate to catch any hydraulic fluid that may issue from the open pipe or wheel cylinder.
2 Wipe the top of the brake master cylinder reservoir and unscrew the cap. Place a piece of polythene sheet over the top of the reservoir and replace the cap. This is to stop hydraulic fluid syphoning out.
3 Using an open ended spanner, carefully unscrew the hydraulic pipe connection union/s to the rear of the wheel cylinder. Note that on the left-hand wheel cylinder two pipes are attached to the wheel cylinder. Note the location of each pipe as these must not be interchanged. To prevent dirt ingress, tape over the pipe ends.
4 Undo and remove the two bolts and washers that secure the wheel cylinder to the brake backplate.
5 Withdraw the wheel cylinder from the front of the brake backplate. Remove the seal on 9 inch (228 mm) brakes (2000 engine).
6 To dismantle the wheel cylinder first ease off each rubber dust cover retaining ring and lift away each rubber dust cover.
7 Carefully lift out each piston together with seal from the wheel cylinder bore. Recover the return springs.
8 Using the fingers only, remove the piston seal from each piston, noting which way round it is fitted (Fig. 9.20). Do not use a metal screwdriver as this could scratch the piston.
9 Inspect the inside of the cylinder for score marks caused by impurities in the hydraulic fluid. If any are found, the cylinder and pistons will require renewal. **Note:** if the wheel cylinder requires renewal always ensure that the replacement is exactly similar to the one removed.
10 If the cylinder is sound, thoroughly clean it out with fresh hydraulic fluid.
11 The old rubber seals will probably be swollen and visibly worn. Smear the new rubber seals with hydraulic fluid and refit to the pistons making sure they are the correct way round with the flap of the seal adjacent to the piston rear shoulder (Fig. 9.20).
12 Wet the cylinder bore with clean hydraulic fluid and insert the return spring. Carefully insert the piston seal end first into the cylinder, making sure that the seals do not roll over as they are initially fitted into the bore.
13 Position the rubber boots on each end of the wheel cylinder and secure in position with the retaining rings.
14 Fit a new ring seal (9 inch (228 mm) brake - 2000 only) onto the rear of the wheel cylinder and position the cylinder in its slot in the backplate. Secure with the two bolts and washers.
15 Reconnect the brake pipe/s to the rear of the wheel cylinder, taking care not to cross thread the union nuts. On the left-hand wheel cylinder make sure the pipes are connected the correct way round as was noted during removal.
16 Refit the brake shoes and drum as described in Section 8 or 9.
17 Refer to Section 2 and bleed the brake hydraulic system.

11 Drum brake backplate - removal and refitting

1   To remove the backplate refer to Chapter 8, Section 5 and remove the axle-shaft (halfshaft).
2   Detach the handbrake cable from the handbrake relay lever.
3   Wipe the top of the brake master cylinder reservoir and unscrew the cap. Place a piece of polythene sheet over the top of the reservoir and replace the cap. This is to stop hydraulic fluid synphoning out.
4   Using an open ended spanner, carefully unscrew the hydraulic pipe connection union/s to the rear of the wheel cylinder. Note that on the left-hand wheel cylinder two pipes are attached to the wheel cylinder. Note the location of each pipe as these must not be interchanged. To prevent dirt ingress tape over the pipe ends.
5   The brake backplate may now be lifted away.
6   Refitting is the reverse sequence to removal. It will be necessary to bleed the brake hydraulic system as described in Section 2.

12 Handbrake - adjustment

1   It is important to check that lack of adjustment is not caused by the cable becoming detached from the body mounted clips, that the equaliser bracket and pivot points are adequately lubricated and that the rear shoe linings have not worn excessively.
2   Chock the front wheels. Jack up the rear of the car and support on firmly based axle stands located under the rear axle. Release the handbrake.
3   Check that there is no free movement at the rear wheel adjustment plungers (Fig. 9.21). If the plungers move, the footbrake should be operated several times until the ratchet is tightened.
4   At the adjusting bracket, on the right-hand side, separate the adjusting nut and sleeve using a screwdriver. Engage the keyed sleeve in the bracket (Fig. 9.22).
5   Now adjust the cable at the right-hand cable to body abutment bracket so as to give a plunger free movement of 0.04 to 0.06 in (1.0 to 1.5 mm) on each brake backplate.
6   Equalise the movement of the plungers by gripping the handbrake at the equaliser bracket and adjusting the position of the cable.
7   Should adjustment of the cable not alter the plunger free movement, it is an indication that the cable is binding or the automatic brake adjuster is not operating correctly - usually due to seizure of the moving parts within the brake unit. It could also be that the adjustment plungers have seized in their locations in the backplate. Further investigation will therefore be necessary.
8   The adjusting nut and keyed sleeve will lock together automatically at the first application of the handbrake.
9   Remove the axle stands and lower the car to the ground.

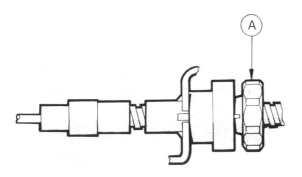

Fig. 9.22. Keyed sleeve engaged in bracket. Adjusting nut (A) (Sec. 12)

13 Handbrake cable - removal and refitting

1   Chock the front wheels, jack up the rear of the car and support on firmly based axle stands located under the rear axle. Release the handbrake. Remove the two rear wheels.
2   From under the vehicle remove the spring clip and withdraw the clevis pin and wave washer from the handbrake lever yoke.
3   Pull back and withdraw the cable from the two floor brackets. Using a pair of pliers withdraw the retaining 'U' shaped clip at the left-hand bracket. Remove the cable from the clips at the radius arms.
4   Remove the brake drums. If they are tight they may be removed using a soft-faced mallet on the outer drum circumference and tapping outwards.
5   Detach the brake cable from each brake unit relay lever and pull the cable through the rear of the backplate.
6   Detach the cable from the equaliser.
7   To refit the cable first feed the cable ends through the rear of the backplate and reconnect to the relay levers. Replace the brake drums.
8   Attach the cable to the underbody brackets and clips on the radius arms. Take care to make sure that the adjuster is correctly located in its bracket (Fig. 9.22).
9   Engage the cable within the groove of the equaliser and then connect the equaliser to the handbrake lever.
10 Refit the rear wheels and referring to Section 12 adjust the handbrake cable.
11 Remove the axle stands and lower the car to the ground.

14 Brake master cylinder - removal and refitting

1   Apply the handbrake and chock the front wheels. Drain the fluid from the master cylinder reservoir and master cylinder by attaching a plastic bleed tube to one of the brake bleed screws. Undo the screw one turn and then pump the fluid out into a clean glass container by means of the brake pedal. Hold the brake pedal against the floor at the end of each stroke and tighten the bleed screw. When the pedal has returned to its normal position loosen the bleed screw and repeat the process until the reservoir is empty.
2   Wipe the area around the two union nuts on the side of the master cylinder body and using an open ended spanner undo the two union nuts. Tape over the ends of the pipes to stop dirt ingress.
3   Undo and remove the two nuts and spring washers that secure the master cylinder to the servo unit. Lift away the master cylinder taking care that no hydraulic fluid is allowed to drip onto the paintwork.
4   Refitting is the reverse sequence to removal. Always start the union nuts before finally tightening the master cylinder nuts. It will be necessary to bleed the hydraulic system: full details will be found in Section 2.

15 Brake master cylinder - dismantling, examination and reassembly

If a replacement master cylinder is to be fitted, it will be necessary to lubricate the seals before fitting to the car as they have a protective coating when originally assembled. Remove the blanking plugs from the hydraulic pipe union seatings. Inject clean hydraulic fluid into the master cylinder and operate the primary piston several times so that the fluid spreads over all the internal working surfaces.
Depress the operating rod to relieve the pressure, and remove the circlip (Fig. 9.23). This is fitted for transportation purposes only.
If the master cylinder is to be dismantled after removal proceed as follows:
1   Remove the reservoir by pulling upwards, and remove the rubber seals.
2   Depress the operating rod to relieve the pressure on the piston stop pin, and remove the pin (Fig. 9.23).
3   Using a compressed air jet, very carefully applied to the rear outlet connection, blow out all the master cylinder internal components. Alternatively, shake out the parts. Take care that adequate precautions are taken to ensure all parts are caught as they emerge.

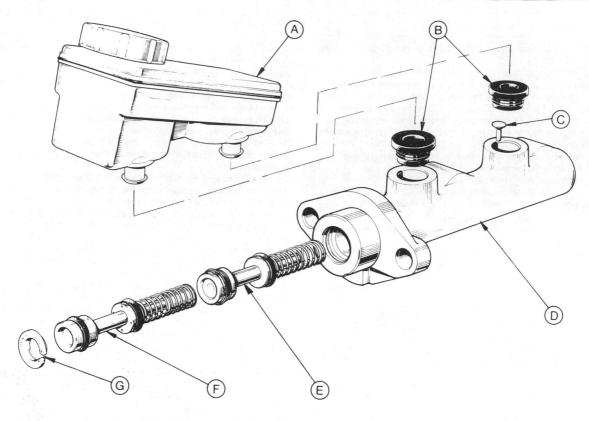

Fig. 9.23. Brake master cylinder (Sec. 15)

A Reservoir
B Reservoir seals

C Piston stop pin
D Master cylinder

E Secondary piston
F Primary piston

G Circlip (used in transportation
   only)

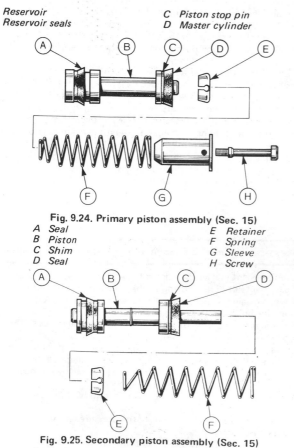

Fig. 9.24. Primary piston assembly (Sec. 15)

A Seal   E Retainer
B Piston   F Spring
C Shim   G Sleeve
D Seal   H Screw

Fig. 9.25. Secondary piston assembly (Sec. 15)

A Seal   D Seal
B Piston   E Retainer
C Shim   F Spring

4 To dismantle the primary piston, unscrew and remove the screw and sleeve. Remove the spring, retainer, seal and shim (Fig. 9.24). Gently lever off the other seal, taking care not to scratch the piston.

5 To dismantle the secondary piston, remove the spring, retainer, seal and shim (Fig. 9.25). Gently lever off the other seal, taking care not to damage the piston.

6 Examine the bore of the cylinder carefully for any signs of scores or ridges. If this is found to be smooth all over new seals can be fitted. If, however, there is any doubt of the condition of the bore, then a new cylinder must be fitted.

7 If examination of the seals shows them to be apparently oversize, or swollen, or very loose on the plungers, suspect oil contamination in the system. Oil will swell these rubber seals, and if one is found to be swollen, it is reasonable to assume that all seals in the braking system will need attention.

8 Thoroughly clean all parts in clean hydraulic fluid or methylated spirits. Ensure that the bypass ports are clear.

9 All components should be assembled wet by dipping in clean brake fluid.

10 Using the fingers only, fit the shim and seals to the secondary piston, ensuring they are the correct way round (Fig. 9.25). Fit the retainer and spring. Check that the master cylinder bore is clean, and smear with clean brake fluid.

11 Wet the secondary piston assembly with clean fluid, and insert into the master cylinder, spring first. Ease the lips of the seals into the cylinder bore taking care they do not roll over.

12 Fit the shim and seals to the primary piston, ensuring they are the correct way round (Fig. 9.24). Fit the retainer, spring, sleeve and screw.

13 Wet the primary piston assembly with clean fluid, and insert into the master cylinder, spring first. Ease the lips of the seals into the cylinder bore taking care they do not roll over.

14 Depress the operating rod and insert the piston stop pin (Fig. 9.23).

15 Check the condition of the front and rear reservoir gaskets and if there is any doubt as to their condition they must be renewed.

16 Replace the hydraulic fluid reservoir.

17 The master cylinder is now ready for refitting to the servo unit. Bleed the complete hydraulic system and road test the car.

Fig. 9.26. Lower dash trim panel screw location (Sec. 16)

16 Brake pedal - removal and refitting

1   Open the bonnet and for safety reasons disconnect the battery.
2   Undo the five screws and remove the lower dash trim panel
(Fig. 9.26).
3   Withdraw the spring clip from the brake servo pushrod to brake
pedal clevis pin. Lift away the clevis pin and the bushes and allow the
pushrod to drop.
4   Detach the brake pedal return spring from the brake pedal bracket.
5   Remove the circlip and float washer and carefully push the shaft
through the bracket and pedal.
6   Lift away the brake pedal. Remove the half bushes from each side
of the brake pedal.
7   Inspect the bushes for signs of wear, and if evident, they must be
renewed. Ensure that the key on each bush engages with the cut-out in
the pedal.
8   Refitting the brake pedal is the reverse sequence to removal.
Lubricate the bushes and shafts with a molybdenum disulphide
grease.
9   Adjust the stop light switch if required, Section 21.

17 Handbrake lever - removal and refitting

If centre console is fitted, refer to Chapter 12 to remove it.

1   Undo and remove the self-tapping screws that secure the handbrake
lever rubber gaiter to the floor. Slide the gaiter up the handbrake lever.
2   Lift away the carpeting from the handbrake area.
3   From under the vehicle remove the spring clip, clevis pin and wave
washer securing the equaliser bracket to the handbrake lever.
4   Undo and remove the two bolts and spring washers that secure
the handbrake lever to the floor. The handbrake lever assembly may
be lifted away from its location on the floor.
5   Refitting is the reverse sequence to removal. Smear the clevis pin
with a little grease. The handbrake lever seal must be installed with
the paint spot uppermost.

18 Vacuum servo unit - description

A vacuum servo unit is fitted into the brake hydraulic circuit in
series with the master cylinder, to provide assistance to the driver when
the brake pedal is depressed. This reduces the effort required by the
driver to operate the brakes under all braking conditions.
The unit operates by vacuum obtained from the induction manifold
and comprises, basically, a booster diaphragm and check valve. The
servo unit and hydraulic master cylinder are connected together so that
the servo unit piston rod acts as the master cylinder pushrod. The
driver's effort is transmitted through another pushrod to the servo
unit piston and its built-in control system. The servo unit piston does
not fit tightly into the cylinder, but has a strong diaphragm to keep
its edges in constant contact with the cylinder wall, so assuring
an air tight seal between the two parts. The forward chamber is held
under vacuum conditions created in the inlet manifold of the engine
and, during periods when the brake pedal is not in use, the controls
open a passage to the rear chamber so placing it under vacuum conditions as well. When the brake pedal is depressed, the vacuum passage
to the rear chamber is cut off and the chamber opened to atmospheric
pressure. The consequent rush of air pushes the servo piston forward
in the vacuum chamber and operates the main pushrod to the master
cylinder.
The controls are designed so that assistance is given under all
conditions and, when the brakes are not required, vacuum in the rear
chamber is established when the brake pedal is released. All air from
the atmosphere entering the rear chamber is passed through a small air
filter.
Under normal operating conditions the vacuum servo unit is
very reliable and does not require overhaul except at very high mileages.
In this case it is far better to obtain a service exchange unit, rather than
repair the original unit.

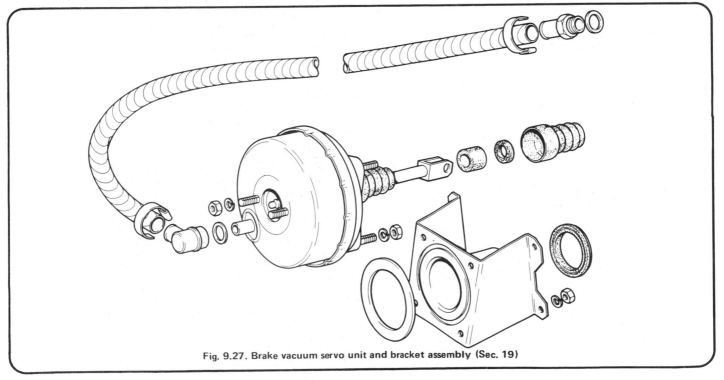

Fig. 9.27. Brake vacuum servo unit and bracket assembly (Sec. 19)

19 Vacuum servo unit - removal and refitting

1   Slacken the clip securing the vacuum hose to the servo unit and carefully draw the hose from its union.
2   Refer to Section 14 and remove the master cylinder.
3   Using a pair of pliers remove the spring clip in the end of the brake pedal to pushrod clevis pin. Lift away the clevis pin and bushes.
4   Undo and remove the nuts and spring washers that secure the servo unit mounting bracket to the bulkhead. Lift away the servo unit and bracket (Fig. 9.27).
5   Undo and remove the four nuts and spring washers that secure the bracket to the servo unit.
6   Refitting the servo unit is the reverse sequence to removal. It will

be necessary to bleed the brake hydraulic system as described in Section 2.

20 Stop light switch - removal and refitting

1   Open the bonnet and, for safety reasons, disconnect the battery.
2   Undo the five screws and remove the lower dash trim panel (Fig. 9.26).
3   Detach the cables from the switch. Undo and remove the locknut, then remove the switch.
4   Refitting the switch is the reverse sequence to removal. The switch should be positioned to operate after 0.2 to 0.6 in (5.0 to 15.0 mm) travel of the brake pedal.

21 Fault diagnosis - braking system

Symptom	Cause	Remedy
Pedal travels almost to floor before brakes operate	Brake fluid level too low	Top up master cylinder reservoir. Check for leaks.
	Caliper leaking	Dismantle caliper, clean, fit new seals and bleed brakes.
	Master cylinder leaking (bubbles in master cylinder fluid)	Dismantle master cylinder, clean and fit new seals. Bleed brakes.
	Brake flexible hose leaking	Examine and fit new hose if old hose leaking. Bleed brakes.
	Brake line fractured	Replace with new brake pipe. Bleed brakes.
	Brake system unions loose	Check all unions in brake system and tighten as necessary. Bleed brakes.
	Pad or shoe linings over 75% worn	Fit replacement pads or shoes.
Brake pedal feels springy	New linings not yet bedded in	Use brakes gently until springy pedal feeling disappears.
	Brake discs or drums badly worn or cracked	Fit new brake discs or drums.
	Master cylinder and/or vacuum servo unit securing nuts loose	Tighten securing nuts, ensure spring washers are fitted.
Brake pedal feels spongy and soggy	Caliper or wheel cylinder leaking	Dismantle caliper or wheel cylinder, clean, fit new seals and bleed brakes.
	Master cylinder leaking (bubbles in master cylinder reservoir)	Dismantle master cylinder, clean and fit new seals and bleed brakes. Renew cylinder if internal walls scored.
	Brake pipe line or flexible hose leaking	Fit new pipeline or hose.
	Unions in brake system loose	Examine for leaks, tighten as necessary.
Excessive effort required to brake car	Pad or shoe linings badly worn	Fit replacement brake shoes and linings.
	New pads or shoes recently fitted - not yet bedded-in	Use brakes gently until braking effort normal.
	Harder linings fitted than standard causing increase in pedal pressure	Remove pads or shoes and replace with normal units.
	Linings and brake drums contaminated with oil, grease or hydraulic fluid	Rectify source of leak, clean brake drums, fit new linings.
	Vacuum servo unit not working	Check vacuum lines and clamps, change check valve.
Brakes uneven and pulling to one side	Linings and discs or drums contaminated with oil, grease or hydraulic fluid	Ascertain and rectify source of leak, clean discs or drums, fit new pads or shoes.
	Tyre pressures unequal	Check and inflate as necessary.
	Radial ply tyres fitted at one end of the car only	Fit radial ply tyres of the same make to all four wheels.
	Brake caliper loose	Tighten backplate securing nuts and bolts.
	Brake pads or shoes fitted incorrectly	Remove and fit correct way round.
	Different type of linings fitted at each wheel	Fit the pads or shoes specified by the manufacturer all round.
	Anchorages for front suspension or rear suspension loose	Tighten front and rear suspension pick-up points.
	Brake discs or drums badly worn, cracked or distorted	Fit new brake discs or drums.

Chapter 10 Electrical system

For modifications, and information applicable to later models, see Supplement at end of manual

Contents

Specifications

Battery

Type	Lead acid 12 volt, negative (−) earth

	1600	**2000**
Capacity		
Manual transmission	38 amp hour	44 amp hour
Automatic transmission	55 amp hour	55 amp hour
Specific gravity (charged)	1.27 to 1.29 at a temperature of 25°C (77°F)	
	(Refer to Section 3)	

The above mentioned batteries are fitted as standard. Higher capacity batteries can be fitted as an option in most instances - consult your Ford dealer.

Starter motor

Inertia	Lucas M35J
Pre-engaged:	
Standard	Lucas M35J
Heavy duty	Lucas 5M90
Number of brushes	4
Brush material	Carbon
Minimum brush length	0.32 in (8 mm)
Brush spring pressure	28 oz (800 gm)
Minimum commutator thickness (face mounted type)	0.08 in (2.05 mm)
Armature endfloat*	0.01 in (0.25 mm)
Type of drive*	Solenoid
Direction of rotation	Clockwise
Maximum current draw	365 amps
Voltage	12

* Not applicable to inertia motor

Alternator
Output

	Wattage	Fitting

Bosch G1-28A and Lucas 15ACR ... ...   28 amps
Bosch K1-35A and Lucas 17ACR ... ...   35 amps
Bosch K1-45A and Lucas 18ACR ... ...   45 amps
Femsa ... ...   32 amps
Maximum continuous speed ... ...   15,000 rev/min
Speed ratio to engine ... ...   1 : 1.9
Minimum brush length:
     Bosch and Lucas ... ...   0.2 in (5 mm)
     Femsa ... ...   0.3 in (7 mm)
Regulating voltage:(4,000 rev/min):
     Bosch and Femsa ... ...   13.7 to 14.5 volts
     Lucas ... ...   14.2 to 14.6 volts

Bulbs

Type	Wattage	Fitting
Headlamps (tungsten) (base model)	40/45	Clip
Headlamps (halogen)	55/60	Clip
Driving lamps	55	Clip
Sidelights	4	Bayonet
Direction indicators	21	Bayonet
Rear lights	5	Bayonet
Stop lights	21	Bayonet
Number plate lamps	4	Bayonet
Reverse lamps	21	Bayonet
Instrument warning lamps/switches	1.3	Glass socket
Instrument illumination	2.6	Glass socket
Automatic selector illumination	1.4	Bayonet
Cigarette lighter illumination	1.4	Bayonet
Interior light(s)	5	Bayonet

1 General description

The electrical system is of the 12 volt negative earth type and the major components comprise a 12 volt battery of which the negative terminal is earthed, an alternator which is driven from the crankshaft pulley, and a starter motor.

The battery supplies a steady amount of current for the ignition, lighting and other electrical circuits and provides a reserve of electricity when the current consumed by the electrical equipment exceeds that being produced by the alternator.

The alternator has its own regulator which ensures a high output if the battery is in a low state of charge or the demand from the electrical equipment is high, and a low output if the battery is fully charged and there is little demand for the electrical equipment.

When fitting electrical accessories to cars with a negative earth system it is important, if they contain silicone diodes or transistors, that they are connected correctly, otherwise serious damage may result to the components concerned. Items such as radios, tape players, electronic ignition systems, electronic tachometer, automatic dipping etc, should all be checked for correct polarity.

It is important that the battery is disconnected before removing the alternator output lead as this is live at all times. Also if body repairs are to be carried out using electric arc welding equipment - the alternator must be disconnected otherwise serious damage can be caused to the more delicate instruments. Do **not** disconnect the battery with the engine running. If 'jumper cables' are used to start the car, they **must** be connected correctly - positive to positive and negative to negative.

2 Battery - removal and refitting

1   The battery is on a carrier fitted to the left-hand wing valance of the engine compartment. It should be removed once every three months for cleaning and testing. Disconnect the negative and then the positive leads from the battery terminals by undoing and removing the plated nuts and bolts (photo). Note that two cables are attached to the positive terminal.

2   Unscrew and remove the bolt, and plain washer that secures the battery clamp plate to the carrier. Lift away the clamp plate. Carefully lift the battery from its carrier and hold it vertically to ensure that none of the electrolyte is spilled.

3   Replacement is a direct reversal of this procedure. **Note: Replace the positive lead before the negative lead and smear the terminals with petroleum jelly to prevent corrosion. Never use an ordinary grease.**

3 Battery - maintenance and inspection

1   Normal weekly battery maintenance consists of checking the electrolyte level of each cell to ensure that the separators are covered by ¼ inch (6 mm) of electrolyte. If the level has fallen, top-up the battery using distilled water only. Do not overfill. If a battery is overfilled or any electrolyte spilled, immediately wipe away the excess as

2.1 Battery cable connections

electrolyte attacks and corrodes any metal it comes into contact with very rapidly.

2   If the battery has the 'Auto-fill' device as fitted on original production of the car, a special topping-up sequence is required. The white balls in the Auto-fill battery are part of the automatic topping-up device which ensures correct electrolyte level. The vent chamber should remain in position at all times except when topping-up or taking specific gravity readings. If the electrolyte level in any of the cells is below the bottom of the filling tube top-up as follows:

a) *Lift off the vent chamber cover.*
b) *With the battery level, pour distilled water into the trough until all the filling tubes and trough are full.*
c) *Immediately replace the cover to allow the water in the trough and tubes to flow into the cells. Each cell will automatically receive the correct amount of water.*

3   As well as keeping the terminals clean and covered with petroleum jelly, the top of the battery, and especially the top of the cells, should be kept clean and dry. This helps prevent corrosion and ensures that the battery does not become partially discharged by leakage through dampness and dirt.

4   Once every three months remove the battery and inspect the battery securing bolts, the battery clamp plate, tray and battery leads for corrosion (white fluffy deposits on the metal which are brittle to touch). If any corrosion is found clean off the deposit with ammonia and paint over the clean metal with an anti-rust/anti-acid paint.

5   At the same time inspect the battery case for cracks. If a crack is found, clean and plug it with one of the proprietary compounds marketed by such firms as Holts for this purpose. If leakage through the crack has been excessive, then it will be necessary to refill the appropriate cell with fresh electrolyte as detailed later. Cracks are frequently caused to the top of the battery case by pouring in distilled water in the middle of winter *after* instead of *before* a run. This gives the water no chance to mix with the electrolyte and so the former freezes and splits the battery case.

6   If topping-up the battery becomes excessive and the case has been inspected for cracks that could cause leakage, but none are found, the battery is being overcharged.

7   With the battery on the bench at the three monthly interval check, measure the specific gravity with a hydrometer to determine the state of charge and condition of the electrolyte. There should be very little variation between the different cells and, if a variation in excess of 0.025 is present it will be due to either:

a) *Loss of electrolyte from the battery at some time caused by spillage or a leak, resulting in a drop in the specific gravity of the electrolyte when the deficiency was replaced with distilled water instead of fresh electrolyte.*
b) *An internal short circuit caused by buckling of the plates or similar malady pointing to the likelihood of total battery failure in the near future.*

8   The specific gravity of the electrolyte for fully charged conditions, at the electrolyte temperature indicated, is listed in Table A. The specific gravity of a fully discharged battery at different temperatures of the electrolyte is given in Table B.

Table A - Specific gravity - battery fully charged

1.268 at 100°F or 38°C electrolyte temperature
1.272 at 90°F or 32°C electrolyte temperature
1.276 at 80°F or 27°C electrolyte temperature
1.280 at 70°F or 21°C electrolyte temperature
1.284 at 60°F or 16°C electrolyte temperature
1.288 at 50°F or 10°C electrolyte temperature
1.292 at 40°F or 4°C electrolyte temperature
1.296 at 30°F or -1.5°C electrolyte temperature

Table B - Specific gravity - battery fully discharged

1.098 at 100°F or 38°C electrolyte temperature
1.102 at 90°F or 32°C electrolyte temperature
1.106 at 80°F or 27°C electrolyte temperature
1.110 at 70°F or 21°C electrolyte temperature
1.114 at 60°F or 16°C electrolyte temperature

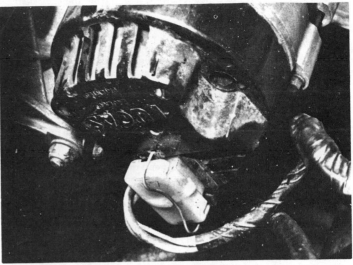

6 Alternator connector plug (Lucas alternator)

1.118 at 50°F or 10°C electrolyte temperature
1.122 at 40°F or 4°C electrolyte temperature
1.126 at 30°F or -1.5°C electrolyte temperature

4   Battery - electrolyte replenishment

1   If the battery is in a fully charged state and one of the cells maintains a specific gravity reading which is 0.025 or more lower than the others, then it is likely that electrolyte has been lost from the cell at some time.

2   Top-up the cell with a solution of 1 part sulphuric acid to 2.5 parts of water. If the cell is already fully topped-up draw some electrolyte out of it with a pipette.

5   Battery - charging

1   In winter time when heavy demand is placed upon the battery, such as when starting from cold and much electrical equipment is continually in use, it is a good idea to occasionally have the battery fully charged from an external source at the rate of 3.5 to 4 amps.

2   Continue to charge the battery at this rate until no further rise in specific gravity is noted over a four hour period.

3   Alternatively, a trickle charger charging at the rate of 1.5 amps can be safely used overnight.

4   Specially rapid 'boost' charges which are claimed to restore the power of the battery in 1 to 2 hours are not recommended as they can cause serious damage to the battery plates through overheating.

5   While charging the battery note that the temperature of the electrolyte should never exceed 100°F (37.8°C).

6   Alternator - general description

The main advantage of an alternator lies in its ability to provide a high charge at low revolutions. Driving slowly in heavy traffic with a dynamo invariably means no charge is reaching the battery. In similar conditions even with the wiper, heater, lights and perhaps radio switched on the alternator will ensure a charge reaches the battery.

The three makes of alternator generate alternating current (ac) which is changed to a direct current (dc) by an internal diode system. They all have a regulator which limits the output to 14 volts maximum at all times. The regulator is mounted internally for Bosch and Lucas, and mounted on the inner wing for Femsa alternators. A warning lamp illuminates if the alternator fails to operate.

The alternator assembly basically consists of a fixed coil winding (stator) in an aluminium housing, which incorporates the mounting lugs. Inside this stator, rotates a shaft wound coil (stator). The shaft is supported at each end by ball race bearings which are lubricated for life.

Slip rings are used to conduct current to and from the rotor field coils via two carbon brushes which bear against them. By keeping the mean diameter of the slip rings to a minimum relative speed between brushes and rings, and hence wear, are also minimal.

The rotor is belt driven from the engine through a pulley keyed to the rotor shaft. A pressed steel fan adjacent to the pulley draws cooling air through the machine. This fan forms an integral part of the alternator specification. It has been designed to provide adequate air flow with a minimum of noise, and to withstand the high stresses associated with the maximum speed. Rotation is clockwise viewed on the drive end.

The brush gear is housed in a moulding, screwed to the outside of the slip ring and bracket. This moulding thus encloses the slip ring and brush gear assembly, and together with the shielded bearing, protects the assembly against the entry of dust and moisture.

The regulator is set during manufacture and requires no further attention.

Electrical connections to external circuits are brought out to Lucas connector blades, these being grouped to accept a moulded connector socket which ensures correct connection (photo). Detail design differences are shown in Fig. 10.1, 10.2 and 10.3.

7 Alternator - routine maintenance

1 The equipment has been designed for the minimum amount of maintenance in service, the only items subject to wear being the brushes and bearings.
2 Brushes should be examined after about 75,000 miles (120,000 km) and renewed if necessary. The bearings are pre-packed with grease for life, and should not require further attention.
3 Check the fan belt every 3,000 miles (5,000 km) for correct adjustment which should be 0.5 inch (13 mm) total movement at the centre of the run between the alternator and water pump pulleys.

8 Alternator - special procedures

Whenever the electrical system of the car is being attended to or external means of starting the engine are used, there are certain precautions that must be taken otherwise serious and expensive damage can result.
1 Always make sure that the negative terminal of the battery is earthed. If the terminal connections are accidentally reversed or if the battery has been reverse charged the alternator diodes will burn out.
2 The output terminal on the alternator marked 'BAT' or B+ must never be earthed but should always be connected directly to the positive terminal of the battery.
3 Whenever the alternator is to be removed or when disconnecting the terminals of the alternator circuit always disconnect the battery earth terminal first.
4 The alternator must never be operated without the battery to alternator cable connected.
5 Should it be necessary to use a booster charger or booster battery to start the engine always double check that the negative cable is connected to negative terminal and the positive cable to positive terminal.

9 Alternator - removal and refitting

1 Disconnect the battery leads.
2 Note the terminal connections at the rear of the alternator and disconnect the plug or multi pin connector.
3 Undo and remove the alternator adjustment arm bolt, slacken the alternator mounting bolts and push the alternator inwards towards the engine. Lift away the fan belt from the pulley.
4 Remove the remaining two mounting bolts and carefully lift the alternator away from the car.
5 Take care not to knock or drop the alternator otherwise this can cause irreparable damage.

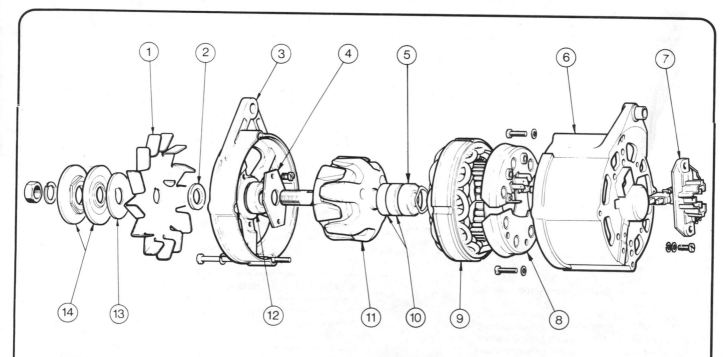

Fig. 10.1. Bosch alternator (Sec. 6 and 11)

1 Fan
2 Spacer
3 Drive end housing
4 Thrust plate
5 Slip ring end bearing
6 Slip ring end housing
7 Brush box and regulator
8 Rectifier (diode) pack
9 Stator
10 Slip rings
11 Rotor
12 Drive end bearing
13 Spacer
14 Pulley

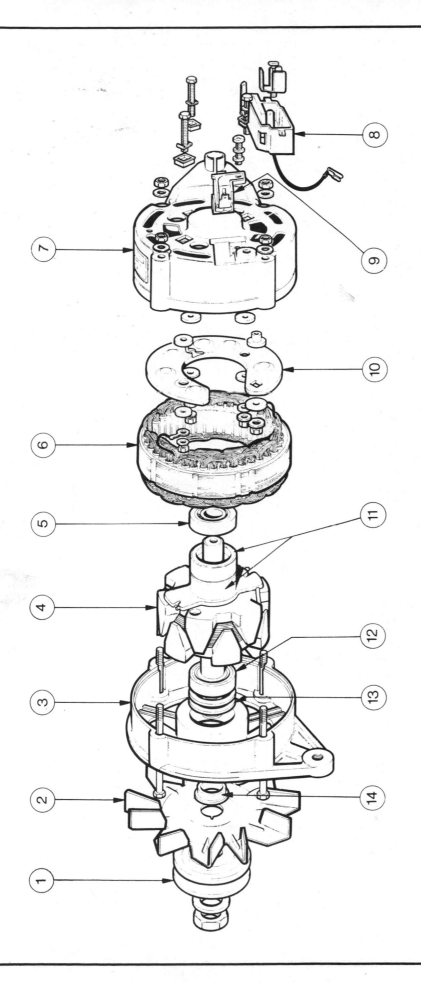

Fig. 10.2. Femsa alternator (Sec. 6 and 12)

1 Pulley
2 Fan
3 Drive end housing
4 Rotor
5 Slip ring end bearing

6 Stator
7 Slip ring end housing
8 Terminal block
9 Brush box
10 Rectifier (diode) pack

11 Slip rings
12 Drive end bearing
13 Thrust washer
14 Spacer

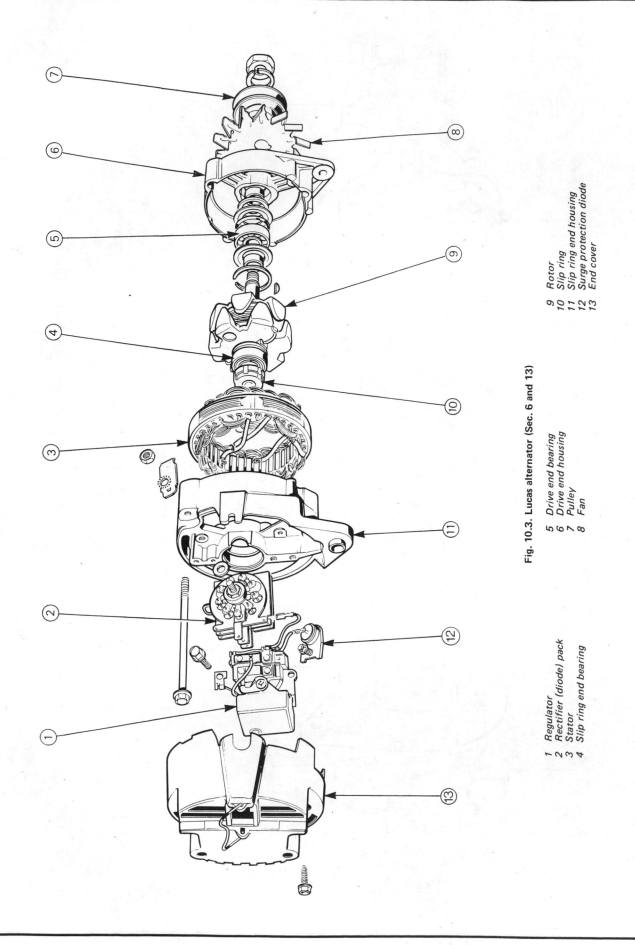

Fig. 10.3. Lucas alternator (Sec. 6 and 13)

1 Regulator
2 Rectifier (diode) pack
3 Stator
4 Slip ring end bearing

5 Drive end bearing
6 Drive end housing
7 Pulley
8 Fan

9 Rotor
10 Slip ring
11 Slip ring end housing
12 Surge protection diode
13 End cover

6   Refitting the alternator is the reverse sequence to removal. Adjust the fan belt so that it has 0.5 inch (13 mm) total movement at the centre of the run between the alternator and water pump pulleys.

10 Alternator - fault finding and repair

Due to the specialist knowledge and equipment required to test or service an alternator it is recommended that if the performance is suspect, the car be taken to an automobile electrician who will have the facilities for such work. Because of this recommendation, information is limited to the inspection and renewal of the brushes. Should the alternator not charge or the system be suspect the following points may be checked before seeking further assistance:
1   Check the fan belt tension, as described in Section 7.
2   Check the battery, as described in Section 3.
3   Check all electrical cable connections for cleanliness and security.

11 Alternator brushes (Bosch) - inspection, removal and refitting

1   Undo and remove the two screws, spring and plain washers that secure the brush box to the rear of the brush end housing (see Fig. 10.1). Lift away the brush box.
2   Check that the carbon brushes are able to slide smoothly in their guides without any sign of binding.
3   Measure the length of the brushes and if they have worn down to 0.2 inch (5 mm) or less, they must be renewed.
4   Hold the brush wire with a pair of engineer's pliers and unsolder it from the brush box. Lift away the two brushes.
5   Insert the new brushes (Fig. 10.4), and check to make sure that they are free to move in their guides. If they bind, lightly polish with a very fine file.
6   Solder the brush wire ends to the brush box taking care that solder is allowed to pass to the stranded wire.
7   Whenever new brushes are fitted new springs should be fitted.
8   Refitting the brush box is the reverse sequence to removal.

12 Alternator brushes (Femsa) - inspection, removal and refitting

1   Disconnect the wire from the brush box at the rear of the alternator, remove the retaining screw and withdraw the brush box (Fig. 10.2).
2   Measure the length of the brushes and if they have worn down to 0.3 in (7 mm) or less, they must be renewed.
3   Insert the new brushes (Fig. 10.5) and check to make sure that they are free to move in their guides. If they bind, lightly polish with a very fine file.
4   Refitting the brush box is the reverse sequence to removal.

13 Alternator brushes (Lucas) - inspection, removal and refitting

1   Refer to Fig. 10.3 and undo and remove the two screws that hold on the end cover. Lift away the end cover.
2   Remove the brush retaining screws (Fig. 10.6) and withdraw the brushes from the brush box.
3   Measure the length of the brushes and if they have worn down to 0.2 in (5 mm) or less, they must be renewed.
4   Insert the new brushes and check to make sure that they are free to move in their guides. If they bind, lightly polish with a very fine file.
5   Reassemble in the reverse order of dismantling. Make sure that leads which may have been connected to any of the screws are reconnected correctly.

14 Starter motor - general description

The starter motors fitted are of Lucas manufacture, and of either the inertial or pre-engaged type.
Both types are series wound, four pole, four brush motors. The bushgear is fully insulated, and comprises wedge shaped brushes actuated by coil springs onto the commutator face. The main casing has two independently fixed end plates. The commutator end plate screws into the main body, while the drive end plate screws into the pole pieces. Access to the brushes is by removing the commutator end plate. The drive pinion fitted to the inertia motor runs on a screwed sleeve with an internal spline (Fig. 10.8). This sleeve, the pinion and the cushion spring are retained on the shaft by a 'C' clip. The pre-engaged type of motor is fitted with a pre-engagement solenoid (Fig. 10.9).

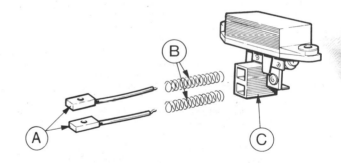

Fig. 10.4. Bosch brushes (A), springs (B) and brush box (C) (Sec. 11)

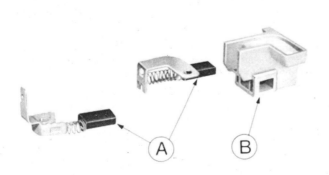

Fig. 10.5. Femsa brushes and springs (A) and brush box (B) (Sec. 12)

Fig. 10.6. Lucas brush retaining screws (Sec. 13)

Incorporated in the pinion assembly is a roller clutch which is able to transmit torque from the starter motor to the engine but not in the reverse direction thereby ensuring that the armature is not driven by the engine at any time.

The solenoid comprises a soft iron plunger, starter switch contacts, main closing winding (series winding) and a hold on (short winding). When the starter ignition switch is operated both the coils are energised in parallel but the closing winding is shorted out by the starter switch contacts when they are closed.

The operating position of the engaging lever in the drive end bracket is pre-set and cannot be altered. This eliminates the adjustment of setting the pinion position to obtain the correct operation of the actuating solenoid. The lever pivots on a non-adjustable pivot pin which is retained in the drive end bracket by a special type of retaining ring which is a spring fit into a groove in the pin.

15 Starter motor - testing on engine

1   If the starter motor fails to operate, then check the condition of the battery by turning on the headlamps. If they glow brightly for several seconds and then gradually dim, the battery is in an uncharged condition.

2   If the headlights continue to glow brightly and it is obvious that the battery is in good condition, then check the tightness of the battery wiring connections (and in particular the earth lead from the battery terminal to its connection on the body frame). If the positive terminal on the battery becomes hot when an attempt is made to work the starter this is a sure sign of a poor connection on the battery terminal. To rectify remove the terminal, clean the mating faces thoroughly and reconnect. Check the connections on the rear of the starter solenoid. Check the wiring with a voltmeter or test lamp for breaks or shorts.

3   *On pre-engaged type starter motors,* test the continuity of the solenoid windings by connecting a test lamp circuit comprising a 12 volt battery and low wattage bulb between the 'STA' terminal and the solenoid body. If the two windings are in order the lamp will light. Next connect the test lamp (fitted with a high wattage bulb) between the solenoid main terminals. Energise the solenoid by applying a 12 volt supply between the unmarked 'Lucar' terminal and the solenoid body. The solenoid should be heard to operate and the test bulb light. This indicates full closure of the solenoid contacts.

4   *On inertia type starter motors,* check the solenoid by bridging the large solenoid terminals with a heavy cable. If the starter motor then operates, the solenoid is at fault.

5   If the battery is fully charged, the wiring in order, and the starter/ ignition switch working and the starter motor still fails to operate, then it will have to be removed from the car for examination. Before this is done, ensure that the starter motor pinion has not jammed in mesh with the flywheel by engaging a gear (not automatic) and rocking the car to-and-fro. This should free the pinion if it is stuck in mesh with the flywheel teeth.

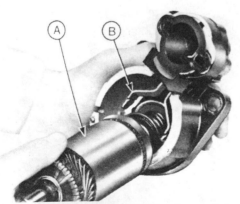

Fig. 10.7. Unhooking the pre-engaged actuating arm (B), armature (A) (Sec. 17)

16 Starter motor - removal and refitting

1   Disconnect the positive and negative terminals from the battery.
2   Make a note of the cable connections to the rear of the solenoid and detach the cable terminals from the solenoid. **Note:** *On inertia starter motors there is only one cable to remove from the motor.*
3   Undo and remove the starter motor securing nuts, bolts and spring washers and lift away the starter motor.
4   Refitting is the reverse sequence to removal.

17 Starter motor (pre-engaged) - dismantling and reassembly

1   Clamp the starter motor in a vice with soft jaws and remove the plastic cap from the commutator end plate.
2   Remove the retaining clip from the end of the armature shaft and discard the clip. Remove the thrust washer.
3   Disconnect and remove the connecting cable from the end of the solenoid. Remove the two securing nuts and washers and guide the solenoid away from the drive end housing. Unhook the solenoid armature from the actuating lever by moving it upwards and away from the lever (Fig. 10.9).
4   Remove the two drive end housing screws and guide the housing and armature assembly away from the body.
5   Remove the armature from the end housing, unhooking the actuating arm from the pinion assembly (Fig. 10.7). Remove the rubber block and sleeve from the housing.
6   Drive the pivot pin from the end housing, and remove the actuating lever. Discard the pivot pin clip, which will be distorted.
7   If it is necessary to dismantle the starter pinion drive, place the armature between soft faces in a bench vice and using a universal puller draw the jump ring from the armature.
8   Tap down the circlip retaining cover and remove the washer, circlip and cover. The pinion assembly may now be removed.
9   Draw the actuating bush towards the pinion so as to expose the circlip and remove the circlip, bush, spring and large washer. It is very important that the one way clutch is not gripped in the vice at the point adjacent to the pinion whilst this is being carried out otherwise the clutch will be damaged.
10 The drive pinion and one way clutch are serviced as a complete assembly so if one part is worn or damaged a new assembly must be obtained.
11 Remove the four commutator end plate screws and carefully tap the plate free from the body. Withdraw the plate slightly, remove the two field winding brushes and remove the plate.
12 To renew the field winding brushes, their flexible connectors must be cut leaving 0.25 in (7 mm) attached to the field coils. Discard the old brushes. Solder new brushes to the flexible connector stubs. Check that the new brushes move freely in their holders.
13 The main terminal stud and its two brushes are available as a unit. To remove, take off the nut, washer and insulator and push the stud and second insulator through the end plate.
14 If cleaning the commutator with petrol fails to remove all the burnt areas and spots, then wrap a piece of glass paper round the commutator and rotate the armature.
15 If the commutator is very badly worn, remove the drive gear, (if still in place on the armature), and mount the armature in a lathe. With the lathe turning at high speed take a very fine cut-out of the commutator and finish the surface by polishing with glass paper. **Do not undercut the mica insulators between the commutator segments. The minimum commutator thickness must never be less than 0.08 in (2 mm).**
16 With the starter motor dismantled, test the four field coils for an open circuit. Connect a 12 volt battery with a 12 volt bulb in one of the leads between the field terminal post and the tapping point of the field coils to which the brushes are connected. An open circuit is proved by the bulb not lighting.
17 If the bulb lights, it does not necessarily mean that the field coils are in order, as there is a possibility that one of the coils will be earthed to the starter yoke or pole shoes. To check this, remove the lead from the brush connector and place it against a clean portion of the starter yoke. If the bulb lights, then the field coils are earthing. Replacement of the field coils calls for the use of a wheel operated screwdriver, a soldering iron, caulking and riveting operations and is beyond the scope of the majority of owners. The starter yoke should

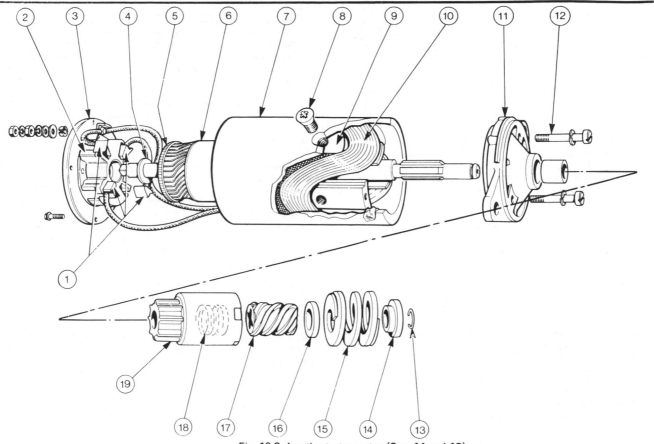

Fig. 10.8. Inertia starter motor (Sec. 14 and 18)

1	Brushes	8	Pole piece retaining screw	15	Cushion spring
2	Brushbox moulding	9	Pole piece	16	Cushion washer
3	Commutator end plate	10	Field winding	17	Screwed sleeve
4	Thrust washer	11	Drive end plate	18	Anti-drift spring
5	Commutator	12	Drive end plate retaining screws	19	Drive pinion
6	Armature	13	'C' clip		
7	Main casing	14	Spring cup		

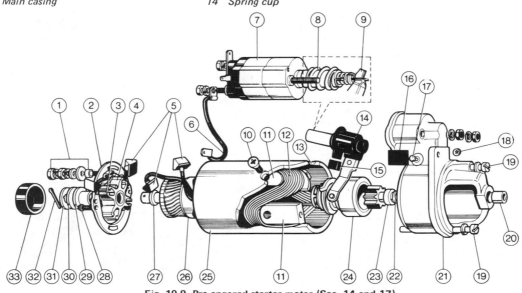

Fig. 10.9. Pre-engaged starter motor (Sec. 14 and 17)

1	Terminal nuts and washers	10	Pole screw	19	Housing retaining screws (2)	27	Thrust washer
2	Commutator end plate	11	Pole shoe	20	Bearing bush	28	Commutator end plate retaining screws (2)
3	Brush housing	12	Field coils	21	Drive end housing	29	Bearing bush
4	Brush springs	13	Field to earth connection	22	Jump ring	30	Thrust plate
5	Brushes	14	Rubber seal	23	Thrust collar	31	Shim washer
6	Connector link, solenoid to starter	15	Rubber dust pad	24	Drive assembly	32	Cotter pin
7	Solenoid unit	16	Rubber dust cover	25	Main casing	33	Dust cover
8	Return spring	17	Pivot pin	26	Armature		
9	Actuating lever	18	Retaining clip				

be taken to a reputable electrical engineering works for new field coils to be fitted. Alternatively purchase an exchange starter motor.

18 If the armature is damaged this will be evident after visual inspection. Look for signs of burning, discolouration, and for conductors that have lifted away from the commutator.

19 With the starter motor stripped down, check the condition of the bushes. They should be renewed when they are sufficiently worn to allow visible side movement of the armature shaft.

20 The old bushes are simply driven out with a suitable drift and the new bushes inserted by the same method. As the bushes are of the phosphor bronze type it is essential that they are allowed to stand in engine oil for at least 24 hours before fitment. If time does not allow, place the bushes in oil at 100°C (212°F) for 2 hours.

21 Reassembly is the reverse sequence to dismantling, but the following points should be noted:

a) *When refitting the drive end housing, the peg on the housing should align with the notch in the casing.*

b) **New** *retaining clips should be fitted to the actuating arm pivot pin and the armature shaft.*

c) *When fitting the clip to the armature shaft end it should be pressed home firmly to eliminate any endfloat in the shaft.*

18 Starter motor (inertia) - dismantling and reassembly

1 The procedure is basically similar to that for the pre-engaged starter motor, Section 17, with the following differences.

2 There is no retaining clip at the commutator end of the armature shaft.

3 The armature, drive end plate and pinion are removed as an assembly after removing the two retaining screws (Fig. 10.8).

4 Remove the drive pinion by compressing the large cushion spring and removing the 'C' clip. (A small proprietary tool is available for this purpose). Remove the spring and drive pinion, then pull the drive end plate from the armature shaft.

19 Flasher circuit - fault tracing and rectification

1 The actual flasher unit consists of a small container positioned at the rear of the instrument panel.

2 If the flasher unit works twice as fast as usual when indicating either right or left turns, this is an indication that there is a broken filament in the front or rear indicator bulb on the side operating too quickly.

3 If the external flashers are working, but the internal flasher warning light has ceased to function, check the filament of the warning bulb and replace as necessary.

4 With the aid of the wiring diagram, check all the flasher circuit connections, if a flasher bulb is sound but does not work.

5 With the ignition switched on, check that the current is reaching the flasher unit by connecting a voltmeter between the 'plug' terminal and earth. If it is found that current is reaching the unit, connect the two flasher unit terminals together and operate the direction indicator switch. If one of the flasher warning lights comes on this proves that the flasher unit itself is at fault and must be replaced as it is not possible to dismantle and repair it.

20 Wiper mechanism - maintenance

1 Renew the screen wiper blades at intervals of 12,000 miles (20,000 km) or 12 months, or more frequently if found necessary.

2 The washer round the wheelbox spindle can be lubricated with several drops of glycerine every 6,000 miles (10,000 km). The screen wiper linkage pivots may be lubricated with a little engine oil.

21 Wiper blades - removal and refitting

1 Lift the wiper arm away from the screen and turn the blade to 90° from the wiper arm.

2 Depress the spring clip, slide the blade down the arm to clear the hook, then slide the blade up the arm and clear of the hook (Fig. 10.10).

3 Replacement is a reversal of this procedure.

22 Wiper arms - removal and refitting

1 Before removing a wiper arm, turn the wiper switch on and off to ensure the arms are in their normal parked position.

2 Unclip the plastic cap from the base of the wiper arm, unscrew the securing nut and remove the washer and wiper arm (Fig. 10.11).

3 With the linkage in the parked position, fit the wiper arm in the correct position, and secure it with the washer and nut. Refit the plastic cap.

23 Wiper mechanism - fault diagnosis and rectification

1 Should the wipers fail, or work very slowly, then check the terminals on the motor for loose connections and make sure the insulation of all wiring has not been damaged, thus causing a short circuit. If this is in order, then check the current the motor is taking by connecting an ammeter in the circuit and turning on the wiper switch. Consumption should be between 2.3 and 3.1 amps.

2 If no current is passing through the motor, check that the switch is operating correctly.

3 If the wiper motor takes a very high current, check the wiper blades for freedom of movement. If this is satisfactory, check the gearbox cover and gear assembly for damage.

4 If the motor takes a very low current ensure that the battery is fully charged. Check the brush gear and ensure the brushes are bearing on the commutator. If not, check the brushes for freedom of movement and, if necessary, renew the tension springs. If the brushes are very worn, they should be replaced with new ones. Check the armature by substitution if this part is suspect.

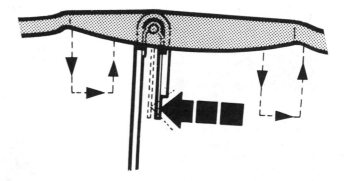

Fig. 10.10. Removing the wiper blade (Sec. 21)

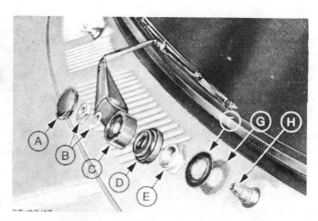

Fig. 10.11. Wiper arm and spindle retaining nuts (Sec. 22 and 24)

A Plastic cap	E Spindle nut
B Nut and washer	F Base washer
C Wiper arm	G Nylon washer
D Spindle nut cover	H Spindle

24.1 Windscreen wiper motor, cover removed

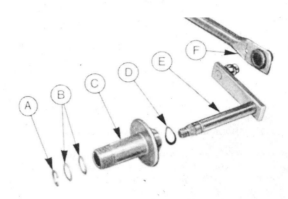

Fig. 10.12. Front wiper spindle components (Sec. 24)

A Circlip   D Wave washer
B Shim and washer   E Pivot shaft
C Bush and housing   F Linkage

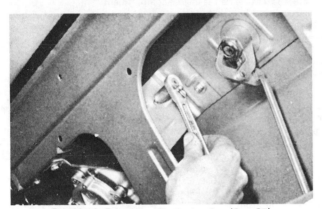

Fig. 10.13. Rear wiper motor bracket (Sec. 25)

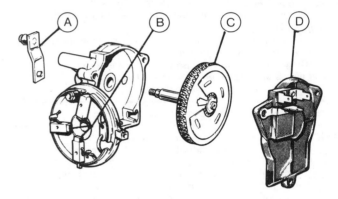

Fig. 10.14. Wiper motor operating arm (A), brushes (B), gear (C) and cover plate (D) (Sec. 26)

24 Wiper motor and linkage (front) - removal and refitting

1   For safety reasons disconnect the battery. Undo and remove the fixing screw and unclip the plastic wiper motor cover. Lift away the cover (photo).
2   Remove the five bolts and lift the wiper linkage cover plate clear. Note that one of these bolts secures the motor earth lead.
3   Undo and remove the bolts that secure the wiper assembly mounting bracket to the scuttle panel; detach the multi-pin plugs from the motor.
4   Carefully lever off the wiper system linkage from the windscreen wiper motor. Undo and remove the three bolts and spring washers that secure the motor to the bracket assembly.
5   Undo and remove the bolts that secure the heater unit and draw the heater unit box to one side just sufficiently for the wiper motor and bracket assembly to be withdrawn.
6   Refer to Section 22 and remove the wiper arms and blades.
7   Carefully unscrew the spindle nuts and washers (Fig. 10.11) and working within the engine compartment lift away the wiper linkage (Fig. 10.12).
8   Refitting is the reverse sequence to removal. Lubricate all moving parts with the exception of the wiper spindles with engine oil. Lubricate the wiper spindles with three drops of glycerine.

25 Wiper motor and linkage (rear) - removal and refitting

1   For safety reasons disconnect the battery. Refer to Section 22, and remove the wiper arm and blade.
2   Lift off the spindle nut cover and remove the spindle nut, washer and seal.

3   Carefully remove the tailgate inner trim panel, and remove the three bolts securing the mounting bracket (Fig. 10.13).
4   Remove the earth lead securing screw, disconnect the multi plug and remove the motor and linkage assembly.
5   Prise the linkage from the motor link, remove the three bolts and detach the wiper motor.
6   Refitting is the reverse sequence to removal.

26 Wiper motor - dismantling, inspection and reassembly

1   Refer to Fig. 10.14 and undo and remove the two crosshead screws that secure the gearbox cover plate to the gearbox.
2   Undo and remove the nut that secures the operating arm to the gear shaft. Lift away the operating arm, wave and plain washers. Note the position of the arm relative to the 'park' cut-out segment of the gear contact plate.
3   Release the spring clips that secure the case and armature to the gearbox. Lift away the case and armature.
4   Wipe away all the grease from inside the gearbox and using a pair of circlip pliers remove the circlip that secures the gear to the shaft. Separate the gear from the shaft.
5   Undo and remove the screw that secures the brush mounting plate, detach the wiring loom plug and remove the brushes.
6   Clean all parts and then inspect the gears and brushes for wear or damage. Lift away the spindle and check for wear in its bush in the gearbox body. Obtain new parts as necessary.
7   Reassembly is the reverse sequence to dismantling. Pack the gearbox with grease.

27 Horn - fault tracing and rectification

1   If the horn works badly or fails completely, first check the wiring
leading to the horn for short circuits and loose connections. Also
check that the horn is firmly secured and that there is nothing lying
on the horn body.
2   Using a test lamp check the wiring to the number 1 fuse on the
fuse box located in the engine compartment. Check that the fuse has
not blown.
3   If the fault is an internal one it will be necessary to obtain a
replacement horn.
4   To remove the horn, disconnect the battery and remove the radiator
grille.
5   Detach the lead at the rear of the horn and then undo and remove
the retaining bolt, spring, horn bracket and star-washer.
6   Refitting the horn is the reverse sequence to removal.

28 Headlight assembly - removal and refitting

1   If the headlight **bulb** only is to be replaced, refer to Section 29.
2   Open the bonnet and for safety reasons, disconnect the battery.
3   Remove the single headlight retaining screw, unclip the adjuster
bracket and lift the assembly forwards (Fig. 10.15).
4   Pull the multi plug from the rear and remove the sidelight bulb by
twisting and pulling clear.
5   Remove the headlight bulb (Section 29) and unclip the headlight
adjusters and the lower location guide.
6   Refitting is a reversal of this procedure, but ensure that the two
adjuster guides are located with the respective body lugs

29 Headlight bulb - removal and refitting

1   For safety reasons, disconnect the battery.
2   From inside the bonnet, pull off the multi plug at the rear of the
headlight. Pull off the rubber gaiter.
3   Twist the bulb retaining ring anti-clockwise (photo) and lift out the
ring and bulb. **Note:** *The glass of the headlight bulb should* **not** *be
touched with the fingers. If it is touched with the fingers it should be
washed with methylated spirit.*
4   Refitting is a reversal of the above procedure.

30 Headlight and auxiliary light alignment

1   It is always advisable to have the lights aligned using special
optical beam setting equipment but if this is not available the following
procedure may be used.

2   Position the car on level ground, 10 ft (3 m) in front of a dark wall
or board. The wall or board must be at right angles to the centre-line of
the car.
3   Draw a vertical line on the board in line with the centre-line of the
car.
4   Bounce the car on its suspension to ensure correct settlement and
then measure the height between the ground and the centre of the
lights.
5   Measure the distance between the centres of the lights to be
adjusted, and mark the board as shown in Figs. 10.16 and 10.19.
6   *Headlights* With the headlights on main beam, cover the other
light(s) to prevent glare. By careful adjustment of the two adjusters at
the rear of the headlight assembly, set the horizontal position until
point 'C' (Fig. 10.16) is at the cross on the aiming board. Adjust the
vertical light position so that the top of the beam pattern just touches
the dotted line (Fig. 10.16).
7   *Auxiliary lights* Turn the auxiliary lights on and cover the other
lights to prevent glare. Slacken the lamp retaining nut and adjust until
the centre of illumination lies at the area shown in Fig. 10.19.

31 Sidelight bulb - removal and refitting

1   The sidelight bulb is fitted within the headlamp assembly, and can
be replaced from inside the engine compartment.
2   Disconnect the sidelight from the headlight assembly by twisting
anti-clockwise and pulling clear (Fig. 10.17). Remove the bayonet
type bulb from the holder.
3   Replace the bulb, then push the holder into the headlight and
twist clockwise to secure. Note that the lugs on the holder are not
symmetrical, so that the holder can only be fitted in one position.

32 Front direction indicator light assembly and bulb - removal and refitting

1   From inside the engine compartment, disconnect the indicator
wire and push it through the inner wing.
2   Working under the wheel arch, undo and remove the two
retaining nuts and push the light assembly forwards away from its
location in the front wing.
3   Refitting is the reverse sequence to removal.
4   If it is necessary to remove the bulb undo and remove the two
crosshead screws that secure the lens to the light body. Lift away the
lens (Fig. 10.18).
5   To detach the bulb press in and turn in an anti-clockwise direction
to release the bayonet fixing and lift away the bulb. Refitting the
bulb and lens is the reverse sequence to removal. Make sure that the
lens gasket is correctly fitted to prevent dirt and water ingress.

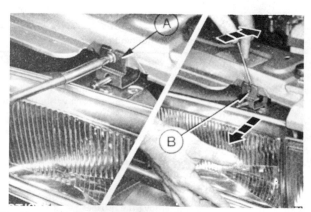

Fig. 10.15. Remove the headlight retaining screw (A) and unclip the
bracket (B) (Sec. 28)

29.3 Headlight bulb retaining ring arms (A)

Fig. 10.16. Headlight alignment (Sec. 30)

A Distance between light centres
B Dipped beam pattern
H Height from ground to headlight centre
X 3.0 in (76 mm)
OO Vehicle centre line

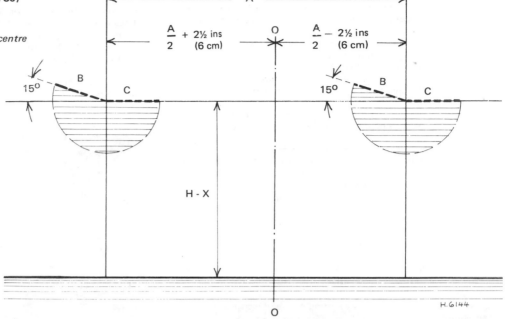

$\frac{A}{2}$ + 2½ ins (6 cm)

$\frac{A}{2}$ − 2½ ins (6 cm)

15°   B   C

15°   B   C

H − X

O

O

H.6144

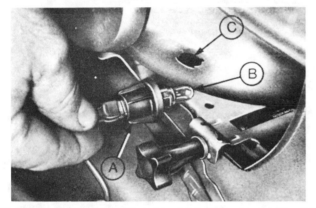

Fig. 10.17. Sidelight bulb (B), holder (A) and location (C) (Sec. 31)

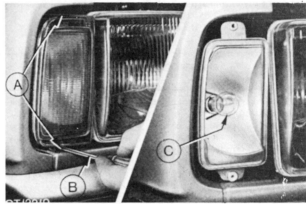

Fig. 10.18. Remove front indicator screws (A) with crosshead screwdriver (B) to remove bulb (C) (Sec. 32)

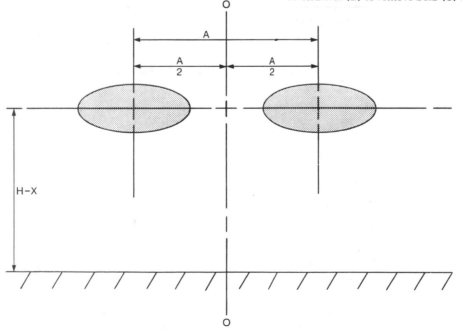

O

A

$\frac{A}{2}$ $\frac{A}{2}$

H−X

O

Fig. 10.19. Auxiliary lamp alignment (Sec. 30)

A Distance between lamp centres   *H Height from ground to lamp centre*   *X 2.0 in (50 mm)*   *OO Vehicle centre line*

33 Rear direction indicator, stop and tail light bulbs - removal and refitting

1 *Saloon* Open the luggage compartment and pull off the protective cover from the rear of the lamp assembly.
2 Press the retaining clip (Fig. 10.20) sideways and remove the bulb plate, then lift out the appropriate bulb. Refitting is the reverse sequence to removal.
3 *Estate car* Remove the two crosshead screws securing the lens to the rear of the vehicle, and renew the appropriate bulb (Fig. 10.21).

34 Rear direction indicator, stop and tail light assembly - removal and refitting

1 *Saloon* Refer to Section 33 to remove the lamp cover and lamp plate.
2 Remove the four retaining nuts and screws, and the earth wire, and lift the lamp assembly from the rear.
3 Refitting is the reverse sequence. Do not forget to reconnect the earth wire.
4 *Estate car* With the rear seat's back folded forward, take out the two crosshead screws from the top edge of the rear trim panel, and unclip the panel.
5 Remove the two light assembly securing nuts and washers and lift away the assembly.
6 Disconnect the wiring after carefully noting which wire goes to which light.
7 Refitting is a reversal of the above procedure.

35 Rear number plate light assembly and bulb - removal and refitting

1 From underneath the bumper, gently squeeze the two plastic clips inwards, and lift out the lamp.
2 Pull off the two Lucar connectors.
3 Gently prise off the lens cover, which is retained by two lugs, lift away the lens and remove the bayonet bulb (Fig. 10.22).
4 Refitting the bulb, lens and assembly is the reverse sequence to removal. Take care to ensure that the lens sealing washer is correctly fitted to prevent dirt and water ingress.

36 Interior light - removal and refitting

1 Very carefully pull the interior light assembly from the location in the roof panel.
2 Disconnect the wires from the terminal connectors and lift away the light unit.
3 If the bulb requires renewal either lift the bulb from its clips (festoon type) or press and turn in an anticlockwise direction (bayonet cap type).
4 Refitting the interior light is the reverse sequence to removal.

37 Instrument cluster and printed circuit - removal and refitting

1 Open and support the bonnet. Disconnect the battery leads.
2 Unclip and remove the steering column upper shroud. Unscrew and remove the lower shroud retaining screws and detach the shroud.
3 Unscrew and remove the crosshead screw to enable the lower facia insulating panel to be lowered clear of the steering column.
4 Loosen (do not remove) the three steering column retaining bolts and lower the column about ¼ in (6 mm).
5 Pull the panel light switch knob free and also the radio control knobs (where fitted). The radio is secured to the panel by two nuts (behind the knobs) and these must be unscrewed and the radio surround panel removed.
6 Unscrew and remove the three lower and three upper instrument cluster/surround bezel retaining screws, then withdraw the bezel from the dashboard. Reach behind the bezel unit, compress the side latches retaining the unit, detach the two multi wiring connectors at the rear of the instruments and detach the three wires to the cigar lighter. Detach the multi loom plugs.

7 Disconnect the wiring connectors to the hazard warning switch and heated rear window switch (where fitted).
8 Compress the speedometer cable connector grooved section as shown in Fig.10.25 and disconnect the cable. Remove the instrument panel unit.
9 Refitting is a reversal of the removal procedure. On completion reconnect the battery and check the operation of the various instruments and switches to ensure that they function correctly.

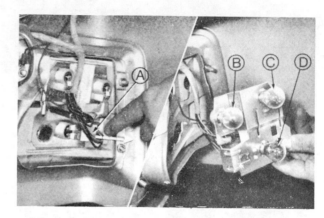

Fig. 10.20. Push the retaining tab (A) sideways to reach the reverse light (B), indicator (C) or stop/tail lamp (D) bulb (Sec. 33)

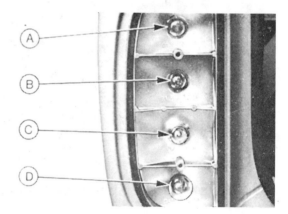

Fig. 10.21. Estate car indicator (A), tail light (B), stop light (C) and reverse light (D) bulbs (Sec. 33)

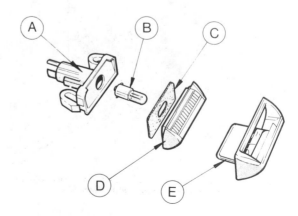

Fig. 10.22. Number plate light body (A), bulb (B), gasket (C), lens (D) and lens cover (E) (Sec. 35)

38 Instrument voltage regulator - removal and refitting

1   Remove the instrument panel, as described in the preceding Section.
2   Unscrew and remove the single screw which secures the voltage regulator to the printed circuit and withdraw it.
3   Refitting is a reversal of this procedure.

39 Instruments, warning lights and illumination lights - removal and refitting

1   Remove the instrument cluster (refer to Section 37).
2   The exact details concerning the number and type of securing nuts and/or screws will vary according to the instrument concerned, but this will be obvious from inspection.
3   Whenever the instrument cluster is dismantled, care must be taken not to crease or tear the printed circuit films, which remove the need for large clusters of wires.
4   When reassembling the instrument cluster, ensure that all printed circuit films and instrument housings are correctly located before tightening the fixings.
5   All light bulb holders should be twisted anti-clockwise for removal. The bayonet bulbs are also twisted anti-clockwise for removal.
6   Refitting the instrument cluster is the reverse sequence to removal.

40 Speedometer inner and outer cable - removal and refitting

1   *Manual gearbox:* Working under the car using a pair of circlip pliers, remove the circlip that secures the speedometer cable to the gearbox extension housing and withdraw the speedometer cable (Fig. 10.26).
    Automatic transmission: Undo and remove the bolt, and spring washer that secures the forked plate to the extension housing. Lift away the forked plate and withdraw the speedometer cable.
2   Remove the clip that secures the speedometer outer cable to the bulkhead.
3   Working under the facia depress the knurled pad on the speedometer cable ferrule and pull the cable from the speedometer head (Fig. 10.25).
4   Remove the grommet that seals the cable to the bulkhead. Withdraw the speedometer cable.
5   Refitting the speedometer cable is the reverse sequence to removal.
6   It is possible to remove the inner cable from the outer cable whilst still attached to the car. Follow the instructions in paragraphs 1 and 3 and pull the inner cable from the outer cable.

41 Steering column switches - removal and refitting

1   Open the bonnet and for safety reasons, disconnect the battery.
2   Unscrew the lower shroud from the steering column and remove it. Then unclip the upper half (Fig. 10.23).

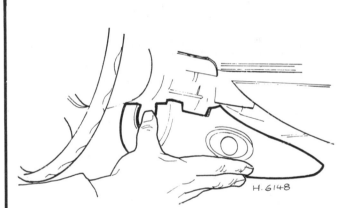

Fig. 10.23. Removing steering column shroud (Sec. 37)

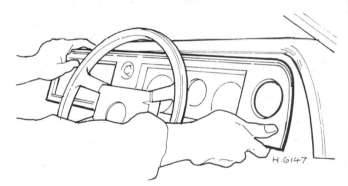

Fig. 10.24. Withdrawing instrument panel bezel (Sec. 37)

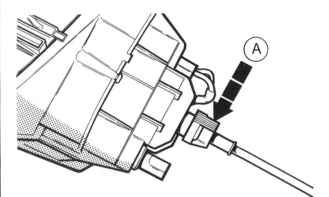

Fig. 10.25. Pressing on the grooved section of the sleeve (A) to release the speedometer cable (Sec. 37)

Fig. 10.26. Remove the circlip (B) and take out the speedometer cable (A) (Sec. 40)

3 Detach the multi pin plugs from the underside of the switch.
4 Undo and remove the two screws and shakeproof washers located on the lever side of the switch and detach the switch assembly from the steering column.
5 Refitting the switch is the reverse sequence to removal.

42 Ignition switch and lock - removal and refitting

1 *The ignition switch* can be removed by unscrewing the lower dash trim panel in the steering column area, and lowering the panel.
2 The switch is then removed by unscrewing the two screws, and disconnecting the multi-plug (Fig. 10.27).
3 *To remove the steering lock,* refer to Chapter 11, Section 24 for the removal of the steering column.
4 Secure the steering column in a vice fitted with jaw protectors and drill out the two shear bolts which retain the two halves of the steering column lock to the column.
5 Commence reassembly by fitting the new lock to the steering column so that the lock tongue engages in the cut-out in the column. Tighten the bolts slightly more than finger-tight and check the operation of the lock by inserting the ignition key. Move the lock assembly fractionally if necessary to ensure smooth and positive engagement when the key is turned.
6 Fully tighten the bolts until the heads shear.
7 Refit the steering column, refer to Chapter 11, Section 24.

43 Instrument panel switches - removal and refitting

1 The switches are removed from the instrument panel by inserting a screwdriver at their lower edge and then levering them from their locations. **Note:** Use a pad of suitable material to prevent damage to the instrument panel (Fig. 10.28).
2 Withdraw the switch far enough to permit the multi-plug to be disconnected.
3 To refit the switch, connect the multi-plug and push the switch firmly into its location.

44 Fuses

1 A fuse block is mounted on the right-hand inner wing panel, under a protective cover (photo).

44.1 Fuse block with outer and inner covers removed

2 The fuses, and their respective circuits are as follows:

Fuse	Size	Function
1	16 amp	Cigarette lighter, clock, interior light(s), hazard flashers, horn, glove compartment light.
2	8 amp	LH side and tail light.
3	8 amp	RH side and tail light, number plate light(s), instrument panel lights.
4	8 amp	Main beam headlights.
5	8 amp	Dipped beam headlights.
6	8 amp	Wiper motor, washer motor, reversing lights.
7	8 amp	Direction indicators, stop lights, instrument cluster, heater motor.

3 Four headlamp fuses are located within the relay, behind the windscreen washer reservoir.

1	16 amp	LH dipped headlight.
2	16 amp	RH dipped headlight.
3	16 amp	RH main beam headlight and LH auxiliary light.
4	16 amp	LH main beam headlight and RH auxiliary light.

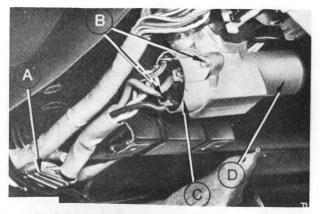

Fig. 10.27. Pull out the multi-plug (A) and remove the two screws (B) to disconnect the ignition switch (C) from the steering lock (D) (Sec. 43)

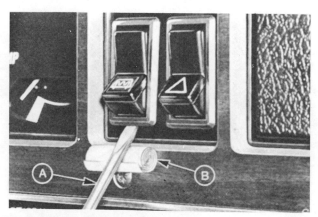

Fig. 10.28. Removing the instrument panel switches using a small screwdriver (A) and protective material (B) (Sec. 44)

4   Two further fuses are located beneath the facia. These are a 16 amp fuse for the heated rear window, located within the relay (Section 46), and a 2 amp (slow blow) fuse in the radio supply lead.
5   Before any fuse that has blown is renewed, it is important to find the cause of the trouble and for it to be rectified, as a fuse acts as a safety device and protects the electrical system against expensive damage should a fault occur.

45 Relays - renewal

1   There are five relays incorporated in the electrical system: headlamp, heated rear window, indicator and hazard flasher, inhibitor switch (automatic transmission) and windscreen wipers.

Headlamp relay
2   This is located within the engine compartment on the side apron panel behind the windscreen washer reservoir.
3   Unplug the washer motor and lift out the reservoir. Unscrew the two crosshead securing screws and lift out the relay.
4   Pull the multi-plug and two double connectors from their terminals, carefully noting the correct connections (Fig. 10.29).

Heated rear window relay
5   This relay is located on the support bracket for the bonnet release lever which is located under the instrument panel (Fig. 10.30).
6   Access to the relay can be facilitated if the instrument panel's lower insulation panel is first removed and the flasher unit extracted from its securing clip.

Indicator and hazard flasher relay
7   This relay is located on the support bracket for the bonnet release lever which is located under the instrument panel (Fig. 10.30).
8   Access to the relay can be facilitated if the instrument panel's lower insulation panel is first removed. The relay can then be pulled from its securing clip.

Inhibitor switch relay
9   This relay is located on the right-hand inner wing panel, and is retained by two crosshead screws.

Windscreen wiper relay
10 This relay is located on the ashtray guide bracket, and is retained by a clip (Fig. 10.31).
11 To remove the relay, first remove the instrument cluster and panel assembly, refer to Section 37.

46 Radios and tape players - installation

A radio or tape player is an expensive item to buy; and will only give its best performance if fitted properly. It is useless to expect concert hall performance from a unit that is suspended from the dashpanel by string with its speaker resting on the back seat or parcel shelf! If you do not wish to do the installation yourself there are many in-car entertainment specialists who can do the fitting for you.
Make sure the unit purchased is of the same polarity as the vehicle. Ensure that units with adjustable polarity are correctly set before commencing installation.
It is difficult to give specific information with regard to fitting, as final positioning of the radio/tape player, speakers and aerial is entirely a matter of personal preference. However, the following paragraphs give guidelines to follow, which are relevant to all installations.

Radios
Most radios are a standardised size of 7 inches wide, by 2 inches deep - this ensures that they will fit into the radio aperture provided in most cars. If your car does not have such an aperture, then the radio must be fitted in a suitable position either in, or beneath, the dashpanel. Alternatively, a special console can be purchased which will fit between the dashpanel and the floor, or on the transmission tunnel. These consoles can also be used for additional switches and instrumentation if required. Where no radio aperture is provided, the following points should be borne in mind before deciding exactly where to fit the unit.

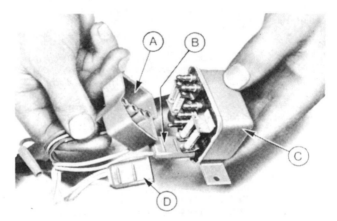

Fig. 10.29. Headlamp relay (Sec. 46)

A   *Multi-connector and cover*
B   *Loom connector*
C   *Relay*
D   *Loom connector*

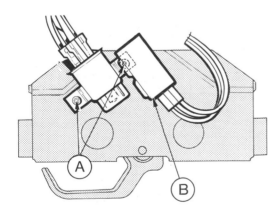

Fig. 10.30. Pull the indicator relay (B) from the spring clip to reach the heated rear window relay screws (A) (Sec. 46)

Fig. 10.31. Pull the wiper relay (A) from the spring clip on the ashtray bracket (B) behind the dash panel (C) (Sec. 46)

a) *The unit must be within easy reach of the driver wearing a seatbelt.*

b) *The unit must not be mounted in close proximity to a tachometer, the ignition switch and its wiring, or the flasher unit and associated wiring.*

c) *The unit must be mounted within reach of the aerial lead, and in such a place that the aerial lead will not have to be routed near the components detailed in the preceding paragraph 'b'.*

d) *The unit should not be positioned in a place where it might cause injury to the car occupants in an accident; for instance, under the dashpanel above the driver's or passenger's legs.*

e) *The unit must be fitted really securely.*

Some radios will have mounting brackets provided together with instructions: others will need to be fitted using drilled and slotted metal strips, bent to form mounting brackets - these strips are available from most accessory stores. The unit must be properly earthed, by fitting a separate earth lead between the casing of the radio and the vehicle frame.

Use the radio manufacturer's instructions when wiring the radio into the vehicle's electrical system. If no instructions are available, refer to the relevant wiring diagram to find the location of the radio 'feed' connection in the vehicle's wiring circuit. A 1-2 amp 'in-line' fuse must be fitted in the radio's 'feed' wire - a choke may also be necessary (see next Section).

The type of aerial used, and its fitted position is a matter of personal preference. In general the taller the aerial, the better the reception. It is best to fit a fully retractable aerial - especially, if a mechanical car-wash is used or if you live in an area where cars tend to be vandalised. In this respect electric aerials which are raised and lowered automatically when switching the radio on or off, are convenient, but are more likely to give trouble than the manual type.

When choosing a site for the aerial the following points should be considered:

a) *The aerial lead should be as short as possible; this means that the aerial should be mounted at the front of the vehicle.*

b) *The aerial must be mounted as far away from the distributor and HT leads as possible.*

c) *The part of the aerial which protrudes beneath the mounting point must not foul the roadwheels, or anything else.*

d) *If possible the aerial should be positioned so that the coaxial lead does not have to be routed through the engine compartment.*

e) *The plane of the panel on which the aerial is mounted should not be so steeply angled that the aerial cannot be mounted vertically (in relation to the 'end-on' aspect of the vehicle). Most aerials have a small amount of adjustment available.*

Having decided on a mounting position, a relatively large hole will have to be made in the panel. The exact size of the hole will depend upon the specific aerial being fitted, although, generally, the hole required is of ¾ inch diameter. On metal bodied cars, a 'tank-cutter' of the relevant diameter is the best tool to be used for making the hole. This tool needs a small diameter pilot hole drilled through the panel, through which, the tool clamping bolt is inserted. On GRP bodied cars, a 'hole saw' is the best tool to use. Again, this tool will require the drilling of a small pilot hole. When the hole has been made the raw edges should be de-burred with a file and then painted, to prevent corrosion.

Fit the aerial according to the manufacturer's instructions. If the aerial is very tall, or if it protrudes beneath the mounting panel for a considerable distance it is a good idea to fit a stay between the aerial and the vehicle frame. This stay can be manufactured from the slotted and drilled metal strips previously mentioned. The stay should be securely screwed or bolted in place. For best reception it is advisable to fit an earth lead between the aerial body and the vehicle frame - this is essential on fibre glass bodied vehicles.

It will probably be necessary to drill one, or two holes through bodywork panels in order to feed the aerial lead into the interior of the car. Where this is the case ensure that the holes are fitted with rubber grommets to protect the cable, and to stop possible entry of water.

Positioning and fitting of the speaker depends mainly on its type. Generally, the speaker is designed to fit directly into the aperture already provided in the car (usually in the shelf behind the rear seats, or in the top of the dashpanel). Where this is the case, fitting the speaker is just a matter of removing the protective grille from the aperture and screwing or bolting the speaker in place. Take great care not to damage the speaker diaphragm whilst doing this. It is a good idea to fit a 'gasket' between the speaker frame and the mounting panel in order to prevent vibration - some speakers will already have such a gasket fitted.

If a 'pod' type speaker was supplied with the radio, the best acoustic results will normally be obtained by mounting it on the shelf behind the rear seat. The pod can be secured to the mounting panel with self-tapping screws.

When connecting a rear mounted speaker to the radio, the wires should be routed through the vehicle beneath the carpets or floor mats preferably through the middle, or along the side of the floorpan, where they will not be trodden on by passengers. Make the relevant connections as directed by the radio manufacturer.

By now you will have several yards of additional wiring in the car; use PVC tape to secure this wiring out of harm's way. Do not leave electrical leads dangling. Ensure that all new electrical connections are properly made (wires twisted together will not do) and completely secure.

The radio should now be working, but before you pack away your tools it will be necessary to 'trim' the radio to the aerial. Follow the radio manufacturer's instructions regarding this adjustment.

Tape players

Fitting instructions for both cartridge and cassette stereo tape players are the same and in general the same rules apply as when fitting a radio. Tape players are not usually prone to electrical interference like radio - although it can occur - so positioning is not so critical. If possible the player should be mounted on an 'even-keel'. Also, it must be possible for a driver wearing a seatbelt to reach the unit in order to change, or turn over, tapes.

For the best results from speakers designed to be recessed into a panel, mount them so that the back of the speaker protrudes into an enclosed chamber within the vehicle (eg; door interiors or the boot cavity).

To fit recessed type speakers in the front doors first check that there is sufficient room to mount the speaker in each door without it fouling the latch or window winding mechanism. Hold the speaker against the skin of the door, and draw a line, around the periphery of the speaker. With the speaker removed draw a second 'cutting' line, within the first, to allow enough room for the entry of the speaker back but at the same time providing a broad seat for the speaker flange. When you are sure that the 'cutting-line' is correct, drill a series of holes around its periphery. Pass a hacksaw blade through one of the holes and then cut through the metal between the holes until the centre section of the panel falls out.

De-burr the edges of the hole and then paint the raw metal to prevent corrosion. Cut a corresponding hole in the door trim panel - ensuring that it will be completely covered by the speaker grille. Now drill a hole in the door edge and a corresponding hole in the door surround. These holes are to feed the speaker leads through - so fit grommets. Pass the speaker leads through the door trim, door skin and out through the holes in the side of the door and door surround. Refit the door trim panel and then secure the speaker to the door using self-tapping screws. **Note:** If the speaker is fitted with a shield to prevent water dripping on it, ensure that this shield is at the top.

'Pod' type speakers can be fastened to the shelf behind the rear seat, or anywhere else offering a corresponding mounting point on each side of the car. If the 'pod' speakers are mounted on each side of the shelf behind the rear seat, it is a good idea to drill several large diameter holes through to the trunk cavity, beneath each speaker - this will improve the sound reproduction. 'Pod' speakers sometimes offer a better reproduction quality if they face the rear window - which then acts as a reflector - so it is worthwhile experimenting before finally fixing the speakers.

47 Radios and tape players - suppression of interference (general)

To eliminate buzzes, and other unwanted noises, costs very little and is not as difficult as sometimes thought. With a modicum of common sense and patience and following the instructions in the following paragraphs, interference can be virtually eliminated.

The first cause for concern is the generator. The noise this makes over the radio is like an electric mixer and the noise speeds up when you rev up the engine (if you wish to prove the point, you can remove

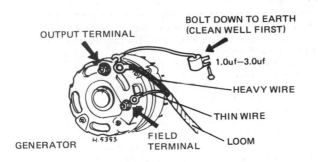

OUTPUT TERMINAL

BOLT DOWN TO EARTH
(CLEAN WELL FIRST)

1.0uf—3.0uf

HEAVY WIRE

THIN WIRE

LOOM

GENERATOR   H.5353   FIELD
TERMINAL

Fig. 10.32. The correct way to connect a capacitor to the generator

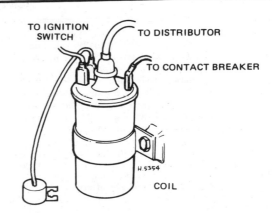

TO IGNITION
SWITCH

TO DISTRIBUTOR

TO CONTACT BREAKER

H.5354

COIL

Fig. 10.33. The capacitor must be connected to the ignition switch
side of the coil

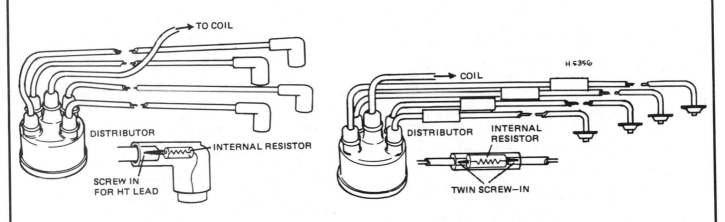

TO COIL

DISTRIBUTOR

INTERNAL RESISTOR

SCREW IN
FOR HT LEAD

H.5356

COIL

DISTRIBUTOR   INTERNAL
RESISTOR

TWIN SCREW—IN

Fig. 10.34. Ignition HT lead suppressors

Resistive spark plug caps (top)

'In-line' suppressors (bottom)

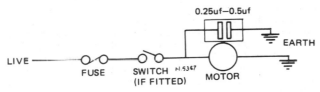

0.25uf—0.5uf

EARTH

LIVE

FUSE   SWITCH   H.5367
(IF FITTED)   MOTOR

Fig. 10.35. Correct method of suppressing electric motors

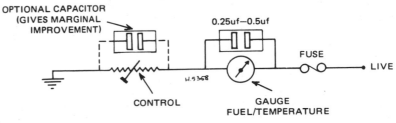

OPTIONAL CAPACITOR
(GIVES MARGINAL
IMPROVEMENT)

0.25uf—0.5uf

FUSE

LIVE

H.5368

CONTROL

GAUGE
FUEL/TEMPERATURE

Fig. 10.36. Method of suppressing gauges and their control units

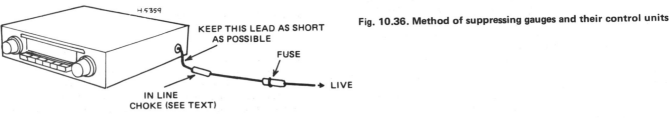

H.5359

KEEP THIS LEAD AS SHORT
AS POSSIBLE

FUSE

LIVE

IN LINE
CHOKE (SEE TEXT)

Fig. 10.37. An 'in-line' choke should be fitted into the live supply lead
as close to the unit as possible

the fanbelt and try it). The remedy for this is simple; connect a 1.0 mf - 3.0 mf capacitor between earth, probably the bolt that holds down the generator base, and the *output* terminal on the alternator. This is most important, for if you connect it to the other terminal you will probably damage the generator permanently (see Fig. 10.32).

A second common cause of electrical interference is the ignition system. Here a 1.0 mf capacitor must be connected between earth and the SW or + terminal on the coil (see Fig. 10.33). This may stop the tick-tick sound that comes over the speaker. Next comes the spark itself.

There are several ways of curing interference from the ignition HT system. One is the use of carbon-cored HT leads as original equipment. Where copper cable is substituted then you must use resistive spark plug caps (see Fig. 10.34) of about 10,000 ohm to 15,000 ohm resistance. If, due to lack of room, these cannot be used, an alternative is to use 'in-line' suppressors - if the interference is not too bad, you may get away with only one suppressor in the coil to distributor line. If the interference does continue (a "clacking" noise) then modify all HT leads.

At this stage it is advisable to check that the radio is well earthed, also the aerial and to see that the aerial plug is pushed well into the set and that the radio is properly trimmed (see preceding Section). In addition, check that the wire which supplies the power to the set is as short as possible and does not wander all over the car. At this stage it is a good idea to check that the fuse is of the correct rating. For most sets this will be about 1 to 2 amps.

At this point the more usual causes of interference have been suppressed. If the problem still exists, a look at the cause of interference may help to pinpoint the component generating the stray electrical discharges.

The radio picks up electromagnetic waves in the air; now some are made by regular broadcasters, and some, which we do not want, are made by the car itself. The home made signals are produced by stray electrical discharges floating around in the car. Common producers of these signals are electrical motors, ie, the windscreen wipers, electric screen washers, electric window winders, heater fan or an electric aerial if fitted. Other sources of interference are flashing turn signals and instruments. The remedy for these cases is shown in Fig. 10.35 for an electric motor whose interference is not too bad and Fig. 10.36 for instrument suppression. Turn signals are not normally suppressed. In recent years, radio manufacturers have included in the line (live) of the radio, in addition to the fuse, an 'in-line' choke. If your circuit lacks one of these, put one in as shown in Fig. 10.37.

All the foregoing components are available from radio stores or accessory stores. If you have an electric clock fitted this should be suppressed by connecting a 0.5 mf capacitor directly across it as shown for a motor in Fig. 10.35.

If after all this, you are still experiencing radio interference, first assess how bad it is, for the human ear can filter out unobtrusive unwanted noises quite easily. But if you are still adamant about eradicating the noise, then continue.

As a first step, a few 'experts' seem to favour a screen between the radio and the engine. This is OK as far as it goes - literally! - for the whole set is screened anyway and if interference can get past that then a small piece of aluminium is not going to stop it.

A more sensible way of screening is to discover if interference is coming down the wires. First, take the live lead; interference can get between the set and the choke (hence the reason for keeping the wires

short). One remedy here is to screen the wire and this is done by buying screened wire and fitting that. The loudspeaker lead could be screened also to prevent 'pick-up' getting back to the radio although this is unlikely.

Without doubt, the worst source of radio interference comes from the ignition HT leads, even if they have been suppressed. The ideal way of suppressing these is to slide screening tubes over the leads themselves. As this is impractical, we can place an aluminium shield over the majority of the lead areas. In a vee- or twin-cam engine this is relatively easy but for a straight engine, the results are not particularly good.

Now for the really impossible cases, here are a few tips to try out. Where metal comes into contact with metal, an electrical disturbance is caused which is why good clean connections are essential. To remove interference due to overlapping or butting panels you must bridge the join with a wide braided earth strap (like that from the frame to the engine/transmission). The most common moving parts that could create noise and should be strapped are, in order of importance:

a) *Silencer to frame*
b) *Exhaust pipe to engine block and frame*
c) *Air cleaner to frame*
d) *Front and rear bumpers to frame*
e) *Steering column to frame*
f) *Bonnet and boot lids to frame*
g) *Hood frame to bodyframe on soft tops*

These faults are most pronounced when (1) the engine is idling, (2) labouring under load. Although the moving parts are already connected with nuts, bolts, etc, these do tend to rust and corrode, thus creating a high resistance interference source.

If you have a 'ragged' sounding pulse when mobile, this could be wheel or tyre static. This can be cured by buying some anti-static powder and sprinkling inside the tyres.

If the interference takes the shape of a high pitched screeching noise that changes its note when the car is in motion and only comes now and then, this could be related to the aerial, especially if it is of the telescopic or whip type. This source can be cured quite simply by pushing a small rubber ball on top of the aerial as this breaks the electric field before it can form; but it would be much better to buy yourself a new aerial of a reputable brand. If, on the other hand, you are getting a loud rushing sound every time you brake, then this is brake static. This effect is most prominent on hot dry days and is cured only by fitting a special kit, which is quite expensive.

In conclusion, it is pointed out that it is relatively easy, and therefore, cheap, to eliminate 95 per cent of all noise, but to eliminate the final 5 per cent is time and money consuming. It is up to the individual to decide if it is worth it. Please remember also, that you cannot get a concert hall performance out of a cheap radio.

Finally, players and eight track players are not usually affected by car noise but in a very bad case, the best remedies are the first three suggestions plus using a 3 - 5 amp choke in the 'live' line and in incurable cases screen the live and speaker wires.

Note: If your car is fitted with electronic ignition, then it is not recommended that either the spark plug resistors or the ignition coil capacitor be fitted as these may damage the system. Most electronic ignition units have built-in suppression and should, therefore, not cause interference.

48 Fault diagnosis - electrical system

Symptom	Cause	Remedy
Starter motor fails to turn engine	Battery discharged	Charge battery.
	Battery defective internally	Fit new battery.
	Battery terminal leads loose or earth lead not securely attached to body	Check and tighten leads.
	Loose or broken connections in starter motor circuit	Check all connections and tighten any that are loose.
	Starter motor switch or solenoid faulty	Test and replace faulty components with new.
	Starter brushes badly worn, sticking, or brush wires loose	Examine brushes, renew as necessary, tighten down brush wires.
	Commutator dirty, worn or burnt	Clean commutator, recut if body burnt.
	Starter motor armature faulty	Overhaul starter motor, fit new armature.
	Field coils earthed	Overhaul starter motor.
Starter motor turns engine very slowly	Battery in discharged condition	Charge battery.
	Starter brushes badly worn, sticking, or brush wires loose	Examine brushes, renew as necessary, tighten down the brush wires.
	Loose wires in starter motor circuit	Check wiring and tighten as necessary.
Starter motor operates without turning engine	Starter motor pinion sticking on the screwed sleeve	Remove starter motor, clean starter motor.
	Pinion or flywheel gear teeth broken or worn	Fit new gear ring to flywheel, and new pinion to starter motor drive.
Starter motor noisy or excessively rough engagement	Pinion or flywheel gear teeth broken or worn	Fit new gear teeth to flywheel, or new pinion to starter motor drive.
	Starter motor retaining bolts loose	Tighten starter motor securing bolts. Fit new spring washer if necessary.
Battery will not hold charge for more than a few days	Battery defective internally	Remove and fit new battery.
	Electrolyte level too low or electrolyte too weak due to leakage	Top-up electrolyte level, test electrolyte specific gravity.
	Plate separators no longer fully effective	Remove and fit new battery.
	Battery plates severely sulphated	Remove and fit new battery.
	Fan/alternator belt slipping	Check belt for wear, renew if necessary, and tighten.
	Battery terminal connections loose or corroded	Check terminals for tightness, and remove all corrosion.
	Alternator not charging properly	Take car to specialist.
	Short in lighting circuit causing continual battery drain	Trace and rectify.
Ignition light fails to go out, battery runs flat in a few days	Fan belt loose and slipping or broken	Check, renew and tighten as necessary.
	Alternator faulty	Take car to a specialist.

Failure of individual electrical equipment to function correctly is dealt with alphabetically, item-by-item, under the headings listed below

Symptom	Cause	Remedy
Fuel gauge gives no reading	Fuel tank empty!	Fill fuel tank.
	Electric cable between tank sender unit and gauge earthed or loose	Check cable for earthing and joints for tightness.
	Fuel gauge case not earthed	Ensure case is well earthed.
	Fuel gauge supply cable interrupted	Check and renew cable if necessary.
	Fuel gauge unit broken	Replace fuel gauge.
Fuel gauge registers full all the time	Electric cable between tank unit and gauge broken or disconnected.	Check over cable and repair as necessary.
Horn operates all the time	Horn push either earthed or stuck down	Disconnect battery earth. Check and rectify source of trouble.
	Horn cable to horn push earthed	Disconnect battery earth. Check and rectify source of trouble.
Horn fails to operate	Blown fuse	Check and renew if broken. Ascertain cause.
	Cable or cable connection loose, broken or disconnected	Check all connections for tightness and cables for breaks.
	Horn has an internal fault	Remove and renew horn.
Horn emits intermittent or unsatisfactory noise	Cable connections loose	Check and tighten all connections.

Fault diagnosis - electrical system (continued)

Symptom	Cause	Remedy
Lights do not come on	Blown fuse	Check and renew fuse.
	If engine not running, battery discharged	Push-start car and charge battery (not automatics).
	Light bulb filament burnt out or bulbs broken	Renew bulbs.
	Wire connections loose, disconnected or broken	Check all connections for tightness and wire cable for breaks.
	Light switch shorting or otherwise faulty	By-pass light switch to ascertain if fault is in switch and fit new switch as appropriate.
Lights come on but fade out	If engine not running battery discharged	Push-start car and charge battery (not automatics).
Lights give very poor illumination	Lamp glasses dirty	Clean glasses.
	Reflector tarnished or dirty	Fit new reflectors.
	Lamps badly out of adjustment	Adjust lamps correctly.
	Incorrect bulb with too low wattage fitted	Remove bulb and renew with correct grade.
	Existing bulbs old and badly discoloured	Renew bulb units.
	Electrical wiring too thin not allowing full current to pass	Re-wire lighting system.
Lights work erratically - flashing on and off, especially over bumps	Battery terminals or earth connection loose	Tighten battery terminals and earth connection.
	Lights not earthing properly	Examine and rectify.
	Contacts in light switch faulty	By-pass light switch to ascertain if fault is in switch and fit new switch as appropriate.
Wiper motor fails to work	Blown fuse	Check and renew fuse if necessary.
	Wire connections loose, disconnected or broken	Check wiper wiring. Tighten loose connections.
	Brushes badly worn	Remove and fit new brushes.
	Armature worn or faulty	If electricity at wiper motor remove and overhaul and fit replacement armature.
	Field coils faulty	Purchase reconditioned wiper motor.
Wiper motor works very slowly and takes excessive current	Commutator dirty, greasy or burnt	Clean commutator thoroughly.
	Drive to wheelboxes bent or unlubricated	Examine drive and straighten out severe curvature. Lubricate.
	Wheelbox spindle binding or damaged	Remove, overhaul, or fit replacement.
	Armature bearings dry or unaligned	Replace with new bearings correctly aligned.
	Armature badly worn or faulty	Remove, overhaul, or fit replacement armature.
Wiper motor works slowly and takes little current	Brushes badly worn	Remove and fit new brushes.
	Commutator dirty, greasy or burnt	Clean commutator thoroughly.
	Armature badly worn or faulty	Remove and overhaul armature or fit replacement.
Wiper motor works but wiper blades remain static	Wheelbox gear and spindle damaged or worn	Examine and if faulty, renew.
	Wiper motor gearbox parts badly worn	Overhaul or fit new gearbox.

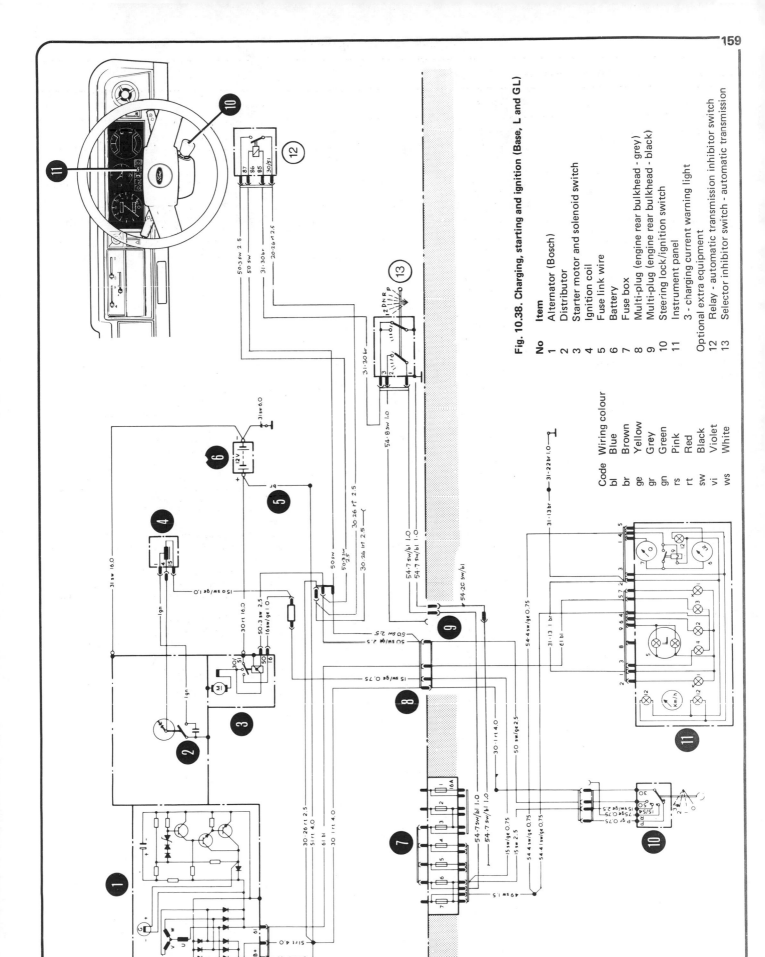

Fig. 10.38. Charging, starting and ignition (Base, L and GL)

No	Item
1	Alternator (Bosch)
2	Distributor
3	Starter motor and solenoid switch
4	Ignition coil
5	Fuse link wire
6	Battery
7	Fuse box
8	Multi-plug (engine rear bulkhead - grey)
9	Multi-plug (engine rear bulkhead - black)
10	Steering lock/ignition switch
11	Instrument panel
3 - charging current warning light
Optional extra equipment
12	Relay - automatic transmission inhibitor switch
13	Selector inhibitor switch - automatic transmission

Code	Wiring colour
bl	Blue
br	Brown
ge	Yellow
gr	Grey
gn	Green
rs	Pink
rt	Red
sw	Black
vi	Violet
ws	White

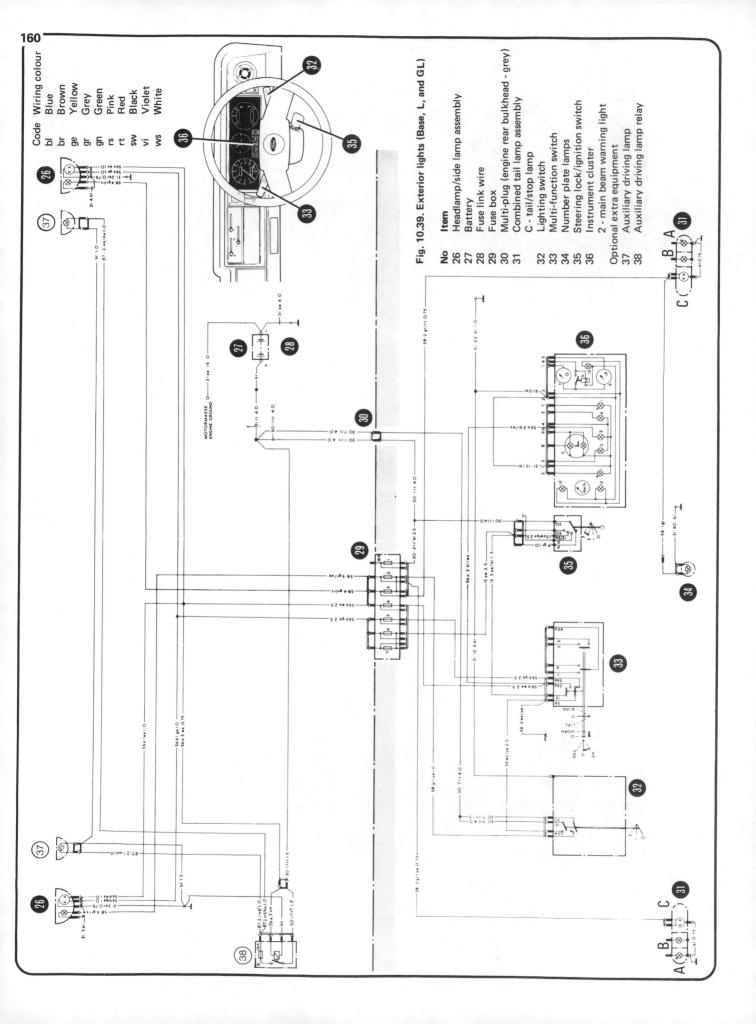

Code	Wiring colour
bl	Blue
br	Brown
ge	Yellow
gr	Grey
gn	Green
rs	Pink
rt	Red
sw	Black
vi	Violet
ws	White

Fig. 10.39. Exterior lights (Base, L, and GL)

No	Item
26	Headlamp/side lamp assembly
27	Battery
28	Fuse link wire
29	Fuse box
30	Multi-plug (engine rear bulkhead - grey)
31	Combined tail lamp assembly
	C - tail/stop lamp
32	Lighting switch
33	Multi-function switch
34	Number plate lamps
35	Steering lock/ignition switch
36	Instrument cluster
	2 - main beam warning light
	Optional extra equipment
37	Auxiliary driving lamp
38	Auxiliary driving lamp relay

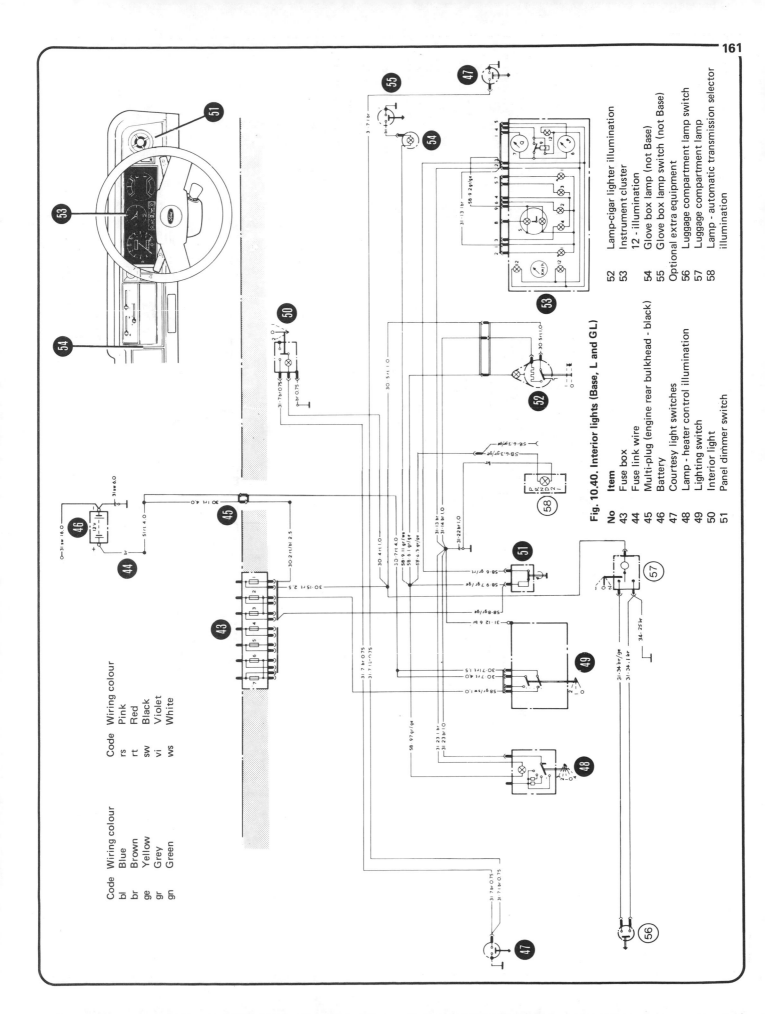

Fig. 10.40. Interior lights (Base, L and GL)

No	Item
43	Fuse box
44	Fuse link wire
45	Multi-plug (engine rear bulkhead - black)
46	Battery
47	Courtesy light switches
48	Lamp - heater control illumination
49	Lighting switch
50	Interior light
51	Panel dimmer switch
52	Lamp-cigar lighter illumination
53	Instrument cluster
	12 - illumination
54	Glove box lamp (not Base)
55	Glove box lamp switch (not Base)
	Optional extra equipment
56	Luggage compartment lamp switch
57	Luggage compartment lamp
58	Lamp - automatic transmission selector illumination

Code	Wiring colour
bl	Blue
br	Brown
ge	Yellow
gr	Grey
gn	Green

Code	Wiring colour
rs	Pink
rt	Red
sw	Black
vi	Violet
ws	White

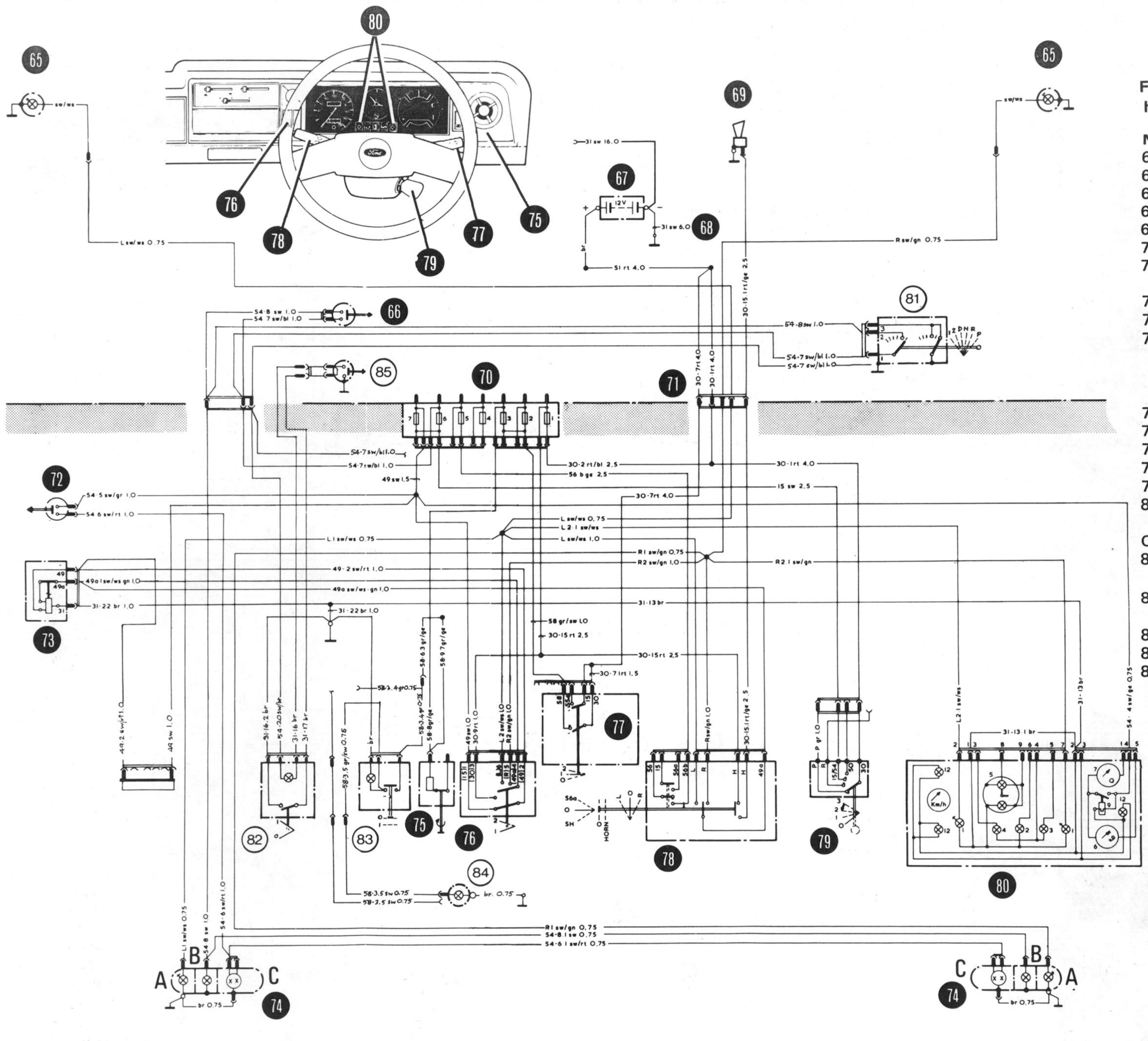

Fig. 10.41. Horn, indicator and hazard lights (Base, L and GL)

No	Item
65	Front flasher lamp
66	Reversing lamp switch
67	Battery
68	Fuse link wire
69	Horn
70	Fuse box
71	Multi-plug (engine rear bulkhead - grey)
72	Stop switch
73	Flasher unit
74	Combined tail lamp assembly
	A - rear flasher lamps
	B - reversing lamps
	C - Tail/stop lamps
75	Panel dimmer switch
76	Hazard flasher switch
77	Lighting switch
78	Multi-function switch
79	Steering lock/ignition switch
80	Instrument cluster
	1 - flasher indicator lamps

Optional extra equipment

No	Item
81	Selector inhibitor switch - automatic transmission
82	Dual circuit brake warning system - test switch
83	Rear fog lamp switch
84	Rear fog lamp
85	Dual circuit brake warning system switch

Code	Wiring colour
bl	Blue
br	Brown
ge	Yellow
gr	Grey
gn	Green
rs	Pink
rt	Red
sw	Black
vi	Violet
ws	White

163

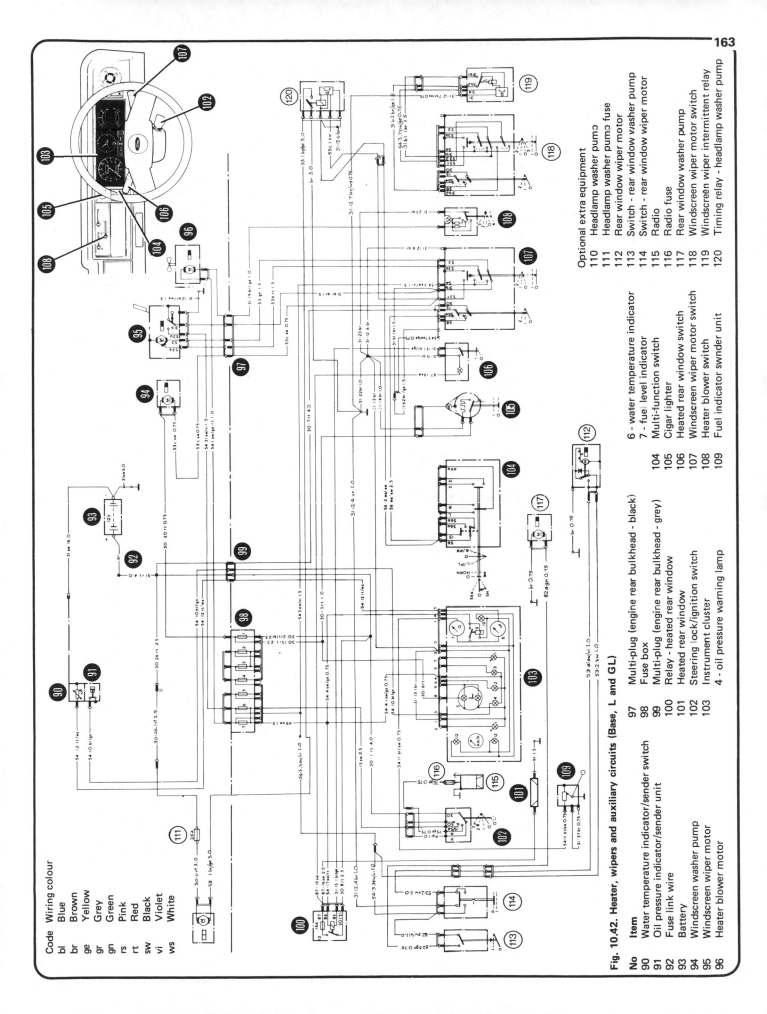

Fig. 10.42. Heater, wipers and auxiliary circuits (Base, L and GL)

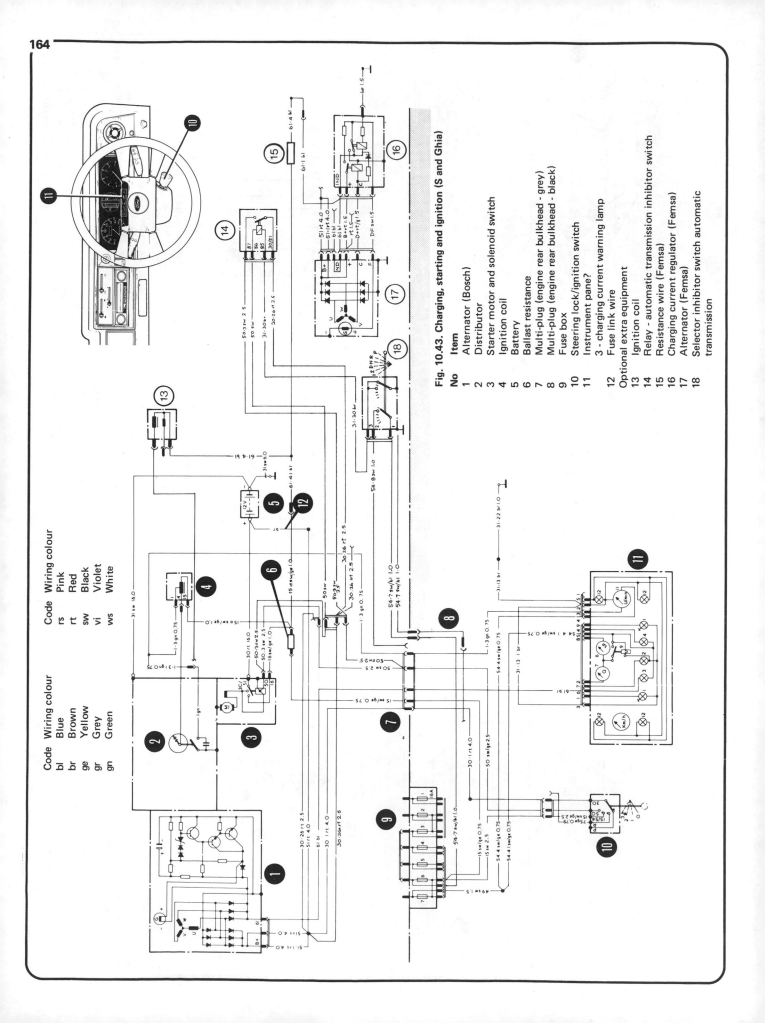

Fig. 10.43. Charging, starting and ignition (S and Ghia)

No	Item
1	Alternator (Bosch)
2	Distributor
3	Starter motor and solenoid switch
4	Ignition coil
5	Battery
6	Ballast resistance
7	Multi-plug (engine rear bulkhead - grey)
8	Multi-plug (engine rear bulkhead - black)
9	Fuse box
10	Steering lock/ignition switch
11	Instrument pane?
3 - charging current warning lamp
12	Fuse link wire
Optional extra equipment
13	Ignition coil
14	Relay - automatic transmission inhibitor switch
15	Resistance wire (Femsa)
16	Charging current regulator (Femsa)
17	Alternator (Femsa)
18	Selector inhibitor switch automatic transmission

Code	Wiring colour
bl	Blue
br	Brown
ge	Yellow
gr	Grey
gn	Green

Code	Wiring colour
rs	Pink
rt	Red
sw	Black
vi	Violet
ws	White

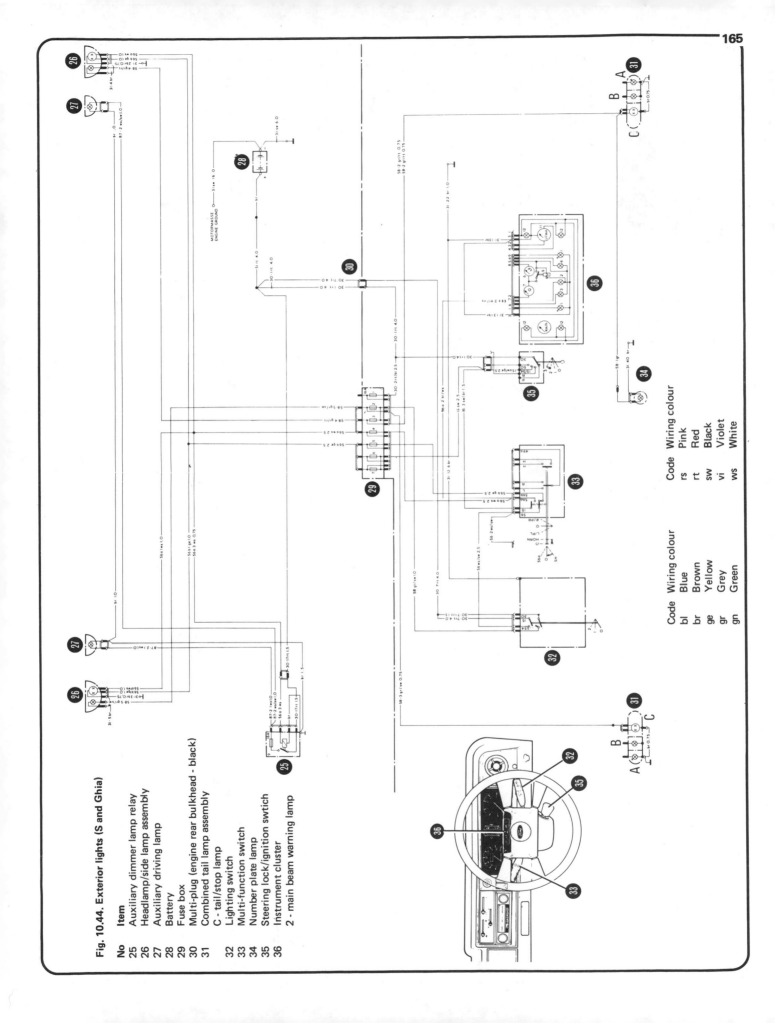

Fig. 10.44. Exterior lights (S and Ghia)

No	Item
25	Auxiliary dimmer lamp relay
26	Headlamp/side lamp assembly
27	Auxiliary driving lamp
28	Battery
29	Fuse box
30	Multi-plug (engine rear bulkhead – black)
31	Combined tail lamp assembly
	C – tail/stop lamp
32	Lighting switch
33	Multi-function switch
34	Number plate lamp
35	Steering lock/ignition switch
36	Instrument cluster
	2 – main beam warning lamp

Code	Wiring colour
bl	Blue
br	Brown
ge	Yellow
gr	Grey
gn	Green

Code	Wiring colour
rs	Pink
rt	Red
sw	Black
vi	Violet
ws	White

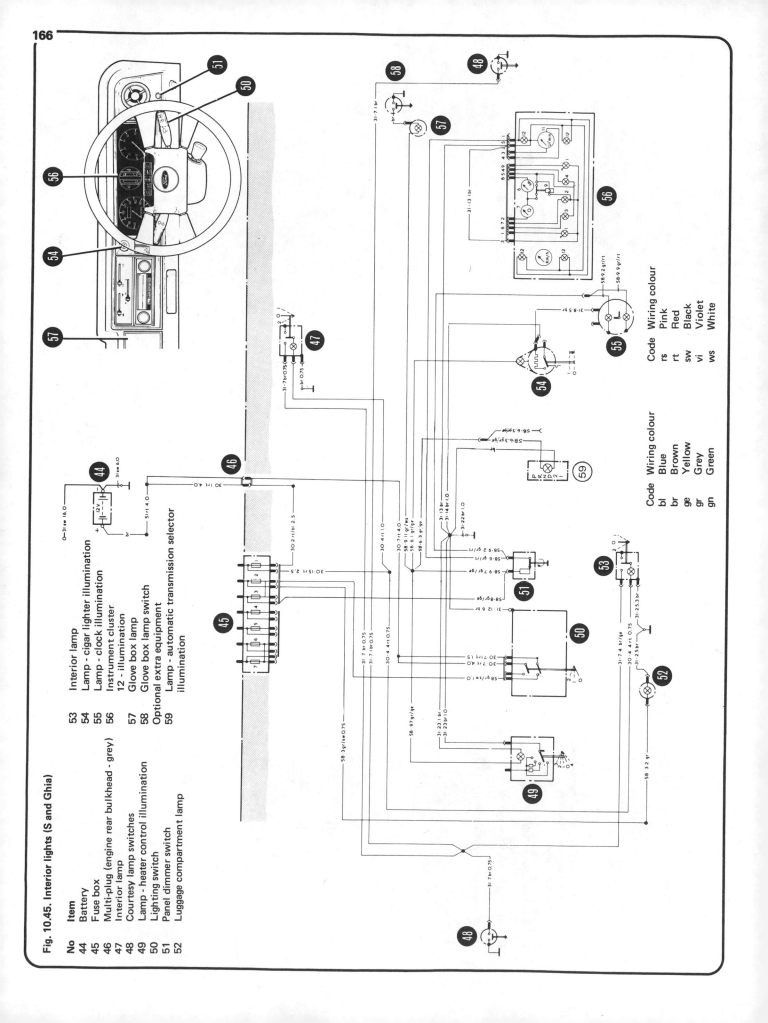

Fig. 10.45. Interior lights (S and Ghia)

No	Item
44	Battery
45	Fuse box
46	Multi-plug (engine rear bulkhead - grey)
47	Interior lamp
48	Courtesy lamp switches
49	Lamp - heater control illumination
50	Lighting switch
51	Panel dimmer switch
52	Luggage compartment lamp
53	Interior lamp
54	Lamp - cigar lighter illumination
55	Lamp - clock illumination
56	Instrument cluster
57	12 - illumination
57	Glove box lamp
58	Glove box lamp switch
59	Optional extra equipment
59	Lamp - automatic transmission selector illumination

Code	Wiring colour
bl	Blue
br	Brown
ge	Yellow
gr	Grey
gn	Green

Code	Wiring colour
rs	Pink
rt	Red
sw	Black
vi	Violet
ws	White

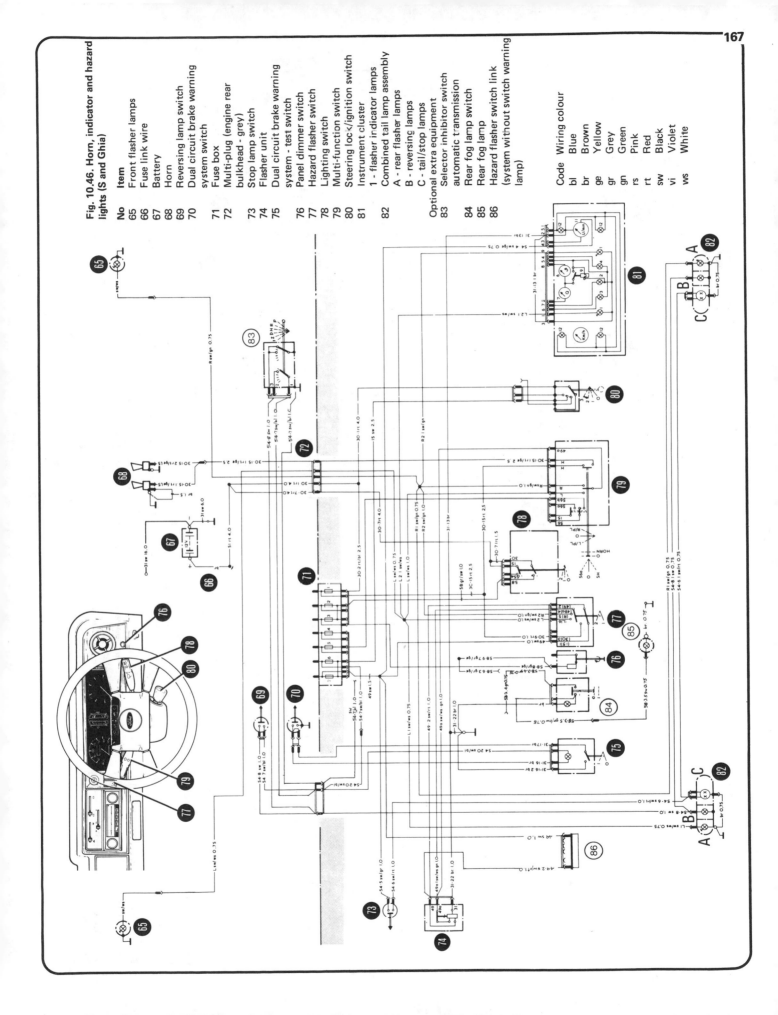

Fig. 10.46. Horn, indicator and hazard lights (S and Ghia)

No	Item
65	Front flasher lamps
66	Fuse link wire
67	Battery
68	Horn
69	Reversing lamp switch
70	Dual circuit brake warning system switch
71	Fuse box
72	Multi-plug (engine rear bulkhead - grey)
73	Stop lamp switch
74	Flasher unit
75	Dual circuit brake warning system - test switch
76	Panel dimmer switch
77	Hazard flasher switch
78	Lighting switch
79	Multi-function switch
80	Steering lock/ignition switch
81	Instrument cluster
	1 - flasher indicator lamps
82	Combined tail lamp assembly
	A - rear flasher lamps
	B - reversing lamps
	C - tail/stop lamps
	Optional extra equipment
83	Selector inhibitor switch automatic transmission
84	Rear fog lamp switch
85	Rear fog lamp
86	Hazard flasher switch link (system without switch warning lamp)

Code	Wiring colour
bl	Blue
br	Brown
ge	Yellow
gr	Grey
gn	Green
rs	Pink
rt	Red
sw	Black
vi	Violet
ws	White

167

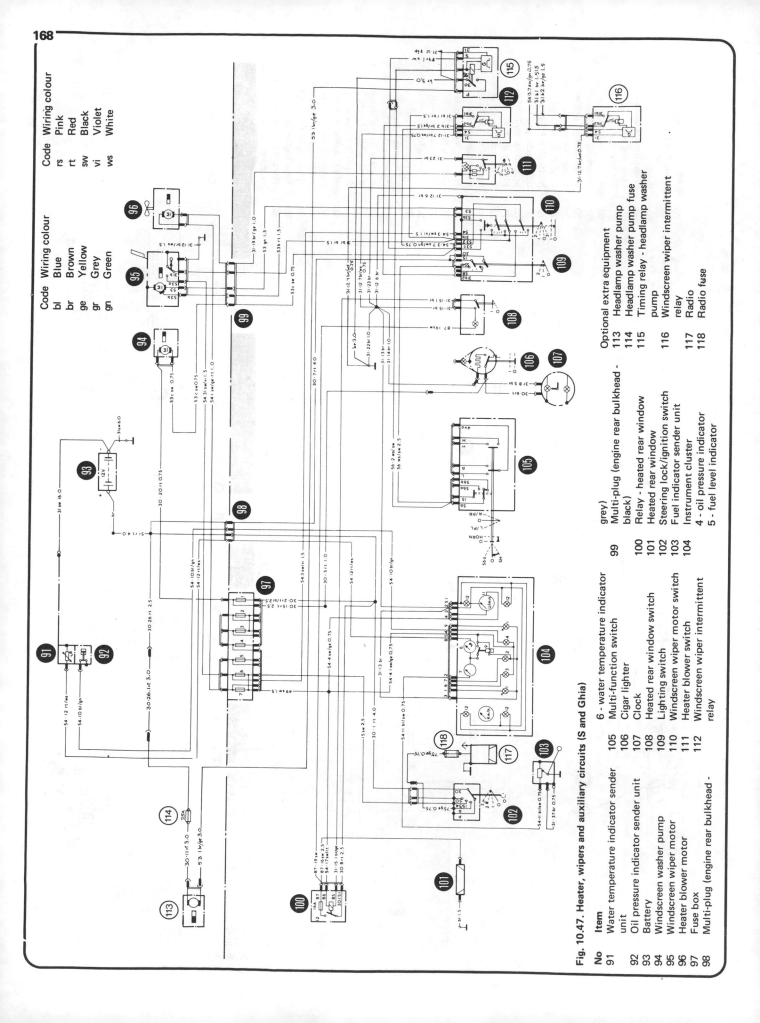

Code	Wiring colour
rs	Pink
rt	Red
sw	Black
vi	Violet
ws	White

Code	Wiring colour
bl	Blue
br	Brown
ge	Yellow
gr	Grey
gn	Green

Fig. 10.47. Heater, wipers and auxiliary circuits (S and Ghia)

No	Item
91	Water temperature indicator sender unit
92	Oil pressure indicator sender unit
93	Battery
94	Windscreen washer pump
95	Windscreen wiper motor
96	Heater blower motor
97	Fuse box
98	Multi-plug (engine rear bulkhead - grey)
99	Multi-plug (engine rear bulkhead - black)
100	Relay - heated rear window
101	Heated rear window
102	Steering lock/ignition switch
103	Fuel indicator sender unit
104	Instrument cluster
	4 - oil pressure indicator
	5 - fuel level indicator
	6 - water temperature indicator
105	Multi-function switch
106	Cigar lighter
107	Clock
108	Heated rear window switch
109	Lighting switch
110	Windscreen wiper motor switch
111	Heater blower switch
112	Windscreen wiper intermittent relay

	Optional extra equipment
113	Headlamp washer pump
114	Headlamp washer pump fuse
115	Timing relay - headlamp washer pump
116	Windscreen wiper intermittent relay
117	Radio
118	Radio fuse

Chapter 11 Suspension and steering

For modifications, and information applicable to later models, refer to Supplement at end of manual

Contents

Specifications

Front suspension

Type	Independent, coil spring, long and short swinging arms. Double acting hydraulic, telescopic shock absorbers
Springs: Identification	Coded with different paint colours. For replacement use spring of same colour

Steering geometry

Toe out	0.04 in (1.00 mm) $\pm$ 0.04 in (1.00 mm)
Castor - standard	$2^o \pm 1^o$
Castor - heavy duty	2° 32' $\pm 1^o$
Camber - standard	-0° 54' $\pm 0^o$ 45'
Camber - heavy duty	-0° 51' $\pm 0^o$ 45'
Max. castor difference LH to RH	0° 45'
Max. camber difference LH to RH	1° 00'

Rear suspension

Type	Radius arms progressive coil springs, hydraulic or gas filled double acting telescopic shock absorbers, stabilizer bar.

Saloon (1600 models)

	Standard	Heavy duty
Colour code	Yellow/violet	Blue/violet
Wire diameter	0.44/0.56 in (11.13/14.28 mm)	0.47/0.59 in (12.05/15.03 mm)
Free length	11.9 in (302.5 mm)	11.5 in (291.5 mm)
Outer diameter	5.08 in (129 mm)	5.08 in (129 mm)
Number of coils	7.5	7.5

Saloon (2000 models)

	Standard	Heavy duty
Colour code	Green/violet	Blue/violet
Wire diameter	0.47/0.57 in (11.9/14.48 mm)	0.47/0.59 in (12.05/15.03 mm)
Free length	11.2 in (284.4 mm)	11.5 in (291.5 mm)
Outer diameter	5.08 in (129 mm)	5.08 in (129 mm)
Number of coils	7.5	7.5

Estate car

	Standard	Heavy duty
Colour code	Pink/violet	Yellow/green
Wire diameter	0.43/0.59 in (10.90/14.92 mm)	0.46/0.60 in (11.65/15.3 mm)
Free length	12.2 in (309 mm)	11.9 in (301 mm)
Outer diameter	5.08 in (129 mm)	5.08 in (129 mm)
Number of coils	7.75	7.75

Steering

Type	Rack and pinion
Method of adjustment	Shims
Turning circle - between walls	34.9 ft (10.64 metres)
Turning circle - between curbs	32.8 ft (10.0 metres)
Lubricant - capacity	0.25 pints (0.15 litres)
Lubricant - type	SAE 90 hypoid

Wheels and tyres

Wheel size	4½J x 13 or 5½J x 13

Tyre pressures - lb/in² (kg/cm²)

	Tyre size	Normally laden * Front	Rear	Fully laden ** Front	Rear
Saloon	165SR x 13	26 (1.8)	26 (1.8)	28 (2.0)	36 (2.5)
	185/70SR x 13	23 (1.6)	23 (1.6)	26 (1.8)	30 (2.1)
Estate	165SR x 13	26 (1.8)	26 (1.8)	28 (2.0)	40 (2.8)
	187/70SR x 13	23 (1.6)	24 (1.7)	26 (1.8)	33 (2.3)
	175SR x 13	21 (1.5)	24 (1.7)	26 (1.8)	40 (2.8)

*Up to three people, plus luggage
** Four or five people, plus luggage

Torque wrench settings

	lb f ft	kg f m
Front suspension		
Crossmember to body bolts	44 - 52	6.0 - 7.0
Stabilizer bar clamp bolts	13 - 18	1.7 - 2.4
Stabilizer bracket to body	13 - 18	1.7 - 2.4
Stub axle ball joints - first tightening	30 - 45	4.1 - 6.2
Stub axle ball joints - final tightening	43 - 66	5.8 - 9.2
Tie bar to lower arm	43 - 50	5.8 - 6.9
Tie bar insulator nuts	46 - 72	6.2 - 9.7
Upper arm pivot bolt	52 - 70	7.1 - 9.6
Lower arm to crossmember	52 - 59	7.1 - 8.2
Shock absorber mounts - top	28 - 35	3.9 - 4.8
Shock absorber mounts - bottom	6 - 9	0.8 - 1.2
Stabilizer bar to tie bar	7 - 9	1.0 - 1.3
Rear suspension		
Upper radius arm to body*	42 - 50	5.8 - 6.9
Upper radius arm to axle*	42 - 50	5.8 - 6.9
Lower radius arm to body*	42 - 50	5.8 - 6.9
Lower radius arm to axle*	42 - 50	5.8 - 6.9
Shock absorber mounts - top	30 - 35	3.9 - 4.8
Shock absorber mounts - bottom	42 - 50	5.8 - 69
Stabiliser bar to radius arm	30 - 35	4.0 - 5.0
Steering		
Steering gear to crossmember	15 - 18	2.1 - 2.4
Track rod end to steering arm	18 - 22	2.5 - 3.0
Coupling to pinion spline	12 - 15	1.7 - 2.1
Universal joint to steering shaft spline	12 - 15	1.7 - 2.1
Steering wheel to steering shaft	20 - 25	2.8 - 3.4
Track rod end locknut	40 - 45	5.5 - 6.3
Track rod end ball housing	33 - 37	4.6 - 5.2
Pinion pre-load cover	13 - 17	1.7 - 2.4
Rack slipper cover	13 - 17	1.7 - 2.4
Pinion turning torque	5 - 15 (lb in)	6 - 17 (kg cm)
Wheel nuts		
Steel wheels	50 - 65	7 - 9
Aluminium wheels	90 - 105	12 - 14

*These bolts must be tightened after the vehicle has been lowered to the ground.

1 General description

The independent front suspension (Fig. 11.2) comprises short and long swinging arms with coil springs and hydraulic double-acting shock-absorbers which operate on the lower swinging arms. The main suspension framework is located on the underbody side members and acts as a mounting point for the wishbone type upper and single lower swinging arms. Attached to the upper frame are rubber bump stops to absorb excessive swinging arm movement. The suspension arms are mounted on rubber bushes and carry the stub axle ball joints at their outer ends.

Located on each axle stub are two taper roller bearings and these run in cups which are pressed into the wheel hubs. To keep the grease in the hub is a spring loaded neoprene seal located in the inner end of the hub. The wheel studs are splined and pressed into the hub flange.

Bolted to the lower arm are rubber mounted tie bars which control the suspension castor angle. The tie bars are connected to a stabilizer bar via a bolt and spacer and bushed at its connection points. It is mounted in split bushes which are clipped to brackets which are bolted to the body side members.

The rear suspension (Fig. 11.1) comprises lower and upper radius arms and coil spring. The two lower radius arms are in position in the axial direction of the vehicle and the two upper radius arms are in a diagonal position so as to absorb any forces created during cornering. All four radius arms are mounted in insulated rubber blocks. Fitted between the rear axle casing and underside of the body are rubber mounted double-acting hydraulic or gas filled telescopic shock absorbers. In addition, a stabilizer bar is fitted which passes along the lower radius arms and across the axle casing.

The coil springs are mounted on the lower radius arms and locate on a rubber ring between the spring and underside of the body.

The steering gear is of the rack and pinion type and is located on the front crossmember by two 'U' shaped clamps, the pinion connected to the steering column by a flexible coupling. Above the flexible coupling the steering column is split by a universal joint that is designed to collapse on impact thus minimising injury to the driver in the event of an accident.

Turning the steering wheel causes the rack to move in a lateral direction and the track rods attached to either end of the rack pass this movement to the steering arms on the stub axle assemblies, thereby moving the roadwheels.

Two adjustments are possible on the steering gear, namely rack slipper bearing adjustment and pinion bearing pre-load adjustment, but the steering gear must be removed from the car to carry out these adjustments. Both adjustments are made by varying the thickness of shim packs.

The two trackrods are adjustable in length to allow adjustment of the toe-in setting and to ensure the wheel lock angles are correct. Lock stops are built into the steering gear and are not adjustable.

2 Front hub bearings - removal and refitting

1   Refer to Chapter 9, Section 5, paragraphs 1, 2, 3, 5 and 6 and remove the disc brake caliper.
2   By judicious tapping and levering remove the dust cap from the centre of the hub.
3   Remove the split pin from the nut retainer and lift away the adjusting nut retainer.
4   Unscrew the adjusting nut and lift away the thrust washer and outer tapered bearing (Fig. 1.3).
5   Pull off the complete hub and disc assembly from the stub axle.
6   From the back of the hub assembly carefully prise out the grease seal noting which way round it is fitted. Lift away the inner tapered bearing.
7   Carefully clean out the hub and wash the bearings with petrol making sure that no grease or oil is allowed to get into the brake disc.
8   Using a soft metal drift carefully remove the inner and outer bearing cups.
9   To fit new cups make sure they are the right way round and using metal tubes of suitable size carefully drift them into position.
10 Pack the cone and roller assembly with grease working the grease well into the cage and rollers. **Note:** Leave the hub and grease seal empty to allow for subsequent expansion of the grease.

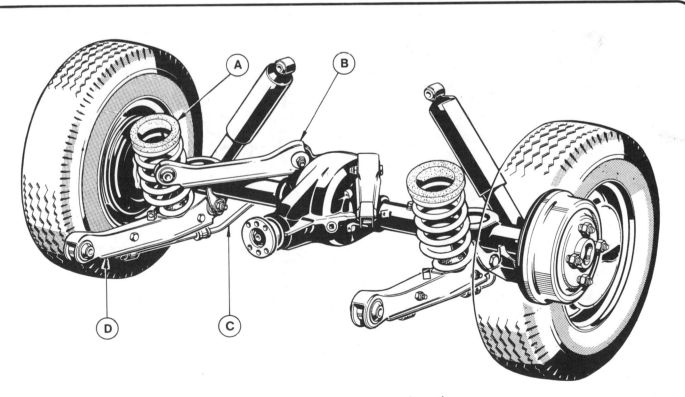

Fig. 11.1. Rear suspension assembly (Sec. 1)

A Coil spring and bush   B Upper radius arm   C Stabilizer bar   D Lower radius arm

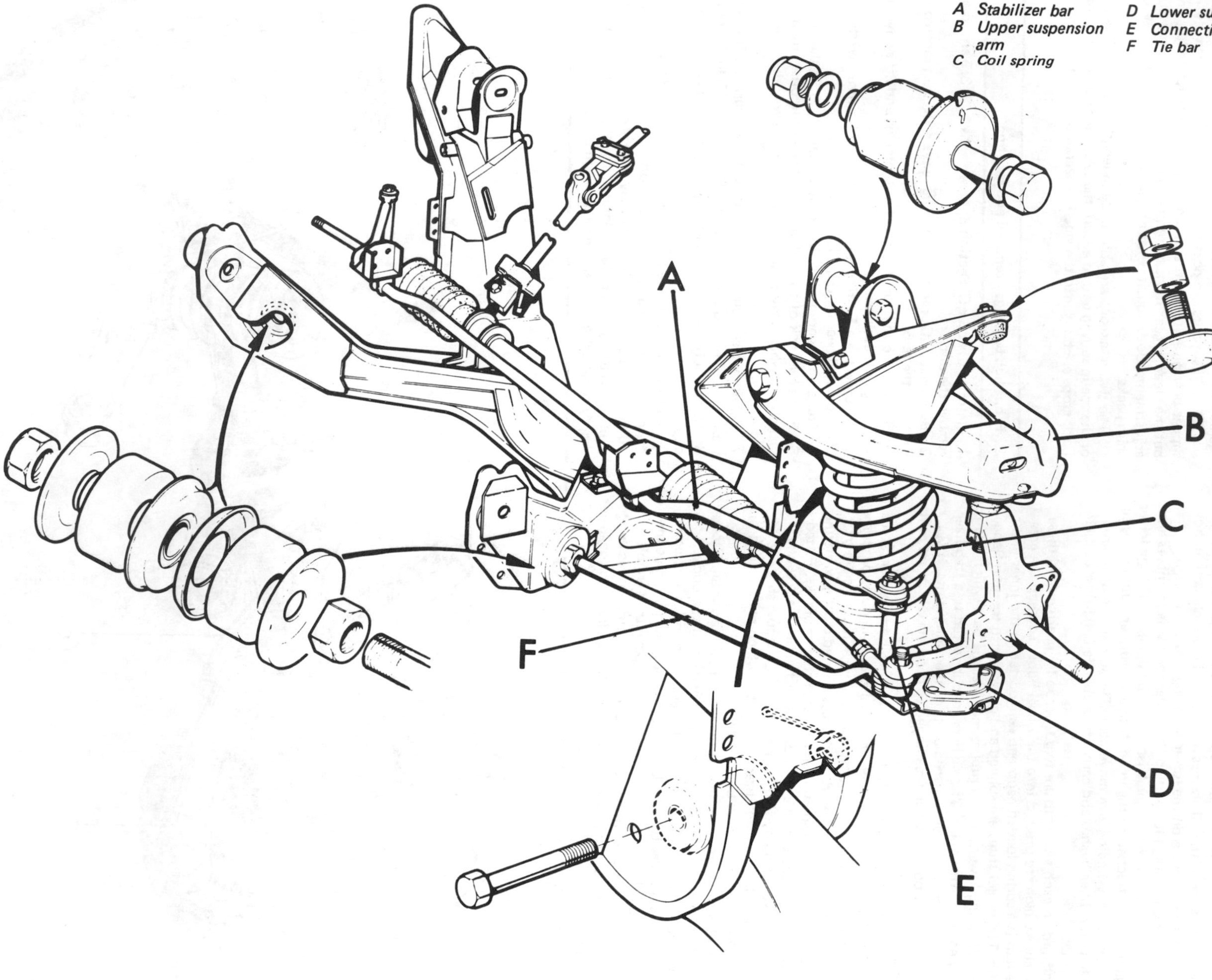

Fig. 11.2. Front suspension assembly (Sec. 1)

A Stabilizer bar
B Upper suspension
   arm
C Coil spring
D Lower suspension arm
E Connecting link
F Tie bar

11 To reassemble the hub first fit the inner bearing and then gently tap the grease seal back into the hub. A new seal must always be fitted as during removal it was probably damaged. The lip must face inwards to the hub.

12 Replace the hub and disc assembly on the stub axle and slide on the outer bearing and thrust washer.

13 Refit the adjusting nut, and tighten it to a torque wrench setting of 27 lb f ft (3.7 kg f m) whilst rotating the hub and disc to ensure free movement and centralisation of the bearings (Fig. 11.4). Slacken the nut back by 90° which will give the required endfloat. Fit the nut retainer and new split pin. Bend over the ears of the split pin.

14 Refit the dust cap to the centre of the hub.

15 Refit the caliper as described in Chapter 9, Section 5.

3 Front hub bearings - adjustment

1 To check the condition of the hub bearings, jack-up the front of the car and support on firmly based stands. Grasp the roadwheel at two opposite points to check for any rocking movement in the wheel hub. Watch carefully for any movement in the steering gear which can easily be mistaken for hub movement.

2 If a front wheel hub has excessive movement, this is adjusted by removing the hub cap and then tapping and levering the dust cap from the centre of the hub.

3 Remove the split pin from the nut retainer and lift away the adjusting nut retainer.

4 If a torque wrench is available tighten the centre adjusting nut to a torque wrench setting of 27 lb f ft (3.73 kg f m) as shown in Fig. 11.4 and then slacken the nut back 90° which will give the required endfloat. Replace the nut retainer and lock with a new split pin.

5 Assuming a torque wrench is not available however, tighten the centre adjusting nut until a slight drag is felt on rotating the wheel. Then loosen the nut very slowly until the wheel turns freely again and there is just a perceptible endfloat. Refit the nut retainer and lock with a new split pin.

6 Refit the dust cap to the centre of the hub.

4 Front hub - removal and refitting

1 Follow the instructions given in Section 2 of this Chapter up to and including paragraph 5.

2 Bend back the locking tab and undo the four bolts holding the hub to the brake disc.

3 If a new hub assembly is being fitted it is supplied complete with new cups and bearings. The bearing cups will already be fitted in the hub. It is essential to check that the cups and bearings are of the same manufacture, this can be done by reading the name on the bearings and by looking at the initial letter stamped on the hub, 'T' stands for Timken and 'S' for Skefco.

4 Clean with scrupulous care the mating surfaces of the hub and check for blemishes or damage. Any dirt or blemishes will almost certainly give rise to disc run-out. Using new locking tabs bolt the disc and hub together and tighten the bolts to a torque wrench setting of 30 - 34 lb f ft (4.15 - 4.70 kg f m).

5 To grease and reassemble the hub assembly follow the instructions given in Section 2, paragraphs 10 onwards.

5 Front axle assembly - removal and refitting

1 Chock the rear wheels, jack-up the vehicle and support the body on firmly based axle stands. Remove the front wheels.

2 Using a garage crane or overhead hoist support the weight of the engine.

3 Wipe the top of the brake master cylinder reservoir and unscrew the cap. Place a piece of polythene sheet over the top of the reservoir and refit the cap. This is to stop hydraulic fluid syphoning out during subsequent operations.

4 Disconnect the flexible brake hoses at the body support brackets (Fig. 11.5).

5 Slacken the steering column clamp plate and carefully withdraw the column.

6 Undo and remove the engine mounting securing nuts at the underside of the mounting (Fig. 11.6). There is one nut to each mounting.

7 Using a garage hydraulic jack or blocks support the weight of the front axle sub-assembly.

Fig. 11.3. Front hub assembly (Sec. 2)

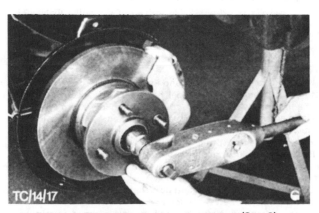

Fig. 11.4. Tightening the hub adjusting nut (Sec. 3)

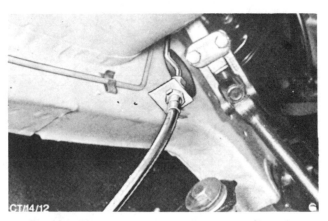

Fig. 11.5. Disconnect the flexible brake hoses (Sec. 5)

Fig. 11.6. Engine mounting stud (nut removed) (Sec. 5)

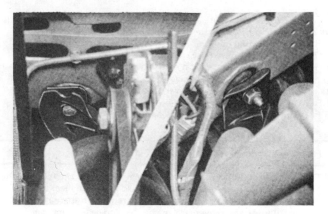

Fig. 11.7. Remove the front axle mounting bolts (Sec. 5)

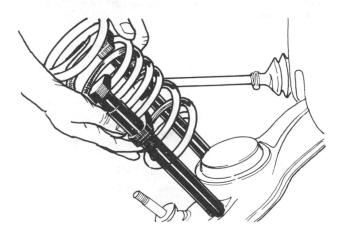

Fig. 11.8. Front coil spring with compressor fitted (Sec. 6)

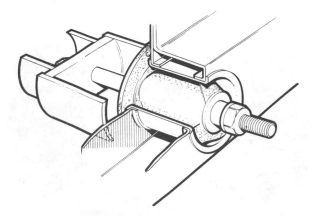

Fig. 11.9. Removing the mounting bush (Sec. 7)

8   Remove the two stabilizer bars to body clamps. Unclip the two
flexible fuel pipes.
9   Undo and remove the bolts which secure the front axle sub-
assembly to the body sidemembers as shown in Fig. 11.7. Carefully
lower the complete assembly and draw forwards from under the front
of the vehicle.
10 Refitting the front axle sub-assembly is the reverse sequence to
removal. It will be necessary to bleed the brake hydraulic
system as described in Chapter 9, Section 2.

---

6   Front axle assembly - overhaul

After high mileage it may be considered necessary to overhaul the
complete front axle assembly. It is far better to remove the complete
unit as described in Section 5 and dismantle it rather than work on it
still mounted on the car. Then proceed as follows:
1   Refer to Chapter 9, Section 5 and remove the caliper.
2   Prise off the hub dust cap and withdraw the split pin and nut
retainer. Undo and remove the nut (Fig. 11.3).
3   Carefully pull the hub and disc assembly from the axle stub.
4   Undo and remove the ball stud securing nuts and then using a
universal ball joint separator release the ball joint taper pins from the
stub axle locations.
5   Next remove the trackrod-ends from their locations on the stub
axles and remove the stub axle assembly as shown in Fig. 11.2.
6   Withdraw the long bolt that secures the upper arm to the axle
frame and lift away the upper arm.
7   It is necessary to compress the spring. For this either make up a
spring compressor tool comprising two parts as shown in Fig. 11.8 or
borrow one from the local Ford garage. Do not attempt to use any
makeshift tools as this can be very dangerous.
8   Using the spring compressors, contract the spring by at least 2 inches
(51 mm).
9   Undo and remove the upper and lower shock absorber retaining
nuts (lower fixing) and bolt (upper fixing). The shock absorber may
now be lifted away through the coil spring and lower arm aperture.
10 Undo and remove the bolts that secure the tie bar to the lower arm.
The lower arm should now be pulled down until there is sufficient
clearances for the coil spring to be lifted away.
11 Bend back the lock tabs and unscrew and remove the four bolts
that secure the steering 'U' shaped rack brackets to the front axle frame.
Lift away the steering rack assembly.
12 Undo and remove the nut and bolt that secures the lower arm to the
front axle frame. Lift away the lower arm.
13 Using a suitable diameter drift or long bolt, piece of metal tube,
packing washers and nut, remove the lower arm bush.
14 The operations described in paragraphs 1 - 13 should now be repeated
for the second front suspension assembly. It will be necessary to
release the coil spring compressor.

15 Undo and remove the nuts that secure the tie bars to the axle frame. Lift away the connecting link, tie bar and stabilizer bar assembly.

16 Undo and remove the nuts and washers from each of the connecting links and part the stabilizer bar from the tie bars.

17 It is now beneficial to cut away the bushes in the tie bar and stabilizer which will make removal far easier.

18 Remove the nuts and washers securing each rubber bump stop. Remove the bump stops.

19 Dismantling is now complete. Wash all parts and wipe dry ready for inspection. Inspect all bushes for signs of wear and all parts for damage or excessive corrosion: if evident, new parts must be obtained. If one coil spring requires renewal the second one must also be renewed as it will have settled over a period of time.

20 During reassembly it is important that none of the rubber mounted bolts are fully tightened until the weight of the vehicle is taken on the front wheels.

21 Replace the rubber bump stops. If they are difficult to insert in their location smear with a little washing up liquid. Bolt the bump stops in position.

22 Fit new end bushes to the stabilizer and tie bar and then locate the connecting links in the stabilizer.

23 Next locate the connecting links in the tie bar and stabilizer bar bushes. Secure with their nut and washers.

24 Screw the nuts on the tie bar ends and follow with the washer together with the bush. Locate the tie bars in their respective positions on the frame and loosely refit the spacer, bush, nut and washer.

25 Using a bench vice and suitable diameter tube fit a new bush to the lower arm. The lower arm pivot bolt is fitted with a nylon nut and split pin. Tighten the nut to 55 lb f ft (7.6 kg f m).

26 Locate the lower arm in the frame and line up the holes with a screwdriver. Refit the pivot bolt and washers making sure that the bolt head is towards the front of the axle frame.

27 Refit the tie bar to the lower suspension arm and retain with the two nuts and bolts.

28 Place the coil spring between the frame and lower arm, with the feathered edge uppermost. Insert the shock absorber through the lower arm and spring and secure the shock absorber in position with the bolt (upper fixing) and nuts (lower fixing).

29 Unscrew the spring compressor and repeat the operations in paragraphs 22 to 28 for the second front suspension assembly.

30 Check the condition of the steering rack mounting rubbers and renew if necessary. Position the steering rack on the axle frame and secure to the mounting brackets with the 'U' clamps. Always use a new locking plate under the bolt heads. Tighten the bolts to a torque wrench setting of 15 - 18 lb f ft (2.1 - 2.4 kg f m) and bend up the locking plate.

31 Place the upper suspension arm on the axle frame, insert the pivot bolt through the arm and frame holes so that the head is towards the front of the axle frame. Secure with the washer and nut. Repeat this operation for the second upper suspension arm.

32 Connect the stub axle assembly to the suspension arm ball joints, locate the trackrod ends in the stub axle, and tighten all the nuts. The trackrod end to steering arm nuts should be tightened to a torque wrench setting of 18 - 22 lb f ft (2.5 - 3 kg f m).

33 Refer to Section 4 and refit the hub and disc assemblies.

34 The complete front axle assembly may now be refitted to the car, as described in Section 5.

35 Check the wheel alignment and steering angles (Section 22).

7 Front axle mounting bushes - removal and refitting

1 Refer to Section 5, and remove the front axle assembly.

2 Using a piece of tube about 4 inches (101.6 mm) long and suitable diameter, a long bolt and nut and packing washers draw the bushes from the side member (Fig. 11.9).

3 Fit new bushes using the reverse procedure. The new bushes must be installed so that the arrows are in alignment with the indentation in the bodyframe. The flange position of the bushes must be: **front bush**, flange located **inside** sidemember; **rear bush**, flange located **outside** sidemember (Fig. 11.10).

4 Refit the front assembly, as described in Section 5.

8 Stub axle - removal and refitting

1 Refer to Section 2 and remove the front hub and disc assembly.

2 Undo and remove the three bolts and spring washers that secure the brake disc splash shield to the stub axle.

3 Extract the split pins and then undo and remove the castellated nuts that secure the three ball joint pins to the stub axle.

4 Using a universal ball joint separator, separate the ball joint pins from the stub axle. Lift away the stub axle.

5 Refitting the stub axle is the reverse sequence to removal. The trackrod end to steering arm retaining nut must be tightened to a torque wrench setting of 18 - 22 lb f ft (2.5 - 3.0 kg f m).

6 If a new stub axle has been fitted it is recommended that the steering geometry and front wheel toe-in be checked. Further information may be found in Section 22.

9 Upper suspension arm - removal and refitting

1 Chock the rear wheels, jack up the front of the car and place on firmly based axle stands. Remove the roadwheel.

2 Disconnect the flexible brake hoses at the body support brackets (Fig. 11.5).

3 Slacken the steering column clamp plate and carefully withdraw the column (see Section 26).

4 Using a garage crane or overhead hoist support the weight of the engine.

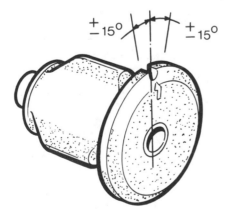

Fig. 11.10. Front axle mounting bush alignment mark (Sec. 7)

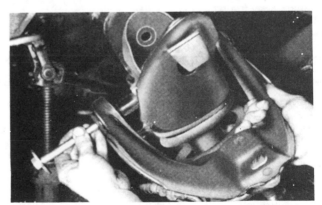

Fig. 11.11. Withdrawing the upper arm pivot bolt (Sec. 9)

5   Undo and remove the engine mounting securing nuts at the underside of the mounting (Fig. 11.6).
6   Using a garage hydraulic jack or blocks, support the weight of the front axle assembly.
7   Unclip the two flexible fuel pipes.
8   Undo and remove the rear bolts which secure the front axle assembly to the body sidemembers. Slacken but do not remove the front securing bolts.
9   Carefully lower the assembly, allowing it to pivot about the front securing bolts.
10 Undo and remove the upper arm to stub axle ball joint nut then using a ball joint separator release the joint. Undo the upper arm pivot bolt nut, withdraw the bolt (Fig. 11.11) and remove the upper arm.
11 Refitting is the reverse sequence of removal but the following points should be noted:

a) *Rubber mounted bolts and nuts should not be fully tightened until the weight of the vehicle is taken on the front wheels.*
b) *The head of the upper arm pivot bolt should be towards the front.*
c) *Check the steering geometry, Section 22.*
d) *It will be necessary to bleed the braking system, Chapter 9, Section 2.*

10 Lower suspension arm - removal and refitting

1   Chock the rear wheels, jack-up the front of the car and place on firmly based axle stands. Remove the roadwheel.
2   Wipe the top of the brake master cylinder reservoir and unscrew the cap. Place a piece of polythene sheet over the top of the reservoir and replace the cap. Disconnect the flexible brake hoses at the body support brackets (Fig. 11.5).
3   It is now necessary to compress the spring. For this either make up a spring compressor tool comprising two parts as shown in Fig. 11.8 or borrow one from the local Ford garage. Do not attempt to use any makeshift tools as this can be very dangerous.
4   Using the spring compressor, contract the spring by at least 2 inches (51 mm).
5   Undo and remove the upper and lower shock absorber retaining nuts (lower fixing) and bolt (upper fixing). The shock absorber may now be lifted away through the coil spring and lower arm aperture.
6   Withdraw the split pin, undo and remove the castellated nut that secures the lower wishbone ball joint pin to the stub axle. Using a universal ball joint separator separate the ball joint pin from the stub axle.
7   The lower suspension arm may now be parted and the coil spring removed.
8   Undo the tie bar locknut and remove the two bolts and nuts that secure the tie bar to the lower arm.
9   Undo and remove the bolt that secures the lower arm to the front axle frame. The suspension arm can now be lifted rearwards and downwards away from the front axle frame.
10 To fit a new bush first remove the old bush by using a piece of tube about 4 inches (101.6 mm) long and suitable diameter, a long bolt and nut and packing washer, draw the bush from the lower suspension arm. Fitting a new bush is the reverse sequence to removal.
11 Refitting the lower suspension arm is the reverse sequence to removal. The lower arm retaining bolts must be tightened once the car has been lowered to the ground.
12 If a new lower steering arm has been fitted it is recommended that the steering geometry and front wheel toe-in be checked. Further information may be found in Section 22.

11 Stabilizer bar - removal and refitting

1   Undo and remove the bolt that secures each stabilizer bar mounting bush clip to the stabilizer bar mounting bracket.
2   Release the clips and then undo and remove the three bolts and spring washers that secure each mounting bracket to the body sidemember.

3   Undo and remove the two nuts, dished washers and upper bushes and detach the connecting links from their locations in the stabilizer bar. The stabilizer bar may now be lifted away from the underside of the car.
4   Refitting the stabilizer bar is the reverse sequence to removal.

12 Stabilizer bar mounting bushes - removal and refitting

1   Undo and remove the bolt that secures each stabilizer bar mounting bush clip to the stabilizer bar mounting brackets.
2   Using a metal bar such as a tyre lever carefully ease the stabilizer bar downwards and push the split mounting bushes and washers clear of their locations.
3   Push the new bushes and washers onto the bar in their approximate positions and then align the bushes with the stabilizer bar mounting brackets and refit the retaining clips and bolts.

13 Stabilizer bar connecting link bush - removal and refitting

1   Refer to Section 11 and remove the stabilizer bar.
2   Using a sharp knife of hacksaw blade cut the cone ends off the connecting link bushes and discard the bushes.
3   Using a bench vice, a piece of tube of suitable diameter and a socket fit the new connecting link bushes by pressing them into the eye of the bar.
4   Refit the stabilizer bar as described in Section 11.

14 Front shock absorber - removal and refitting

1   Chock the rear wheels, jack-up the front of the car and place on firmly based stands. Remove the roadwheel.
2   Locate a small jack under the lower suspension arm and partially compress the coil spring.
3   Undo and remove the shock absorber top mounting bolt.
4   Undo and remove the two nuts that secure the shock absorber lower mounting. The shock absorber may now be lifted away through the coil spring and lower arm aperture.
5   Examine the shock absorber for signs of damage to the body, distorted piston rod, loose mounting or hydraulic fluid leakage which, if evident, means a new unit should be fitted.
6   To test for shock absorber efficiency, hold the unit in the vertical position and gradually extend and contract the unit between its maximum and minimum limit ten times. It should be apparent that there is equal resistance on both directions of movement. If this is not apparent a new unit should be fitted - always renew the shock absorbers in pairs.
7   Refitting the shock absorbers is the reverse sequence to removal.

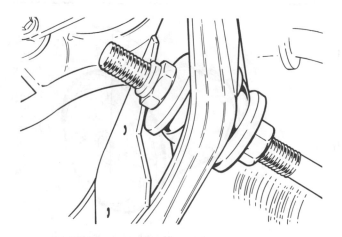

Fig. 11.12. Tie bar end mounting (Sec. 15)

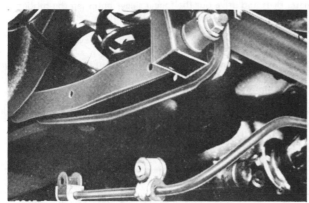

Fig. 11.13. Rear stabilizer bar removal from lower radius arm (Sec. 16)

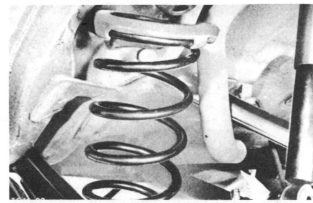

Fig. 11.14. Removing the rear suspension spring and bush (Sec. 16)

Fig. 11.15. Using a nut and packing (A) with a tube (C) to remove the bush (B) (Sec. 17)

Fig. 11.16. Fitting spacer to rear shock absorber lower mounting bolt (Sec. 18)

15 Tie bar - removal and refitting

1   Chock the rear wheels, jack-up the front of the car and place on firmly based axle stands. Remove the roadwheel.
2   Undo and remove the bolts that secure the tie bar to the lower suspension arm.
3   Extract the split pin from the end of the bar. Undo and remove the forward of the two nuts that secure the tie bar to the chassis frame member.
4   Disconnect the stabilizer bar connecting link.
5   Remove the bush and spacer assembly from the threaded end of the tie bar. Lift away the tie bar (Fig. 11.12).
6   If it is necessary to fit new bushes, use a sharp knife or hacksaw blade and cut the cone ends from the tie bar bush. Discard the old bush.
7   Using a tube of suitable diameter, a socket and bench vice, fit a new tie bar end bush.
8   Refitting the tie bar is the reverse sequence to removal. It is recommended that the steering geometry and front wheel toe-in be checked. Further information will be found in Section 22.

16 Rear spring - removal and refitting

1   Chock the front wheels, jack up the rear of the car and support the **body** on firmly based stands. Remove the rear wheels.
2   Using a suitable jack to relieve any tension on the through bolts, remove the stabilizer bar from the lower radius arm (Fig. 11.13).
3   Position the jack under the lower arm to remove the tension, and remove the front through bolt. Lower the jack and ease out the coil spring and rubber bush, noting its location (Fig. 11.14).

4   Refitting is the reverse of this procedure. The lower arm bolt should be fitted from the outside, and the stabilizer bar bolts from the inside. Do not tighten the nuts fully until the weight of the car is on its wheels.
5   If one coil spring requires renewal the second one must also be renewed as it will have settled over a period of time. Make sure, by referring to a Ford dealer, that the correct type of spring is fitted.

17 Rear suspension upper radius arm - removal and refitting

1   Chock the front wheels, jack-up the rear of the car and support the body on firmly based stands. Remove the rear wheels.
2   Disconnect the stabilizer bar from the radius arm and swing it to one side.
3   Jack-up the rear axle so that the shock absorber can be disconnected from the axle mounting.
4   Lower the jack and press the coil spring from its upper retainer. Now twist the spring from its lower retainer.
5   Again jack-up the rear axle and having relieved the radius arm bolts of any strain, remove the bolts and withdraw the radius arm.
6   Should it be necessary to fit new mounting insulator bushes the bushes may be removed using a piece of tube about 4 inches (101.6 mm) long and suitable diameter, a long bolt and nut and packing washers and drawing out the old bushes (Fig. 11.15).
7   Fitting new bushes is the reverse procedure as was used for removal.
8   The upper arm bolts should be fitted from the outside, the stabilizer bar bolts from the inside, and the shock absorber bolt from the front, with the spacer located as in (Fig. 11.16). Do not tighten the nuts fully until the weight of the car is on its wheels.

18 Rear suspension lower radius arm - removal and refitting

1   Chock the front wheels, jack-up the rear of the car and support the body on firmly based axle stands. Remove the rear wheels.
2   Disconnect the stabilizer bar from the radius arm and swing it to one side.
3   Jack-up the rear axle and disconnect the shock absorber lower mounting.
4   Lower the jack and press the coil spring from the upper retainer. Twist the spring from the lower retainer.
5   Remove the radius arm pivot bolts and withdraw the arm.'
6   Should it be necessary to fit new mounting insulator bushes, the bushes may be removed using a piece of tube about 4 inches (101.6 mm) long and suitable diameter, a long bolt and nut and packing washers and drawing out the old bushes (Fig. 11.15).
7   Fitting new bushes is the reverse procedure as was used for removal. **Note:** the two bushes are of different diameters.
8   Refitting the lower radius arm is the reverse sequence to removal. The upper spring rubber bush **must** be refitted correctly. The lower arm bolts should be fitted from the outside, the stabilizer bar bolts from the inside and the shock absorber bolt from the front, with the spacer located as in Fig. 11.16. Do not tighten the nuts fully until the weight of the car is on its wheels.

19 Rear shock absorber - removal and refitting

1   Chock the front wheels, jack-up the rear of the car and support the axle on firmly based stands. Remove the rear wheel.

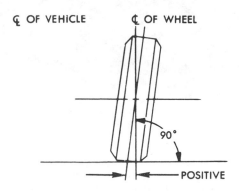

Fig. 11.17. Camber diagram (Sec. 22)

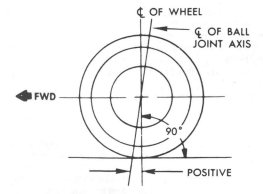

Fig. 11.18. Castor diagram (Sec. 22)

2   Undo and remove the shock absorber upper and lower mounting nuts and bolt. Lift away the shock absorbers.
3   Should it be necessary to fit new rubber bushes, use a suitable diameter drift and drive out the spacer sleeve and then the rubber bushes. Refitting new bushes is the reversal of the removal sequence.
4   Examine the shock absorber for signs of damage to the body, distorted piston rod or hydraulic leakage which, if evident, means a new unit should be fitted.
5   To test for damper efficiency hold the unit in the vertical position and gradually extend and contract the unit between its maximum and minimum limits ten times. It should be apparent that there is equal resistance in both directions of movement. If this is not apparent a new unit should be fitted; always renew shock absorbers in pairs.
6   Refitting the shock absorber is the reverse sequence to removal (Fig. 11.16).

20 Rear stabilizer bar - removal and refitting

1   Remove the bolts which secure each end of the stabilizer bar to the radius arms (Fig. 11.13)
2   Unscrew the self-locking nuts and withdraw the front and rear mounting brackets together with the insulating bushes.
3   Bushes are renewed in a similar manner to those for the shock absorbers, by first removing the metal spacer. The use of a little brake fluid will facilitate installation of the rubber bush.

21 Steering - lubrication

1   Lubrication of the rack and pinion during normal service operation is not necessary, the lubricant is contained in the assembly by rubber gaiters. However, should a loss occur due to a leak from the rack housing or rubber gaiters then the correct amount of oil should be inserted using an oil can. Obviously before replenishment is carried out the source of leak must be found and rectified.
2   To top-up the oil in the rack and pinion assembly, remove the clip from the rubber gaiter on the right-hand end of the steering rack housing and rotate the steering wheel until the rack is in the normal straight ahead position. Allow any remaining oil to seep out so that it is not overfilled. Using an oil can filled with Hypoy 90 type gear oil insert the nozzle into the end of the rack housing and refill with not more than 0.25 pint (0.14 litre) of oil.
3   Reposition the gaiter and tighten the clip quickly to ensure minimum loss of oil and then move the steering wheel from lock to lock very slowly to distribute the oil in the housing.
    Important: If at any time the car is raised from the ground and the front wheels are clear and suspended, do not use any excessive force or rapid movement when moving the wheels, especially from one lock to the other, otherwise damage could occur to the steering mechanism.

22 Front wheel - alignment and steering angles

1   Accurate front wheel alignment is essential to prevent excessive steering and tyre wear. Before considering the steering/suspension geometry, check that the tyres are correctly inflated, that the front wheels are not buckled, the hub bearings are not worn or incorrectly adjusted and that the steering linkage is in good order, without slackness or wear at the joints.
2   Wheel alignment consists of four factors:
    Camber, which is the angle at which the front wheels are set from the vertical when viewed from the front of the car. Positive camber is the amount (in degrees) that the wheels are tilted outwards at the top from the vertical (Fig. 11.17).
    Castor, is the angle between the steering axis and a vertical line when viewed from each side of the car. Positive castor is when the steering axis is inclined rearward (Fig. 11.18).
    Steering axis inclination, is the angle, when viewed from the front of the car between the vertical and an imaginary line drawn between the upper and lower suspension control arm ball joints (Fig. 11.19).
    Toe setting, is the amount by which the distance between the front inside edges of the roadwheels (measured at hub height) differs from the diametrically opposite distance measured between the rear inside edges of the front roadwheels (Fig. 11.20 shows toe-out).

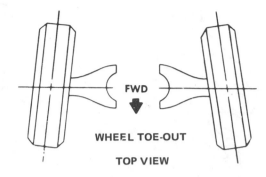

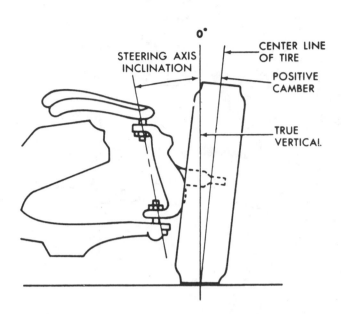

Fig. 11.19. Steering axis inclination diagram (Sec. 22)

Fig. 11.20. Toe-out diagram (Sec. 22)

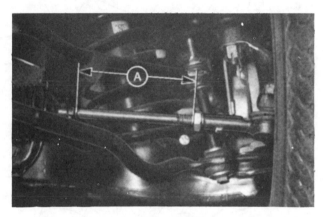

Fig. 11.21. Adjustable track rod length (A) (Sec. 22)

3 Due to the need for special gauges it is not normally within the scope of the home mechanic to check and adjust any steering angle except toe. Where suitable equpiment can be borrowed however, adjustment can be carried out in the following way, setting the tolerances to those given in Specifications.

4 Before carrying out any adjustment, place the vehicle on level ground, tyres correctly inflated and the front roadwheels are set in the 'straight-ahead' position. Make sure that all suspension and steering components are securely attached and without wear in the moving parts.

The camber and steering axis inclination angles are set in production and they cannot be altered or adjusted. Any deviation from the angles specified must therefore be due to collision damage or gross wear in the components.

5 *To adjust the castor angle,* release the tie bar nuts and screw them in, or out, as necessary (Fig. 11.12).

6 *To adjust the toe,* (which must always be carried out after adjustment of the castor angle - where required), make or obtain a toe gauge. One can be made up from a length of tubing or bar, cranked to clear the sump, clutch or torque converter bellhousing and having a screw and locknut at one end.

7 Use the gauge to measure the distance between the two inner wheel rims (at hub height and at the rear of the roadwheels).

8 Push or pull the vehicle to rotate the roadwheels through 180° (half a turn) and then measure the distance between the inner wheel rims (at hub height and at the front of the roadwheels). This last measurement will differ from the first by the amount specified in the Specifications Section. This represent the correct toe-setting of the front wheels.

9 Where the toe is found to be incorrect, loosen the locknuts on both the trackrod ends, also release the screws on the steering bellow clips (Fig. 11.21).

10 Turn each trackrod in the same direction by not more than one quarter turn at a time and then recheck the toe. When the adjustment is correct, tighten the locknuts without moving the trackrods and make sure that the trackrod ends are in their correct plane (centre position of arc of travel).

11 Tighten the steering bellows clips making sure that the bellows have not twisted during the adjustment operations.

12 It is important to always adjust each trackrod equally.
Where new components have been fitted, adjust the length of each trackrod so that they are equal and the front roadwheels in approximately the 'straight-ahead' position, before commencing final setting with the gauge.

23 Steering wheel - removal and refitting

1 With the front wheels in the straight-ahead position note the position of the spokes of the steering wheel and mark the hub of the steering wheel and inner shaft to ensure correct positioning upon refitting.

2 Carefully prise out the steering wheel insert and using a socket or box spanner of the correct size slacken the steering wheel nut but leave it two or three turns on the thread.

3 Remove the wheel by thumping the rear of the rim adjacent to the spokes with the palms of the hands which should loosen the hub splines from the steering shaft spline. Fully remove the nut and lift off the steering wheel.

4 Replacement is the reverse procedure to removal. Correctly align the two marks previously made to ensure correct positioning of the spikes. Do not thump the steering wheel when refitting as it could cause the inner shaft to collapse. Refit the nut and tighten to a torque wrench setting of 20 - 25 lb f ft (2.8 - 3.4 kg f m).

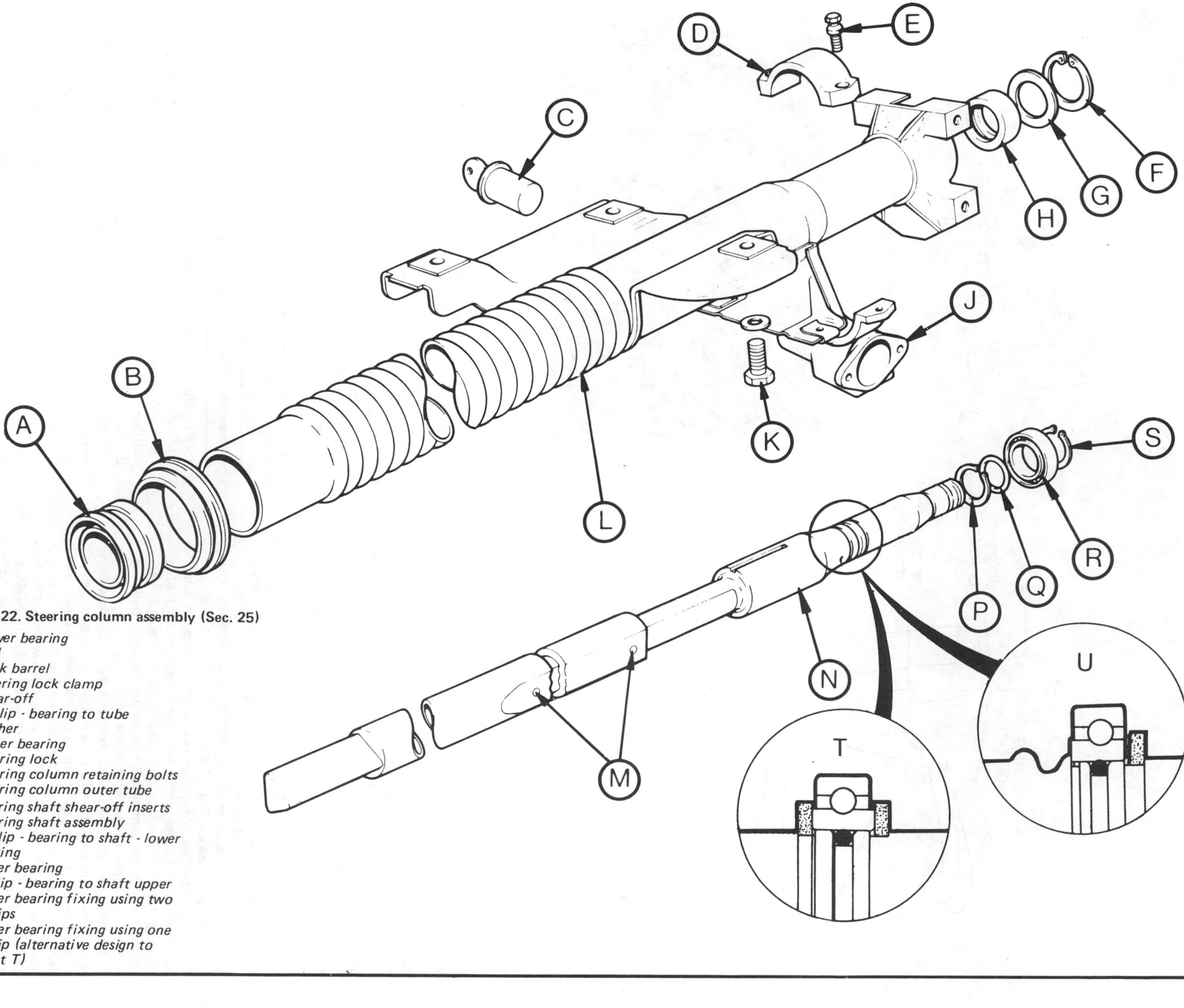

Fig. 11.22. Steering column assembly (Sec. 25)

A   Lower bearing
B   Seal
C   Lock barrel
D   Steering lock clamp
E   Shear-off
F   Circlip - bearing to tube
G   Washer
H   Upper bearing
J   Steering lock
K   Steering column retaining bolts
L   Steering column outer tube
M   Steering shaft shear-off inserts
N   Steering shaft assembly
P   Circlip - bearing to shaft - lower
Q   'O' ring
R   Upper bearing
S   Circlip - bearing to shaft upper
T   Upper bearing fixing using two
    circlips
U   Upper bearing fixing using one
    circlip (alternative design to
    insert T)

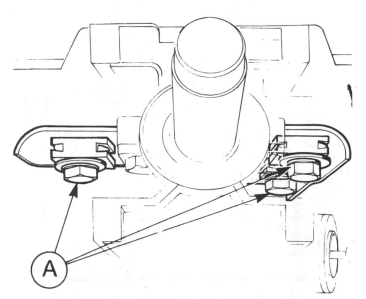

Fig. 11.23. Steering column retaining bolts (Sec. 24)

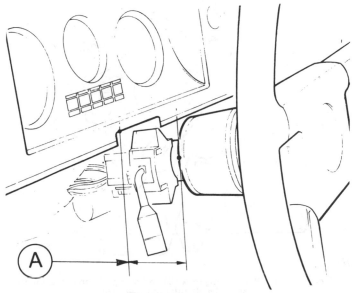

Fig. 11.24. Checking the steering column assembly location (Sec. 24)

24 Steering column assembly - removal and refitting

1 Disconnect the battery and then working within the engine compartment, bend back the locktabs on the flexible coupling clamp plate. Slacken both bolts, extract one and swing the clamp plate to one side.
2 Refer to Section 23 and remove the steering wheel.
3 Unscrew and remove the steering column lower shroud and remove it, then unclip the upper shroud.
4 Unscrew and remove the dash lower insulation panel.
5 Remove the two bolts each from the wiper switch, light switch and multi-function switch. Note that one wiper switch bolt also has an earth wire.
6 Remove the section of air duct which passes over the steering column.
7 Remove the two screws which secure the wiring harness plug to the bottom of the ignition switch.
8 Remove the upper and lower steering column bracket bolts (Fig. 11.20) lower the column and then withdraw it through the vehicle interior.
9 Installation is the reverse of removal, but before tightening the column bracket bolts (Fig. 11.22), ensure that the dimension A shown in Fig. 11.24 is 2.87 - 3.03 in (73 - 77 mm).

25 Steering column shaft - removal and refitting

1 Refer to Section 24 and remove the steering column assembly.
2 Drill out the steering lock mounting bolt heads and remove the lock.
3 Lift away the lower bearing cover. Using a pointed chisel carefully prise open the staking and ease out the lower bearing.
4 With a pair of circlip pliers contract and withdraw the circlip and plain washer from the top end of the shaft.
5 Withdraw the steering shaft complete with the upper bearing from the column assembly (Fig. 11.22).
6 Using circlip pliers remove the upper bearing retaining circlip then remove the upper bearing. Remove the lower retaining circlip, where fitted.

7 Refitting is the reverse of removal. To fit the steering lock, position the clamp as shown in Fig. 11.25 ensuring that the lock tongue engages in the hole in the column tube. Tighten the new retaining bolts until the heads break off.

26 Steering column flexible coupling and universal joint assembly - removal and refitting

1 Undo and remove the nut, clamp bolt and spring washer that secures the flexible coupling bottom half to the pinion shaft (Fig. 11.26).
2 Bend back the locktabs and undo and remove the two bolts securing the universal joint lock bar to the lower steering shaft. Lift away the tab washer and lock bar.
3 The lower steering shaft may now be lifted away.
4 To refit place the lower steering shaft in its approximate fitted position and align the master splines on the shaft and pinion. Connect the shaft to the pinion.
5 Position the triangular clamp on the bottom of the steering column and secure with the clamp bar bolts and tab washer. Tighten the bolts fully and lock by bending up the tabs.
6 Refit the flexible coupling bottom half clamp bolt spring washer and nut. Tighten to a torque wrench setting of 12 - 15 lb f ft (1.7 - 2.1 kg f m).

27 Rack and pinion steering gear - removal and refitting

1 Before starting this operation set the steering wheel to the straight-ahead position.
2 Jack-up the front of the car and place blocks under the wheels. Lower the car slightly so that the trackrods are in a near horizontal position.
3 Undo and remove the nut, bolt the spring washer that secures the flexible coupling bottom half clamp to the pinion shaft.

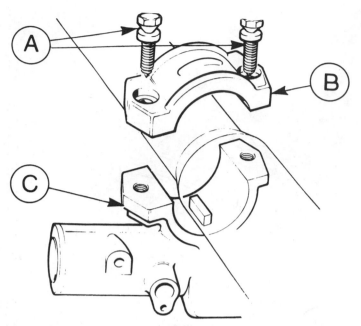

Fig. 11.25. Fit the steering lock (C) and clamp (B) and retain with 'shear-head' bolts (A) (Sec. 25)

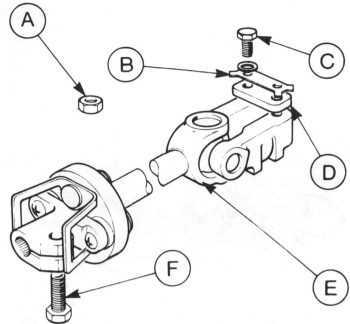

Fig. 11.26. Steering flexible coupling assembly (Sec. 26)

A Nut
B Lock tab
C Clamp bolt

D Clamp plate
E Universal joint
F Clamp bolt

4 Bend back the lock tabs and then undo and remove the bolts that secure the steering gear assembly to the mountings on the front axle frame. Lift away the bolts, lock washers and 'U' shaped clamps.
5 Withdraw the split pins and undo and remove the castellated nuts from the ends of each trackrod where they join the steering arms. Using a universal ball joint separator, separate the trackrod ball pins from the steering arms and lower the steering gear assembly downwards out of the car.
6 Before replacing the steering gear assembly make sure the wheels have remained in the straight-ahead position. Also check the condition of the mounting rubbers round the housing and if they appear worn or damaged they must be renewed.
7 Check that the steering rack is also in the straight-ahead position. This can be done by ensuring that the distances between the ends of both trackrods and the rack housing on both sides are the same.
8 Place the steering gear assembly in its location on the front axle frame and at the same time mate up the splines on the pinion shaft with the splines in the clamp on the steering column flexible column. There is a master spline so make sure these are in line.
9 Replace the two 'U' shaped clamps using new locking tabs under the bolts, tighten the bolts to a torque wrench setting of 12 - 15 lb f ft (1.7 - 2.0 kg f m). Bend up the locking tabs.
10 Refit the trackrod ends into the steering arms, replace the castellated nuts and tighten them to a torque wrench setting of 18 - 22 lb f ft (2.5 - 3.0 kg f m). Use new split pins to lock the nuts.
11 Tighten the clamp bolt on the steering column flexible coupling to a torque wrench setting of 12 - 15 lb f ft (1.7 - 2.1 kg f m), having first double checked that the pinion is correctly located in on the splines.
12 Jack-up the car, remove the blocks from under the wheels and lower the car to the ground. The toe setting must now be checked and further information will be found in Section 22.

28 Rack and pinion steering gear - adjustments

1 For the steering gear to function correctly, two adjustments are necessary. These are pinion bearing pre-load and rack damper adjustment. Care must be taken not to overtighten otherwise seizure may take place. Double check all readings.
2 To carry out these adjustments, remove the steering gear from the car as described in Section 27, then mount the steering gear assembly in a soft jawed vice so that the pinion is in a horizontal position and the rack damper cover plate to the top.
3 Remove the rack damper cover plate by undoing and removing the two retaining bolts and spring washers. Lift away the cover plate, gasket and shims. Also remove the small spring and the yoke which bears onto the rack.
4 Now remove the pinion bearing pre-load cover plate from the base of the pinion, by undoing and removing the two bolts and spring washers. Lift away the cover plate, gasket and shims.
5 To set the pinion bearing pre-load replace the cover plate with the thick shim against the cover plate, and at least two thin shims. Leave out the gasket, tighten the retaining bolts to compress the shim pack, then slacken the bolts until the cover plate just contacts the shims.
6 Using feeler gauges, measure the gap between the cover plate and the pinion housing. This should be between 0.011 and 0.014 in (0.28 and 0.35 mm). Take several readings near each bolt to ensure that the cover plate is parallel and note the final (average) reading. To bring the gap within tolerance, change the thinner shims as necessary from the selection available.
7 Shims are available in the following thicknesses:

Part No.	Material	Thickness
71BB - 3K544 - AA	Steel	0.005 in (0.13 mm)
71BB - 3K544 - BA	Steel	0.007 in (0.19 mm)
71BB - 3K544 - CA	Steel	0.010 in (0.25 mm)
71BB - 3K544 - DA	Steel	0.092 in (2.35 mm)
71BB - 3K544 - LA	Steel	0.002 in (0.05 mm)
71BB - 3581 - AA	Buna coated flexoid	0.01 in (0.254 mm)

8 Remove the cover plate, fit a new gasket make sure that the oil seal lips are packed with grease. Refit the cover plate.
9 Apply sealant to the bolt threads and then screw in the bolts and tighten them to a torque of 16 lbf/ft (22 Nm).

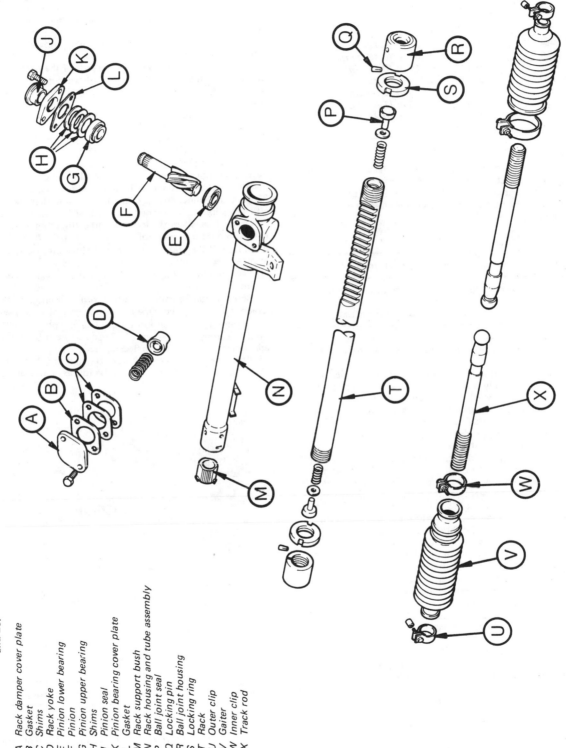

Fig. 11.27. Rack and pinion steering gear (Sec. 28 and 29)

A Rack damper cover plate
B Gasket
C Shims
D Rack yoke
E Pinion lower bearing
F Pinion
G Pinion upper bearing
H Shims
J Pinion seal
K Pinion bearing cover plate
L Gasket
M Rack support bush
N Rack housing and tube assembly
P Ball joint seal
Q Locking pin
R Ball joint housing
S Locking ring
T Rack
U Outer clip
V Gaiter
W Inner clip
X Track rod

10 To reset the rack damper adjustment, replace the yoke in its location on the rack and make sure it is fully home. Using a straight edge and feeler gauges, measure the distance between the top of the yoke and the surface of the pinion housing. Make a note of this dimension.

11 Assemble a shim pack including the gasket whose thickness is greater than the measurement obtained in paragraph 10, by between 0.002 - 0.005 in (0.050 - 0.125 mm). Shim thickness available are listed below.

Part No.	Material	Thickness
71BB - 3N597 - AA	Steel	0.005 in (0.127 mm)
71BB - 3N597 - BA	Steel	0.007 in (0.19 mm)
71BB - 3N 597 - CA	Steel	0.010 in (0.25 mm)
71BB - 3N597 - DA	Steel	0.015 in (0.38 mm)
71BB - 3N597 - EA	Steel	0.020 in (0.50 mm)
71BB - 3N597 - FA	Steel	0.060 in (1.5 mm)
71BB - 3N 598 - AA	Buna coated flexoid	0.010 in (0.25 mm)

12 Fit the spring into the recess in the yoke. Place the shim pack so that the gasket will be next to the cover plate and refit the cover plate. Apply a little Loctite or similar sealing compound to the bolt threads. Tighten down the bolt to a torque wrench setting of 13- 17 lb f ft (1.7 - 2.4 kg f m).

29 Rack and pinion steering gear - dismantling and reassembly

1 Remove the steering gear assembly from the car as described in Section 27.

2 Undo the trackrod ball joint locknuts and unscrew the ball joints. Lift away the plain washer and remove the locknut. To assist in obtaining an approximate correct setting for trackrod adjustment mark the threads or count the number of turns required to undo the ball joint.

3 Slacken off the clips securing the rubber gaiter to each track rod and rack housing end. Carefully pull off the gaiters. Have a quantity of rag handy to catch the oil which will escape when the gaiters are removed. **Note:** on some steering gear assemblies soft iron wire is used instead of clips. Always secure the gaiter with clips.

4 To dismantle the steering gear assembly it is only necessary to remove the trackrod which is furthest away from the pinion.

5 To remove the trackrod place the steering gear assembly in a soft jawed vice. Working on the trackrod ball joint carefully drill out the pin that secures the ball housing to the locknut (Fig.11.27). Great care must be taken not to drill too deeply or the rack will be irreparably damaged. The hole should be about 0.375 in (9.525 mm) deep.

6 Hold the locknut with a spanner, then grip the ball housing with a mole wrench and undo it from the threads on the rack.

7 Take out the spring and ball seat from the recess in the end of the rack and then unscrew the locknut from the threads on the rack. The spring and ball seat must be renewed during reassembly.

8 Undo and remove the two bolts and spring washers that secure the pinion cover plate. Lift away the cover, shims and gaskets. Remove the pinion and upper bearing.

9 Undo and remove the two bolts and spring washers that secure the rack damper cover. Lift away the cover, gasket shims, springs and yoke.

10 With the pinion removed, withdraw the complete rack assembly with one trackrod still attached from the pinion end of the casing.

11 The remaining pinion bearing assembly may now be removed from the rack housing.

12 It is always advisable to withdraw the rack from the pinion end of the rack housing. This avoids passing the rack teeth through the bush at the other end of the casing and causing possible damage.

13 Carefully examine all parts for signs of wear or damage. Check the condition of the rack support bush at the opposite end of the casing from the pinion. If this is worn renew it. If the rack or pinion teeth are in any way damaged a new rack and pinion will have to be obtained.

14 Take the pinion seal off the top of the casing and replace it with a new seal.

15 To commence reassembly fit the lower pinion bearing and thrust washer into their recess in the casing.

16 Replace the rack in the housing from the pinion end and position it in the straight-ahead position by equalising the amount it protrudes at either end of the casing.

17 Replace the remaining pinion bearing and thrust washer onto the pinion and fit the pinion into its housing so that the larger master-spline on the pinion shaft is parallel to the rack and on the right-hand side of the pinion.

18 Replace the rack damper yoke, springs, shims, gasket and cover plate.

19 To replace the track rod that has been removed, start by fitting a new spring and ball seat to the recess in the end of the rack shaft and replace the locknut onto the threads of the rack.

20 Lubricate the ball, ball seat and ballhousing with a small amount of Hypoy 90 type gear oil. Then slide the ballhousing over the track-rod and screw the housing onto the rack threads keeping the trackrod in the horizontal position until the trackrod starts to become stiff to move.

21 Using a normal spring balance hook it round the trackrod 0.25 in (6 mm) from the end and check the effort required to move it from the horizontal position.

22 By adjusting the tightness of the ballhousing on the rack threads the effort required to move the trackrod must be set at 5 lb (2.8 kg).

23 Tighten the locknut up to the housing and then recheck that the effort required to move the trackrod is still correct at 5 lb (2.8 kg).

24 On the line where the locknut and ballhousing met, drill a 0.125 in (3.175 mm) diameter hole which must be 0.375 in (9.525 mm) deep. Even if the two halves of the old hole previously drilled out align, a new hole must be drilled (Fig. 11.28).

25 Tap a new retaining pin into the hole and peen the end over to secure it.

26 Refit the rubber gaiters and trackrod ends ensuring that they are replaced in exactly the same position from which they were removed.

27 Remove the rack damper cover plate and pour in 0.25 pint (0.15 litre) of Hypoy 90 type gear oil. Then carry out both steering gear adjustments as described in Section 28.

28 After the steering gear has been refitted to the car the toe must be checked. Further information will be found in Section 22.

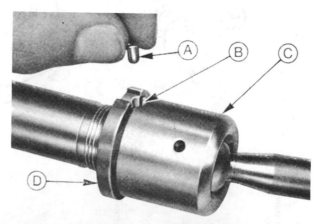

Fig. 11.28. Locking the track rod balljoint housing (C) and lock ring (D) with a locking pin (A) in the new hole (B) (Sec. 29)

30 Steering rack rubber gaiter - removal and refitting

1 Jack-up the front of the car and place blocks under the wheels. Lower the car slightly so that the trackrods are in a near horizontal position.

2 Withdraw the split pin and undo the castellated nut holding the ball joint taper pin to the steering arm. Using a universal ball joint separator part the taper pin from the steering arm.

3 Undo the trackrod ball joint locknut and unscrew the ball joint. To assist in obtaining an approximate correct setting for trackrod adjustment mark the threads or count the number of turns required to undo the ball joint.

4   Slacken off the clips securing the rubber gaiter to the trackrod and rack housing end. Carefully pull off the gaiter. Have a quantity of rag handy to catch the oil which will escape when the gaiters are removed. **Note:** on some steering gear assemblies soft iron wire is used instead of clips. Always secure the gaiter with clips.

5   Fitting a new rubber gaiter is now the reverse sequence to removal. It will be necessary to refill the steering gear assembly with Hypoy 90 type gear oil. Full information will be found in Section 21.

6   It is recommended that the toe-setting be checked at the earliest opportunity. Further information will be found in Section 22.

31 Trackrod end - removal and refitting

Full information will be found in Section 30, omitting paragraphs 4 and 5.

32 Wheels and tyres

1   The roadwheels are of either pressed steel or aluminium alloy construction, and the tyres are of the radial ply type.

2   Check the tyre pressure weekly, including the spare.

3   The wheel nuts should be tightened to the appropriate torque as shown in the Specifications, and it is an advantage if a smear of grease is applied to the wheel stud threads.

4   Every 6,000 miles (10,000 km) the roadwheels should be moved round the vehicle (this does not apply where the wheels have been balanced on the vehicle) in order to even out the tyre tread wear (this procedure is not recommended for fabric belted radials). To do this, remove each wheel in turn, clean it thoroughly (both sides) and remove any flints which may be embedded in the tread). Check the tread wear pattern which will indicate any mechanical or adjustment faults in the suspension or steering components. Examine the wheel bolt holes for elongation or wear. If such conditions are found, renew the wheel.

5   Renewal of the tyres should be carried out when the thickness of the tread pattern is worn to a minimum of 1/16 inch or the wear indicators (if incorporated) are visible.

6   The method of moving the tyres depends on whether the spare (5th) wheel is brought into the rotational pattern. Always adjust the front and rear tyre pressures after moving the wheels round as previously described.

7   Have all wheels balanced initially and again halfway through the useful life of the tyres.

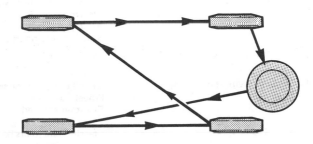

Fig. 11.29. Tyre rotation pattern (Sec. 32)

Fault diagnosis overleaf

33 Fault diagnosis - suspension and steering

Symptom	Cause	Remedy
Steering feels vague, car wanders and floats at speed	Tyre pressures uneven Dampers worn Spring broken Steering gear ball joints badly worn Suspension geometry incorrect Steering mechanism free play excessive Front suspension and rear axle pick-up points out of alignment	Check pressures and adjust as necessary. Test, and replace if worn. Renew spring. Fit new ball joints. Check and rectify. Adjust or overhaul steering mechanism. Normally caused by poor repair work after a serious accident. Extensive rebuilding necessary.
Stiff and heavy steering	Tyre pressure too low No oil in steering gear Front wheel toe-in incorrect Suspension geometry incorrect Steering gear incorrectly adjusted too tightly Steering column badly misaligned	Check pressures and inflate tyres. Top up steering gear. Check and reset toe-in. Check and rectify. Check and re-adjust steering gear. Determine cause and rectify (usually due to bad repair after severe accident damage and difficult to correct).
Wheel wobble and vibration	Seized ball joints or swivels Wheel nuts loose Front wheels and tyres out of balance Steering ball joints badly worn Hub bearings badly worn Steering gear free play excessive Front springs weak or broken	Renew. Check and tighten as necessary. Balance wheels and tyres and add weights as necessary. Replace steering gear ball joints. Remove and fit new hub bearings. Adjust and overhaul steering gear. Inspect and overhaul as necessary.

Chapter 12 Bodywork and fittings

For modifications, and information applicable to later models, see Supplement at end of manual

Contents

Specifications

Overall length
Saloon	172.7 in (4384 mm)
Estate	176.7 in (4484 mm)

Overall width ... ...
67 in (1700 mm)

Overall height
Saloon	53.7 in (1362 mm)
Estate	53.8 in (1366 mm)

Wheel base ... ...
101.6 in (2579 mm)

Track
Front	56 in (1422 mm)
Rear	56 in (1422 mm)

Luggage capacity
Saloon	11.8 cu ft (0.33 cu m)
Estate	34 cu ft (0.96 cu m)
Seat flat	64 cu ft (1.81 cu m)

1 General description

The combination body and underframe is of all steel welded construction. This makes a very strong and torsionally rigid shell.

The Cortina is available in either saloon or estate version with a seating capacity of five adults. The windscreen is slightly curved and is zone toughened for additional driver and passenger safety. In the event of windscreen shattering this 'zone' breaks into much larger pieces than the rest of the screen thus giving the driver much better vision than would otherwise be possible.

The Aeroflow type of ventilation system is fitted. Air drawn in through a grille on the scuttle can either be heated or pass straight into the car. Used air passes out through a grille behind the rear side windows.

The estate cars have the same engine, technical and general specifications as the saloon car except for the counterbalanced tailgate fitted with a lock.

Although the wheelbase for the saloon and estate car versions is the same, the overall length of the estate car is longer.

For additional occupant safety thick padding is used to surround the top of the dash panel.

2 Maintenance - bodywork and underframe

1 The condition of your car's bodywork is of considerable importance as it is upon this that the second-hand value of the car will mainly depend. It is much more difficult to repair neglected bodywork than to renew mechanical assemblies. The hidden portions of the body, such as the wheel arches, the underframe and the engine compartment are equally important, although obviously not requiring such frequent attention as the immediately visible paintwork.

2 Once a year or every 12,000 miles (20,000 km) it is a sound scheme to visit your local main agent and have the underside of the body steam cleaned. All traces of dirt and oil will be removed and the underside can then be inspected carefully for rust, damaged hydraulic pipes, frayed electrical wiring and similar maladies.

3 At the same time, the engine compartment should be cleaned in a similar manner. If steam cleaning facilities are not available then brush a water soluble cleanser over the whole engine and engine compartment with a stiff paint brush, working it well in where there is an accumulation of oil and dirt. Do not paint the ignition system, and protect it with oily rags when the cleanser is washed off. As the cleanser is washed away it will take with it all traces of oil and dirt, leaving the engine looking clean and bright.

4 The wheel arches should be given particular attention as under sealing can easily come away here and stones and dirt thrown up from the roadwheels can soon cause the paint to chip and flake, and so allow rust to set in. If rust is found, clean down to the bare metal with wet and dry paper, apply an anti-corrosive coating such as zinc primer or red lead, and renew the paintwork and undercoating.

5 The bodywork should be washed once a week or when dirty. Thoroughly wet the car to soften the dirt and then wash the car down with a soft sponge and plenty of clean water. If the surplus dirt is not washed off very gently, in time it will wear paint down as surely as wet and dry paper. It is best to use a hose if this is available. Give the car a final wash down and then dry with a soft chamois leather to prevent the formation of spots.

6 Spots of tar and grease thrown up from the road can be removed by a rag dampened with petrol.

7 Once every six months, or more frequently if wished, give the bodywork and chromium trim a thoroughly good wax polish. If a chromium cleaner is used to remove rust on any of the car's plated parts remember that the cleaner also removes part of the chromium, so use sparingly.

3 Maintenance - upholstery and carpets

1 Remove the carpets or mats and thoroughly vacuum clean the interior of the car every three months or more frequently, if necessary.

2 Beat out the carpets and vacuum clean them if they are very dirty. If the upholstery is soiled apply an upholstery cleaner with a damp sponge and wipe off with a clean dry cloth.

4 Maintenance - PVC external roof covering

Under no circumstances try to clean any external PVC roof covering with detergents, caustic soaps or spirit cleaners. Plain soap and water is all that is required, with a soft brush to clean dirt that may be ingrained. Wash the covering as frequently as the rest of the car.

5 Minor body damage - repair

The photo sequences on pages 198 and 199 illustrate the operations detailed in the following sub-sections.

Repair of minor scratches in the car's bodywork

If the scratch is very superficial, and does not penetrate to the metal of the bodywork, repair is very simple. Lightly rub the area of the scratch with a paintwork renovator (eg; T-Cut), or a very fine cutting paste, to remove loose paint from the scratch and to clear the surrounding bodywork of wax polish. Rinse the area with clean water.

Apply touch-up paint to the scratch using a thin paint brush, continue to apply thin layers of paint until the surface of the paint in the scratch is level with the surrounding paintwork. Allow the new paint at least two weeks to harden; then blend it into the surrounding paintwork by rubbing the paintwork, in the scratch area, with a paintwork renovator (eg; T-Cut) or a very fine cutting paste. Finally, apply wax polish.

An alternative to painting over the scratch is to use a paint transfer. Use the same preparation for the affected area; then simply pick a patch of a suitable size to cover the scratch completely. Hold the patch against the scratch and burnish its backing paper; the patch will adhere to the paintwork, freeing itself from the backing paper at the same time. Polish the affected area to blend the patch into the surrounding paintwork. Where the scratch has penetrated right through to the metal of the bodywork, causing the metal to rust, a different repair technique is required. Remove any loose rust from the bottom of the scratch with a penknife, then apply rust inhibiting paint (eg; Kurust) to prevent the formation of rust in the future. Using a rubber or nylon applicator fill the scratch with bodystopper paste. If required, this paste can be mixed with cellulose thinners to provide a very thin paste which is ideal for filling narrow scratches. Before the stopper-paste in the scratch hardens, wrap a piece of smooth cotton rag around the top of a finger. Dip the finger in cellulose thinners and then quickly sweep it across the surface of the stopper-paste in the scratch; this will ensure that the surface of the stopper-paste is slightly hollowed. The scratch can now be painted over as described earlier in this Section.

Repair of dents in the car's bodywork

When deep denting of the car's bodywork has taken place, the first task is to pull the dent out, until the affected bodywork almost attains its original shape. There is little point in trying to restore the original shape completely, as the metal in the damaged area will have stretched on impact and cannot be reshaped fully to its original contour. It is better to bring the level of the dent up to a point which is about 1/8 inch (3 mm) below the level of the surrounding bodywork. In cases where the dent is very shallow anyway, it is not worth trying to pull it out at all.

If the underside of the dent is accessible, it can be hammered out gently from behind, using a mallet with a wooden or plastic head. Whilst doing this, hold a suitable block of wood firmly against the impact from the hammer blows and thus prevent a large area of bodywork from being 'belled-out'.

Should the dent be in a section of the bodywork which has a double skin or some other factor making it inaccessible from behind, a different technique is called for. Drill several small holes through the metal inside the dent area - particularly in the deeper sections. Then screw long self-tapping screws into the holes just sufficiently for them to gain a good purchase in the metal. Now the dent can be pulled out by pulling on the protruding heads of the screws with a pair of pliers.

The next stage of the repair is the removal of the paint from the damaged area, and from an inch or so of the surrounding 'sound' bodywork. This is accomplished most easily by using a wire brush or abrasive pad on a power drill, although it can be done just as effectively by hand using sheets of abrasive paper. To complete the preparations for filling, score the surface of the bare metal with a screwdriver or the tang of a file, or alternatively, drill small holes in the affected area. This will provide a really good 'key' for the filler paste.

To complete the repair see the Section on filling and respraying.

Repair of rust holes or gashes in the car's bodywork

Remove all paint from the affected area and from an inch or so of the surrounding 'sound' bodywork, using an abrasive pad or a wire brush on a power drill. If these are not available a few sheets of abrasive paper will do the job just as effectively. With the paint removed you will be able to gauge the severity of the corrosion and therefore decide whether to replace the whole panel (if this is possible) or to repair the affected area. Replacement body panels are not as expensive as most people think and it is often quicker and more satisfactory to fit a new panel than to attempt to repair large areas of corrosion.

Remove all fittings from the affected area except those which will act as a guide to the original shape of the damaged bodywork (eg, headlamp shells etc.,). Then, using tin snips or a hacksaw blade, remove all loose metal and any other metal badly affected by corrosion. Hammer the edges of the hole inwards in order to create a slight depression for the filler paste.

Wire brush the affected area to remove the powdery rust from the surface of the remaining metal. Paint the affected area with rust inhibiting paint (eg; Kurust); if the back of the rusted area is accessible treat this also.

Before filling can take place it will be necessary to block the hole in some way. This can be achieved by the use of one of the following materials: Zinc gauze, Aluminium tape or Polyurethane foam.

Zinc gauze is probably the best material to use for a large hole. Cut a piece to the approximate size and shape of the hole to be filled. Then position it in the hole so that the edges are below the level of the surrounding bodywork. It can be retained in position by several blobs of filler paste around its periphery.

Aluminium tape should be used for small or very narrow holes. Pull a piece off the roll and trim it to the approximate size and shape required, then pull off the backing paper (if used) and stick the tape over the hole; it can be overlapped if the thickness of one piece is insufficient. Burnish down the edges of the tape with the handle of a screwdriver or similar, to ensure that the tape is securely attached to the metal underneath.

Polyurethane foam is best used where the hole is situated in a section of bodywork of complex shape, backed by a small box section (eg; where the sill panel meets the rear wheel arch - most cars). The usual mixing procedure for this foam is as follows: Put equal amounts of fluid from each of the two cans provided in the kit, into one container. Stir until the mixture begins to thicken, then quickly pour this mixture into the hole, and hold a piece of cardboard over the larger apertures. Almost immediately the polyurethane will begin to expand, gushing frantically out of any small holes left unblocked. When the foam hardens it can be cut back to just below the level of the surrounding bodywork with a hacksaw blade.

Bodywork repairs - filling and respraying

Before using this Section, see Section on dent, deep scratch, rust hole, gash repairs.

Many types of bodyfiller are available, but generally speaking those proprietary kits which contain a tin of filler paste and a tube of resin hardener (eg; Holts Cataloy) are best for this type of repair. A wide, flexible plastic or nylon applicator will be found invaluable for imparting a smooth and well contoured finish to the surface of the filler.

Mix up a little filler on a clean piece of card or board - use the hardener sparingly (follow the maker's instructions on the packet) otherwise the filler will set very rapidly.

Using the applicator, apply the filler paste to the prepared area; draw the applicator across the surface of the filler to achieve the correct contour and to level the filler surface. As soon as a contour that approximates to the correct one is achieved, stop working the paste - if you carry on too long the paste will become sticky and begin to 'pick-up' on the applicator. Continue to add thin layers of filler paste at twenty-minute intervals until the level of the filler is just 'proud' of the surrounding bodywork.

Once the filler has hardened, excess can be removed using a Surform plane or Dreadnought file. From then on, progressively finer grades of abrasive paper should be used, starting with a 40 grade production paper and finishing with 400 grade 'wet-and-dry' paper. Always wrap the abrasive paper around a flat rubber, cork, or wooden block - otherwise the surface of the filler will not be completely flat. During the smoothing of the filler surface the 'wet-and-dry' paper should be periodically rinsed in water. This will ensure that a very smooth finish is imparted to the filler at the final stage.

At this stage the 'dent' should be surrounded by a ring of bare metal which in turn should be encircled by the finely 'feathered' edge of the good paintwork. Rinse the repair area with clean water, until all of the dust produced by the rubbing-down operation is gone.

Spray the whole repair area with a light coat of grey primer - this will show up any imperfections in the surface of the filler. Repair these imperfections with fresh filler paste or bodystopper, and once more smooth the surface with abrasive paper. If bodystopper is used, it can be mixed with cellulose thinners to form a really thin paste which is ideal for filling small holes. Repeat this spray and repair procedure until you are satisfied that the surface of the filler, and the feathered edge of the paintwork are perfect. Clean the repair area with clean water and allow to dry fully.

The repair area is now ready for spraying. Paint spraying must be carried out in a warm, dry, windless and dust free atmosphere. This condition can be created artificially if you have access to a large indoor working area, but if you are forced to work in the open, you will have to pick your day very carefully. If you are working indoors, dousing the floor in the work area with water will 'lay' the dust which would otherwise be in the atmosphere. If the repair area is confined to one body panel, mask off the surrounding panels; this will help to minimise the effects of a slight mis-match in paint colours. Bodywork fittings (eg; chrome strips, door handles etc), will also need to be removed or masked off. Use genuine masking tape and several thicknesses of newspaper for the masking operation.

Before commencing to spray, agitate the aerosol can, thoroughly, then spray a test area (an old tin, or similar) until the technique is mastered. Cover the repair area with a thick coat of primer; the thickness should be built up using several thin layers of paint rather than one thick one. Using 400 grade 'wet-and-dry' paper, rub down the surface of the primer until it is really smooth. While doing this, the work area should be thoroughly doused with water, and the 'wet-and-dry' paper periodically rinsed in water. Allow to dry before spraying on more paint.

Spray on the top coat, again building up the thickness by using several thin layers of paint. Start spraying in the centre of the repair area and then, using a circular motion, work outwards until the whole repair area and about 2 inches of the surrounding original paintwork is covered. Remove all masking material 10 to 15 minutes after spraying on the final coat of paint.

Allow the new paint at least two weeks to harden fully; then using a paintwork renovator (eg; T-Cut) or a very fine cutting paste, blend the edges of the new paint into the existing paintwork. Finally, apply wax polish.

6 Major body damage - repair

1 Because the body is built on the monocoque principle and is integral with the underframe, major damage must be repaired by competent mechanics with the necessary welding and hydraulic straightening equipment.
2 If the damage has been serious it is vital that the body is checked for correct alignment as otherwise the handling of the car will suffer and many other faults such as excessive tyre wear and wear in the transmission and steering may occur.
3 There is a special body jig which most large body repair shops have and to ensure that all is correct it is important that this jig be used for all major repair work.

7 Maintenance - hinges and locks

Once every 3000 miles (5000 km) or 3 months, the door, bonnet and boot or tailgate hinges and locks should be given a few drops of oil from an oil can. The door striker plates can be given a thin smear of grease to reduce wear and to ensure free movement.

8 Front bumper - removal and installation

1 Open the bonnet and remove the radiator grille, as described in Section 32.

2 Undo and remove the bolt, washer and spacer assemblies
that secure the wrap round ends of the bumper bar. Then unscrew the
two bolts that secure the under-riders to the body (Fig. 12.1).
3 The front bumper assembly may now be lifted away taking care
not to scratch the paintwork on the front wings.
4 If it is necessary to detach the under-riders from the bumper bar,
undo and remove the nut and washers that secure the bracket and
under-rider to the bumper bar.
5 Refitting the bumper bar and under-riders is the reverse sequence
to removal. Do not fully tighten the fixings until the bumper bar is
perfectly straight and correctly located.

9 Rear bumper - removal and installation

1 Press in the two plastic lugs securing the number plate lights, remove
the lights and place to one side.
2 Open the luggage compartment lid and roll back the matting. Undo
and remove the bolts and washers that secure the bumper bar brackets
to the body (Fig. 12.2).
3 The rear bumper may now be lifted away taking care not to scratch
the paintwork on the rear wings.
4 If it is necessary to detach the under-riders and brackets undo and
remove the bolts, spring and plain washers.
5 Refitting the bumper bar and under-riders is the reverse sequence
to removal. Do not fully tighten the fixings until the bumper bar is
perfectly straight and correctly located.

10 Windscreen glass - removal and installation

1 If you are unfortunate enough to have a windscreen shatte., or
should you wish to renew your present windscreen, fitting a replacement
is one of the jobs which the average owner is advised to leave to
a professional. For the owner who wishes to attempt the job himself
the following instructions are given.
2 Cover the bonnet with a blanket or cloth to prevent accidental
damage and remove the windscreen wiper blades and arms as detailed
in Chapter 10.
3 Put on a pair of lightweight shoes and get onto one of the front
seats. An assistant should be ready to catch the glass as it is released
from the body aperture.
4 Place a piece of soft cloth between the soles of your shoes and
the windscreen glass and with both feet on one top corner of the
windscreen push firmly.
5 When the weatherstrip has freed itself from the body aperture flange
in that area repeat the process at frequent intervals along the top edge
of the windscreen until from outside the car the glass and weatherstrip
can be removed together.
6 If you are having to replace your windscreen due to a shattered
screen, remove all traces of sealing compound from the weatherstrip
and body flange.
7 Now is the time to remove all pieces of glass if the screen has
shattered. Use a vacuum cleaner to extract as much as possible. Switch
on the heater boost motor and adjust the screen controls to 'screen
defrost' but watch out for flying pieces of glass which might have
blown out of the ducting.
8 Carefully inspect the rubber moulding for signs of splitting or
deterioration.
9 To refit the glass first fit the weatherstrip onto the glass with the
joint at the lower edge.
10 Insert a piece of thick cord into the channel of the weatherstrip
with the two ends protruding by at least 12 inches (300 mm) at the
bottom centre of the screen.
11 Mix a concentrated soap and water solution and apply to the flange
of the windscreen aperture.
12 Offer up the screen to the aperture, and with an assistant press
the rubber surround hard against one end of the cord, moving round
the windscreen and so drawing the lip over the windscreen flange of
the body. Keep the draw cord parallel to the windscreen. Using the
palms of the hands, thump on the glass from the outside to assist the
lip in passing over the flange and to seat the screen correctly onto the
aperture.

13 To ensure a good watertight joint apply some Seelastik SR51
between the weatherstrip and the body and press the weatherstrip
against the body to give a good seal.
14 Any excess Seelastik may be removed with a petrol moistened
cloth.
15 Lubricate the finisher strip groove with the soap and water solution
and insert the strip.
16 Refit the wiper arms and blades and do not forget the Road Fund
Tax disc.

11 Door rattles - tracing and rectification

1 The most common cause of door rattle is a misaligned, loose or
worn striker plate; however other causes may be:

     a) *Loose door or window winder handles;*
     b) *Loose or misaligned door lock components;*
     c) *Loose or worn remote control mechanism.*

2 It is quite possible for door rattles to be the result of a combination
of the above faults so a careful examination should be made to determine
their exact cause.

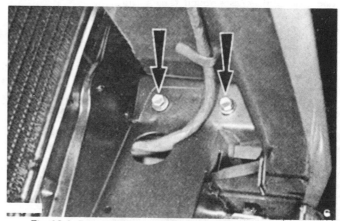

Fig. 12.1. Remove the front bumper retaining bolts (Sec. 8)

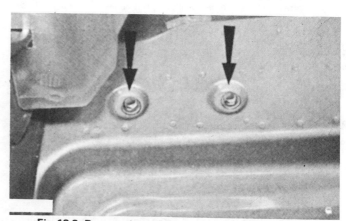

Fig. 12.2. Remove the rear bumper retaining bolts (Sec. 9)

14.1 Remove the trim to expose the retaining screw

3 If striker plate wear or misalignment is the cause, the plate should be renewed or adjusted as necessary. The procedure is detailed in Section 13.
4 Should the window winder handle rattle, this can be easily rectified by inserting a rubber washer between the escutcheon and door trim panel.
5 If the rattle is found to be emanating from the door lock it will in all probability mean that the lock is worn and therefore should be replaced with a new lock unit, as described in Section 15 or 16.
6 Lastly, if it is worn hinge pins causing rattles they should be renewed.

12 Front and rear door - removal and installation

1 Using a pencil, accurately mark the outline of the hinge relative to the door. Remove the two bolts that secure each hinge to the pillar and lift away the complete door.
2 For storage it is best to stand the door on an old blanket and allow it to lean against a wall also suitably padded at the top to stop scratching.
3 Refitting the door is the reverse sequence to removal. If, after refitting, adjustment is necessary, it should be done at the hinges to give correct alignment, or the striker rest if the door either moves up or down on final closing.

13 Door striker plate - removal, refitting and adjustment

1 If it is wished to renew a worn striker plate, mark its position on the door pillar so a new plate can be fitted in the same position.
2 To remove the plate simply undo and remove the four crosshead screws which hold the plate in position. Lift away the plate.
3 Replacement of the door striker plate is the reverse sequence to removal.
4 To adjust the striker plate, close the door to the first of the two locking positions. Check that the edges of the lock plate and the striker plate are parallel, and that the rear edge of the door stands 0.25 in (6.0 mm) proud of the body. Move the striker plate as necessary.
5 With the lock 'open', check the clearance at 'A' in Fig. 12.3. This can be checked by placing a ball of plasticine on the striker post and carefully closing the door. The dimension 'A' should be set to 0.08 in (2.0 mm) by carefully moving the striker plate **vertically** as required.

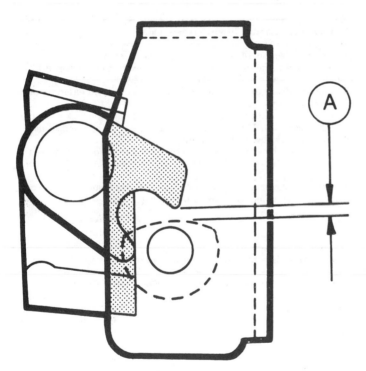

Fig. 12.3. Check the door striker plate adjustment (Sec. 13)

A = 0.08 in (2.0 mm)

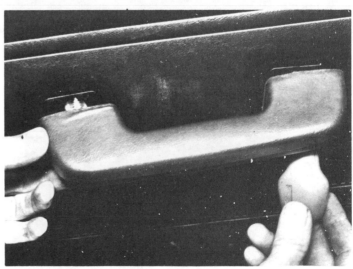

14.3 Remove the two armrest securing screws

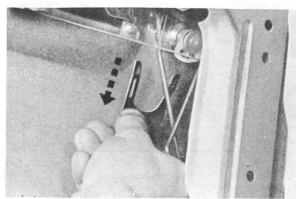

Fig. 12.4. Remove the exterior lock retaining clip (Sec. 15)

Fig. 12.5. Remove the lock rod crank by driving out the pin (Sec. 16)

Fig. 12.6. Disengage the interior handle rod from the rear door lock (Sec. 16)

14 Door trim - removal and refitting

1   Using a knife or thin bladed screwdriver, carefully prise the plastic trim from its recesses in the window winder handle. This will expose the handle retaining screw (photo).
2   Wind up the window and note the position of the handle. Undo and remove the crosshead retaining screw and lift away the handle.
3   Undo and remove the two crosshead screws that secure the door pull. Lift away the door pull. Unscrew the interior lock knob (photo).
4   Using a screwdriver, carefully remove the door lock remote control housing bezel by sliding the bezel towards the hinge end of the door. Lift away the bezel.
5   Insert a thin strip of metal with all the sharp edges removed, or a thick knife blade, between the door and the trim panel. This will release one or two of the trim panel retaining clips without damaging the trim. The panel can now be gently eased off by hand.
    Note that where a map pocket is fitted the trim panel is in two halves. Lack of care when releasing the trim clips could result in the fabric tearing.
6   Carefully remove the plastic weatherproof sheeting. Removal is now complete.
7   Replacement is generally a reversal of the removal procedure.
Note: When replacing the panel ensure that each of the trim panel retaining clips is firmly located in its hole by sharply striking the panel in the approximate area of each clip with the palm of the hand. This will make sure the trim is seated fully.

15 Door lock assembly (front) - removal and refitting

1   Refer to Section 14 and remove the door interior trim.
2   Remove the interior handle by sliding forward to disengage it from the door. Remove the interior knob by unscrewing.
3   Working inside the door shell carefully prise the two exterior control rods from their locations in the lock assembly (Fig. 12.7).
4   Remove the three lock securing screws and push the lock assembly into the door shell. The assembly should be manoeuvred to disengage the interior lock rod, and the interior handle rod.
5   To remove the exterior handle, remove the two crosshead screws from inside the door shell. To remove the exterior lock, pull down and remove the retaining clip (Fig. 12.4).
6   Refitting the door lock assembly is the reverse sequence to removal. Lubricate all moving parts with a little grease.

16 Door lock assembly (rear) - removal and refitting

1   Refer to Section 14 and remove the door interior trim.
2   Remove the interior lock rod crank from the door shell by drifting out the retaining pin with a suitable pin punch (Fig. 12.5).
3   Prise the exterior handle rod from its location in the lock assembly. Remove the interior door handle by sliding it forward to disengage it from the door.
4   Remove the three lock securing screws and push the lock assembly into the door shell. Turn the interior handle rod to disengage it from the lock (Fig. 12.6). Remove the lock
5   The exterior handle may be removed after unscrewing the two crosshead screws from inside the door shell.
6   Refitting the door lock assembly is the reverse sequence. Lubricate all moving parts with a little grease.

17 Door glass and regulator - removal and refitting

1   Using a screwdriver carefully ease out the door inner and outer weatherstrips from their retaining clips on the door panel.
2   Undo and remove the two screws that secure the door glass to the window regulator. On rear doors, remove the two screws (Fig. 12. 8) and remove the window frame extension channels. Tilt the glass and remove it upwards from the inside of the door (Fig. 12.9).

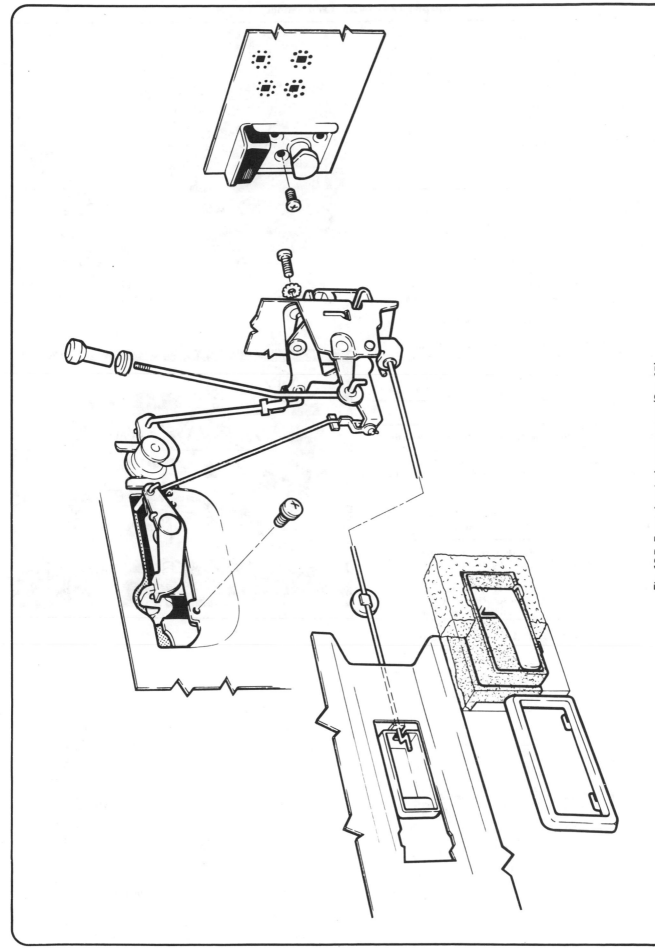

Fig. 12.7. Front door lock components (Sec. 15)

3   Remove the three pairs of screws and the retaining clip on front doors (photo), or remove the five screws on rear doors (Fig. 12.10). and lift away the regulator mechanism.

4   Should it be necessary to remove the glass run channel, start at the front lower frame end and carefully ease the glass run channel from its location in the door frame.

5   Refitting the door glass and regulator is the reverse sequence to removal. Lubricate all moving parts with a little grease. Before refitting the trim panel check the operation and alignment of the glass and regulator and adjust if necessary. When all is correct fully tighten all securing bolts.

18 Bonnet - removal and installation

1   Open the bonnet and support it open using the bonnet stay. To act as a datum for refitting, mark the position of the hinges relative to the bonnet inner panel.

2   With the assistance of a second person hold the bonnet in the open position and release the stay.

3   Undo and remove the two bolts, spring and plain washers that secure each hinge to the bonnet taking care not to scratch the top of the wings.

4   Lean the bonnet up against a wall, suitably padded to stop scratching the paint.

5   Refitting the bonnet is the reverse sequence to removal. Any adjustments necessary can be made either at the hinges or the bonnet catch.

19 Bonnet lock - adjustment

1   Should it be necessary to adjust the bonnet catch first slacken the locknut securing the shaft in position.

2   Using a wide bladed screwdriver, screw the shaft in, or out, as necessary until the correct bonnet front height is obtained. Tighten the locknut.

20 Bonnet release cable - removal, refitting and adjustment

1   Unscrew the five screws securing the dash lower trim panel.

2   Detach the direction indicator flasher unit and the heated rear window relay from their mountings (See Chapter 10).

3   Through the holes in the side of the bonnet release lever bracket, insert a screwdriver and **slacken** the bracket securing screws.

4   Lift off the bracket and disengage the bonnet release cable.

5   Refer to Section 32 and remove the radiator grille.

6   Slacken the cable clamp bolt (Fig. 12.11) and unhook and cable from the lock spring.

Fig. 12.8. Removing the window extension channel screws (Sec. 17)

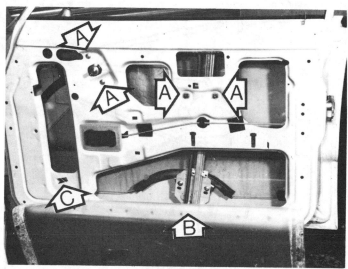

17.3 Remove the regulator screws on face of door (A), on underside of door (B) and retaining clip (C)

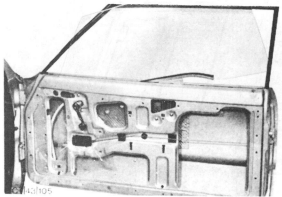

Fig. 12.9. Removing the door window glass to the inside (Sec. 17)

Fig. 12.10. Rear door window regulator retaining screws (Sec. 17)

7 Unclip the cable from its retaining clips around the engine compartment and pull through into the vehicle interior.
8 Installation is the reverse of removal ensuring that the bulkhead rubber grommet is correctly located.
9 The cable should be adjusted to give the dimension shown in Fig. 12.11, and the clamp bolt (Fig. 12.12) tightened.

21 Boot lid - removal and installation

1 Open the boot lid to its fullest extent. To act as a datum for refitting, mark the position of the hinge relative to the lid inner panel.
2 With the assistance of a second person hold the boot in the open position and then undo and remove the two bolts, spring and plain washers that secure each hinge to the boot lid. Lift away the boot lid taking care not to scratch the top of the rear wings.
3 Lean the boot lid up against a wall, suitably padded to avoid scratching the paint.
4 Refitting the boot lid is the reverse sequence to removal. Any adjustment necessary can be made at the hinge.

22 Boot lid lock - removal and refitting

1 Open the boot lid and carefully withdraw the spring clip located at the end of the lock spindle.
2 Undo and remove the three bolts and spring washers that secure the lock to the boot lid (Fig. 12.13). Lift away the lock assembly.
3 Refitting the lock assembly is the reverse sequence to removal, noting that a small clearance is necessary at A in Fig. 12.13.

23 Boot lid lock striker plate - removal

1 Open the boot lid and with a pencil mark the outline of the striker plate relative to the inner rear panel to act as a datum for refitting.
2 Undo and remove the two bolts with spring and plain washers that secure the striker plate. Lift away the striker plate (Fig. 12.13).
3 Refitting the striker plate is the reverse sequence to removal. Line up the striker plate with the previously made marks and tighten the securing bolts.

24 Tailgate assembly - removal and installation

1 Open the tailgate and with a pencil mark the outline of the hinges relative to the inner panel.
2 With the assistance of a second person hold the tailgate in position and then undo and remove the bolts, spring and plain washers that secure each hinge to the tailgate. Lift away the tailgate taking care not to scratch the side panels.
3 Refitting the tailgate is the reverse sequence to removal. Any adjustment may be made at the hinges.

25 Tailgate lock - removal and refitting

1 Use a wide bladed screwdriver or a thick knife blade between the tailgate and the trim panel. This will release one or two of the trim panel retaining clips without damaging the trim. The panel can now be gently eased out by hand.

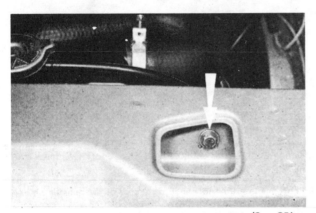

Fig. 12.11. Slacken the bonnet cable clamp bolt (Sec. 20)

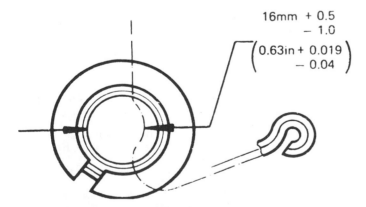

$$16mm \begin{array}{c} + 0.5 \\ - 1.0 \end{array}$$

$$\left(0.63in \begin{array}{c} + 0.019 \\ - 0.04 \end{array} \right)$$

Fig. 12.12. Setting dimension for the bonnet release spring (Sec. 20)

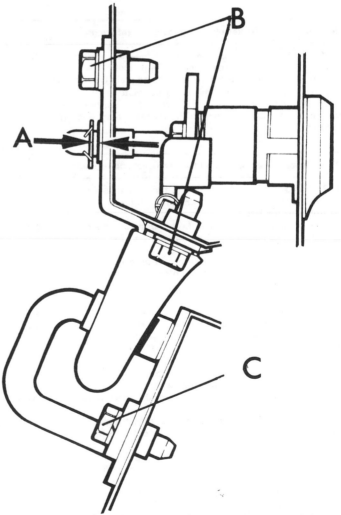

Fig. 12.13. Boot lock retaining bolts (B), spring clip clearance (A) and striker plate retaining bolts (C) (Sec. 22 and 23)

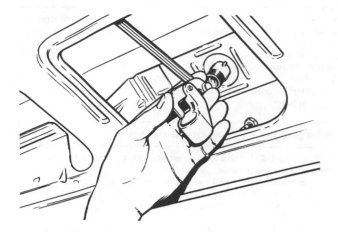

Fig. 12.14. Remove the linkage from the tailgate lock barrel (Sec. 25)

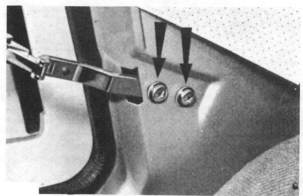

Fig. 12.15. Remove the opening quarter window catch screws (Sec. 29)

2   Undo and remove the large hexagonal nut that retains the lock linkage to the handle, and remove the linkage (Fig. 12.14).
3   Remove the three screws securing the lock and handle assembly, and lift away from the tailgate.
4   To refit the lock assembly is the reverse sequence to removal.

26 Tailgate lock striker plate - removal and refitting

1   Open the tailgate and with a pencil mark the outline of the striker plate relative to the luggage compartment floor.
2   Undo and remove the bolts, spring and plain washers that secure the striker plate and lift away the striker plate.
3   Refitting the striker plate is the reverse sequence to removal. Line up the striker plate with the previously made mark and tighten the securing bolts.

27 Tailgate hinge and torsion bar - removal and refitting

1   Refer to Section 24 and remove the tailgate assembly.
2   With a pencil mark the outline of the hinge and torsion bar assembly to the body.
3   Undo and remove the four bolts, spring and plain washers that secure the hinge and torsion bar assembly to the body and lift away the assembly.
4   Refitting the tailgate hinge and torsion bar assembly is the reverse sequence to removal. Line up the hinge with the previously made mark and tighten the securing bolts.

28 Fixed rear quarter window glass (two-door) - removal and refitting

1   Using a blunt screwdriver carefully ease the moulding from the weatherstrip.
2   An assistant should now be ready to catch the glass as it is released from the body aperture. Working inside the car push on the glass next to the weatherstrip so releasing it from the aperture flange. Lift away the glass and weatherstrip.
3   Remove the weatherstrip and clean off all traces of sealer. Inspect the weatherstrip for signs of splitting or deterioration and, if evident, a new weatherstrip must be obtained.
4   To refit the glass assembly first fit the moulding to its groove in the weatherstrip and apply a little sealer to the groove in which the glass seats. Fit the glass to the weatherstrip.
5   Fit a draw cord in the weatherstrip to body groove and position the glass to the aperture. Working inside the car, pull on the draw cord whilst the assistant pushes on the glass so drawing the lip over the flange.

Fig. 12.16. Drift out the window catch roll pin (Sec. 29)

29 Opening rear quarter window glass (two-door) - removal and refitting

1   Pull off the interior trim panel to the rear of the quarter window. Unscrew the catch retaining screw exposed (Fig. 12.15).
2   Open the window approximately 30° and gently rock up and down to disengage the hinges from the rubbers.
3   Carefully support the glass with the catch resting on a wooden block and drift out the roll pin (Fig. 12.16).
4   The catch stud is supplied fitted to the window. Refitting of the window is the reverse of the removal procedure.

30 Rear window glass - removal and refitting

1   Undo and remove the self-tapping screws that secure the front edge of the rear seat cushion to the heel plate. Lift out the cushion taking care not to damage the upholstery or headlining.
2   Open the boot lid and undo and remove the screws that secure the top of the rear seat backrest to the body. Carefully lift away the backrest.
3   Remove the retainers and bend back the lock tabs securing the rear parcel shelf. Lift away the parcel shelf.
4   Place a blanket over the boot lid so that it is not accidentally scratched and remove the rear window glass using the same procedure as for the front windscreen. Further information will be found in Section 10, paragraphs 3 to 6 inclusive.
5   Refitting the rear window glass is similar to the refitting of the front windscreen. Refer to Section 10, paragraphs 8 to 16 inclusive.
6   Take care not to damage the element if a heated window is fitted.

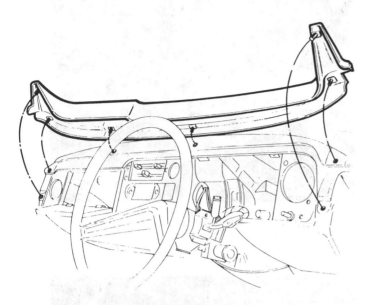

Fig. 12.17. Crash padding securing points (Sec. 33)

Fig. 12.18. Remove the heater motor plug and speedometer cable from its clip (Sec. 34)

31 Tailgate window glass - removal and refitting

The procedure for removal and replacement of the tailgate window glass is basically identical to that for the windscreen glass. Refer to Section 10, paragraphs 3 to 6 and 8 to 16.

32 Radiator grille - removal and installation

1 Open the bonnet and support in the open position. Undo and remove the crosshead screws that secure the radiator grille to the front body panels. Lift away the radiator grille. Refitting is the reverse sequence to removal but take care to locate the grille tabs in their respective slots in the front lower panel.

33 Instrument panel crash padding - removal and installation

1 Refer to Chapter 10, Section 37 and remove the instrument cluster.
2 Remove the glove compartment lock striker, and the lid.
3 Remove the glove compartment securing screws, pull the assembly forward, disconnect the lamp leads and remove the assembly.
4 Remove the air vent surround and then remove the two exposed air vent securing screws and pull the vent from the facia so that the hose can be disconnected from it.
5 Access to the crash pad securing nuts can now be obtained through the apertures. Installation is a reversal of removal (Fig. 12.17).

34 Heater assembly - removal and installation

1 Refer to Chapter 2 and drain the cooling system.
2 Locate the multi-pin plug connector for the heater unit blower motor and detach the plug from the socket, disconnect the speedometer drive cable from the clip on the heater assembly (Fig. 12.18).
3 Slacken the clips that secure the heater water pipes to the heater unit. Note which way round the pipes are fitted and carefully withdraw the two pipes.
4 Undo and remove the self tapping screws that secure the heater unit to the bulkhead. Their locations are shown in Fig. 12.19.
5 Remove the lower dash insulation panel, remove the bolt from the temperature control valve bracket (Fig. 12.20), and withdraw the control and bracket. Withdraw the heater from the bulkhead.
6 Note that there are three gaskets located between the heater housing flange and if these are damaged they must be renewed (Fig. 12.21 items B, M, N).

Fig. 12.19. Remove the four heater retaining screws (Sec. 34)

Fig. 12.20. Remove the temperature control valve bracket (Sec. 34 and 36)

This sequence of photographs deals with the repair of the dent and paintwork damage shown in this photo. The procedure will be similar for the repair of a hole. It should be noted that the procedures given here are simplified — more explicit instructions will be found in the text

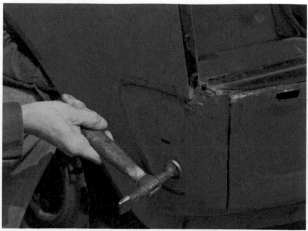

In the case of a dent the first job — after removing surrounding trim — is to hammer out the dent where access is possible. This will minimise filling. Here, the large dent having been hammered out, the damaged area is being made slightly concave

Now all paint must be removed from the damaged area, by rubbing with coarse abrasive paper. Alternatively, a wire brush or abrasive pad can be used in a power drill. Where the repair area meets good paintwork, the edge of the paintwork should be 'feathered', using a finer grade of abrasive paper

In the case of a hole caused by rusting, all damaged sheet-metal should be cut away before proceeding to this stage. Here, the damaged area is being treated with rust remover and inhibitor before being filled

Mix the body filler according to its manufacturer's instructions. In the case of corrosion damage, it will be necessary to block off any large holes before filling — this can be done with aluminium or plastic mesh, or aluminium tape. Make sure the area is absolutely clean before ...

... applying the filler. Filler should be applied with a flexible applicator, as shown, for best results; the wooden spatula being used for confined areas. Apply thin layers of filler at 20-minute intervals, until the surface of the filler is slightly proud of the surrounding bodywork

Initial shaping can be done with a Surform plane or Dreadnought file. Then, using progressively finer grades of wet-and-dry paper, wrapped around a sanding block, and copious amounts of clean water, rub down the filler until really smooth and flat. Again, feather the edges of adjoining paintwork

The whole repair area can now be sprayed or brush-painted with primer. If spraying, ensure adjoining areas are protected from over-spray. Note that at least one inch of the surrounding sound paintwork should be coated with primer. Primer has a 'thick' consistency, so will find small imperfections

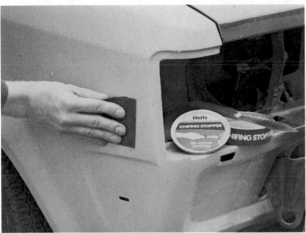

Again, using plenty of water, rub down the primer with a fine grade wet-and-dry paper (400 grade is probably best) until it is really smooth and well blended into the surrounding paintwork. Any remaining imperfections can now be filled by carefully applied knifing stopper paste

When the stopper has hardened, rub down the repair area again before applying the final coat of primer. Before rubbing down this last coat of primer, ensure the repair area is blemish-free — use more stopper if necessary. To ensure that the surface of the primer is really smooth use some finishing compound

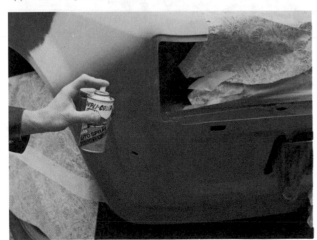

The top coat can now be applied. When working out of doors, pick a dry, warm and wind-free day. Ensure surrounding areas are protected from over-spray. Agitate the aerosol thoroughly, then spray the centre of the repair area, working outwards with a circular motion. Apply the paint as several thin coats

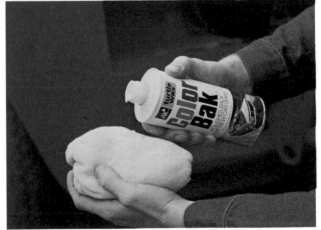

After a period of about two weeks, which the paint needs to harden fully, the surface of the repaired area can be 'cut' with a mild cutting compound prior to wax polishing. When carrying out bodywork repairs, remember that the quality of the finished job is proportional to the time and effort expended

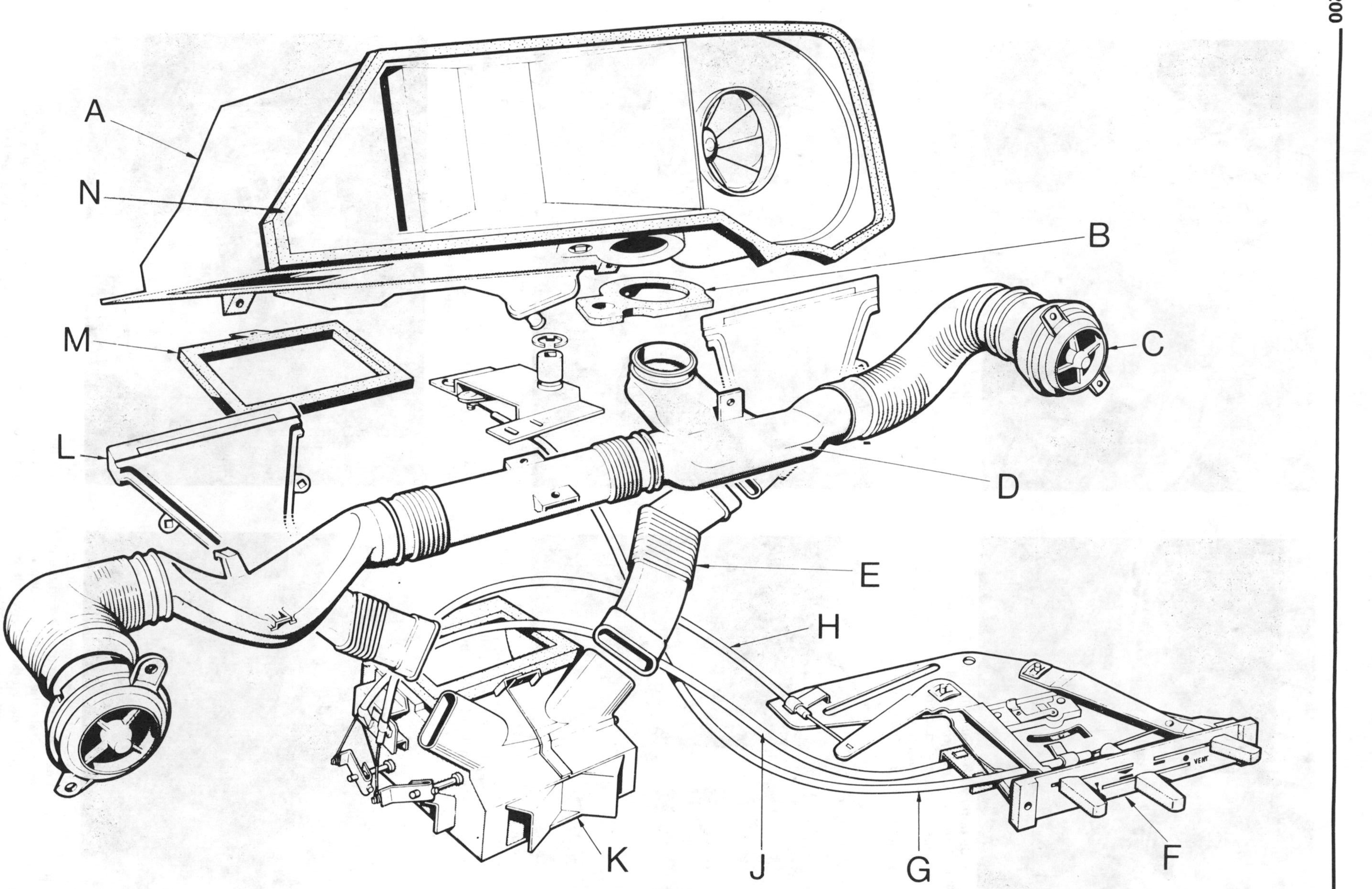

Fig. 12.21. Heating system components (Sec. 34)

A   Heater assembly
B   Ambient air duct/control valve shaft
    gasket
C   Air vent
D   Ambient air duct

E   Demister
F   Control panel
G   Temperature control valve Bowden
    cable
H   Air distribution valve Bowden cable

J   Air inlet valve Bowden cable
K   Air distribution valve assembly
L   Demister vent
M   Heating system air duct gasket
N   Heater assembly gasket

Fig. 12.22. Remove the heater radiator lower panel bolts (Sec. 35)

Fig. 12.23. Remove the heater motor assembly (Sec. 35)

Fig. 12.24. Remove the Bowden cables from the air distribution valve (Sec. 36)

Fig. 12.25. Location of heater motor resistance plate rivets (Sec. 36)

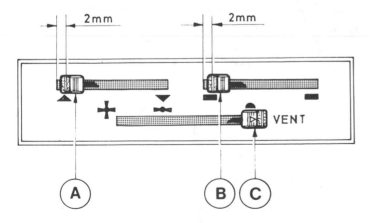

Fig. 12.26. Move the air distribution lever (A), the air temperature lever (B) and the boost fan switch (C) to the positions shown (Sec. 37)

7   To refit the heater assembly, stick on three new gaskets to the heater joint face. If the original gaskets are to be retained apply some sealer to the free face of the gasket pack.

8   Move the flap located in the centre of the heater housing and the control lever inside the car to either the 'cold' or 'hot' position.

9   Fit the heater to the bulkhead and connect the quadrant of the control valve pivot. Secure the heater with the self tapping screws.

10 Refit the water drain pipe and reconnect the multi-pin plug to the blower motor, refit the speedometer cable.

11 Reconnect the two hoses to the heater unit and secure with the clips.

12 Refill the cooling system as described in Chapter 2.

35 Heater assembly - dismantling and reassembly

1   Refer to Section 34 and remove the heater assembly.

2   Undo and remove the two bolts that secure the heater radiator lower panel to the main casing. Lift away the lower panel (Fig. 12.22).

3   Carefully slide out the heater radiator together with its foam rubber packing.

4   Undo and remove the three bolts that secure the blower motor baseplate and lift away the blower motor assembly (Fig. 12.23).

5   Inspect the heater radiator for signs of leaks which, if evident, may be repaired in a similar manner used for the engine cooling system radiator as described in Chapter 2. It is a good policy to reverse flush the radiator to remove any sediment.

6   Reassembling the heater assembly is the reverse sequence to removal.

7   It is possible to remove the heater radiator and the blower motor whilst the heater assembly is still fitted in the car.

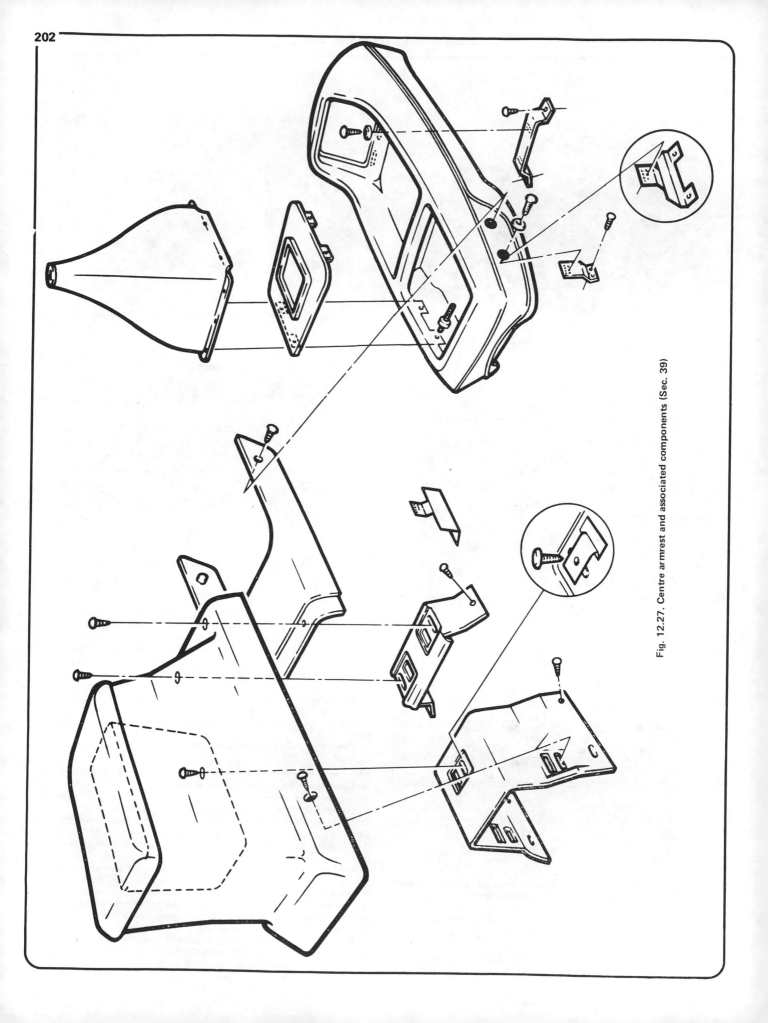

Fig. 12.27. Centre armrest and associated components (Sec. 39)

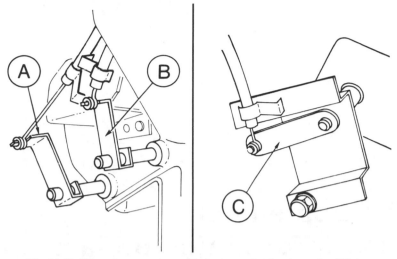

Fig. 12.28. Move the air inlet valve (A), the air distribution valve (B)
and the temperature control valve (C) to the positions shown (Sec. 37)

36 Heater controls - removal, refitting and adjustment

1   Refer to Chapter 10, Section 37 and remove the instrument panel.
2   Remove the lower dash insulation panel, and remove the Bowden
cables from the temperature control valve (Fig. 12.20) and the air
distribution valve assembly (Fig. 12.24).
3   Unscrew the three control panel securing screws, disconnect the
electric cables at the rear and remove the control assembly complete
with Bowden cables.
4   If required, remove the Bowden cables from the controls, and the
resistance plate by drilling out the rivets (Fig. 12.25).
5   Refitting is a reversal of the above procedure.
6   To adjust the control cables, set the upper heater controls to a
point approximately 0.1 in (2 mm) from their stops, and lock the
booster switch in the 'vent' position by pulling outwards (Fig. 12.26).
Set the heater flaps in their end positions and clamp the cable sheaths
with the spring clips (Fig. 12.28).

37 Trinket tray - removal and installation

1   Remove the four screws (two each side) and lift off the tray.
Refitting is a reversal of this procedure.

38 Centre console - removal and installation

1   Refer to Section 39 and remove the centre armrest if fitted.
2   Prise out the clock (or the blanking plate) and disconnect the
clock leads.
3   Unscrew and remove the two screws accessible through the clock
aperture and the two located at the rear sides of the console.
4   Unscrew the gearlever knob, or remove the 'T' handle from
the selector lever, and lift up the centre console.
5   Refitting is a reversal of this procedure.

39 Centre armrest - removal and installation

1   Position the front seats as required to remove one armrest
retaining screw from each side (Fig. 12.27).
2   Open the armrest lid, and remove the screw from the bottom of the
box.
3   Remove the two screws from the front of the armrest, and lift the
armrest forward over the handbrake lever.
4   Refitting is a reversal of this procedure.

Chapter 13 Supplement:
Revisions and information on later models

Contents

1 Introduction

This Chapter contains the modifications made on the 1.6 and 2.0 litre Cortina models that were produced from 1978 to 1982. In most instances the modifications are on models built from August 1979 and these models are known as the Cortina 80 range. One or two amendments to the original manual have also been included in this Chapter although wherever possible any alterations have been made in the Chapter concerned. The principal modification points on the Cortina 80 are outlined in Fig. 13.1.

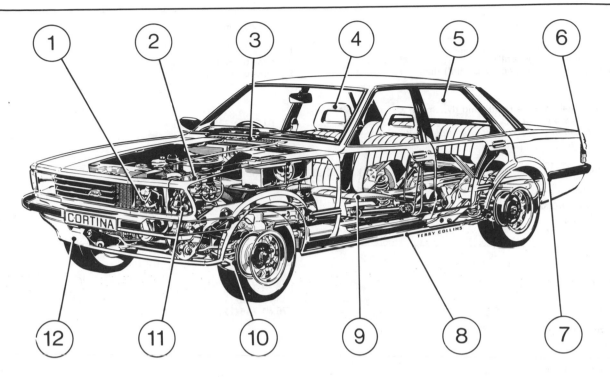

Fig. 13.1 Cortina 80 model showing principal modifications (Sec 1)

1 Viscous coupled thermostatic fan
2 Variable venturi carburettor
3 Improved heating/ventilation
4 New style headrests
5 Enlarged glass area
6 Wrap around tail lights with integral fog lights (Saloons only)

7 Plastic bumper end caps (front and rear)
8 Improved corrosion protection
9 Redesigned seats
10 Revised spring settings
11 Wrap around front indicators
12 Deepened front spoiler

---

2 Specifications

The following data are those which differ from the details given in the Specifications at the start of the Chapter concerned

Engine – 1980 models

	Fan declutched	Fan engaged
Maximum PS (kW) @ rpm:		
1.6 HC	75.5 (55.5) @ 5500	73.5 (54.0) @ 5300
1.6 2V*	92.5 (68.0) @ 5900	91.0 (67.0) @ 5700
2000 HC	102.0 (75.0) @ 5400	101.0 (74.0) @ 5200
Maximum torque in lbf ft (kgf m) @ rpm:		
1.6 HC	87.7 (12.1) @ 2800	86.2 (11.9) @ 2700
1.6 2V*	93.1 (12.9) @ 4000	92.4 (12.8) @ 4000
2000 HC	114.5 (15.8) @ 4000	113.0 (15.6) @ 4000

Engine with Weber 2V carburettor (Ghia)
Cylinder head (all models)
Valve seat angle .... 46°

Cooling system

Fan type (Aug 79 on) .... Thermo viscous fan clutch
Thermostat:
Starts to open .... 89° to 93°C (192° to 200°F)
Fully open .... 103° to 106°C (217° to 223°F)
Fan belt tension .... 0.4 in (10 mm) deflection midway between alternator and water pump pulleys

Torque wrench settings	lbf ft	kgf m
Fan to viscous clutch	6 to 9	0.8 to 1.0

Carburation (1600 cc only, except Ghia)

Carburettor type .... Ford variable venturi (VV)
Part number:
Manual transmission 79HF-9510-KCB
Automatic transmission 79HF-9510-KDB

Idle speed	800 ± 25 rpm
Idle CO%	1.5 ± 0.5
Metering rod code number	FAJ
Choke gauge diameter (twist drill)	3.4 mm (0.135 in)
Choke fast idle/pull down gauge (twist drill) diameter ...	3.7 mm (0.145 in)

Ignition system

Ignition timing initial advance (static and dynamic)*	
1600 with VV carburettor	12° BTDC at 800 rev/min
*Distributor vacuum hose disconnected and plugged	

Clutch

Adjustment method	Automatic from August 1979
Diameter (1.6 2V)	8.46 in (215 mm)

Automatic transmission

Fluid type (see text)	Ford specification SQM-2C9010-A

Rear axle

Axle type (2000 Estate)	Salisbury type A
Axle ratio:	
1600 (optional)	3.78 : 1 (34/9)
2000 Saloon	3.45 : 1 (38/11)
2000 Estate	3.75 : 1 (45/12)

Electrical system

Bulb wattage:	
Interior light	10
Luggage compartment	10
Glovebox	2
Side repeaters (where fitted)	4

Power-assisted steering (when fitted)

Type	Power-assisted rack-and-pinion
Ratio	17.73 : 1
Fluid type	Automatic transmission fluid (Castrol TQF or equivalent)

Steering angles 1980 on

Toe	0 to 0.8 in (0 to 2.0 mm)
Castor:	
Saloon – standard	Nominal 1° 40', acceptable 0° 55' to 2° 55'
Saloon – heavy duty	Nominal 2° 17', acceptable 1° 17' to 3° 32'
Estate – standard	Nominal 1° 57', acceptable 1° 12' to 3° 12'
Estate – heavy duty	Nominal 2° 17', acceptable 1° 17' to 3° 32'
Estate – business	Nominal 1° 21', acceptable 0° 21' to 2° 36'
Camber*:	
Saloon – standard	Nominal 0° 53', acceptable 0° 08' to 1° 38'
Saloon – heavy duty	Nominal 0° 51'; acceptable 0° 06' to 1° 36'
Estate – standard	Nominal 0° 53', acceptable 0° 08' to 1° 38'
Estate – heavy duty	Nominal 0° 51', acceptable 0° 06' to 1° 36'
Estate – business	Nominal 0° 54', acceptable 0° 09' to 1° 39'
*Castor values positive, camber angles negative	
Maximum side to side variation:	
Castor	0° 45'
Camber	1° 00'

Torque wrench settings

	lbf ft	kgf m
Steering coupling clamp bolts	12 to 15	1.7 to 2.1
Steering coupling pinch-bolt	12 to 15	1.7 to 2.1
Pressure hose unions	19 to 23	2.7 to 3.2
Return hose unions	12 to 15	1.7 to 2.1
Pulley hub retaining bolt	15 to 20	2.0 to 2.7
Steering rack mounting bolts	32 to 37	4.4 to 5.1
Track-rod end locknuts	42 to 50	5.7 to 6.8
Track-rod end-to-steering arm	18 to 22	2.5 to 3.0
Track-rod end ball housing	33 to 37	4.6 to 5.2

3 Engine

General modifications to the 1980 range

1 The 1.6 and 2.0 litre engines fitted to the Cortina 80 models have changed very little compared with the original engines fitted to the Mk IV model. The piston rings and valve springs are now of low friction type, but these apart, no significant changes have been introduced. Although the engines now have increased power and greater economy, these factors are due to the fitting of a thermo viscous fan and a variable choke carburettor. These items are dealt with in the following Sections.

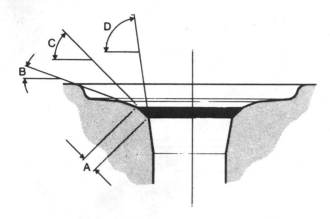

Fig. 13.2 Valve seat cutting diagram (Sec 3)

A   Valve seat width
B   Top relief angle
C   Valve seat angle
D   Bottom relief angle

Valve seat angles

2   On all engines built from 1980 on it is essential that any refacing of the valve seats is carried out in accordance with the angles shown in Fig. 13.2.

A	Valve seat width	0.06 to 0.08 in (1.5 to 2.0 mm)
B	Top relief angle	35°
C	Valve seat angle	46°
D	Bottom relief angle	65°

Crankshaft front oil seal – renewal

3   This operation can be carried out with the engine in the vehicle.
4   Remove the timing belt and crankshaft sprocket as described in Section 10 and 18 of Chapter 1.
5   If an oil seal removal tool is available, extract the crankshaft oil seal. Without the special tool, it may be possible to prise it out or to drill it and screw in self-tapping screws which will act as leverage points.
6   If the oil seal cannot be removed using one of these methods then the sump pan will have to be removed (Section 13, Chapter 1).
7   Unbolt the oil seal housing and auxiliary shaft front cover and gasket. The oil seal can then be driven out.
8   Clean the oil seal seat recess and drive a new seal into position. A socket is useful for this job. Check that the seal lip is towards the engine and has been lightly greased.
9   Refit the housing and cover using a new gasket. Check that the bottom face of the housing is flush with the block.
10 Refit the sump pan, timing belt and crankshaft sprocket all as described in Chapter 1.

4   Cooling system

Thermo viscous fan – description

1   To increase engine performance and provide better fuel economy a thermo viscous fan clutch is now fitted to all models (from 1980 on). This type of fan has several advantages over the type orginally used and these are:

(a) Engine warms up faster
(b) Less power required to drive the belt, therefore increased fanbelt life, more engine power and better fuel economy
(c) Fan operation is quieter

2   The fan itself is manufactured in plastic and is of multi-blade design. It is mounted on a viscous coupling whose operation is thermostatically controlled. On initial start-up when the engine is cold the fan rotates at 'idle' speed irrespective of engine speed. As the engine warms up the bi-metallic element in the fan hub actuates the control valve in the fan unit; this in turn progressively opens up the inlet port, allowing fluid into the rotor chamber (Fig. 13.3). This increases the fan drive torque and the fan speed increases accordingly.
3   The fluid is transferred into the fluid reservoir (at the front) by the rotational action of the rotor, and a ram pump. The fluid is kept in the reservoir until the engine starts to warm up, when it is progressively transferred into the rotor chamber as previously described.
4   The unit is not repairable and therefore should it become defective it must be renewed.

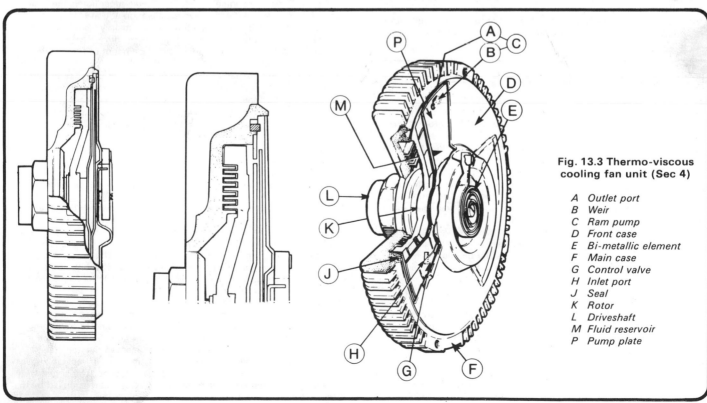

Fig. 13.3 Thermo-viscous cooling fan unit (Sec 4)

A   Outlet port
B   Weir
C   Ram pump
D   Front case
E   Bi-metallic element
F   Main case
G   Control valve
H   Inlet port
J   Seal
K   Rotor
L   Driveshaft
M   Fluid reservoir
P   Pump plate

Thermo viscous fan – removal and refitting

5 Removal of the thermo viscous fan necessitates the use of a special spanner with which to unscrew the unit from the water pump hub. An ordinary 32 mm (1.25 in) open jaw spanner can be modified to suit and reference to the illustration (Fig. 13.4) shows that the spanner must be cranked by 0.5 in (12 mm) at the point indicated. The jaw thickness of the spanner is also important and must not exceed 0.196 in (5 mm).

6 Hold and support the water pump pulley to prevent it rotating. Engage the special spanner over the fan clutch unit and unscrew it; *a left-hand thread is employed* so turn the spanner *clockwise* viewed from the front to loosen it.

7 Unscrew and remove the four fan-to-clutch bolts and separate the fan and clutch.

8 Refitting is a reversal of the removal process. When assembling the fan to the clutch, tighten the retaining bolts to the specified torque. This is most critical as the aluminium clutch housing may be damaged if this figure is exceeded.

Coolant expansion tank – description

9 A coolant expansion tank is now fitted and this assists the cooling system in retaining the correct volume of coolant. The tank is connected to the radiator by a pipe which is attached to the radiator filler neck. As the coolant temperature rises it expands and some flows into the expansion tank. This then returns when the engine cools.

10 Only check the coolant level when the engine is cold, otherwise the coolant flow between the radiator and expansion tank may be interrupted and an incorrect level reading taken.

11 The coolant level must be checked at the radiator filler neck, *not* at the expansion tank. Should topping up be required, top it up at the radiator to the base of the filler neck.

12 The coolant level in the expansion tank should never exceed 1/4 full. If the level exceeds this and approaches the top of the tank the radiator cap is probably at fault, giving an incorrect pressure, and this must therefore be checked and renewed if defective.

Coolant expansion tank – removal and refitting

13 To remove the expansion tank, allow the engine to cool and remove the expansion tank cap.

14 Unscrew and remove the two retaining screws and remove the tank, lifting it clear of its location lug in the mounting.

15 Any coolant left in the tank can be emptied into a clean container for re-use if required.

16 Refitting is a reversal of the removal procedure. On completion check the coolant level in the radiator and top up if necessary.

---

5 Fuel system

Variable venturi (VV) carburettor – description

1 Due to the anti-pollution regulations being introduced in various countries, Ford have developed a new variable choke carburettor of their own design which is more efficient than the previously used fixed jet Motorcraft carburettor. The new carburettor gives an increase in performance and improved petrol consumption; because it supplies a leaner mixture to the combustion chambers, the exhaust CO emissions are also reduced. These improvements are basically due to improved fuel atomisation and improved air/fuel mixture ratio under normal operating conditons. Known as the Ford VV (variable venturi) carburettor, it operates in the following manner.

2 Fuel is supplied to the carburettor via a needle valve which is actuated by the float. When the fuel level is low in the float chamber in the carburettor, the float drops and opens the needle valve. When the correct fuel level is reached the float will close the valve and shut off the fuel supply.

3 The float level on this type of carburettor is not adjustable since minor variations in the fuel level do not affect the performance of the carburettor. The valve needle is prevented from vibrating by means of a ball and light spring and to further ensure that the needle seals correctly it is coated in a rubber-like coating of Viton.

4 The float chamber is vented internally via the main jet body and carburettor air inlet, thus avoiding the possibility of petrol vapour escaping into the atmosphere.

5 The air/fuel mixture intake is controlled by the air valve which is opened or closed according to the operating demands of the engine.

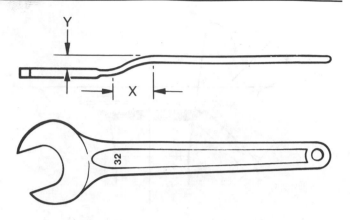

Fig. 13.4 Special spanner for thermo-viscous fan removal (Sec 4)

X = 1.0 in (25.0 mm)   Y = 0.5 in (12.0 mm)

The valve is actuated by a diaphragm which in turn opens or closes according to the vacuum supplied through the venturi between the air valve and the throttle butterfly. As the air valve and diaphragm are connected they open or close correspondingly.

6 When the engine is idling the air intake requirement is low and therefore the valve is closed, causing a high air speed over the main jet exit. However as the throttle plate is opened, the control vacuum (depression within the venturi) increases and is diverted to the diaphragm which then releases the air valve to balance the control spring and control vacuum.

7 When the throttle is opened further this equality of balance is maintained as the air valve is progressively opened to equalise the control spring and control vacuum force throughout the speed range.

8 Fuel from the float chamber is drawn up the pick-up tube and then regulated through two jets and the tapered needle and into the engine. The vacuum within the venturi draws the fuel. This is shown in Fig. 13.9. At low engine speeds the needle taper enters the main jet to restrict the fuel demand. On acceleration and at higher engine speeds the needle is withdrawn through the main jet by the action of the air valve to which it is attached. As the needle is tapered, the amount by which it is moved regulates the amount of fuel passing through the main jet.

9 The sonic idle system as used on other Ford fixed jet carburettors is also employed in the VV type, with 70% of the idle fuel mixture supplied via the sonic idle system and 30% from the main system. When idling, fuel is drawn through the main pick-up tube (Fig. 13.10), passes through the idle jet and then mixes with the air stream being supplied from the air bleed in the main jet body. The air/fuel mixture then passes on through the inner galleries to the mixture control screw which regulates the fuel supply at idle. This mixture then mixes with the air form the bypass idle channel and finally enters the inlet manifold via the sonic discharge tube at an accelerated rate of flow.

10 Throttle actuation is via a progressive linkage which has a cam and roller mechanism. The advantage of this system is that a large initial throttle pressure allows only a small throttle plate opening. As the throttle is opened up and approaches its maximum travel the throttle plate movement accelerates accordingly. This system aids economy, gives a good engine response through the range on smaller engines, and enables the same size of carburettor to be employed on other models in the range.

11 To counterbalance the drop in vacuum when initially accelerating, a restrictor is fitted into the air passage located between the control vacuum areas and the control diaphragm. This restrictor causes the valve to open slowly when an increase in air flow is made which in turn causes a higher vacuum for a brief moment in the main jet, caused by the increase in air velocity. This increase in vacuum causes the fuel flow to increase thus preventing a 'flat spot'. The larger amounts of fuel required under heavy acceleration are supplied by the accelerator pump.

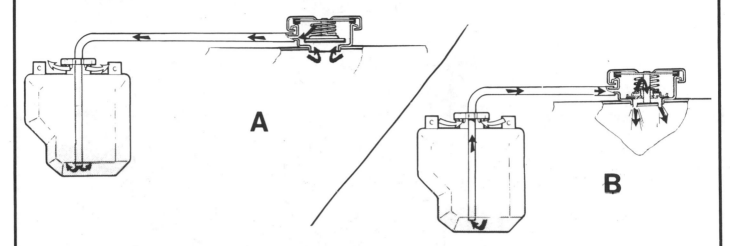

Fig. 13.5 Cooling system expansion tank (Sec 4)

A   Flow to tank (pressure valve open)
B   Return from tank (vacuum valve open)

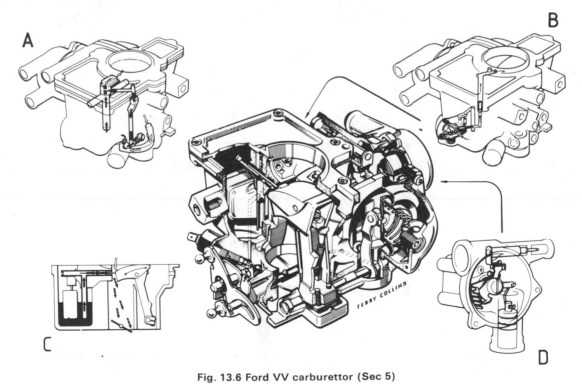

Fig. 13.6 Ford VV carburettor (Sec 5)

A   Sonic idle system   C   Main jet system
B   Accelerator pump system   D   Automatic choke system

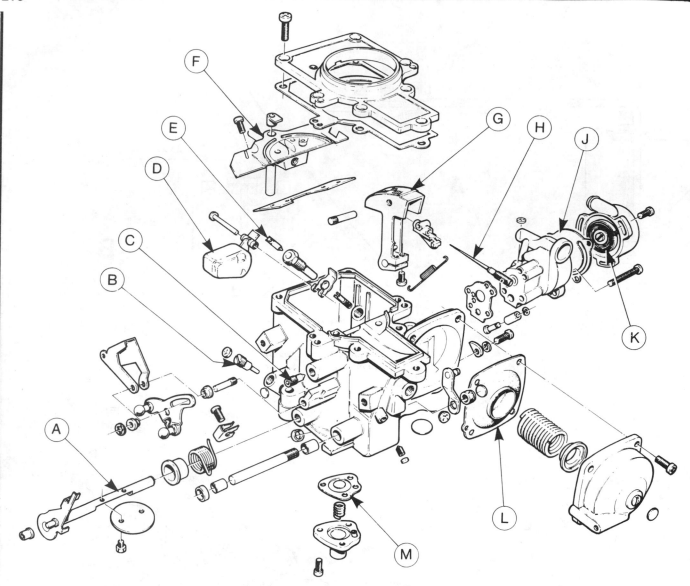

Fig. 13.7 Exploded view of VV carburettor (Sec 5)

A Throttle spindle
B Mixture screw
C Bypass leak adjuster

D Float
E Needle valve
F Main jet body

G Air valve
H Meter rod (needle)
J Choke unit

K Bi-metal coil
L Vacuum diaphragm
M Accelerator pump diaphragm

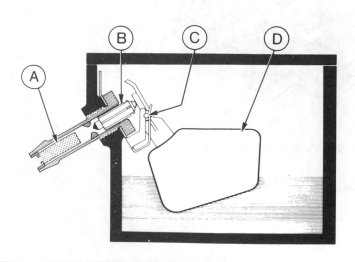

Fig. 13.8 VV fuel inlet valve and float (Sec 5)

A Filter
B Needle valve
C Float pivot
D Float

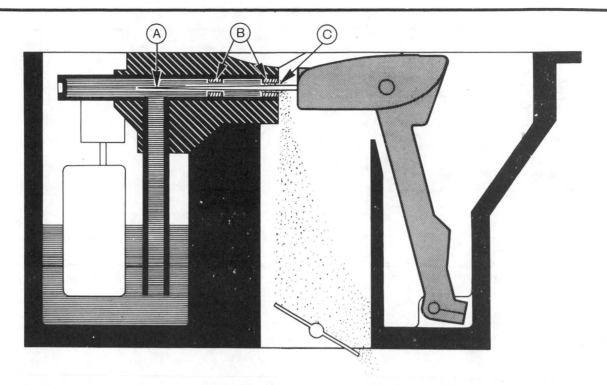

Fig. 13.9 Main jet supply system (Sec 5)

A   Tapered needle   B   Main and secondary jets   C   Fuel outlet

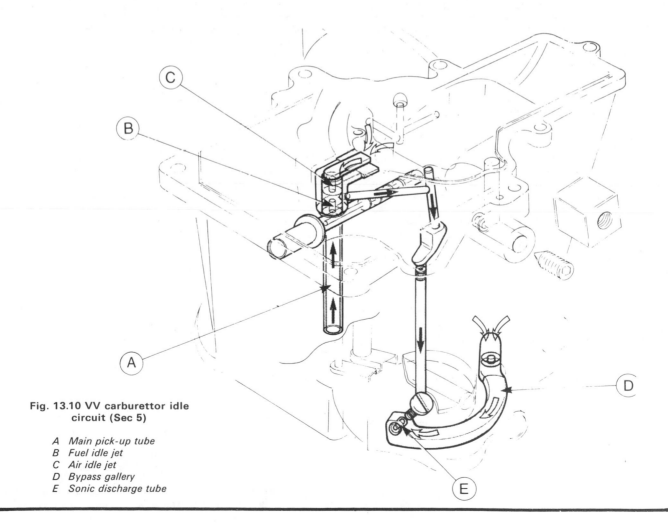

**Fig. 13.10 VV carburettor idle
circuit (Sec 5)**

A   Main pick-up tube
B   Fuel idle jet
C   Air idle jet
D   Bypass gallery
E   Sonic discharge tube

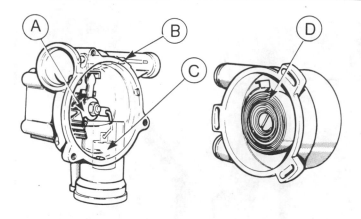

Fig. 13.11 Automatic choke unit (Sec 5)

A   Operating linkage   C   Pull-down piston
B   Needle valve   D   Bi-metallic coil

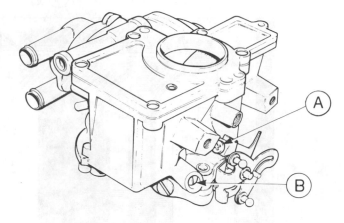

Fig. 13.12 VV carburettor adjustment screws (Sec 5)

A   Throttle (idle) speed screw   B   Mixture (idle) screw

12 The accelerator pump injects fuel into the venturi direct when acceleration causes a drop in manifold pressure. This richening of the mixture prevents engine hesitation under heavy acceleration. The accelerator pump is a diaphragm type and is actuated from vacuum obtained from under the throttle plate. During acceleration the vacuum under the throttle plate drops, the diaphragm return spring closes the diaphragm and the fuel in the pump is fed via the inner galleries through the one-way valve and into the venturi. The system incorporates a back bleeder and vacuum break air hole. Briefly explained, the back bleed allows any excess fuel vapour to return to the float chamber when prolonged idling causes the carburettor temperature to rise and the fuel in the accelerator pump reservoir to become overheated. The vacuum break air hole allows air into the pump outlet pipe to reduce the vacuum at the accelerator pump jet at high speed. Too much fuel would otherwise enter the accelerator pump system.

13 A fully automatic choke system is fitted, whereby engine coolant is fed through the choke unit. According to the temperature of the coolant, the bi-metal spring in the unit opens or closes. This in turn actuates the choke mechanism, which consists of a variable needle jet and a variable supply of air. Fuel to the choke jet is fed from the main pick-up tube via the internal galleries within the main jet body. When the bi-metal spring is contracted (engine cold), it pulls the tapered needle from the jet to increase the fuel delivery rate. The spring expands as the engine warms up and the needle reduces the fuel supply as it re-enters the jet. The choke air supply is supplied via the venturi just above the throttle plate. The fuel mixes with the air in the choke air valve, whence it is delivered to the engine.

14 A choke pull-down system is employed whereby if the engine is under choke but is only cruising, ie not under heavy loading, the choke is released. This is operated by the vacuum piston which is connected to the choke spindle by levers.

15 Last but not least, an anti-dieseling valve is visible on the outside of the body of the carburettor. This valve shuts off the fuel supply to the idle system when the engine is turned off and so prevents the engine running on or 'dieseling'. The solenoid valve is actuated electrically. When the ignition is turned off, it allows a plunger to enter and block the sonic discharge tube to stop the supply of fuel into the idle system. When the ignition is switched on the solenoid is actuated and the plunger is withdrawn from the tube.

16 It should be noted that the VV carburettor is not interchangeable with fixed choke carburettors as fitted to other Ford models. The manifold and throttle linkages, and also the ignition timing, are all different to suit the VV carburettor.

VV carburettor – adjustment

17 The engine must have reached its normal running temperature before making any adjustments.

18 For normal maintenance there are two carburettor settings possible: the idle speed adjustment and the mixture setting adjustment.

19 To deal with the idle speed adjustment first, this is similar to that on the Ford fixed venturi type carburettors dealt with in Chapter 3. Adjustment is made with the throttle stop screw (Fig. 13.12). To increase the idle speed tighten the screw, to decrease it unscrew it. If available use a tachometer to set the idle speed.

20 The mixture adjustment screw is covered with a 'tamperproof' plug. This should not normally be removed as the mixture setting was preset at the factory. If necessary, however, the plug can be prised free from its housing and the mixture screw adjusted to achieve the specified CO level. To weaken the mixture, tighten the screw; to richen the mixture turn the screw anti-clockwise. If an exhaust gas analyser is not available, turn the screw to achieve the smoothest idle, without hunting or misfiring. It may be necessry to readjust the throttle stop screw during this operation.

VV carburettor – air filter element renewal

21 The air cleaner element on this carburettor must be renewed at the specified service intervals. To remove the element proceed as follows.

22 Raise and support the bonnet. Unscrew and remove the air cleaner retaining screws (photo). The cover can now be unclipped from the cleaner body to detach it, after removing the single retaining screw. As the body tends to move with the cover when you try to unclip it, you may find it easier if you remove the complete air cleaner unit and then detach the cover. When removing the unit you will have to detach the air cleaner to manifold ducting (this just pulls free), and as the unit is raised from the carburettor disconnect the vacuum feed pipes (photo).

23 With the cover removed, lift out and discard the old element. Wipe out the filter body using a clean non-fluffy rag and then insert the new element (photo).

24 Relocate the cover, clipping it into position around its outer edge, making sure it is correctly located. Where the unit was fully removed, reconnect the vacuum hoses underneath, and as the unit is located onto the carburettor ensure that the special gasket is in position. Reconnect the air hose and ducting and make secure by tightening the three retaining screws.

VV carburettor – removal and refitting

25 Remove the air cleaner unit as described above.

26 Disconnect the solenoid feed wire (check that ignition is off).

27 Disconnect the throttle cable from the carburettor. Prise free the balljoint retaining clip using a screwdriver (photo), then compress the cable location retaining clips to release the cable from its location bracket (photo).

28 Disconnect the main fuel supply pipe to the carburettor and plug it to prevent fuel leakage and the ingress of dirt.

5.22A Air cleaner retaining screws (arrowed)

5.27A Removing throttle balljoint clip

5.22B Vacuum hose connections on underside of air cleaner casing

5.27B Throttle cable retainer clips (arrowed) at bracket

5.23 Air cleaner element

29 Disconnect the distributor vacuum pipe at the carburettor.
30 The auto choke inlet and outlet hoses can now be detached, but first release the radiator cap to ensure that the cooling system is not still under pressure. As the two hoses are disconnected from the choke body, plug them to prevent coolant leakage.
31 The carburettor is retained in position on the manifold by two diagonally opposed studs and nuts (photo). Remove the nuts and washers and then carefully lift the carburettor clear over the studs (photo).
32 Refitting the carburettor is a reversal of the removal procedure, but note the following:

(a) Always use a new carburettor-to-manifold gasket
(b) Make sure that the gasket faces are clean
(c) Do not overtighten the carburettor retaining nuts but ensure that they are secure
(d) Replace the original fuel supply hose crimped clip with a suitable worm drive clip
(e) Check that all hoses and connections are secure
(f) On completion check the engine idle speed and fuel mixture setting as described above

5.31A Unscrewing carburettor mounting nut

5.34 Removing carburettor top cover

5.31B Removing carburettor from manifold

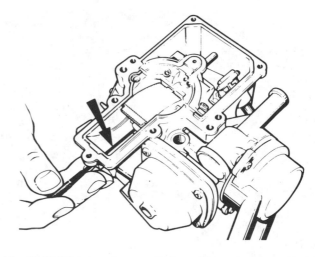

Fig. 13.13 Withdrawing needle from VV carburettor (Sec 5)

VV carburettor – dismantling and reassembly

Note: *Before attempting to overhaul a well worn carburettor, ensure that spares are available and reasonably priced. It may be both quicker and cheaper to obtain a complete carburettor on an exchange basis.*

33 Before dismantling the carburettor clean it off externally and prepare a suitable work space on the bench to lay out the respective components in order of appearance.

34 Unscrew and remove the seven carburettor cover retaining screws. Carefully lift the cover clear trying not to break the gasket. Remove the gasket (photo).

35 Drain any remaining fuel from the float chamber.

36 If the variable choke metering rod (or needle) is to be removed, prise the tamperproof plug from the body and insert a suitable screwdriver through the hole. Unscrew the metering rod and withdraw it (Fig. 13.13).

37 To remove the main jet body, unscrew the four retaining screws (photo), and carefully lift the body clear, noting gasket. If the metering rod is still in position, retract it as far as possible from the jet, press the float down and carefully pull the jet body clear of the metering rod (photo). Great care must be taken here not to bend or distort the rod in any way.

5.37A Main jet body retaining screws (arrowed)

5.37B Withdrawing main jet body

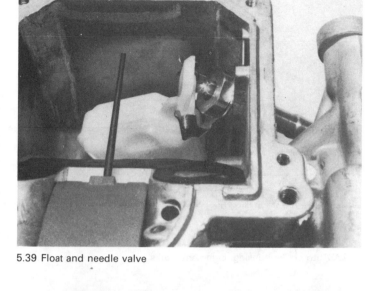

5.39 Float and needle valve

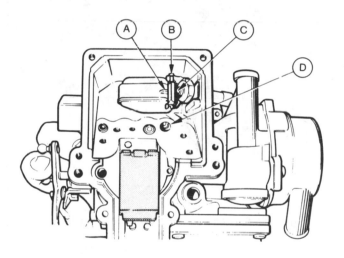

Fig. 13.14 VV carburettor with cover removed (Sec 5)

A Float
B Float pivot pin
C Fuel inlet needle valve

D Accelerator pump discharge
    passage

5.40A Control diaphragm circlip (arrowed)

38 The accelerator pump outlet one-way valve ball and weight can now be extracted by inverting the carburettor body.
39 Withdraw the float pivot pin followed by the float and needle valve (photo).
40 Unscrew and remove the four screws retaining the control diaphragm housing. Carefully detach the housing, spring, and seat, taking care not to split or distort the diaphragm. Fold back the diaphragm rubber from the flange. Using a small screwdriver, prise free the retaining clip to release the diaphragm. Pull the clip in a safe place to prevent it getting lost before reassembly (photos).
41 Now remove the accelerator pump by unscrewing the three retaining screws. Remove the housing and spring.
42 To remove the choke housing, note its postional markings, unscrew the retaining screws and carefully withdraw the housing (photos). Unscrew the solenoid unit.
43 The carburettor is now dismantled and the various components can be cleaned and inspected.

5.40B Removing control diaphragm

5.42A Auto choke housing alignment marks

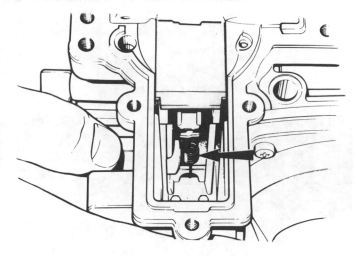

Fig. 13.15 Metering rod spring (Sec 5)

5.42B Choke housing cover and gasket

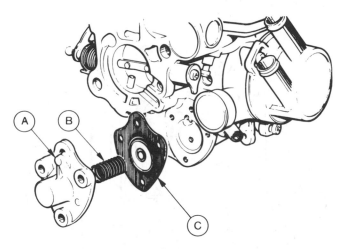

Fig. 13.16 Accelerator pump components (Sec 5)

A Housing   C Diaphragm
B Return spring

44 Check the body and components for signs of excessive wear and/or defects and renew as necessary. In particular inspect the main jet in the body. Excessive wear is present if the body is oval. Also pay particular attention to the air valve and linkage, the throttle plate (butterfly), its spindle and the throttle linkages for wear.
45 The diaphragm rubber must be in good condition and not split or perished. Check also that the metering rod spring is correctly fitted to the air valve (Fig. 13.15).
46 Renew all gaskets and seals during assembly and ensure that the mating surfaces are perfectly clean.
47 Commence assembly by refitting the accelerator pump. Locate the gasket face of the diaphragm towards the pump housing; when in position it must not be distorted at all.
48 Reconnect the diaphragm to the control linkage and retain by fitting the circlip. This is fiddly and requires a steady hand and a little patience. Check that the clip is fully engaged when in position.
49 As the diaphragm is fitted ensure that the double holes on one corner align with the corresponding holes in the carburettor body (photo). With the diaphragm in position, relocate the housing and spring and insert the retaining screws to secure. Take care not to distort the diaphragm as the housing is tightened.

5.49 Diaphragm hole alignment

50 If removed, refit the mixture adjustment screw, but don't relocate the tamperproof plug yet as the mixture must be adjusted when the engine is restarted. Do not overtighten the screw! Back off the screw three full turns.

51 Insert the float needle, the float and the pivot pin. When installing the needle valve the spring-loaded ball must face towards the float.

52 Locate the accelerator pump ball and weight into the discharge gallery, fit a new gasket into position and then refit the main jet body. If the metering rod is already in position, retract and raise it to re-engage the main jet housing over the rod and then lower it into position. Do not force or bend the rod in any way during this operation. Tighten the jet body retaining screws. If the metering rod is still to be fitted, do not fully tighten the jet body retaining screws until after the jet is fitted and known to be centralised.

53 If still to be fitted, slide the metering rod into position and screw it in until the rod shoulder aligns with the main body vertical face. Do not overtighten the rod. Should it bend during assembly, try re-centralising the jet main body, then tighten the retaining screws.

54 Plug the metering rod extraction hole in the carburettor body.

55 Position the new top cover gasket in position and refit the top cover. Tighten the retaining screws progressively and evenly (photo).

56 The auto choke housing can be refitted to complete assembly. Ensure that the body alignment marks correspond and as it is fitted engage the bi-metal coil with the middle choke lever slot (photo). Use a new gasket. Refit the three retaining screws and before tightening check that the body alignment markings correspond. To check or adjust the auto choke, see below.

57 Refit the carburettor onto the inlet manifold and tune and adjust it as described previously.

VV carburettor – automatic choke adjustment

58 To do this job accurately you will require a CO meter and a tachometer, but if the following instructions are followed carefully a satisfactory adjustment can be made.

59 Renew the air cleaner unit.

60 Unscrew the three screws retaining the choke housing in position and withdraw the housing.

61 To check the choke gauging you will require a twist drill 3.4 mm (0.135 in) diameter to act as a gauge rod.

62 Using a small screwdriver, prise free the tamperproof plug from the point indicated in Fig. 13.17 then looking through the vacant plug hole turn the lever so that the central shaft drilling aligns with the hole in the carburettor housing.

63 Insert the twist drill through the plug hole and fully locate into the choke center shaft.

64 Slacken off the choke linkage to shaft nut (Fig. 13.18).

65 Rotate the choke lever clockwise to its stop and then retighten the retaining nut (but don't overtighten it!).

66 Extract the gauge drill and then check the choke pull-down/fast idle as follows (do not refit the tamperproof plug just yet).

67 With a small pair of pliers, bend the operating lever to the position shown in Fig. 13.19 to ensure that the lever doesn't restrict the vacuum piston movement.

68 To prevent the pull-down lever moving while it is being bent, insert a twist drill into the hole in the choke housing just above the piston bore (Fig. 13.20).

69 Now look down the choke gauge hole and rotate the choke operating lever so that the central shaft drilling aligns with the hole in the housing.

70 Insert a 3.7 mm (0.145 in) diameter twist drill down into the gauge hole and into the central shaft. For models built after 1981 use a 4.3 mm (0.169 in) diameter drill.

71 Push the vacuum piston down to the bottom of its travel whilst holding the choke lever in the fully anti-clockwise position. Check that there is a small clearance between the pull-down lever and the bi-metal choke lever. If not, bend back the lever as previously described.

72 To make the adjustment, push the vacuum piston fully down (Fig. 13.21), hold the bi-metal lever in the fully anti-clockwise position and check that the pulldown lever is **JUST** touching the bi-metal lever without applying pressure to it. After rechecking the setting, remove the twist drill and fit a new tamperproof plug.

73 Locate a new gasket and engage the bi-metal coil in the central slot of the choke lever then loosely fit the choke housing, with the fixing screws finger tight. Turn the choke housing to align the single cover mark with the centre of the three index marks on the carburettor

5.55 Main jet body gasket

5.56 Middle slot of choke lever (arrowed)

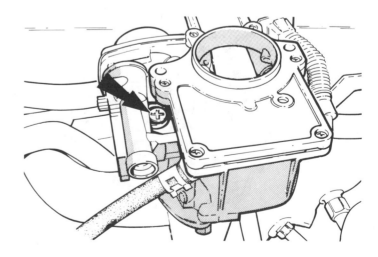
Fig. 13.17 Tamperproof plug (central shaft alignment) (Sec 5)

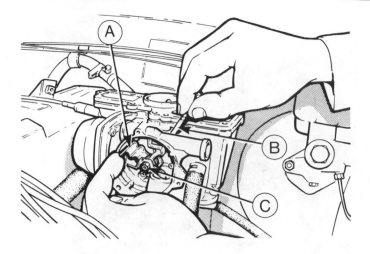

Fig. 13.18 Automatic choke operating lever (A), twist drill (B) and nut (C) (Sec 5)

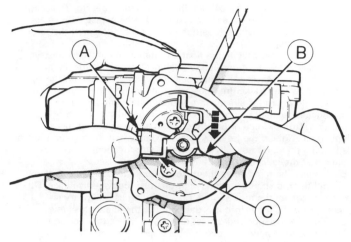

Fig. 13.21 Choke bi-metal lever (A), vacuum piston (B) pushed down, and pull-down lever (C) in contact with lever (A) (Sec 5)

Fig. 13.19 Operating lever bent (Sec 5)

body. Tighten the housing screws. Turning the choke housing anti-clockwise is towards rich and clockwise is in the lean direction.

VV carburettor – automatic choke unit – removal and refitting

74 Remove the air cleaner unit.

75 Release any pressure in the cooling system by unscrewing the radiator cap, then detach the auto choke coolant inlet and outlet hose at the carburettor.

76 Unscrew and remove the three screws retaining the choke housing in position. Withdraw the housing and bi-metal coil.

77 Unscrew and remove the three screws retaining the choke unit in the choke body of the carburettor (Fig. 13.22). Withdraw the choke unit.

78 Refitting of the choke unit is a reversal of the removal procedure, but check and if necessary adjust the auto choke pull-down/fast idle setting and the choke gauging as described above.

79 When refitting the choke bi-metal coil body make sure that the alignment marks correspond and engage the coil tag in the middle slot of the choke lever as it is fitted.

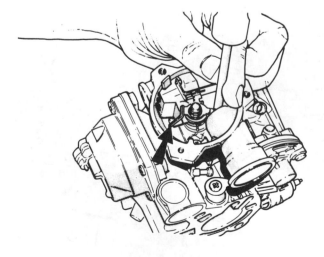

Fig. 13.20 Twist drill used to retain choke pull-down lever while it is being bent (Sec 5)

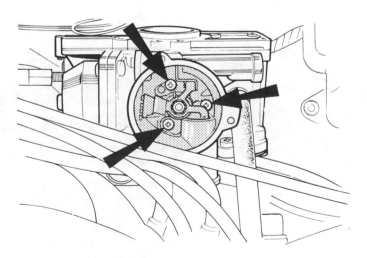

Fig. 13.22 Choke unit retaining screws (Sec 5)

Weber twin venturi carburettor – modifications
80 From approximately May 1981 the Weber twin venturi carburettor fitted to 2.0 litre engines has been modified to improve cold start and cold drive operation. The modifications comprise a revised accelerator pump discharge nozzle and the inclusion of a low vacuum enrichment device known as a ported vacuum switch (Fig. 13.23). These modifications do not affect the servicing or overhaul procedures described in Chapter 3.

6 Ignition system

Spark control system
1 This arrangement was devised to overcome poor driveability and acceleration problems from cold start on 1.6 litre models fitted with a Ford VV carburettor. The system may be fitted in the following way if not already so equipped during production.
2 Disconnect the battery.
3 Remove the original vacuum hose which runs between the distributor vacuum unit and the carburettor.
4 Drain the cooling system as described in Chapter 2.

5 Obtain the following parts:

Ported vacuum switch EIAZ – 8A564D or D70E – 8A564 – AIA Adaptor 74HF – 9C704 – AA

6 Screw the vacuum switch into the adaptor, tightening to 19 lbf ft (27 Nm) and having a final angled setting as shown in Fig. 13.26.
7 Cut a 1.0 in (25.4 mm) section from the centre of the run of the lower automatic choke coolant hose.
8 Fit the switch/adaptor assembly into the cut auto-choke hose and secure with hose clips.
9 Cut a length of vacuum hose into the various lengths specified in Fig. 13.27.
10 Assemble the hoses as shown, making sure that the white and black sides of the fuel trap and the spark sustain valve are correctly orientated.
11 Connect the vacuum hoses to the ported vacuum switch.
12 Connect hose (1) to the carburettor and hose (6) to the distributor vacuum unit.
13 It is important that the vacuum hose to the carburettor passes over the choke housing and that the CARB outlet of the fuel trap is lower than the DIST outlet of the trap. Use suitable straps to arrange this.
14 Refill the cooling system. Reconnect the battery.

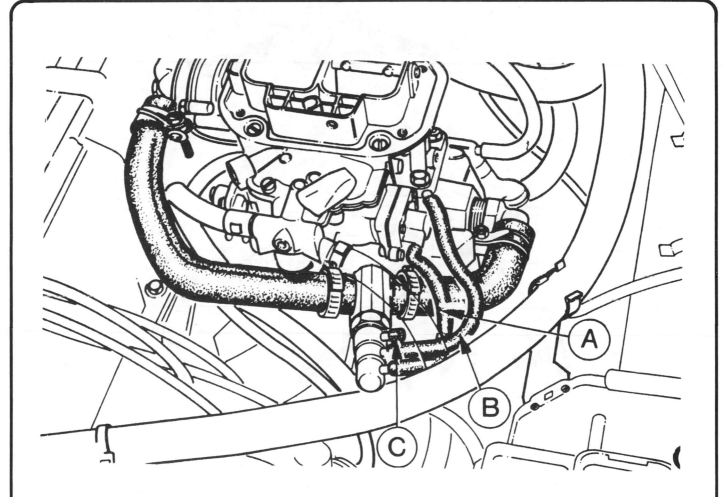

Fig. 13.23 Ported vacuum switch and associated components with Weber carburettor (Sec 5)

A   Vacuum hose   B   Vacuum hose   C   Blanking plug

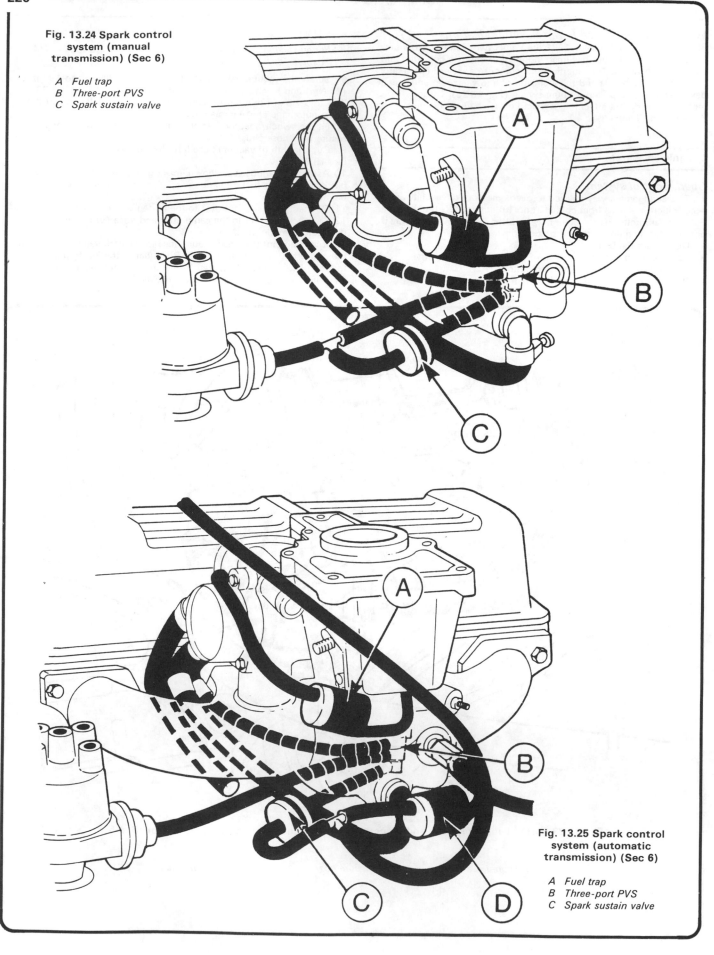

Fig. 13.24 Spark control system (manual transmission) (Sec 6)

A   Fuel trap
B   Three-port PVS
C   Spark sustain valve

Fig. 13.25 Spark control system (automatic transmission) (Sec 6)

A   Fuel trap
B   Three-port PVS
C   Spark sustain valve

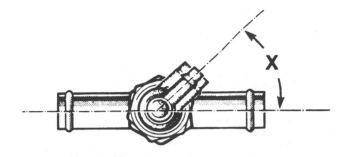

Fig. 13.26 Vacuum switch adaptor setting (Sec 6)

X = 45°

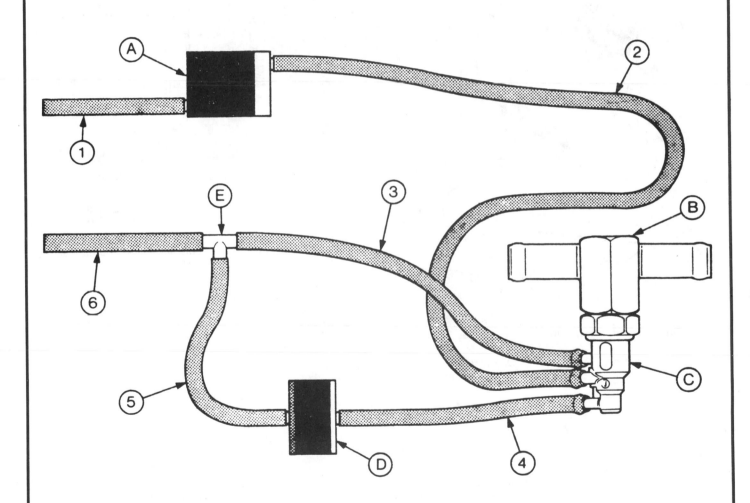

Fig. 13.27 Spark control system components (in service fitting) (Sec 6)

A   *Fuel trap*
B   *Adaptor*
C   *Three-port PVS*
D   *Spark sustain valve*
E   *Hose T-piece*

1   *Hose length = 70.0 mm*
2   *Hose length = 580.0 mm*
3   *Hose length = 200.0 mm*

4   *Hose length = 110.0 mm*
5   *Hose length = 110.0 mm*
6   *Hose length = 70.0 mm*

7 Clutch

Automatically adjusted clutch cable – description

1 All 1980 models fitted with manual transmission have an auto-matically adjusted clutch operating cable, the adjustment being taken up by a device fitted to the clutch pedal. The main components of this device are shown in Fig. 13.28.

2 The pedal operates the cable and release lever in the noromal manner, but when the pedal pressure is released and the pawl is not in mesh on the quadrant, the cable tension is taken up by the spring located between the quadrant and clutch pedal. As the pedal is depressed, the pawl will engage itself into the nearest quadrant teeth.

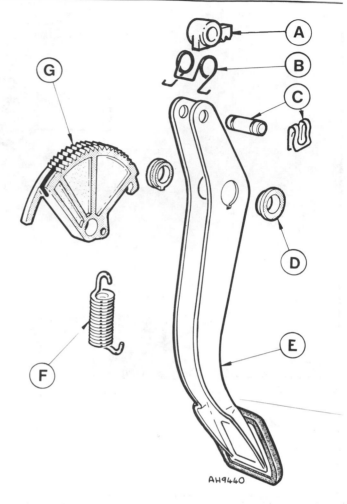

Fig. 13.29 Clutch pedal and cable adjustment components (Sec 7)

A Pawl
B Tension spring (pawl)
C Pin and clip
D Bushes

E Pedal
F Tension spring (quadrant)
G Quadrant

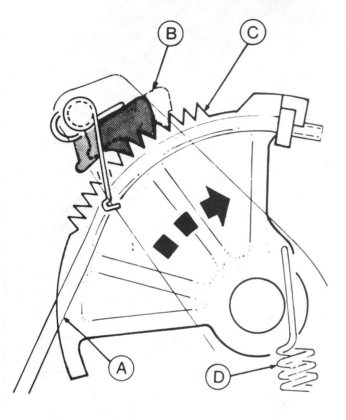

Fig. 13.28 Automatic clutch adjuster (Sec 7)

A Clutch cable
B Pawl

C Quadrant
D Tension spring

Automatically adjusted clutch cable – removal and refitting

3 Jack up and raise the front of the car. Supplement with axle stands or blocks to make secure. If ramps or a pit are available use these instead. Ensure handbrake is fully applied.

4 Working underneath the car, prise back the clutch release lever rubber gaiter from the clutch housing.

5 Pull the cable downwards in front of the release lever. Hold the lever and detach the cable. remove the clutch release lever rubber damper.

6 Working inside the car, push the driver's seat right back for extra room and then unclip and remove the dash lower trim panel.

7 Pull the cable through and detach it from the pedal adjustment mechanism quadrant (Fig. 13.30) Withdraw the cable through the aperture between the pedal mechanism and pedal, then extract the cable through the engine compartment.

8 Refitting is a reverse of the removal procedure. However, it will be found easier to reconnect the clutch cable to the release lever if the pedal is held away from the floor by wedging a suitable piece of

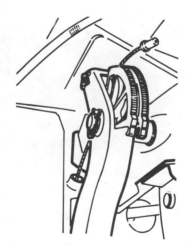

Fig. 13.30 Cable end fitting at clutch pedal (Sec 7)

wood between the two. Then, using a suitable metal plate or
screwdriver blade, hold the pawl away from the quadrant teeth so
that the quadrant can be rotated to provide sufficient free play for
cable reconnection at the release lever.
9 When assembled, again lift the pawl clear of the quadrant against
spring pressure, then rotate the quadrant so that when released, the
pawl is on the smooth face of the quadrant as shown in Fig. 13.31.

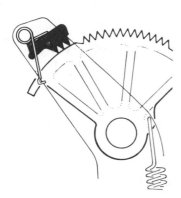

**Fig. 13.31 Pawl located on smooth face of clutch pedal
quadrant (Sec 7)**

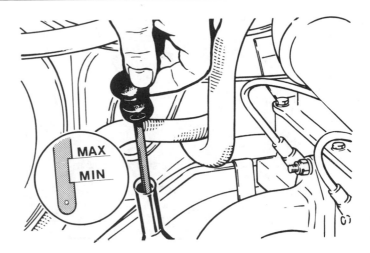

**Fig. 13.32 Later type automatic transmission fluid dipstick
(Sec 8)**

*Clutch pedal/automatic adjustment mechanism –
removal and refitting*
10 Refer to the previous sub-section and disconnect the clutch
operating cable from the release lever and from the pedal quadrant,
but do not fully remove it.
11 Prise free the pedal shaft locking clip and washer and then
withdraw the pedal assembly from the shaft, pulling it sideways.
12 To dismantle the pedal assembly, extract the spindle bushes, lift
out the quadrant and tension spring, then withdraw the pawl pivot,
the pawl and its spring.
13 Remove any parts that may be in need of replacement, in
particular the tension and pawl springs and the quadrant/pedal
bushes.
14 Refitting is the reversal of the removal and dismantling sequence.
Lubricate the quadrant and pedal pivot with a small amount of
graphite grease. Refer to the details given in paragraphs 8 and 9.

8 Automatic transmission

Automatic transmission fluid – level checking
1 Automatic transmission models manufactured from May 1979
onwards incorporate an increase in transmission fluid level in conjunction with a modified fluid level dipstick (Fig. 13.32). The level
check procedure has also been revised as follows.
2 Before checking the fluid level drive the car for approximately 5
miles (8 km) to bring the transmission fluid up to normal operating
temperature.
3 Park the car on level ground and apply the handbrake.
4 With the engine idling, move the selector lever through all
positions three times. Now select P position and wait one to two
minutes.
5 With the engine still idling, open the bonnet and withdraw the
transmission dipstick. Wipe it clean, re-insert it, withdraw it for the
second time and read off the level. The fluid level should be between
the MAX and MIN notches on the dipstick.
6 If necessary, top up the transmission with the specified fluid
through the dipstick tube.
7 Always keep the exterior of the transmission and the dipstick tube
clean and free from dirt and grit.

Automatic transmission fluid specification
8 From approximately September 1980 an improved automatic
transmission fluid has been introduced and carries the Ford specification SQM-2C9019-A. This fluid is known as type CJ fluid and

must not be mixed with the earlier SQM-2C9007-AA type, or
transmission damage may occur. Models filled with the new fluid are
identified by their red dipstick/filler tube. Models filled with the earlier
type fluid have a black or bright finish filler tube and a black dipstick.
The earlier type fluid will still be available for use in transmissions
manufactured before September 1980.
9 When topping up the transmission always ensure that the correct
type of fluid according to dipstick/filler tube colour, is used.

9 Propeller shaft

Flexible coupling
1 From 1980 on 1.6 and 2.0 litre models with manual or automatic
tramsmission are fitted with a two-piece driveshaft and flexible
coupling.
2 The flexible coupling will expand if unbolted and removed.
3 In order to align the bolt holes when refitting the coupling, use a
large worm drive hose clip around the coupling to compress it.

10 Braking system

General information
1 Certain improvements have been made to the braking system of
1980 models. The brake fluid reservoir is now manufactured in
see-through plastic and it is therefore no longer necessary to remove
the filler cap to check the fluid level. Maximum and minimum levels
are marked on the side of the reservoir; the fluid level must be
maintained between the two marks at all times.
2 The rear brake backplates now incorporate an aperture to allow
the ear brake linings to be inspected for wear without removing the
brake drums (Fig. 13.33).
3 All models manufactured from early 1979 on are equipped with a
brake fluid level warning light system.
4 The differential valve assembly was fitted to early Cortina models
and has now been superseded by a brake pressure control valve. The
removal and refitting procedure for both units is similar, as described
below. The brake pressure control valve is however a sealed unit and
cannot be dismantled for overhaul.
5 The improvements mentioned above do not affect the servicing or
overhaul procedures of the brake system as described in Chapter 9.

Differential valve assembly – removal and refitting
6 Wipe the top of the brake master cylinder reservoir and unscrew
the cap. Place a thin piece of polythene over the top of the reservoir
and refit the cap. This will prevent loss of hydraulic fluid during
subsequent operations.

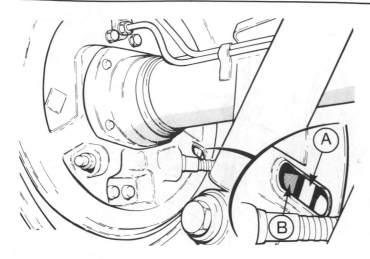

Fig. 13.33 Brake shoe lining inspection hole (Sec 10)

A   Drum   B   Shoe

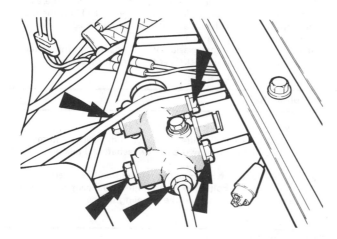

Fig. 13.34 Brake pressure differential valve pipe unions (Sec 10)

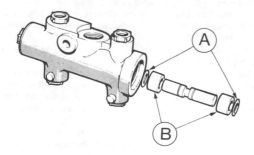

Fig. 13.35 Brake pressure differential valve components (Sec 10)

A   Rubber seals   B   Sleeves

7   Wipe the area around the valve assembly and then unscrew the pipe unions from the valve. Tape or plug the ends of the pipes to prevent dirt ingress.
8   Disconnect the warning light switch plug from the side of valve body.
9   Undo and remove the retaining nut and bolt, and lift away the valve.
10 Refitting is the reverse sequence to removal. Bleed the hyudraulic system as described in Chapter 9 after refitting.

Differential valve assembly – dismantling and reassembly

11 Before dismantling the valve obtain an overhaul kit consisting of new rubber seals. Do not re-use the old seals after dismantling.
12 Unscrew the warning light switch unit and remove it from the side of the valve body.
13 Undo and remove the piston retaining bolt and copper sealing washer.
14 Using a small screwdriver inserted through the pipe union, carefully push out the piston complete with sleeves and rubber seals.
15 Wash the valve and internal components in clean hydraulic fluid and dry with a lint-free cloth. Carefully examine the valve bore, piston and sleeves for scoring or wear and, if apparent, renew the complete valve assembly.
16 Begin reassembly by lubricating all the parts in clean hydraulic fluid.
17 Slide the two sleeves onto the piston and retain them in place with new rubber seals.
18 Insert the piston assembly into the valve bore, then refit the retaining nut and copper washer.
19 Finally screw in the warning light switch and tighten it fully.
20 The valve can now be refitted to the car as described in the previous Section.

Additional bleeding methods

21 The following methods may be used to bleed the brake hydraulic system as alternatives to the procedure described in Chapter 9.

Bleeding – using one-way valve kit

22 There are a number of one-man, one-way brake bleeding kits available from motor accessory shops. It is recommended that one of these kits is used wherever possible as it will greatly simplify the bleeding operation and also reduce the risk of air or fluid being drawn back into the system quite apart from being able to do the work without the help of an assistant.
23 To use the kit, connect the tube to the bleedscrew and open the screw one half a turn.
24 Depress the brake pedal fully and slowly release it. The one-way valve in the kit will prevent expelled air from returning at the end of each pedal downstroke. Repeat this operation several times to be sure of ejecting all air from the system. Some kits include a translucent container which can be positioned so that the air bubbles can actually be seen being ejected from the system.
25 Tighten the bleed screw, remove the tube and repeat the operations on the remaining brakes.
26 On completion, depress the brake pedal. If it still feels spongy repeat the bleeding operations as air must still be trapped in the system.

Bleeding – using a pressure bleeding kit

27 These kits too are available from motor accessory shops and are usually operated by air pressure from the spare tyre.
28 By connecting a pressurised container to the master cylinder fluid reservoir, bleeding is then carried out by simply opening each bleed screw in turn and allowing the fluid to run out, rather like turning on a tap, until no air is visible in the expelled fluid.
29 By using this method, the large reserve of hydraulic fluid provides a safeguard against air being drawn into the master cylinder during bleeding which often occurs if the fluid level in the reservoir is not maintained.
30 Pressure bleeding is particularly effective when bleeding 'difficult' systems or when bleeding the complete system at time of routine fluid renewal.
31 Discard brake fluid which has been expelled. It is almost certain to be contaminated with moisture, air and dirt making it unsuitable for further use. Clean fluid should always be stored in an airtight container as it absorbs moisture readily (hygroscopic) which lowers

its boiling point and could affect braking performance under severe conditions.

Handbrake cable – adjustment

32   As from September 1982, a new type of handbrake cable adjuster has been fitted.

33   The knurled locknut is released simply by unscrewing it with the fingers. When tightening after adjustment, which is carried out by turning the adjuster sleeve, hold the sleeve and tighten the locknut onto it until two clicks are heard indicating that the locking tangs have engaged.

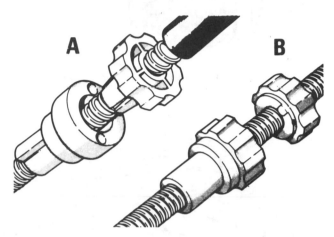

Fig. 13.36 Two types of handbrake cable adjuster (Sec 10)

A Earlier type   B Later type

11   Electrical system

Front direction indicator lights – bulb renewal

1   On 1980 models the front indicator lights were changed and are now individual units separate from the headlights. They are immediately recognisable, being larger than the older type, and are of the 'wrap-around' type making them visible from the side as well. To replace a bulb proceed as follows.

2   Raise and support the bonnet.

3   The lens/unit retaining nut is accessible in the engine compartment at the front on the side concerned. Unscrew the nut (photo) whilst simultaneously supporting the lens/unit.

11.3 Front direction indicator lamp fixing screw (arrowed)

4   Remove the lens/unit from the panel aperture and extract the bulbholder. The bayonet fitting bulb can now be removed for replacement (photos).

5   Refitting is a reversal of the removal procedure. Check that the rubber cover is fully fitted over the bulbholder. On completion test the indicator for satisfactory operation.

11.4A Withdrawing front direction indicator lamp

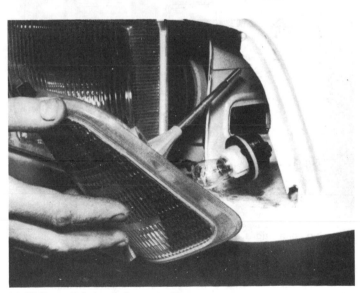

11.4B Front direction indicator bulb

Rear combination lights – bulb renewal

6   The 1980 Saloon models have a redesigned tail light unit on each side and each unit now incorporates foglights. (The 1980 Estate models retain the original type rear light units but a separate rear foglamp is now fitted – see below). To remove a unit and change a bulb on the later type light units proceed as follows.

7   Open the boot lid and remove the complete bulbholder unit by gripping it and pushing it sideways as shown (Fig. 13.37). When it is clear of the lamp body clips, remove it.

8   The defective bulb can now be removed and replaced.

9   If the complete lamp body is to be removed, detach the two multi-plugs and then unscrew and remove the screws, nuts and washers that secure the lamp body (Fig. 13.38).

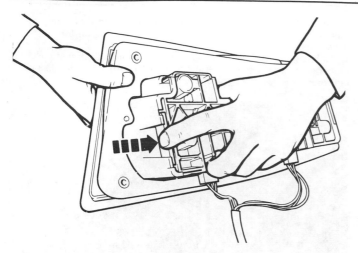

Fig. 13.37 Rear combination light removal – press retaining tang (arrowed) (Sec 11)

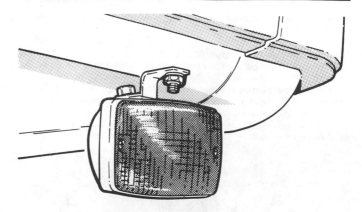

Fig. 13.39 Rear foglight (Estate version) (Sec 11)

Fig. 13.38 Rear lamp cluster fixing screws (Sec 11)

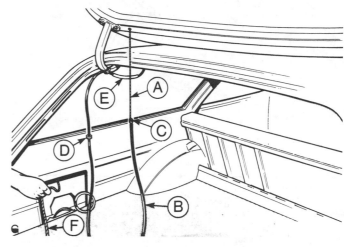

Fig. 13.40 Renewal of rear screen washer hose (Sec 11)

A Cord   D Grommet
B Hose   E Protective sleeve
C Cord taped to hose   F Cord

10 Refitting is a reversal of the removal procedure. Check that the multi-plug connections are secure, and check the operation of all rear lights on completion.

Rear foglight (Estate models) – removal and refitting
11 A foglight is now fitted to the rear, directly under the bumper, on 1980 Estate models.
12 To replace a bulb, simply unscrew the two lens retaining screws and detach the lens for access to the bulb which has a bayonet type fixing.
13 To remove the complete unit, disconnect the wiring to the light unit, unscrew the unit retaining nut and serrated washer and lower the unit.
14 Refitting is a reversal of the removal procedure. Check the operation of the light on completion.

Rear windscreen washer hoses (Estate) – renewal
15 Open the tailgate and carefully prise free the trim panel which is attached to the tailgate by snap clips.
16 Remove the rear load space trim panel in a similar fashion, then disconnect the hose from the nozzle and attach a length of cord to the hose. Unclip the hose from the transmission clips in the tailgate and carefully pull through the hose and cord.
17 Remove the side panel access cover to the reservoir (photo), detach the reservoir retaining strap and lift it clear.

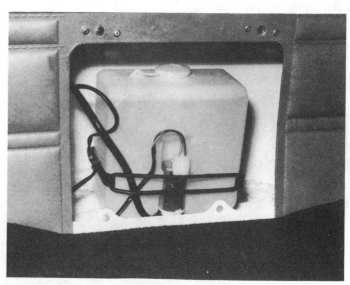

11.17 Rear screen washer reservoir (Estate) cover panel removed

18 Detach the hose from the washer unit pump and tie some cord to the end of the hose. Pull the hose carefully through the pillar and remove the hose. The cord is left in place through the body channel to pull the new hose through.

19 Fitting of the new hose is a reversal of the removal process. Ensure that the hose connections are secure and top up the reservoir. Check the operation of the washer and wiper before refitting the trim panels.

Reversing light switch

20 The reversing light switch is located in the gear selector extension housing, in line with the lever. If renewal is necessary simply engage neutral, detach the connecting cable to the switch and unscrew the switch to remove it from the extension. Photo 3.8 in Chapter 6 shows the extension and the reversing light switch. Refitting is a reversal of the removal procedure.

Ignition switch lock barrel – removal and refitting

21 Disconnect the battery leads.

22 Unscrew and unclip the upper and lower steering column shrouds.

23 Turn the ignition key to position 1 (accessories) to align the key barrel retaining clip with the keyway register in the housing. Use a scriber or fine punch and depress the leaf spring in the cylinder through the hole (Fig. 13.41), simultaneously pulling on the key to withdraw the cylinder and lock barrel. Agitate the key slightly to the right and left to ease removal.

24 With the key fully located in the barrel, remove the circlip and check that its seat on the barrel is in good condition.

25 If the key is fully withdrawn from the barrel the springs and wards will be disconnected from the barrel.

26 Refitting the key, lock cylinder and barrel is a reversal of the removal procedure, but note the following:

(a) Withdraw the key by 0.2 in (5 mm) to set the ward as shown in order to reassemble the barrel and cylinder. The barrel will only fit in one position

(b) When assembled check that the key can be turned to all positions. Excessive force should not be necessary to assemble the lock barrel unit

(c) Turn the key to positon 1 and locate the circlip. The gap in the circlip must be in line with the cylinder keyway register (Fig. 13.42)

(d) Fit the cylinder unit into the housing and check that it is fully seated with the leaf spring engaged in the housing slot

(e) Reconnect the battery leads and check the operation of the steering lock and the ignition key functions

Windscreen wipers

27 As from 1980 some models are fitted with either intermittent wipe action or flick wiper action windscreen wipers.

28 The intermittent wipe action operates via a relay unit which is located on the underside of the instrument panel. The intermittent wipe action allows a sweep delay of about 5 seconds.

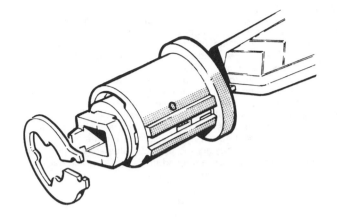

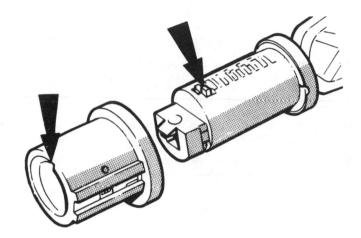

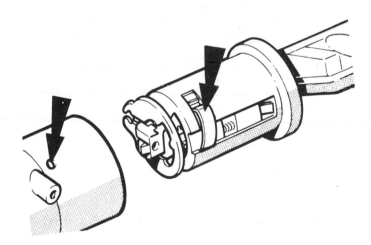

Fig. 13.42 Ignition lock reassembly stages (Sec 11)

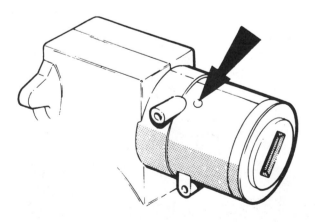

Fig. 13.41 Lock cylinder leaf spring hole (Sec 11)

29 The flick action is obtained via the wiper switch which when pressed down against spring pressure, will operate the wipers until the pressure on the switch is released. The wipers then automatically return to the parked position.

30 Removal and replacement procedures are identical with those given for the earlier types in Chapter 10. It is of course important to quote the car model, and also its year, when ordering any replacement parts, to ensure getting the correct type.

Heated seats

31 On some models, heated front seats are available as an optional extra. The seats themselves are basically the same but heater pads are inserted under the seat trim, one to the seat back and one to the seat section. Both pads are secured to the seat foam padding tie-rods by three hob rings at one end and tapes at the other.

32 Power is supplied to each pad via a relay located within the upper control console near the heated seat switch.

33 The pads themselves require no maintenance. If for any reason the seats become wet, this will not affect the seat pads.

34 Removal of the pads is best left to a Ford dealer since it requires the removal of the seat trim. It is also essential that the pads be correctly fitted since if they are too tight, no allowance is given for seat stretch. If fitted too loose the pad may wrinkle which could cause the element to short circuit.

Clock – removal and refitting

35 Disconnect the battery.

36 Using two screwdrivers, inserted at opposite sides under the clock bezel, lever the clock from the centre console.

37 Disconnect the leads from the rear of the clock.

38 Refitting is a reversal of removal.

Load space lamp switch (Estate) – removal and refitting

39 Disconnect the battery.

40 Open the tailgate and remove the trim panel from the roof.

41 Unscrew the two nuts which hold the switch to the tailgate hinge.

42 Withdraw the switch and disconnect the leads.

43 Refitting is a reversal of removal.

Windscreen wiper delay relay – renewal

44 On vehicles so equipped, the relay is located behind the facia panel.

45 For access to the relay, remove the facia under cover panel from the driver's side and then reach up and unclip the relay from its bracket.

46 Disconnect the multi-plug.

47 Refit the new relay by reversing the removal operations.

Headlamp washer system

48 This consists of a reservoir, pump and nozzles.

49 To remove the pump, first disconnect the battery.

50 Disconnect the multi-plug from the windscreen washer pump.

51 Remove the fluid reservoir cap and the headlamp wash pump bypass return pipe.

52 Pull the windscreen washer pipe from the pump outlet.

53 Disconnect the large bore pipe which runs between the reservoir and the headlamp washer pump.

54 Disconnect the pipe from the pump and plug the pipe to avoid fluid loss.

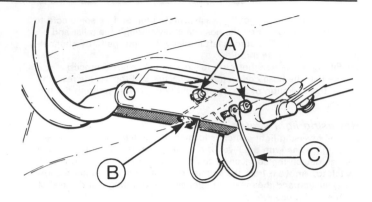

Fig. 13.44 Load space lamp switch (Sec 11)

A   Switch fixing nuts   C   Earth lead
B   Switch

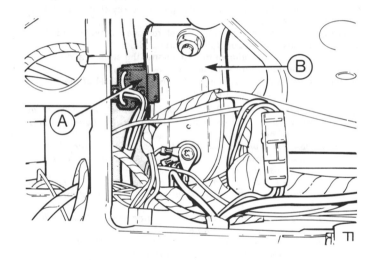

Fig. 13.45 Windscreen wiper delay relay (Sec 11)

A   Relay   B   Bracket

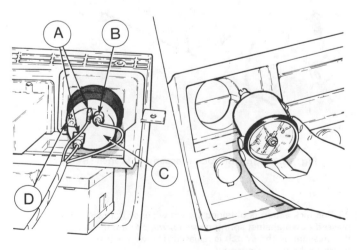

Fig. 13.43 Clock removal (Sec 11)

A   Leads   C   Clock
B   Illumination   D   Retaining clip

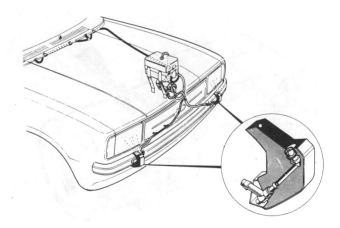

Fig. 13.46 Headlamp wash system (Sec 11)

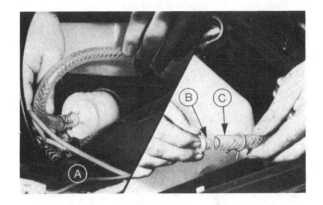

Fig. 13.47 Disconnecting headlamp washer pump (Sec 11)

A   Disconnecting hose   C   Hose from reservoir
B   Hose plug

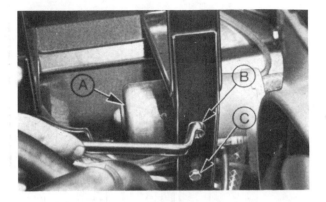

Fig. 13.48 Unbolting pump (Sec 11)

A   Pump   C   Lower securing bolts
B   10.0 mm ring spanner

55 Remove the washer reservoir. ·
56 Unclip the hose from the headlamp washer pump outlet.
57 Unbolt the headlamp washer pump, disconnect the multi-plug and remove the pump and return hose.
58 The headlamp washer nozzles are an integral part of the bumper overrider and if necessary, they must be renewed as an assembly.
59 The nozzles can be adjusted using a suitable tool to provide a wash pattern as shown in Fig. 13.50.

Heated rear window – precautions and repair
60 The tailgate or rear window elements are fixed to the interior surface of the glass.
61 Clean the glass with water and a leather or soft cloth. Avoid solvents or abrasive cleaners.
62 Rub the glass in the direction of the filaments and avoid scratching them with rings on the fingers.
63 Never stick labels over the element and do not pack luggage so that it rubs against the glass.
64 If the element is damaged, it can probably be repaired with one of the special conductive paints available from motor stores.

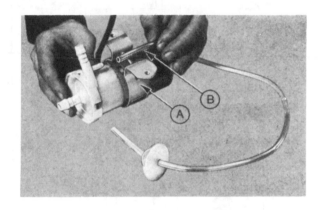

Fig. 13.49 Headlamp washer pump (Sec 11)

A   Pump   B   Bypass (return) hose

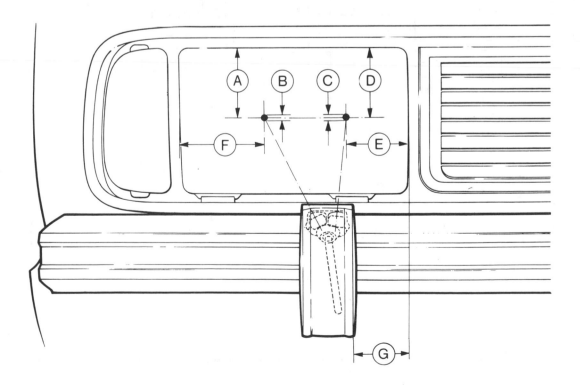

Fig. 13.50 Headlamp wash pattern (Sec 11)

A = 3.2 in (80.0 mm)
B = 0.31 in (8.0 mm)
C = 0.31 in (8.0 mm)
D = 3.2 in (80.0 mm)
E = 2.8 in (70.0 mm)
F = 3.4 in (85.0 mm)
G = 2.3 in (58.0 mm)

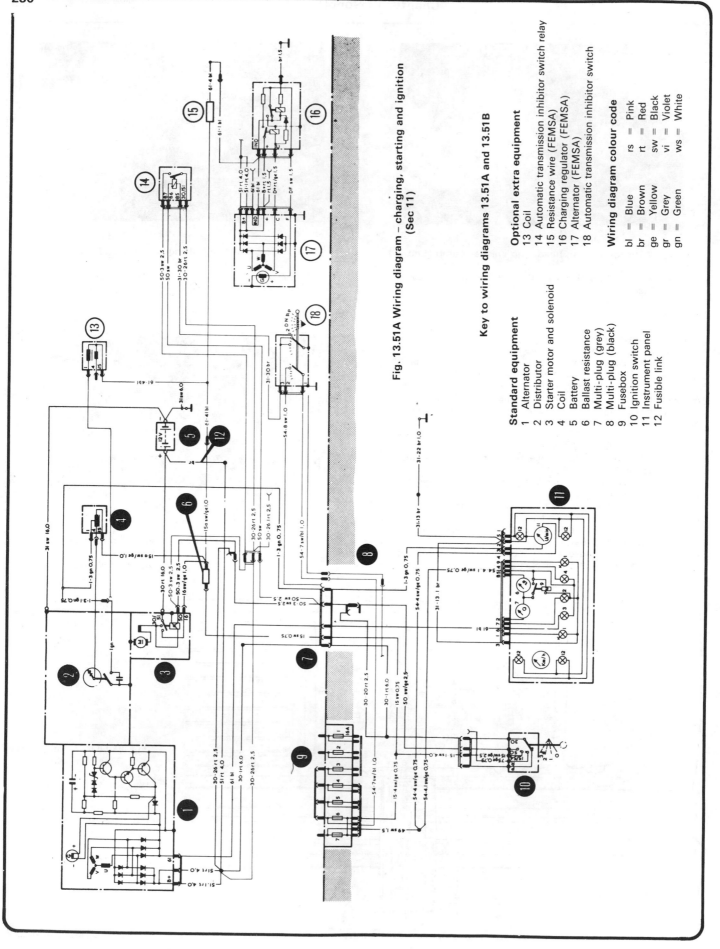

Fig. 13.51A Wiring diagram – charging, starting and ignition (Sec 11)

Key to wiring diagrams 13.51A and 13.51B

Standard equipment
1 Alternator
2 Distributor
3 Starter motor and solenoid
4 Coil
5 Battery
6 Ballast resistance
7 Multi-plug (grey)
8 Multi-plug (black)
9 Fusebox
10 Ignition switch
11 Instrument panel
12 Fusible link

Optional extra equipment
13 Coil
14 Automatic transmission inhibitor switch relay
15 Resistance wire (FEMSA)
16 Charging regulator (FEMSA)
17 Alternator (FEMSA)
18 Automatic transmission inhibitor switch

Wiring diagram colour code

bl	=	Blue	rs	=	Pink
br	=	Brown	rt	=	Red
ge	=	Yellow	sw	=	Black
gr	=	Grey	vi	=	Violet
gn	=	Green	ws	=	White

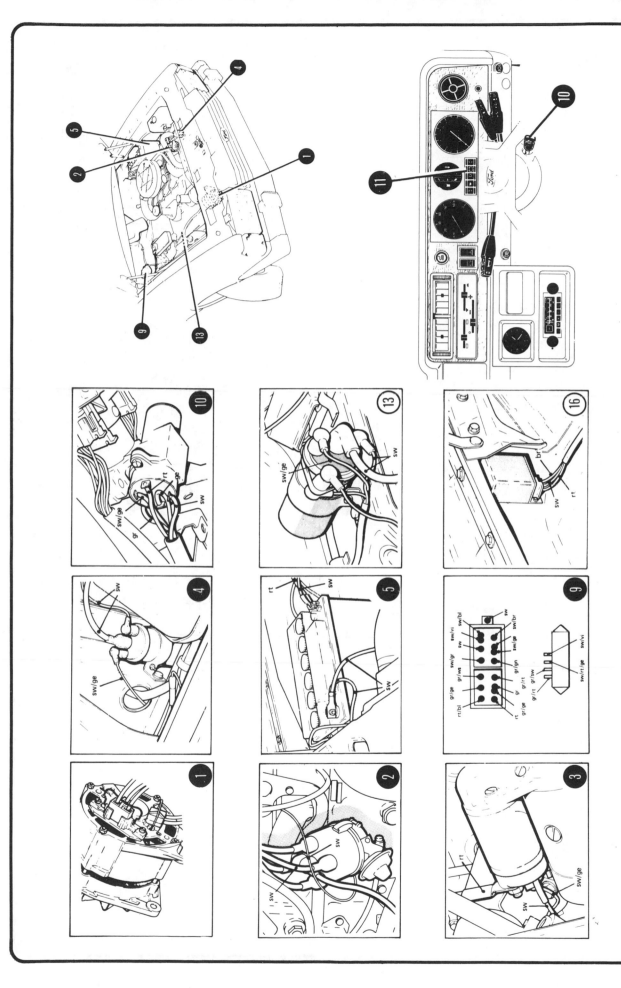

Fig. 13.51B Component connections, charging, starting and ignition (Sec 11)

Key to wiring diagrams 13.52A and 13.52B

25 Auxiliary lamp dimmer relay
26 Headlamp/sidelamp assembly
27 Auxiliary lamp
28 Battery
29 Fusebox
30 Multi-plug (black)
31 Stop/tail lamp (B) and tail
    lamp (C) assembly
32 Lighting switch
33 Multi-function switch
34 Number plate lamp
35 Ignition switch
36 Instrument cluster

Wiring diagram colour code

bl = Blue	rs = Pink
br = Brown	rt = Red
ge = Yellow	sw = Black
gr = Grey	vi = Violet
gn = Green	ws = White

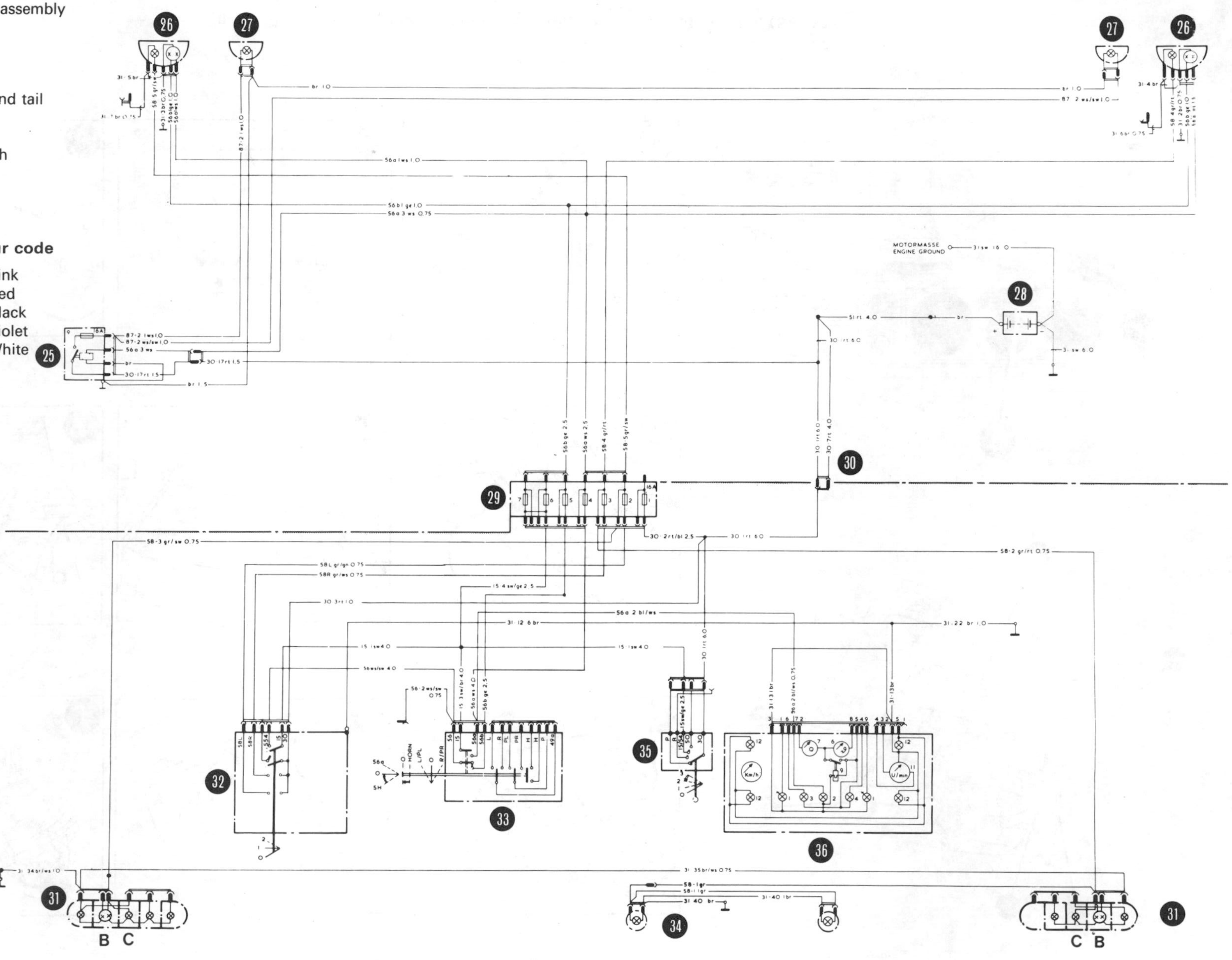

Fig. 13.52A Wiring diagram – exterior lighting (Sec 11)

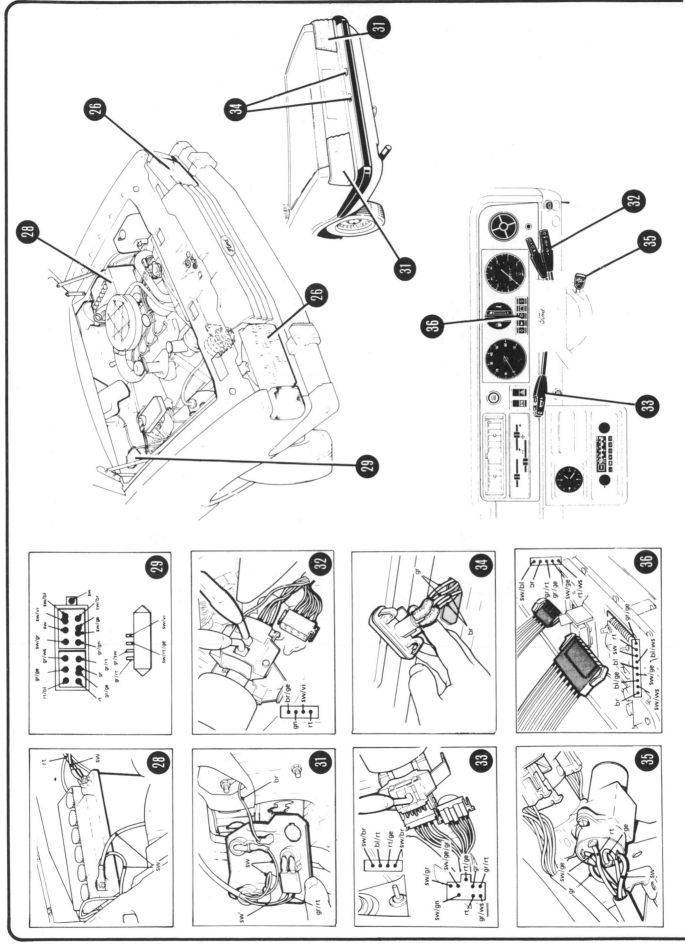

Fig. 13.52B Component connections – exterior lighting (Sec 11)

234

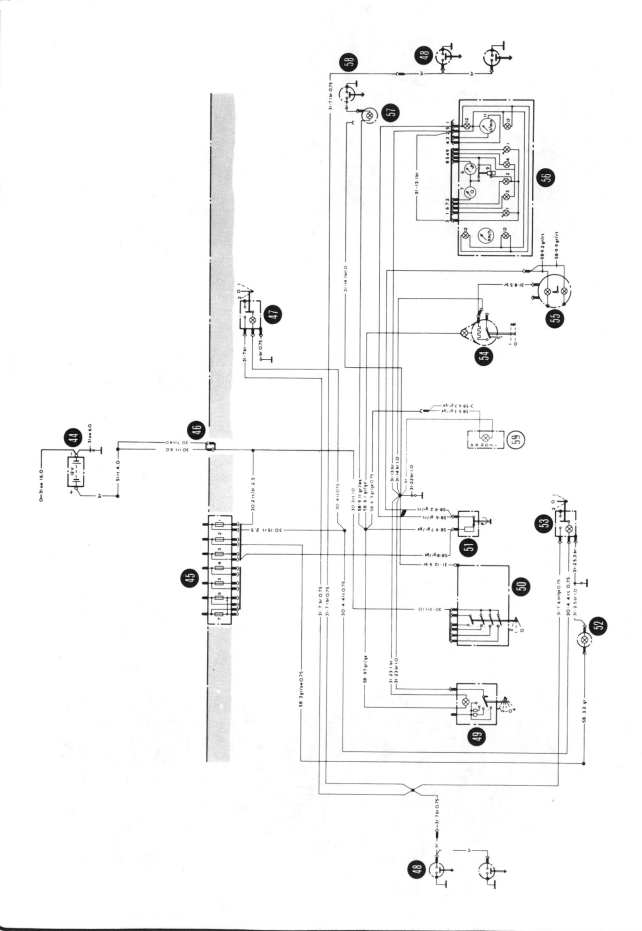

Fig. 13.53A Wiring diagram – interior lighting (Sec 11)

Key to wiring diagrams 13.53A and 13.53B

44 Battery
45 Fusebox
46 Multi-plug (grey)
47 Interior lamp
48 Door switches for interior lamp
49 Heater control lamp
50 Lighting switch
51 Panel dimmer switch
52 Luggage area lamp
53 Interior lamp
54 Cigar lighter lamp
55 Clock lamp
56 Instrument cluster
57 Glovebox lamp
58 Glovebox lamp switch
59 Automatic transmission selector lamp (when fitted)

Wiring diagram colour code

bl = Blue   rs = Pink
br = Brown   rt = Red
ge = Yellow   sw = Black
gr = Grey   vi = Violet
gn = Green   ws = White

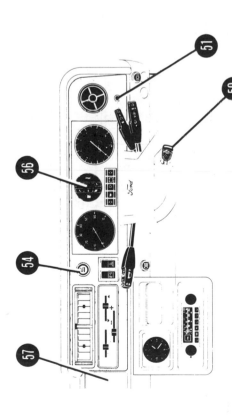

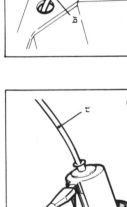
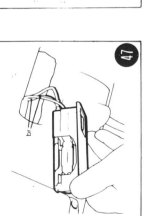
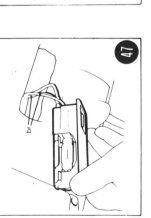

Fig. 13.53B Component connections – interior lighting (Sec 11)

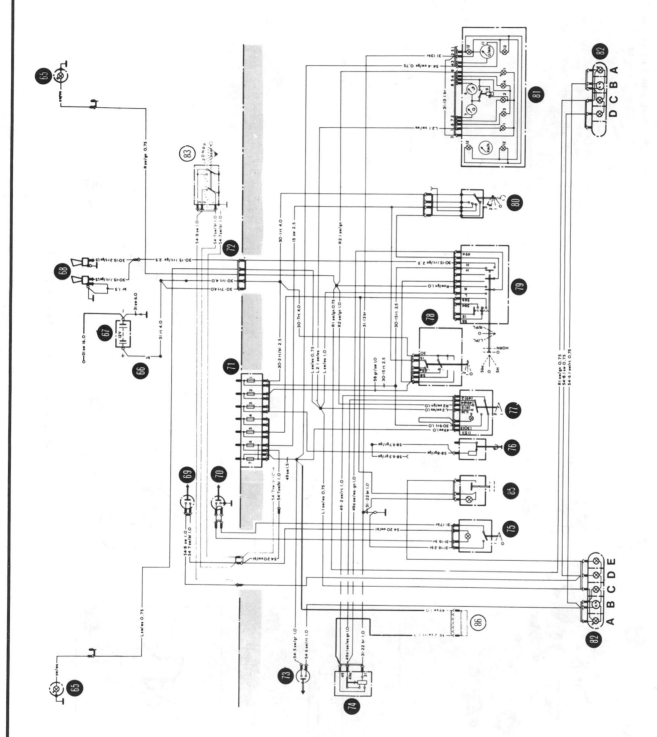

Fig. 13.54A Wiring diagram – horn, direction indicators and hazard warning lights (Sec 11)

Key to wiring diagrams 13.54A and 13.54B

65 Front flasher lamps
66 Fusible link
67 Battery
68 Horn
69 Reversing lamp switch
70 Brake warning switch
71 Fusebox
72 Multi-plug (grey)
73 Stoplamp switch
74 Flasher unit
75 Brake warning test switch
76 Panel dimmer switch
77 Hazard flasher switch
78 Lighting switch
79 Multi-function switch
80 Ignition switch
81 Instrument cluster switch
82 Tail lamp assembly:
  A Rear flasher lamp
  B Stop/tail lamp
  C Tail lamp
  D Reversing lamp
  E Rear fog lamp
83 Automatic transmission inhibitor switch (if fitted)
85 Rear fog lamp switch and warning lamp
86 Hazard flasher link (if no switch warning lamp)

Wiring diagram colour code

bl = Blue		rs = Pink
br = Brown		rt = Red
ge = Yellow		sw = Black
gr = Grey		vi = Violet
gn = Green		ws = White

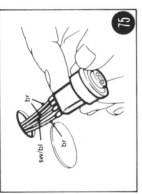
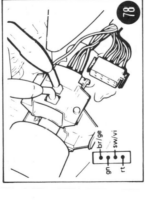

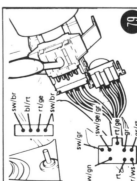

Fig. 13.54B Component connections – horn, direction indicators and hazard warning lights (Sec 11)

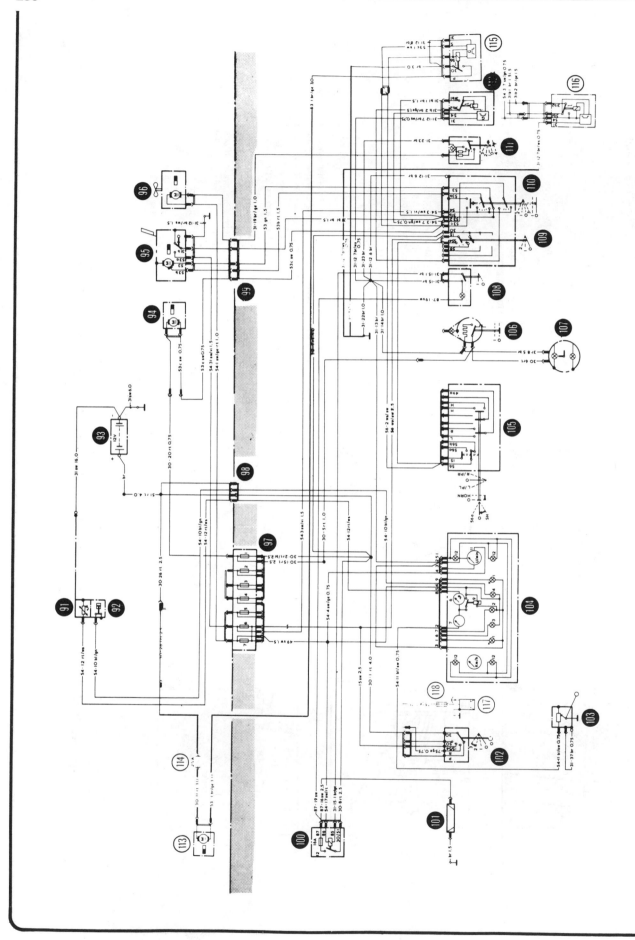

Fig. 13.55A Wiring diagram – heater, wiper and ancillary circuits (Sec 11)

Key to wiring diagrams 13.55A and 13.55B

91 Water temperature sender
92 Oil pressure sender
93 Battery
94 Windscreen washer pump
95 Windscreen wiper motor
96 Heater blower motor
97 Fusebox
98 Multi-plug (grey)
99 Multi-plug (black)
100 Heated rear window relay
101 Heated rear window
102 Ignition switch
103 Fuel gauge sender
104 Instrument cluster
105 Multi-function switch
106 Cigar lighter
107 Clock
108 Heated rear window switch
109 Lighting switch
110 Windscreen wiper switch
111 Heater blower switch
112 Windscreen wiper intermittent relay
113 Headlamp washer pump*
114 Headlamp washer pump fuse*
115 Headlamp washer pump timing relay*
116 Windscreen wiper intermittent relay*
117 Radio*
118 Radio fuse*
* If fitted

Wiring diagram colour code

bl	= Blue	rs	= Pink
br	= Brown	rt	= Red
ge	= Yellow	sw	= Black
gr	= Grey	vi	= Violet
gn	= Green	ws	= White

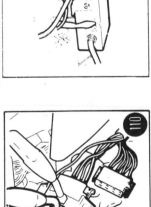
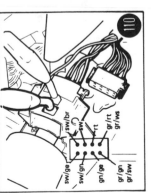
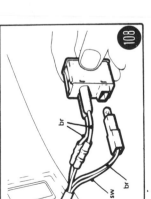
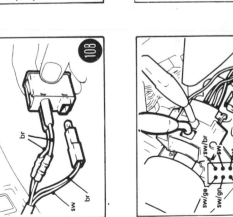

Fig. 13.55B Component connections – heater, wiper and ancillary circuits (Sec 11)

12 Suspension and steering

General modifications to 1980 models

1   A few minor modifications have been made to the suspension system for 1980 Cortinas. The front anti-roll bar is of larger diameter, the spring rates have been changed and the rear shock absorbers on all models are now gas filled.

2   Vehicles fitted with the 'S-pack' or (for Estate models) the 'Business pack' have uprated suspension components and tyres. (The 'S-pack also includes various trim and instrumentation improvements; the Business pack, more prosaically, includes larger brake drums and a strengthened rear axle casing.)

3   Removal and refitting of the suspension components is described in Chapter 11. Uprated components are removed and refitted in the same way as their regular counterparts, but it is important when ordering spare parts to specify if your vehicle is fitted with the S-pack or Business pack. Similarly, not all the 1980 parts are interchangeable with earlier ones, so always specify precisely the year and model of the vehicle concerned when ordering spares.

Maintenance and inspection

4   The suspension and steering components must be checked at 6000 mile (9600 km) intervals for signs of wear, damage or general deterioration. Any defective items must be attended to without delay.

5   Run the vehicle onto ramps, over an inspection pit or jack up and support as applicable.

6   The front and rear suspension check points are shown in Figs. 13.56 and 13.57.

7   Check the condition of the front and rear suspension arm bushes for signs of wear or deterioration. Also check the shock absorber mounting bushes. Renew as necessary.

8   Clean and inspect the steering balljoint covers and gaiters; if they are split or damaged, renew them. It is unlikely that the gaiters themselves can be obtained without purchasing the complete balljoint. Check the balljoints for wear.

9   Check all suspension securing all bolts and nuts for correct tightening torque in accordance with the figures specified in Chapter 11. Check that all split-pins are located and secure.

10   Check the shock absorbers for effective action by applying a downward hand pressure to each body corner in turn. On release, the body should return to its normal height and not continue to bounce. Where the shock absorbers are felt to be weak they must be renewed. They must also be renewed if they show signs of leaking – they cannot be repaired.

11   Check the steering rack bellows for signs of leakage, splits or perishing and renew the gaiters if necessary.

12   Every 36 000 miles (57 000 km) (or three years, whichever is first) the suspension balljoints must be lubricated as shown in Fig. 13.58 using a grease gun with a tapered nozzle. Clean the area around the balljoint, remove the plug and inject the grease. Refit each plug after greasing and wipe away any excess grease from around the joints.

13   Wear in the suspension arm lower balljoint may be checked if the front end of the car is raised and supported on stands and the lower arm checked for up and down movement preferably using a dial gauge.

14   If this movement exceeds 3.0 mm (0.118 in) renew the balljoint using a repair kit. To do this, remove the roadwheel and then cut off the upper leads from the balljoint fixing rivets.

15   Unscrew the two bolts which hold the radius rod and the anti-roll bar to the suspension arm.

16   Extract the split pin, unscrew the castle nut and then separate the balljoint from the suspension arm using a suitable splitter tool.

17   Remove the balljoint components.

18   Commence refitting by first cleaning the mounting surfaces. Then remove the gaiter and retainer plate from the new balljoint.

19   Offer the new balljoint to the underside of the suspension arm and then locate the gaiter and retainer plate. Check that the lip of the gaiter is under the retainer plate recess.

20   Fit the securing bolts so that their heads are uppermost. Tighten the nuts to 22 lbf ft (30 Nm).

21   Wipe the ball-stud clean and connect it to the hub barrier. Screw on the castellated nut to 37 lbf ft (50 Nm). Insert a new split pin, tightening the nut slightly to align the split pin hole if necessary.

22   Reconnect the radius rod and anti-roll bar, fit the roadwheel and lower the vehicle.

23   If the tyres show signs of uneven wear but no faults or appreciable wear can be found in the steering and suspension components, it is likely that the steering geometry is out of alignment. In this case refer to Chapter 11, Section 22, and check the alignment and steering angles as prescribed.

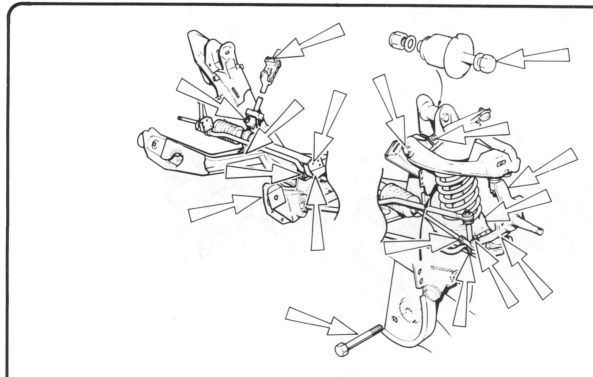

Fig. 13.56 Front suspension and steering check points (Sec 12)

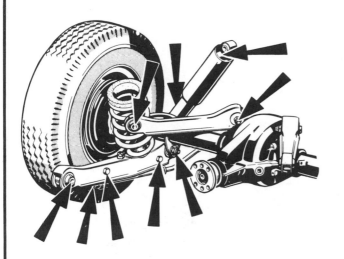

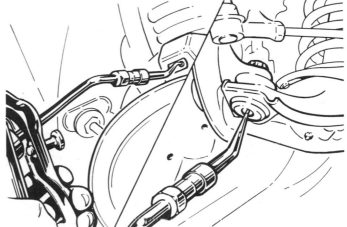

Fig. 13.57 Rear suspension check points (Sec 12)

Fig. 13.58 Lubricating suspension balljoints (Sec 12)

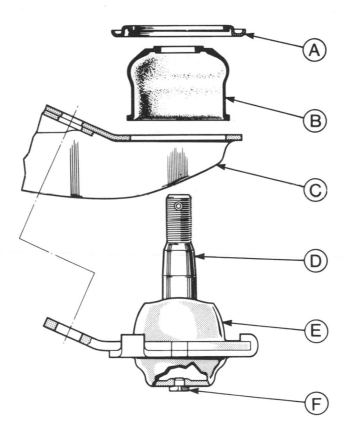

Fig. 13.59 Front suspension arm balljoint repair kit (Sec 12)

A   Retainer plate   C   Suspension arm   E   Balljoint
B   Gaiter   D   Ball stud   F   Plug

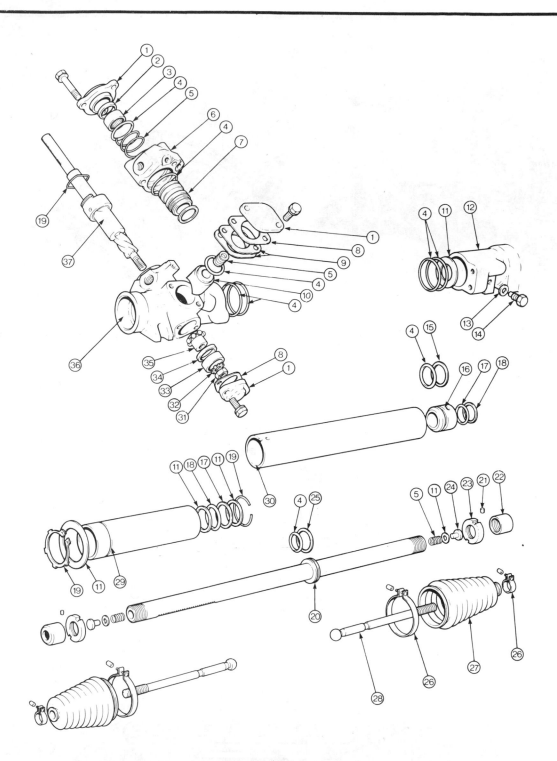

Fig. 13.60 Exploded view of power-assisted steering gear (Sec 12)

1 Cover plate	11 Washer	20 Rack	29 Rack tube
2 Bush	12 Bearing end housing	21 Locking pin	30 Rack housing
3 Roller bearing	13 Aluminium washer	22 Ball housing	31 Nut
4 O-ring	14 Housing retaining peg	23 Locking ring	32 Tab washer
5 Spring	15 Split nylon washer	24 Ball seat	33 Spacer
6 Control valve housing	16 Rack support bush	25 Nylon piston ring	34 Outer bearing race
7 Control valve spool	17 Grooved seal	26 Gaiter clip	35 Lower pinion bearing
8 Gasket	18 Flat seal	27 Gaiter	36 Pinion end housing
9 Shims	19 Circlip	28 Track-rod	37 Pinion
10 Rack slipper			

Power-assisted steering system – description

24 Power-assisted steering is available as an optional extra on certain models. The pump which provides the hydraulic pressure for power assistance is driven from the crankshaft pulley; twin drivebelts are fitted.

25 The DIY mechanic is recommended to confine his attention to those items listed below. Complete dismantling of the steering gear is not recommended due to the need for special tools on reassembly.

26 Scrupulous cleanliness must be observed when dealing with the power-assisted steering system. The entry of even small particles of dirt into the hydraulic system may cause malfunction or rapid wear.

Power-assisted steering system – routine maintenance

27 At the specified intervals, check the fluid level as follows. Remove the reservoir filler cap/dipstick. Wipe the dipstick with a non-fluffy cloth and refit the cap, then remove the cap and check the level of the fluid on the dipstick.

28 One side of the dipstick is marked *Full Cold* and the other side *Full Hot*. Top-up, if necessary, with the specified power steering fluid (automatic transmission fluid) to the appropriate mark on the dipstick.

29 Where topping-up is necessary, check all hoses and pipes in the system for leakage and rectify as required.

30 Check the tension and condition of the drivebelts regularly and re-tension or renew as necessary as described in Chapter 2. Note that if one belt breaks in service, *both* should be renewed, as the remaining belt will have been over-stressed.

31 Set the steering wheel to the straight-ahead position.

32 Jack-up the front of the car and place blocks under the wheels, then lower the car slightly so that the track-rods are in a near horizontal position. Remove the engine splash, if fitted.

33 Disconnect the fluid feed and return pipes from the control valve and drain the fluid into a container. Plug the ends of the pipes and the openings in the control valve to prevent the entry of dirt.

34 Bend back the lock tabs on the coupling clamp plate, loosen the bolts and remove the clamp plate. Remove the bolt clamping the lower end of the coupling assembly to the pinion shaft, disengage the assembly from the pinion shaft and lift it out.

35 Withdraw the split pins and remove the castellated nuts from the ends of the track-rods where they are attached to the steering arms. Using a universal balljoint separator, detach the track-rod ballpins from the steering arms.

36 Bend back the lock tabs, withdraw the split pins, then undo the nuts and remove the rack to crossmember securing bolts.

37 Remove the fan shroud securing screws and lift the shroud out of the engine compartment.

38 Remove the right-hand engine mounting securing nut and jack-up the engine approximately 5 in. (125 mm). Move the rack to the left-hand side, and guide the right-hand track-rod over the top of the stabilizer bar, then remove the steering gear assembly from the right-hand side.

39 Before refitting the steering gear assembly make sure the wheels are still in the straight-ahead position.

40 Check that the steering rack is in the centre of its travels. This can be done by ensuring that the distance between the ends of both track-rods and the rack housing on both sides is the same.

41 Slide the assembly in from the right-hand side of the car, and fit the steering coupling on the pinion shaft, with the master splines aligned, then loosely fit the clamp bolt and nut. Fit the steering gear assembly securing bolts using new locking tabs.

42 Fit the coupling clamp to the lower end of the steering shaft, fit new locking plate and refit the bolts loosely.

43 Tighten the steering gear-to-crossmember securing bolts to the specified torque and fit new split pins.

44 Reconnect the track-rod ends to the steering arms and tighten the castellated nuts to the specified torque. Fit new pins.

45 Lower the engine and tighten the right-hand engine mounting nut.

46 Reconnect the power steering fluid feed and return pipes to the control valve.

47 Tighten the clamp bolts on the steering shaft flexible coupling and on the pinion shaft to the specified torque.

48 Refit the engine splash shield (if fitted) and the fan shroud.

49 Jack-up the car, remove the support blocks and lower the car to the ground.

50 Top-up the power steering fluid reservoir with the specified fluid and bleed the system as described below.

51 Check and adjust the toe-in as described in Chapter 11.

Power-assisted steering pump – removal and refitting

52 Remove the pump drivebelts (refer to Chapter 2 if necessary).

53 Disconnect the fluid feed and return pipes from the pump and drain the fluid into a container. Plug the ends of the pipes and the openings in the pump.

54 To remove the pump from the mounting bracket requires a special wrench, but it is just as easy to undo the bracket-to-engine mounting bolts using a standard spanner and remove the pump and bracket as an assembly.

55 Refitting is the reverse of the removal procedure. Adjust the belt tension as described in Chapter 2. Top-up the reservoir with the specified power steering fluid and bleed the steering system as described below.

Power-assisted steering hydraulic system – bleeding

56 After any of the hydraulic unions have been disconnected, or if the fluid level in the reservoir has been allowed to fall so far that air has been introduced into the system, bleeding will be necessary. Proceed as follows.

57 Fill the reservoir to the maximum level with the specified power steering (automatic transmission type) fluid, and jack-up the front of the car.

58 Wait for at least two minutes after filling the reservoir, then start the engine and run it at approximately 1500 rpm.

59 Whilst an assistant slowly turns the steering wheel from lock-to-lock, top-up the reservoir until the level is stabilized and air bubbles can no longer be seen in the fluid. Fit the filler cap. **Note:** *When the car is raised from the ground with the front wheels clear and suspended, do not use any force or rapid movement when moving the wheels from lock-to-lock as this will cause rack oil pressure to build up and burst or force off the rubber gaiters.*

Power-assisted steering fluid cooler – removal and refitting

60 Remove the five radiator grille securing screws and lift out the grille.

61 Loosen the power steering hoses securing clamps and pull the hoses off the cooler. Position the hoses with the ends pointing upwards to minimise fluid loss.

62 Remove the two bolts securing the cooler to the front panel and lift out the cooler.

63 Refitting is the reverse of the removal procedure. Top-up the reservoir and bleed the steering system as described.

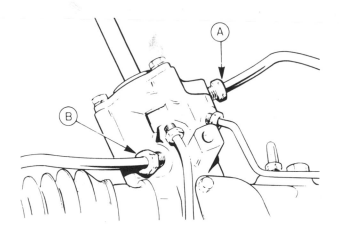

Fig. 13.61 Pipeline connections at power-steering gear (Sec 12)

A *Fluid supply pipe*   B *Fluid return pipe*

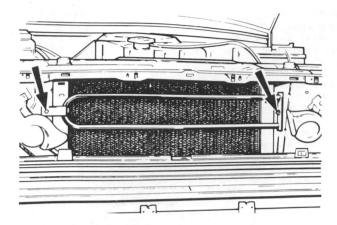

Fig. 13.62 Power-assisted steering fluid cooler (Sec 12)

Fixing bolts (arrowed)

Power-assisted steering gear – bellows renewal

64 It is possible to renew the bellows without removing the steering gear from the vehicle.

65 The procedure is virtually identical to that described for manual steering in Chapter 11, Section 30, but it is important that after the original bellows have been removed, the steering should be turned from lock-to-lock to expel all the old oil.

66 Refill the rack housing with 0.33 pints (0.20 litres) of SAE 40 engine oil by slipping the spout of an oil gun under each bellows neck in turn.

Rear shock absorbers – removal and refitting

67 As stated at the beginning of this Section the rear shock absorbers fitted to all models are now of the gas-filled type.

68 The Removal and refitting of these units varies slightly from the procedures described in Chapter 11.

69 First jack up the rear of the car and support it on axle stands positioned clear of the rear axle.

70 Place another jack beneath the shock absorber mounting on the rear axle and jack up the axle slightly.

71 Undo and remove the shock absorber upper and lower mounting nuts and bolts, and lift away the shock absorber.

72 With the unit removed from the car the procedure for inspection, testing and renewal of the rubber bushes is the same as described in Chapter 11.

73 Refitting the shock absorber is the reverse sequence to removal. Note that the lower mounting boss is offset relative to the shock absorber body and that this offset must be positioned closest to the axle casing (Fig. 13.63).

Wheels and tyres – general care and maintenance

74 Wheels and tyres should give no real problems in use provided that a close eye is kept on them with regard to excessive wear or damage. To this end, the following points should be noted.

75 Ensure that tyre pressures are checked regularly and maintained correctly. Checking should be carried out with the tyres cold and not immediately after the vehicle has been in use. If the pressures are checked with the tyres hot, an apparently high reading will be obtained owing to heat expansion. Under no circumstances should an attempt be made to reduce the pressures to the quoted cold reading in this instance, or effective underinflation will result.

76 Underinflation will cause overheating of the tyre owing to excessive flexing of the casing, and the tread will not sit correctly on the road surface. This will cause a consequent loss of adhesion and excessive wear, not to mention the danger of sudden tyre failure due to heat build-up.

77 Overinflation will cause rapid wear of the centre part of the tyre tread coupled with reduced adhesion, harsher ride, and the danger of shock damage occurring in the tyre casing.

78 Regularly check the tyres for damage in the form of cuts or

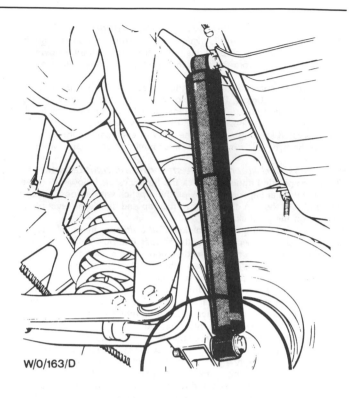

W/0/163/D

Fig. 13.63 Rear shock absorber offset lower mounting (Sec 12)

bulges, especially in the sidewalls. Remove any nails or stones embedded in the tread before they penetrate the tyre to cause deflation. If removal of a nail *does* reveal that the tyre has been punctured, refit the nail so that its point of penetration is marked. Then immediately change the wheel and have the tyre repaired by a tyre dealer. Do *not* drive on a tyre in such a condition. In many cases a puncture can be simply repaired by the use of an inner tube of the correct size and type. If in any doubt as to the possible consequences of any damage found, consult your local tyre dealer for advice.

79 Periodically remove the wheels and clean any dirt or mud from the inside and outside surfaces. Examine the wheel rims for signs of rusting, corrosion or other damage. Light alloy wheels are easily damaged by 'kerbing' whilst parking, and similarly steel wheels may become dented or buckled. Renewal of the wheel is very often the only course of remedial action possible.

80 The balance of each wheel and tyre assembly should be maintained to avoid excessive wear, not only to the tyres but also to the steering and suspension components. Wheel imbalance is normally signified by vibration through the vehicle's bodyshell, although in many cases it is particularly noticeable through the steering wheel. Conversely, it should be noted that wear or damage in suspension or steering components may cause excessive tyre wear. Out-of-round or out-of-true tyres, damaged wheels and wheel bearing wear/ maladjustment also fall in this category. Balancing will not usually cure vibration caused by such wear.

81 Wheel balancing may be carried out with the wheel either on or off the vehicle. If balanced on the vehicle, ensure that the wheel-to-hub relationship is marked in some way prior to subsequent wheel removal so that it may be refitted in its original position.

82 General tyre wear is influenced to a large degree by driving style – harsh driving and acceleration or fast cornering will all produce more rapid tyre wear. Interchanging of tyres may result in more even wear, but this should only be carried out where there is no mix of tyre types on the vehicle. However, it is worth bearing in mind that if this is completely effective, the added expense of replacing a complete set of tyres simultaneously is incurred, which may prove financially restrictive for many owners.

83 Front tyres may wear unevenly as a result of wheel misalignment.

The front wheels should always be correctly aligned according to the settings specified by the vehicle manufacturer.

84 Legal restrictions apply to the mixing of tyre types on a vehicle. Basically this means that a vehicle must not have tyres of differing construction on the same axle. Although it is not recommended to mix tyre types between front axle and rear axle, the only legally permissible combination is crossply at the front and radial at the rear. When mixing radial ply tyres, textile braced radials must always go on the front axle, with steel braced radials at the rear. An obvious disadvantage of such mixing is the necessity to carry two spare tyres to avoid contravening the law in the event of a puncture.

85 In the UK, the Motor Vehicles Construction and Use Regulations apply to many aspects of tyre fitting and usage. It is suggested that a copy of these regulations is obtained from your local police if in doubt as to the current legal requirements with regard to tyre condition, minimum tread depth, etc.

13 Bodywork

Modifications to the 1980 range

1   The following items listed below are detail changes which affect the 1980 range of Cortinas. In most instances these items are not interchangeable with their earlier counterparts and it is therefore essential to quote your car's year and models when ordering replacement parts.

Windscreen and door glass

2   A laminated windscreen is now fitted as standard equipment. The total glass area has been increased to improve forward and rearward vision. Side vision has also been improved by extending the door openings into the roof.

Bumpers

3   The 1980 models now have plastic end caps on each side of the bumpers at the front and rear. These give additional side and corner protection to the bodywork.

4   To remove a bumper quarter section, use a block of wood as shown in Fig. 13.64. Butting it against the edge of the quarter section, tap the section free, using only hand pressure on the wood block. When the quarter section is free from its bumper clips, disengage it from the body securing clip.

5   The body clips may be removed by twisting them through 90°.

6   Where overriders are fitted, these will have to be detached first before removing the corner mouldings. Refit in reverse order, sliding the section into engagement with its retaining clips. Check for security when fitted.

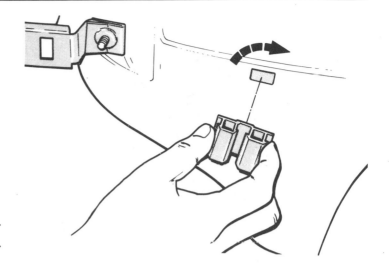

Fig. 13.65 Bumper to body clip (Sec 13)

7   An alternative method of removing the plastic end caps may be used if the complete bumper assembly is first removed from the vehicle. The spring clips which secure the end caps may be squeezed and the cap pulled off the bumper bar.

Sliding roof – adjustment

8   To adjust the sliding roof first open it about halfway, then detach the trim panel at the front of the sliding roof. The trim is secured by clips. Close the roof when the trim is free and then slide the trim panel fully rearwards.

9   Keeping the roof closed, loosen the adjusting clamps at the front and rear. These are shown in Fig. 13.66.

10 Adjustment to the sliding panel height is made by moving the mountings forwards or rearwards as required. The heights should be as follows:

Front: Flush to 0.040 in (1 mm) below main roof front edge
Rear: Flush to 0.040 in (1 mm) above main roof rear edge

11 To adjust the roof winder mechansim, the roof must be closed. Unscrew and remove the two spacer washers and screw retaining the winder handle. Note the handle position and remove it.

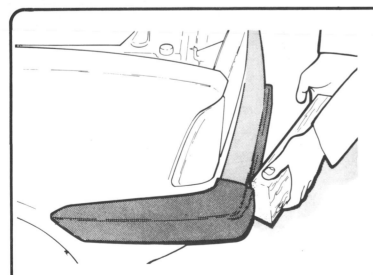

Fig. 13.64 One method of removing bumper quarter sections (Sec 13)

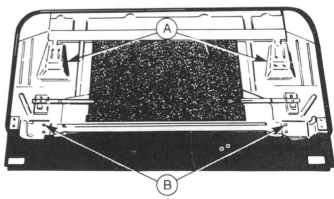

Fig. 13.66 Sliding roof mounting slides (Sec 13)

A   Front   B   Rear

Fig. 13.67 Sunroof winder mechanism (Sec 13)

12 Unscrew and remove the winder gear unit (Fig. 13.67).
13 Wind the gear unit clockwise to its full extent, then wind it back by about 1/2 turn. Refit the unit.
14 Refit the winder handle, aligning it in its original fitted position, and make secure with washers and screw. Check the operation of the sliding roof and if satisfactory refit the front trim panel. When in position make sure that it is secure and that no material protrudes onto the front guide rail.

Sliding roof – removal and refitting

15 Open the roof panel. Unscrew and remove the four screws which secure the deflector to the cable covers. Extract the deflector. Unscrew and remove the front cable cover, noting that the central screws are of the normal threaded type whilst the others are self-tapping type.
16 Prise free the upper and lower cable location clips as shown (Fig. 13.68).
17 Unscrew the guide rail cover screws on each side, then carefully prise free the guide rail covers.
18 Remove the front guide retaining screws.

19 Carefully pull the roof along the rails to the almost closed position, then lift the guide rails and slide the roof free (complete with guide rails). This part of the operation is best achieved with the aid of an assistant to avoid damaging the roof.
20 If the cables and guides are to be renewed, detach them from the roof panel. The cables should normally be renewed when the assembly is dismantled, especially if the roof mechanism is known to be faulty.
21 Refitting is a reversal of the removal procedure, but note the following special points:

(a) When the roof is back in position ensure that the rear guide rail pegs engage in the holes in the rear body section
(b) When locating the cables into the winder unit make sure that the lower clips are between the cable and guide. The top clip fits over the whole assembly
(c) The front cable cover section must initially be only loosely secured until after the roof has been adjusted as described above.

Sliding roof weatherstrip – removal and renewal

22 Half open the roof, carefully unclip the trim panel at the front of the roof. Slide the trim panel rearwards.
23 Remove the four clamp bolts and disconnect the two roof-to-guide rail mounting slides at the front (Fig. 13.69). The spring arms can now be swung away from the rear roof mounting brackets as shown In Fig. 13.70. Unscrew the two rear mounting brackets-to-roof panel bolts and pull off the lockplates. Lift clear the sliding roof panel with the aid of an assistant to avoid damaging it.
24 Unscrew and remove the seven self-tapping screws retaining the rear seal sponge mounting plate and remove the plate. Two of these screws are under the anti-rattle pads.
25 Prise free the two plastic guide peg covers at the rear on each side and then pull the weatherstrip free. The insulator padding can be cut carefully from the roof panel lower face and can if desired be re-used.
26 Clean the insulator pad surface of the roof panel, smear on an even layer of adhesive and apply the insulator padding carefully into position.
27 Clean the rear sponge mounting plate, apply some sealer to the plate weatherstrip location, then fit the weatherstrip carefully into position.
28 Refit the rear sponge mounting plate and the plastic guide peg covers, then carefully insert the roof panel back into position. Before

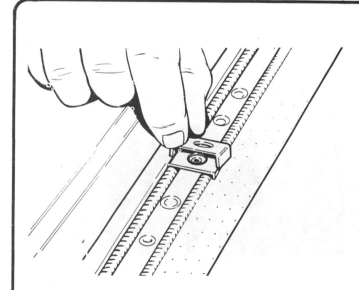

Fig. 13.68 Sunroof cable locating clips (Sec 13)

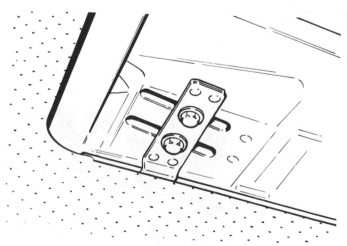

Fig. 13.69 Sunroof front mounting clamp bolts (Sec 13)

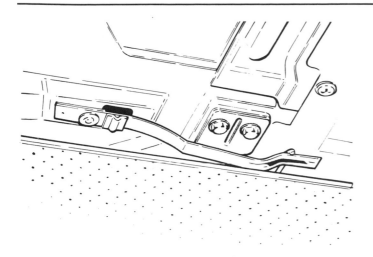

Fig. 13.70 Sunroof spring arms clear of rear mounting bracket (Sec 13)

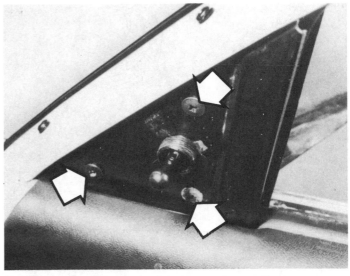

13.35 Remote control mirror retaining screws (arrowed)

fitting the roof panel, check that the rear mounting brackets are fully forward and against the stops.
29 Refit the rear mounting bracket lockplates and secure the mountings to the roof panel.
30 Relocate the spring arms, then fit the front mounting slides in the guide rail and loosely attach to the sliding roof.
31 Close the roof and adjust it as described above.
32 Check the roof operation before tightening the cover screws. Open the roof partially, slide the trim panel back into position and relocate. When fitting ensure that the material does not snag on the front guide rail when fitting under it. Clip the panel into position to complete.

Door mirror – removal and refitting
33 Prise free the triangular trim panel on the inside using a screwdriver or other suitable tool, and use a piece of thin cardboard or paper to protect the paintwork when levering.
34 On models equipped with the remote control type mirror, the bezel over the control knob can sometimes be difficult to unscrew by finger pressure. To remove the bezel Ford recommend using a special tool (Ford number 41-014) and this is shown in Fig. 13.71. This tool would not be too difficult to make up if need be.
35 Unscrew and remove the three retaining screws and remove the mirror from the door (photo).
36 Refitting is a reversal of the removal procedure.

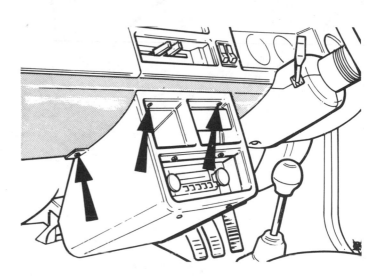

Fig. 13.72 Centre console fixing screws (Sec 13)

Upper central console – removal and refitting
37 Disconnect the battery leads.
38 Unscrew and remove the four console retaining screws in the positions indicated in Fig. 13.72. Withdraw the console sufficiently to disconnect the wiring to the radio and clock (as applicable).
39 Refitting is the reversal of the removal sequence.

Heating and ventilation
40 The heating and ventilation system on the Cortina 80 series has been updated and now incorporates central fresh air vents and side window demisting. The heater unit itself is basically the same as on the earlier models and its removal and refitting instructions remain unchanged, as do the controls and their adjustments.

Central ventilation panel – removal and refitting
41 Disconnect the battery leads.
42 Disconnect and remove the dash lower left-hand trim panel, which is retained by 2 or 3 clips and a couple of metal tags.
43 Remove the instrument panel as described in Chapter 10.
44 Unscrew and remove the two vent screws, pull the vent from its location and detach the air supply hose.
45 Refitting is the reversal of the removal process. On completion check the operation of all instruments and controls.

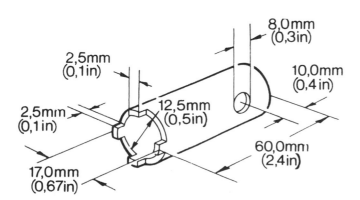

Fig. 13.71 Remote control door mirror removal tool (Sec 13)

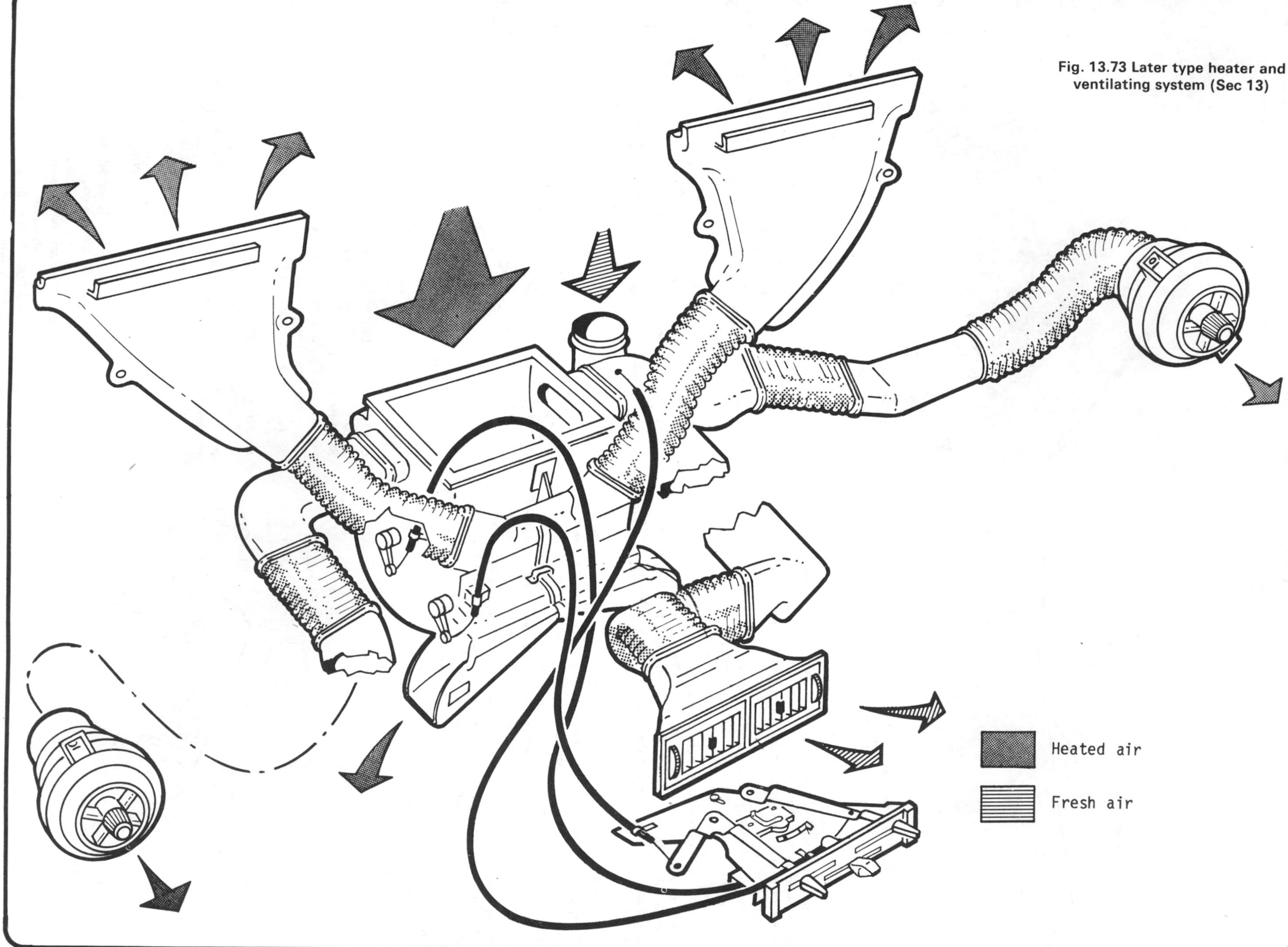

Fig. 13.73 Later type heater and ventilating system (Sec 13)

Heated air

Fresh air

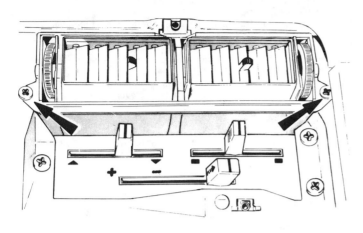

Fig. 13.74 Centre vent fixing screws (Sec 13)

Cable-type window regulator mechanism – removal and refitting

46 An improved cable-operated window regulator mechanism has been introduced on all models produced from the beginning of 1981.

47 To remove the regulator from the door first remove the door trim as described in Chapter 12.

48 Remove the screws securing the regulator handle fixing and the upper and lower channel mounting to the door panel. Now undo and remove the two screws securing the regulator to the door glass bracket. Support the door glass and remove the regulator from the lower aperture in the door.

49 To refit the regulator, position the mechanism in the door and loosely refit all the retaining screws.

50 Wind the window up fully and tighten the regulator-to-door glass bracket retaining screws. If working on the front door, preload the door glass, before tightening the screws, by gently levering down the upper rear corner of the glass with a screwdriver.

51 Now wind the window down two turns of the regulator handle and tighten the handle fixing and upper channel mounting screws. On the front door push the upper channel rearwards before tightening the screws.

52 Wind the window down all the way and tighten the lower channel mounting screws.

53 The door trim can now be refitted as described in Chapter 12.

Front seat – removal and refitting

54 Push the seat fully forward and remove the rear bolts from the seat slides.

55 Push the seat fully to the rear and unscrew and remove the front bolts.

56 Remove the seat from the vehicle.

Rear seat – removal and refitting

57 At the lower front edge of the seat cushion, bend back the covering flaps and extract the securing screws.

58 Remove the cushion from the vehicle interior.

59 To remove the seat back feel under its lower edge and straighten the retaining tangs.

60 Working within the luggage boot, unscrew the seat back fixing nuts.

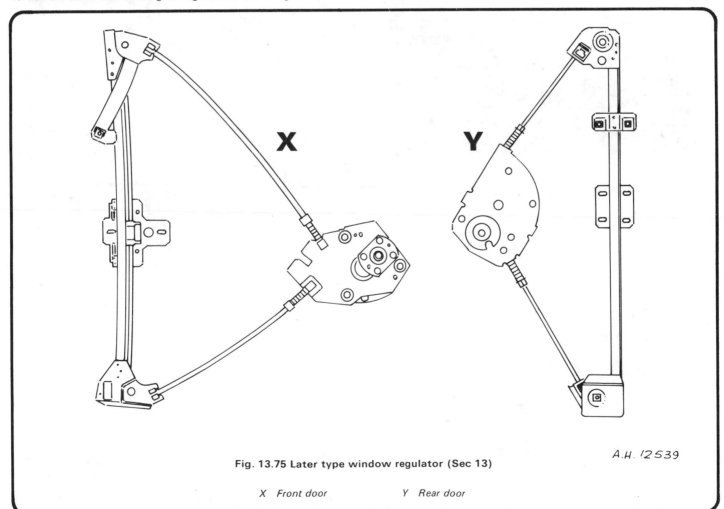

Fig. 13.75 Later type window regulator (Sec 13)

A.H. 12539

X   Front door   Y   Rear door

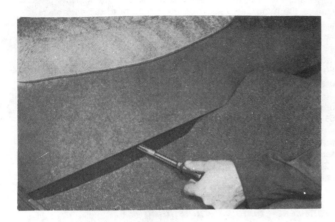

Fig. 13.76 Rear seat cushion fixing screw (Sec 13)

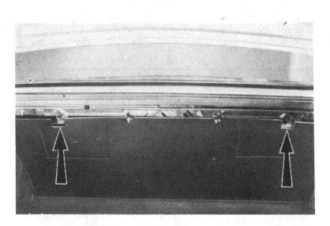

Fig. 13.77 Rear seat back fixing nuts (Sec 13)

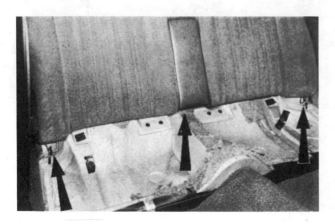

Fig. 13.78 Rear seat back retaining tangs (Sec 13)

61 Return to the vehicle interior, pull the seat back towards the front of the vehicle and remove it.

62 Refitting of both front and rear seats is a reversal of removal.

Seat belts

63 Inertia reel seat belts are fitted to the front seats only, but rear seat belts are optionally available.

64 Regularly inspect the belts for fraying or cuts. Cleaning should be done using warm water and detergent only. Never use solvents or other cleaners.

Front seat belts – removal

65 The belt stalk is secured to the seat bracket with Torx type bolts while a single bolt secures the reel.

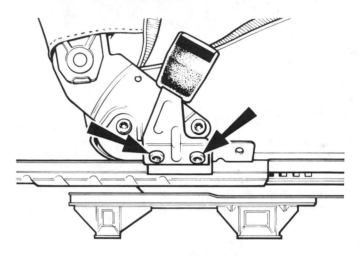

Fig. 13.79 Front seat belt stalk attachment (Sec 13)

Fig. 13.80 Seat belt reel fixing bolt (Sec 13)

66 On two-door cars, the belt is secured to a lower anchorage rail.

67 The upper anchor bolt is accessible after having prised off its plastic cover.

68 Never alter the original fitted sequence of the belt anchor bolt and allied components.

Rear seat belts – removal

69 The belt anchor bolts can be reached after removal of the rear seat cushion.

70 The belt reel is located within the luggage boot on Saloon models and at the side of the luggage area on estate versions.

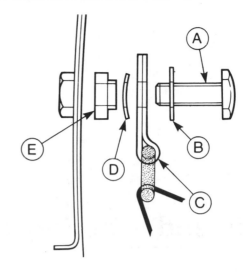

Fig. 13.82 Seat belt upper anchor bolt and associated components (Sec 13)

A Bolt	D Wave washer
B Flat washer	E Spacer
C Anchor plate	

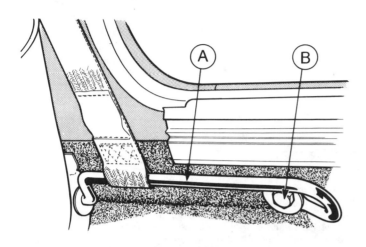

Fig. 13.81 Front seat belt anchorage rail (Sec 13)

Fault diagnosis – power-assisted steering

Symptom	Reason(s)
Lack of power assistance	Pump belt needs adjustment Hoses or pipes restricted Fluid level low Hydraulic system may require bleeding of air Low fluid pressure perhaps caused by worn pump
Poor self-centering	Return fluid hose or pipe restricted Control valve spool sticking Stiff operation of rack caused by damaged rack piston or seals
Noisy operation of steering pump	Fluid level low Pump belt slack Flow control valve defective or worn pump components

Tools and working facilities

Introduction

A selection of good tools is a fundamental requirement for anyone contemplating the maintenance and repair of a motor vehicle. For the owner who does not possess any, their purchase will prove a considerable expense, offsetting some of the savings made by doing-it-yourself. However, provided that the tools purchased are of good quality, they will last for many years and prove an extremely worthwhile investment.

To help the average owner to decide which tools are needed to carry out the various tasks detailed in this manual, we have compiled three lists of tools under the following headings: *Maintenance and minor repair, Repair and overhaul,* and *Special.* The newcomer to practical mechanics should start off with the *Maintenance and minor repair* tool kit and confine himself to the simpler jobs around the vehicle. Then, as his confidence and experience grow, he can undertake more difficult tasks, buying extra tools as, and when, they are needed. In this way, a *Maintenance and minor repair* tool kit can be built-up into a *Repair and overhaul* tool kit over a considerable period of time without any major cash outlays. The experienced do-it-yourselfer will have a tool kit good enough for most repair and overhaul procedures and will add tools from the *Special* category when he feels the expense is justified by the amount of use to which these tools will be put.

It is obviously not possible to cover the subject of tools fully here. For those who wish to learn more about tools and their use there is a book entitled *How to Choose and Use Car Tools* available from the publishers of this manual.

Maintenance and minor repair tool kit

The tools given in this list should be considered as a minimum requirement if routine maintenance, servicing and minor repair operations are to be undertaken. We recommend the purchase of combination spanners (ring one end, open-ended the other); although more expensive than open-ended ones, they do give the advantages of both types of spanner.

> *Combination spanners - 10, 11, 12, 13, 14 & 17 mm*
> *Adjustable spanner - 9 inch*
> *Engine sump/gearbox/rear axle drain plug key*
> *Spark plug spanner (with rubber insert)*
> *Spark plug gap adjustment tool*
> *Set of feeler gauges*
> *Brake bleed nipple spanner*
> *Screwdriver - 4 in long x ¼ in dia (flat blade)*
> *Screwdriver - 4 in long x ¼ in dia (cross blade)*
> *Combination pliers - 6 inch*
> *Hacksaw (junior)*
> *Tyre pump*
> *Tyre pressure gauge*
> *Grease gun with adaptor for front suspension balljoints*
> *Oil can*
> *Fine emery cloth (1 sheet)*
> *Wire brush (small)*
> *Funnel (medium size)*

Repair and overhaul tool kit

These tools are virtually essential for anyone undertaking any major repairs to a motor vehicle, and are additional to those given in the *Maintenance and minor repair* list. Included in this list is a comprehensive set of sockets. Although these are expensive they will be found invaluable as they are so versatile - particularly if various drives are included in the set. We recommend the ½ in square-drive type, as this can be used with most proprietary torque wrenches. If you cannot afford a socket set, even bought piecemeal, then inexpensive tubular box spanners are a useful alternative.

The tools in this list will occasionally need to be supplemented by tools from the *Special* list.

> *Sockets (or box spanners) to cover range in previous list*
> *Reversible ratchet drive (for use with sockets)*
> *Extension piece, 10 inch (for use with sockets)*
> *Universal joint (for use with sockets)*
> *Torque wrench (for use with sockets)*
> *'Mole' wrench - 8 inch*
> *Ball pein hammer*
> *Soft-faced hammer, plastic or rubber*
> *Screwdriver - 6 in long x 56 in dia (flat blade)*
> *Screwdriver - 2 in long x 56 in square (flat blade)*
> *Screwdriver - 1½ in long x ¼ in dia (cross blade)*
> *Screwdriver - 3 in long x ⅛ in dia (electricians)*
> *Pliers - electricians side cutters*
> *Pliers - needle nosed*
> *Pliers - circlip (internal and external)*
> *Cold chisel - ½ inch*
> *Scriber*
> *Scraper*
> *Centre punch*
> *Pin punch*
> *Hacksaw*
> *Valve grinding tool*
> *Steel rule/straight-edge*
> *Allen keys*
> *Selection of files*
> *Wire brush (large)*
> *Axle-stands*
> *Jack (strong trolley or hydraulic type)*

Special tools

The tools in this list are those which are not used regularly, are expensive to buy, or which need to be used in accordance with their manufacturers' instructions. Unless relatively difficult mechanical jobs are undertaken frequently, it will not be economic to buy many of these tools. Where this is the case, you could consider clubbing together with friends (or joining a motorists' club) to make a joint purchase, or borrowing the tools against a deposit from a local garage or tool hire specialist.

The following list contains only those tools and instruments freely available to the public, and not those special tools produced by the vehicle manufacturer specifically for its dealer network. You will find occasional references to these manufacturers' special tools in the text of this manual. Generally, an alternative method of doing the job without the vehicle manufacturers' special tool is given. However, sometimes, there is no alternative to using them. Where this is the case and the relevant tool cannot be bought or borrowed, you will have to entrust the work to a franchised garage.

Valve spring compressor
Piston ring compressor
Balljoint separator
Universal hub/bearing puller
Impact screwdriver
Micrometer and/or vernier gauge
Dial gauge
Stroboscopic timing light
Dwell angle meter/tachometer
Universal electrical multi-meter
Cylinder compression gauge
Lifting tackle
Trolley jack
Light with extension lead

Buying tools

For practically all tools, a tool factor is the best source since he will have a very comprehensive range compared with the average garage or accessory shop. Having said that, accessory shops often offer excellent quality tools at discount prices, so it pays to shop around.

Remember, you don't have to buy the most expensive items on the shelf, but it is always advisable to steer clear of the very cheap tools. There are plenty of good tools around at reasonable prices, so ask the proprietor or manager of the shop for advice before making a purchase.

Care and maintenance of tools

Having purchased a reasonable tool kit, it is necessary to keep the tools in a clean serviceable condition. After use, always wipe off any dirt, grease and metal particles using a clean, dry cloth, before putting the tools away. Never leave them lying around after they have been used. A simple tool rack on the garage or workshop wall, for items such as screwdrivers and pliers is a good idea. Store all normal wrenches and sockets in a metal box. Any measuring instruments, gauges, meters, etc, must be carefully stored where they cannot be damaged or become rusty.

Take a little care when tools are used. Hammer heads inevitably become marked and screwdrivers lose the keen edge on their blades from time to time. A little timely attention with emery cloth or a file will soon restore items like this to a good serviceable finish.

Working facilities

Not to be forgotten when discussing tools, is the workshop itself. If anything more than routine maintenance is to be carried out, some form of suitable working area becomes essential.

It is appreciated that many an owner mechanic is forced by circumstances to remove an engine or similar item, without the benefit of a garage or workshop. Having done this, any repairs should always be done under the cover of a roof.

Wherever possible, any dismantling should be done on a clean, flat workbench or table at a suitable working height.

Any workbench needs a vice: one with a jaw opening of 4 in (100 mm) is suitable for most jobs. As mentioned previously, some clean dry storage space is also required for tools, as well as for lubricants, cleaning fluids, touch-up paints and so on, which become necessary.

Another item which may be required, and which has a much more general usage, is an electric drill with a chuck capacity of at least 56 in (8 mm). This, together with a good range of twist drills, is virtually essential for fitting accessories such as mirrors and reversing lights.

Last, but not least, always keep a supply of old newspapers and clean, lint-free rags available, and try to keep any working area as clean as possible.

Spanner jaw gap comparison table

Jaw gap (in)	Spanner size
0.250	$\frac{1}{4}$ in AF
0.276	7 mm
0.313	$\frac{5}{16}$ in AF
0.315	8 mm
0.344	$\frac{11}{32}$ in AF; $\frac{1}{8}$ in Whitworth
0.354	9 mm
0.375	$\frac{3}{8}$ in AF
0.394	10 mm
0.433	11 mm
0.438	$\frac{7}{16}$ in AF
0.445	$\frac{3}{16}$ in Whitworth; $\frac{1}{4}$ in BSF
0.472	12 mm
0.500	$\frac{1}{2}$ in AF
0.512	13 mm
0.525	$\frac{1}{4}$ in Whitworth; $\frac{5}{16}$ in BSF
0.551	14 mm
0.563	$\frac{9}{16}$ in AF
0.591	15 mm
0.600	$\frac{5}{16}$ in Whitworth; $\frac{3}{8}$ in BSF
0.625	$\frac{5}{8}$ in AF
0.630	16 mm
0.669	17 mm
0.686	$\frac{11}{16}$ in AF
0.709	18 mm
0.710	$\frac{3}{8}$ in Whitworth; $\frac{7}{16}$ in BSF
0.748	19 mm
0.750	$\frac{3}{4}$ in AF
0.813	$\frac{13}{16}$ in AF
0.820	$\frac{7}{16}$ in Whitworth; $\frac{1}{2}$ in BSF
0.866	22 mm
0.875	$\frac{7}{8}$ in AF
0.920	$\frac{1}{2}$ in Whitworth; $\frac{9}{16}$ in BSF
0.938	$\frac{15}{16}$ in AF
0.945	24 mm
1.000	1 in AF
1.010	$\frac{9}{16}$ in Whitworth; $\frac{5}{8}$ in BSF
1.024	26 mm
1.063	$1\frac{1}{16}$ in AF; 27 mm
1.100	$\frac{5}{8}$ in Whitworth; $\frac{11}{16}$ in BSF
1.125	$1\frac{1}{8}$ in AF
1.181	30 mm
1.200	$\frac{11}{16}$ in Whitworth; $\frac{3}{4}$ in BSF
1.250	$1\frac{1}{4}$ in AF
1.260	32 mm
1.300	$\frac{3}{4}$ in Whitworth; $\frac{7}{8}$ in BSF
1.313	$1\frac{5}{16}$ in AF
1.390	$\frac{13}{16}$ in Whitworth; $\frac{15}{16}$ in BSF
1.417	36 mm
1.438	$1\frac{7}{16}$ in AF
1.480	$\frac{7}{8}$ in Whitworth; 1 in BSF
1.500	$1\frac{1}{2}$ in AF
1.575	40 mm; $\frac{15}{16}$ in Whitworth
1.614	41 mm
1.625	$1\frac{5}{8}$ in AF
1.670	1 in Whitworth; $1\frac{1}{8}$ in BSF
1.688	$1\frac{11}{16}$ in AF
1.811	46 mm
1.813	$1\frac{13}{16}$ in AF
1.860	$1\frac{1}{8}$ in Whitworth; $1\frac{1}{4}$ in BSF
1.875	$1\frac{7}{8}$ in AF
1.969	50 mm
2.000	2 in AF
2.050	$1\frac{1}{4}$ in Whitworth; $1\frac{3}{8}$ in BSF
2.165	55 mm
2.362	60 mm

Fault diagnosis

Introduction

The vehicle owner who does his or her own maintenance according to the recommended schedules should not have to use this section of the manual very often. Modern component reliability is such that, provided those items subject to wear or deterioration are inspected or renewed at the specified intervals, sudden failure is comparatively rare. Faults do not usually just happen as a result of sudden failure, but develop over a period of time. Major mechanical failures in particular are usually preceded by characteristic symptoms over hundreds or even thousands of miles. Those components which do occasionally fail without warning are often small and easily carried in the vehicle.

With any fault finding, the first step is to decide where to begin investigations. Sometimes this is obvious, but on other occasions a little detective work will be necessary. The owner who makes half a dozen haphazard adjustments or replacements may be successful in curing a fault (or its symptoms), but he will be none the wiser if the fault recurs and he may well have spent more time and money than was necessary. A calm and logical approach will be found to be more satisfactory in the long run. Always take into account any warning signs or abnormalities that may have been noticed in the period preceding the fault – power loss, high or low gauge readings, unusual noises or smells, etc – and remember that failure of components such as fuses or spark plugs may only be pointers to some underlying fault.

The pages which follow here are intended to help in cases of failure to start or breakdown on the road. There is also a Fault Diagnosis Section at the end of each Chapter which should be consulted if the preliminary checks prove unfruitful. Whatever the fault, certain basic principles apply. These are as follows:

Verify the fault. This is simply a matter of being sure that you know what the symptoms are before starting work. This is particularly important if you are investigating a fault for someone else who may not have described it very accurately.

Don't overlook the obvious. For example, if the vehicle won't start, is there petrol in the tank? (Don't take anyone else's word on this particular point, and don't trust the fuel gauge either!) If an electrical fault is indicated, look for loose or broken wires before digging out the test gear.

Cure the disease, not the symptom. Substituting a flat battery with a fully charged one will get you off the hard shoulder, but if the underlying cause is not attended to, the new battery will go the same way. Similarly, changing oil-fouled spark plugs for a new set will get you moving again, but remember that the reason for the fouling (if it wasn't simply an incorrect grade of plug) will have to be established and corrected.

Don't take anything for granted. Particularly, don't forget that a 'new' component may itself be defective (especially if it's been rattling round in the boot for months), and don't leave components out of a fault diagnosis sequence just because they are new or recently fitted. When you do finally diagnose a difficult fault, you'll probably realise that all the evidence was there from the start.

Electrical faults

Electrical faults can be more puzzling than straightforward mechanical failures, but they are no less susceptible to logical analysis if the basic principles of operation are understood. Vehicle electrical wiring exists in extremely unfavourable conditions – heat, vibration and chemical attack – and the first things to look for are loose or corroded connections and broken or chafed wires, especially where the wires pass through holes in the bodywork or are subject to vibration.

All metal-bodied vehicles in current production have one pole of the battery 'earthed', ie connected to the vehicle bodywork, and in nearly all modern vehicles it is the negative (–) terminal. The various electrical components – motors, bulb holders etc – are also connected to earth, either by means of a lead or directly by their mountings. Electric current flows through the component and then back to the battery via the bodywork. If the component mounting is loose or corroded, or if a good path back to the battery is not available, the circuit will be incomplete and malfunction will result. The engine and/or gearbox are also earthed by means of flexible metal straps to the body or subframe; if these straps are loose or missing, starter motor, generator and ignition trouble may result.

Assuming the earth return to be satisfactory, electrical faults will be due either to component malfunction or to defects in the current supply. Individual components are dealt with in Chapter 10. If supply wires are broken or cracked internally this results in an open-circuit, and the easiest way to check for this is to bypass the suspect wire temporarily with a length of wire having a crocodile clip or suitable connector at each end. Alternatively, a 12V test lamp can be used to verify the presence of supply voltage at various points along the wire and the break can be thus isolated.

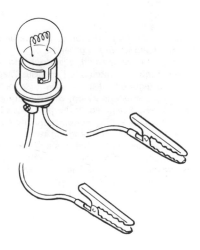

Simple test lamp useful for tracing electrical faults

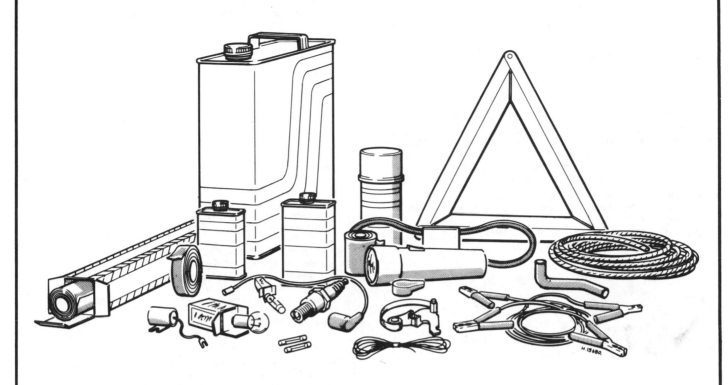

Carrying a few spares can save a long walk!

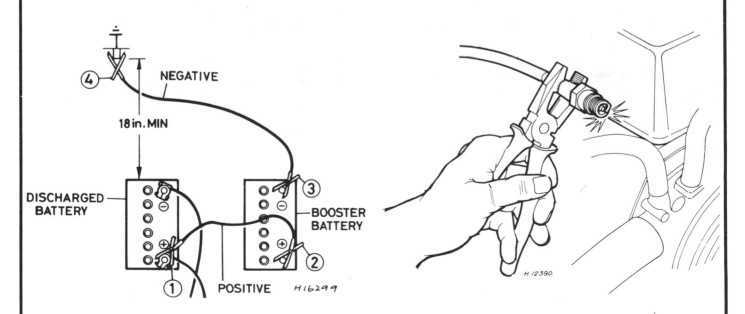

Jump start lead connections for negative earth vehicles —
connect leads in order shown

Crank engine and check for spark. Note use of insulated
tool

If a bare portion of a live wire touches the bodywork or other earthed metal part, the electricity will take the low-resistance path thus formed back to the battery: this is known as a short-circuit. Hopefully a short-circuit will blow a fuse, but otherwise it may cause burning of the insulation (and possibly further short-circuits) or even a fire. This is why it is inadvisable to bypass persistently blowing fuses with silver foil or wire.

Spares and tool kit

Most vehicles are supplied only with sufficient tools for wheel changing; the *Maintenance and minor repair* tool kit detailed in *Tools and working facilities*, with the addition of a hammer, is probably sufficient for those repairs that most motorists would consider attempting at the roadside. In addition a few items which can be fitted without too much trouble in the event of a breakdown should be carried. Experience and available space will modify the list below, but the following may save having to call on professional assistance:

Spark plugs, clean and correctly gapped
HT lead and plug cap – long enough to reach the plug furthest from the distributor
Distributor rotor, condenser and contact breaker points
Drivebelt(s) – emergency type may suffice
Spare fuses
Set of principal light bulbs
Tin of radiator sealer and hose bandage
Exhaust bandage
Roll of insulating tape
Length of soft iron wire
Length of electrical flex
Torch or inspection lamp (can double as test lamp)
Battery jump leads
Tow-rope
Ignition waterproofing aerosol
Litre of engine oil
Sealed can of hydraulic fluid
Emergency windscreen
'Jubilee' clips
Tube of filler paste

If spare fuel is carried, a can designed for the purpose should be used to minimise risks of leakage and collision damage. A first aid kit and a warning triangle, whilst not at present compulsory in the UK, are obviously sensible items to carry in addition to the above.

When touring abroad it may be advisable to carry additional spares which, even if you cannot fit them yourself, could save having to wait while parts are obtained. The items below may be worth considering:

Clutch and throttle cables
Cylinder head gasket
Alternator brushes
Fuel pump repair kit
Tyre valve core

One of the motoring organisations will be able to advise on availability of fuel etc in foreign countries.

Engine will not start

Engine fails to turn when starter operated
Flat battery (recharge, use jump leads, or push start)
Battery terminals loose or corroded
Battery earth to body defective
Engine earth strap loose or broken
Starter motor (or solenoid) wiring loose or broken
Automatic transmission selector in wrong position, or inhibitor switch faulty
Ignition/starter switch faulty
Major mechanical failure (seizure)
Starter or solenoid internal fault (see Chapter 10)

Starter motor turns engine slowly
Partially discharged battery (recharge, use jump leads, or push start)
Battery terminals loose or corroded
Battery earth to body defective

Engine earth strap loose
Starter motor (or solenoid) wiring loose
Starter motor internal fault (see Chapter 10)

Starter motor spins without turning engine
Flat battery
Starter motor pinion sticking on sleeve
Flywheel gear teeth damaged or worn
Starter motor mounting bolts loose

Engine turns normally but fails to start
Damp or dirty HT leads and distributor cap (crank engine and check for spark)
Dirty or incorrectly gapped distributor points (if applicable)
No fuel in tank (check for delivery at carburettor)
Excessive choke (hot engine) or insufficient choke (cold engine)
Fouled or incorrectly gapped spark plugs (remove, clean and regap)
Other ignition system fault (see Chapter 4)
Other fuel system fault (see Chapter 3)
Poor compression (see Chapter 7)
Major mechanical failure (eg camshaft drive)

Engine fires but will not run
Insufficient choke (cold engine)
Air leaks at carburettor or inlet manifold
Fuel starvation (see Chapter 3)
Ballast resistor defective, or other ignition fault (see Chapter 4)

Engine cuts out and will not restart

Engine cuts out suddenly – ignition fault
Loose or disconnected LT wires
Wet HT leads or distributor cap (after traversing water splash)
Coil or condenser failure (check for spark)
Other ignition fault (see Chapter 4)

Engine misfires before cutting out – fuel fault
Fuel tank empty
Fuel pump defective or filter blocked (check for delivery)
Fuel tank filler vent blocked (suction will be evident on releasing cap)
Carburettor needle valve sticking
Carburettor jets blocked (fuel contaminated)
Other fuel system fault (see Chapter 3)

Engine cuts out – other causes
Serious overheating
Major mechanical failure (eg camshaft drive)

Engine overheats

Ignition (no-charge) warning light illuminated
Slack or broken drivebelt – retension or renew (Chapter 2)

Ignition warning light not illuminated
Coolant loss due to internal or external leakage (see Chapter 2)
Thermostat defective
Low oil level
Brakes binding
Radiator clogged externally or internally
Electric cooling fan not operating correctly
Engine waterways clogged
Ignition timing incorrect or automatic advance malfunctioning
Mixture too weak

Note: *Do not add cold water to an overheated engine or damage may result*

Low engine oil pressure

Gauge reads low or warning light illuminated with engine running
Oil level low or incorrect grade
Defective gauge or sender unit
Wire to sender unit earthed
Engine overheating
Oil filter clogged or bypass valve defective
Oil pressure relief valve defective
Oil pick-up strainer clogged
Oil pump worn or mountings loose
Worn main or big-end bearings

Note: *Low oil pressure in a high-mileage engine at tickover is not necessarily a cause for concern. Sudden pressure loss at speed is far more significant. In any event, check the gauge or warning light sender before condemning the engine.*

Engine noises

Pre-ignition (pinking) on acceleration
Incorrect grade of fuel
Ignition timing incorrect
Distributor faulty or worn
Worn or maladjusted carburettor
Excessive carbon build-up in engine

Whistling or wheezing noises
Leaking vacuum hose
Leaking carburettor or manifold gasket
Blowing head gasket

Tapping or rattling
Incorrect valve clearances
Worn valve gear
Worn timing belt
Broken piston ring (ticking noise)

Knocking or thumping
Unintentional mechanical contact (eg fan blades)
Worn drivebelt
Peripheral component fault (generator, water pump etc)
Worn big-end bearings (regular heavy knocking, perhaps less under load)
Worn main bearings (rumbling and knocking, perhaps worsening under load)
Piston slap (most noticeable when cold)

General repair procedures

Whenever servicing, repair or overhaul work is carried out on the car or its components, it is necessary to observe the following procedures and instructions. This will assist in carrying out the operation efficiently and to a professional standard of workmanship.

Joint mating faces and gaskets

Where a gasket is used between the mating faces of two components, ensure that it is renewed on reassembly, and fit it dry unless otherwise stated in the repair procedure. Make sure that the mating faces are clean and dry with all traces of old gasket removed. When cleaning a joint face, use a tool which is not likely to score or damage the face, and remove any burrs or nicks with an oilstone or fine file.

Make sure that tapped holes are cleaned with a pipe cleaner, and keep them free of jointing compound if this is being used unless specifically instructed otherwise.

Ensure that all orifices, channels or pipes are clear and blow through them, preferably using compressed air.

Oil seals

Whenever an oil seal is removed from its working location, either individually or as part of an assembly, it should be renewed.

The very fine sealing lip of the seal is easily damaged and will not seal if the surface it contacts is not completely clean and free from scratches, nicks or grooves. If the original sealing surface of the component cannot be restored, the component should be renewed.

Protect the lips of the seal from any surface which may damage them in the course of fitting. Use tape or a conical sleeve where possible. Lubricate the seal lips with oil before fitting and, on dual lipped seals, fill the space between the lips with grease.

Unless otherwise stated, oil seals must be fitted with their sealing lips toward the lubricant to be sealed.

Use a tubular drift or block of wood of the appropriate size to install the seal and, if the seal housing is shouldered, drive the seal down to the shoulder. If the seal housing is unshouldered, the seal should be fitted with its face flush with the housing top face.

Screw threads and fastenings

Always ensure that a blind tapped hole is completely free from oil, grease, water or other fluid before installing the bolt or stud. Failure to do this could cause the housing to crack due to the hydraulic action of the bolt or stud as it is screwed in.

When tightening a castellated nut to accept a split pin, tighten the nut to the specified torque, where applicable, and then tighten further to the next split pin hole. Never slacken the nut to align a split pin hole unless stated in the repair procedure.

When checking or retightening a nut or bolt to a specified torque setting, slacken the nut or bolt by a quarter of a turn, and then retighten to the specified setting.

Locknuts, locktabs and washers

Any fastening which will rotate against a component or housing in the course of tightening should always have a washer between it and the relevant component or housing.

Spring or split washers should always be renewed when they are used to lock a critical component such as a big-end bearing retaining nut or bolt.

Locktabs which are folded over to retain a nut or bolt should always be renewed.

Self-locking nuts can be reused in non-critical areas, providing resistance can be felt when the locking portion passes over the bolt or stud thread.

Split pins must always be replaced with new ones of the correct size for the hole.

Special tools

Some repair procedures in this manual entail the use of special tools such as a press, two or three-legged pullers, spring compressors etc. Wherever possible, suitable readily available alternatives to the manufacturer's special tools are described, and are shown in use. In some instances, where no alternative is possible, it has been necessary to resort to the use of a manufacturer's tool and this has been done for reasons of safety as well as the efficient completion of the repair operation. Unless you are highly skilled and have a thorough understanding of the procedure described, never attempt to bypass the use of any special tool when the procedure described specifies its use. Not only is there a very great risk of personal injury, but expensive damage could be caused to the components involved.

Conversion factors

Length (distance)

Inches (in)	X	25.4	= Millimetres (mm)	X	0.0394 = Inches (in)
Feet (ft)	X	0.305	= Metres (m)	X	3.281 = Feet (ft)
Miles	X	1.609	= Kilometres (km)	X	0.621 = Miles

Volume (capacity)

Cubic inches (cu in; in^3)	X	16.387	= Cubic centimetres (cc; cm^3)	X	0.061 = Cubic inches (cu in; in^3)
Imperial pints (Imp pt)	X	0.568	= Litres (l)	X	1.76 = Imperial pints (Imp pt)
Imperial quarts (Imp qt)	X	1.137	= Litres (l)	X	0.88 = Imperial quarts (Imp qt)
Imperial quarts (Imp qt)	X	1.201	= US quarts (US qt)	X	0.833 = Imperial quarts (Imp qt)
US quarts (US qt)	X	0.946	= Litres (l)	X	1.057 = US quarts (US qt)
Imperial gallons (Imp gal)	X	4.546	= Litres (l)	X	0.22 = Imperial gallons (Imp gal)
Imperial gallons (Imp gal)	X	1.201	= US gallons (US gal)	X	0.833 = Imperial gallons (Imp gal)
US gallons (US gal)	X	3.785	= Litres (l)	X	0.264 = US gallons (US gal)

Mass (weight)

Ounces (oz)	X	28.35	= Grams (g)	X	0.035 = Ounces (oz)
Pounds (lb)	X	0.454	= Kilograms (kg)	X	2.205 = Pounds (lb)

Force

Ounces-force (ozf; oz)	X	0.278	= Newtons (N)	X	3.6 = Ounces-force (ozf; oz)
Pounds-force (lbf; lb)	X	4.448	= Newtons (N)	X	0.225 = Pounds-force (lbf; lb)
Newtons (N)	X	0.1	= Kilograms-force (kgf; kg)	X	9.81 = Newtons (N)

Pressure

Pounds-force per square inch (psi; lbf/in^2; lb/in^2)	X	0.070	= Kilograms-force per square centimetre (kgf/cm^2; kg/cm^2)	X	14.223 = Pounds-force per square inch (psi; lbf/in^2; lb/in^2)
Pounds-force per square inch (psi; lbf/in^2; lb/in^2)	X	0.068	= Atmospheres (atm)	X	14.696 = Pounds-force per square inch (psi; lbf/in^2; lb/in^2)
Pounds-force per square inch (psi; lbf/in^2; lb/in^2)	X	0.069	= Bars	X	14.5 = Pounds-force per square inch (psi; lbf/in^2; lb/in^2)
Pounds-force per square inch (psi; lbf/in^2; lb/in^2)	X	6.895	= Kilopascals (kPa)	X	0.145 = Pounds-force per square inch (psi; lbf/in^2; lb/in^2)
Kilopascals (kPa)	X	0.01	= Kilograms-force per square centimetre (kgf/cm^2; kg/cm^2)	X	98.1 = Kilopascals (kPa)

Torque (moment of force)

Pounds-force inches (lbf in; lb in)	X	1.152	= Kilograms-force centimetre (kgf cm; kg cm)	X	0.868 = Pounds-force inches (lbf in; lb in)
Pounds-force inches (lbf in; lb in)	X	0.113	= Newton metres (Nm)	X	8.85 = Pounds-force inches (lbf in; lb in)
Pounds-force inches (lbf in; lb in)	X	0.083	= Pounds-force feet (lbf ft; lb ft)	X	12 = Pounds-force inches (lbf in; lb in)
Pounds-force feet (lbf ft; lb ft)	X	0.138	= Kilograms-force metres (kgf m; kg m)	X	7.233 = Pounds-force feet (lbf ft; lb ft)
Pounds-force feet (lbf ft; lb ft)	X	1.356	= Newton metres (Nm)	X	0.738 = Pounds-force feet (lbf ft; lb ft)
Newton metres (Nm)	X	0.102	= Kilograms-force metres (kgf m; kg m)	X	9.804 = Newton metres (Nm)

Power

Horsepower (hp)	X	745.7	= Watts (W)	X	0.0013 = Horsepower (hp)

Velocity (speed)

Miles per hour (miles/hr; mph)	X	1.609	= Kilometres per hour (km/hr; kph)	X	0.621 = Miles per hour (miles/hr; mph)

Fuel consumption*

Miles per gallon, Imperial (mpg)	X	0.354	= Kilometres per litre (km/l)	X	2.825 = Miles per gallon, Imperial (mpg)
Miles per gallon, US (mpg)	X	0.425	= Kilometres per litre (km/l)	X	2.352 = Miles per gallon, US (mpg)

Temperature

Degrees Fahrenheit = (°C x 1.8) + 32   Degrees Celsius (Degrees Centigrade; °C) = (°F - 32) x 0.56

*It is common practice to convert from miles per gallon (mpg) to litres/100 kilometres (l/100km),
where mpg (Imperial) x l/100 km = 282 and mpg (US) x l/100 km = 235

Index